Arieh A. Ullmann
Alfred Lewis
Editors

Privatization and Entrepreneurship: The Managerial Challenge in Central and Eastern Europe

"This is a provocative, challenging collection of papers that comes at an opportune, but difficult time. Privatization in Central and Eastern Europe is moving toward the 'end game.' The easy tasks are finished, the learning by doing period is over, the quick and dirty deals are completed. Now the tough cases must be handled, with much more public attention than earlier cases received. Now the true managerial and entrepreneurial challenges must be met, to finish the privatization task and to make newly privatized enterprises competitive in domestic and world markets. This collection provides useful insights for this task, and a well-organized guide to the themes, questions, and arguments that will shape practice in the future.

The five-part organization is clear and helps to organize the diverse views and topics covered in the individual papers. Part I, particularly the first chapter, does an excellent job of setting the frame and outlining the issues involved in privatization. The challenges outlined in Parts II and III provide a helpful entrée to the strategic issues presented in Part IV.

In sum, this is an important work that will be useful to scholars of privatization, policy makers, and practitioners alike. It adds significant detail and context to our understanding of a complex and highly politicized process, and comes at a time when broader understanding of the process is crucial to future success."

William K. Holstein, PhD
Distinguished Service Professor,
School of Business,
State University of New York
at Albany; Founding Director,
Center for Private Enterprise
Development, Budapest, Hungary

"This book offers a fascinating range of perspectives on economic transition. There are ideas here for everyone engaged in transforming the business organizations of previously communist-controlled countries. The case studies of restructuring and new start-ups are also particularly relevant for contemporary thinking about Chinese economic reforms."

Simon Johnson
Associate Professor,
Fuqua School of Business,
Duke University

The Haworth Press, Inc.

Privatization and Entrepreneurship
The Managerial Challenge in Central and Eastern Europe

INTERNATIONAL BUSINESS PRESS
Erdener Kaynak, PhD
Executive Editor

Privatization and Entrepreneurship
The Managerial Challenge in Central and Eastern Europe

Arieh A. Ullmann
Alfred Lewis
Editors

International Business Press
An Imprint of The Haworth Press, Inc.
New York • London

Published by

International Business Press, an imprint of The Haworth Press, Inc., 10 Alice Street, Binghamton, NY 13904-1580

Cover designed by Donna M. Brooks.

Library of Congress Cataloging-in-Publication Data

Privatization and entrepreneurship : the managerial challenge in Central and Eastern Europe / Arieh A. Ullmann, Alfred Lewis, editors.
    p. cm.
Includes bibliographical references and index.
ISBN 1-56024-972-2 (hard : alk. paper)
    1. Management–Europe, Central. 2. Post-communism–Europe, Central. 3. Management–Europe, Eastern. 4. Post-communism–Europe, Eastern. I. Ullmann, Arieh A., 1945- . II. Lewis, Alfred, 1961- .
HD70.C36P75 1996   96-28115
658'.00947–dc20   CIP

CONTENTS

ABOUT THE EDITORS

Arieh A. Ullmann, PhD, is Associate Professor of Management in the School of Management, Binghamton University, State University of New York. He has published numerous books, articles, and cases on management and international operations and has been involved in projects on Hungarian regional economic development, Romanian entrepreneurship training, and Russian small business development. Dr. Ullmann was formerly a Research Fellow at the Science Center Berlin, Germany, and a Research Assistant at the Federal Institute of Technology, Zurich, Switzerland. He has also taught at the Free University, Berlin, the University of Maryland, Berlin, and Haifa University, Israel.

Alfred Lewis, PhD, is Associate Provost and teaches Strategic Management and International Finance and Trade at Binghamton University, State University of New York. Dr. Lewis serves on the editorial board of the *Journal of European Business and Economic Development* and is a reviewer for several other journals. His research interests include policy issues, political-economic dimensions of international trade, and the global trend toward trade bloc formations. His work has been published in the *Journal of Strategic Change, European Research, Journal of European Business and Economic Development, Business and the Contemporary World*, and the *International Review of Strategic Management*.

ABOUT THE CONTRIBUTORS

Patrick Arens is director of, and management consultant at, Pentium Business Consultants, R.L. Brasov, Romania. He is also a doctoral student at the Vrije University, Amsterdam. Mr. Arens' research interests include the process of strategic change for enterprises in transitional economies.

Douglas L. Bartley is a retired associate professor of management. Prior to entering academia, he was a personnel director for H. J. Heinz in the United States for 17 years, and was vice president for manufacturing of a Heinz subsidiary in Brazil. He is the author of *Job Evaluation: Wage and Salary Administration* (Addison-Wesley), among other books. He currently is a volunteer management consultant for Volunteers in Overseas Cooperative Assistance, Washington, DC. He has worked extensively in Eastern Europe and the former Soviet Union on the privatization of manufacturing enterprises.

Keith D. Brouthers is an assistant professor in strategic management at the Vrije University, Amsterdam. Dr. Brouthers' research interests include international strategy, and foreign direct investment in Central and Eastern Europe. Dr. Brouthers has published in leading international management journals in the United States and Europe.

Jacob M. Chacko is an associate professor of marketing in the College of Business and Public Administration at the University of North Dakota. He has published in *Business and the Contemporary World, American Business Review, Business and Public Affairs, SAM Advanced Management Journal,* and the *Midwestern Business and Economic Review.* Professors Chacko and Chelminski are currently in the process of writing a book on doing business in Eastern Europe.

Piotr Chelminski is a lecturer of marketing in the College of Business and Public Administration at the University of North Dakota. His research has appeared in *Business and the Contemporary World, SAM Advanced Management Journal, Business and Public Affairs,* and *Management Research News.*

Wade Danis is currently a doctoral student in strategy and international business at Indiana University at Bloomington. His work experience includes six years in retail buying and merchandising, and two years managing a not-for-profit consulting firm that serviced minority-owned small businesses in New York City. After earning his MBA in 1993, Mr. Danis moved to Hungary, where he worked for a large electronics manufacturing firm as an in-house consultant. Prior to returning to the United States in 1995, Mr. Danis spent five months at Warsaw University in Poland, where he taught entrepreneurship and strategy. His research interests include strategic management in transition economies, particularly those of the former Soviet-bloc countries of Central and Eastern Europe.

James H. Davis is an assistant professor in the College of Business Administration, University of Notre Dame. He earned his PhD in corporate strategy and organization theory from the University of Iowa. His research interests include corporate governance, stewardship theory, and trust.

Julio O. De Castro is an assistant professor of strategy and organization management at the University of Colorado at Boulder. Professor De Castro's research examines the process of privatization of state-owned enterprises and of technology transfer, from the perspective of the firm and its strategy, and with a particular interest in developing and former communist countries. Professor De Castro received the 1994-95 Robert S. McNamara Fellowship from the World Bank to study the process of privatization of state-owned enterprises in the Dominican Republic.

G. Scott Erickson is an assistant professor of marketing and international business at Ithaca College, Ithaca, NY. He received his PhD in Business and Economics from Lehigh University. Current research interests include innovation and patent law, international retailing, and international trade controls.

Norman Frohlich is a professor in the faculty of management at the University of Manitoba and a senior researcher at the Manitoba Centre for Health Policy and Evaluation. His research interests and publications fall within the areas of public choice, experimental economics, distributive justice, and health policy. He has published numerous articles and three books, the most recent of which is *Choosing Justice: An Experimental Approach to Ethical Theory* (University of California Press, 1992), co-authored with Professor Joe A. Oppenheimer.

Jane K. Giacobbe-Miller is an associate professor of management at the University of Massachusetts at Amherst. Her research focuses on work values and attitudes in U.S. culture and their relationship to workplace behaviors. She has consulted extensively with industry in the design of compensation and other human resource management systems.

Andrew Gross is a professor of marketing and international business at Cleveland State University, where he has taught for 25 years. He was a Fulbright senior scholar in Hungary in 1989 and 1992, and has served as visiting professor at McGill University and McMaster University in Canada, the University of New South Wales in Australia, and the Budapest University of Economic Sciences. He has published in numerous journals and is co-author of three books. He is an active consultant for industry and government in the United States and abroad. He was a founding partner of Predicasts, Inc., a pioneering firm in the information industry. Dr. Gross serves on the board of several journals, is active in civic groups, and has published three books and over fifty articles in marketing and international business journals.

Frank L. Hefner earned his PhD in economics at the University of Kansas. He is an assistant professor at the College of Charleston. His current research interests include economic impact models and transitional economies.

Robert D. Hisrich is the A. Malachi Mixon III Chair and a professor of entrepreneurial studies at the Weatherhead School of Management, Case Western Reserve University. He is also president of H & B Associates, a marketing and management consulting firm he founded. Mr. Hisrich has authored 12 books and over 120 articles on marketing, entrepreneurship, venture capital, and international business. He is a consultant to start-up, medium-size, and Fortune 1000 companies and has designed and delivered management and entrepreneurial programs to U.S. and foreign businesses and governments. Presently he is establishing a university/industry program in Hungary, developing a high school teachers entrepreneurship training program in Russia, and establishing a business school and Model Republic in Cheboksary (Russia).

Devi Jankowicz is a reader in management, and director of the Central and Eastern European Centre, at Teesside Business School, University of Teesside, United Kingdom. Originally trained in occupational psychology and in management cybernetics, he has drawn on personal construct psychology in recent years in order to research and understand the process of management development in Central and Eastern Europe.

John L. Kmetz is an associate professor of management at the University of Delaware. He was director of the university's USAID contract for management training in Bulgaria in 1991 and 1992, and managed a USAID program for energy planning in Panama. He teaches international business (graduate and undergraduate) on campus and in Europe. His research interests include organizational transitions in Europe, technology change in organizations, and management research methodology.

Fritz Kröger, after an apprenticeship in a bank, studied business administration at the University of Mannheim and Saarbrücken, where in 1973 he completed his doctorate. He joined A. T. Kearney in 1976. In 1986 he became a partner and was promoted to vice president. Since 1990 he has been head of the Berlin office. Dr. Kröger is a member of several boards of directors and supervisory boards. His work is in the area of strategic management on a global scope. In recent years he has worked extensively in the area of restructuring large conglomerates in Central and Eastern Europe.

David W. Lutz is a research associate in the Center for Christian Social Thought and Management, University of St. Thomas (MN). He earned his PhD in philosophy at the University of Notre Dame. His current research interests include the history of moral philosophy and the philosophy of corporate governance.

Robert D. Lynch is a professor of management and director of the Small Business Institute in the School of Business Administration at Rowan College of New Jersey. Before joining the School of Business he served in executive operations management positions at RCA and Westinghouse Electric and also operated his own small business. He was the founding director of the Management Institute at Rowan and served in that position from 1974 to 1996. Dr. Lynch received his PhD from Carnegie Mellon University and his MBA from Rutgers University.

Valeri V. Makoukha is a professor of economics and Pro-Rector of the Pedagogical University in Veronezh, Russia. His past research has included studies in international economics and of food problems in developing countries. He has worked as an interpreter to the Soviet Economic Mission and was Counselor to the Ministry of Education in Cuba. In 1994 he received an eight-month scholar grant from the International Research and Exchange Board to study small business activities in the United States where he was a visiting lecturer in the School of Business Administration at Roman College. He received his Kandidat degree in economics from the Leningrad Pedagogical Institute.

Patrick J. Marx is currently a graduate student in the MS accounting program at Binghamton University, Binghamton, NY, and is working at Universal Instruments on special projects for the chief financial officer. He graduated from the University of Virginia with a BS in finance in 1990. For two years, he worked as a financial analyst for the Energy Recovery Fund, a small venture capital fund that invested in small capitalization oil and gas companies in North America and the U.K. North Sea. In 1992, he became the project director in Romania for Romanian Christian Enterprises and served as the financial director of a print shop, Multimedia International, for one and a half years.

Michael K. Mauws is currently completing his PhD in organizational analysis at the University of Alberta. He is also CEO of Westward Industries, a firm specializing in the manufacture of small, fuel-efficient vehicles. His research interests include how we organize, why we organize, and what happens when we organize.

Christoph B. Melchers is managing director of the IFM Freiburg – Institute for Psychological Impact Research – Dr. C. B. Melchers Ltd. (Germany). After receiving his diploma in psychology in 1973 he worked as a research assistant at the University of Cologne, where he received his PhD in 1977. His research interests are in the areas of advertising and public relations, psychology of the media, the arts, culture, and everyday life. A psychotherapist, he was a co-founder of morphological market psychology and of IFM Freiburg. As part of IFM's research projects, he is involved in examining cultural change in eastern Germany and in Central and Eastern Europe.

Daniel J. Miller is an assistant professor of management at Central Connecticut State University in New Britain, Connecticut. His research areas are executive compensation and decision making. He has worked as a consultant for several businesses in the areas of strategic planning and employee relations.

Lynn E. Miller is a professor in the department of management at La Salle University in Philadelphia, Pennsylvania. Her comparative research extends earlier work focusing on individual and organizational determinants of job satisfaction and performance in the United States.

Michael S. Minor is an associate professor of marketing and international business at the University of Texas-Pan American, Edinburg, TX. He has published a *South Carolina Essays in International Business* monograph and has also published in the *Journal of International Business Studies, International Studies of Management and Organization, Risk Analysis, Journal of Consumer Marketing*, and elsewhere. He has done research on privatization for the Transnational Corporations and Management Division of the United Nations.

Karen L. Newman is an associate professor in the School of Business at Georgetown University, Washington, DC. She specializes in organizational behavior. Her current research focuses on management transitions in the Czech Republic, ethical work climates, and high performance work groups in a variety of cultures. She has published in such journals as the *Academy of Management Journal, Industrial Relations, Public Administration Review, Social Justice Research, Case Research Journal*, and *Human Relations*. Professor Newman has a PhD from the University of Chicago.

Stanley D. Nollen is a professor in the School of Business at Georgetown University in Washington, DC. He specializes in international business and business economics. His research interests focus on business in emerging market economies, including case studies among Czech companies. One of these cases has been published in the *Case Research Journal*. Professor Nollen has a PhD from the University of Chicago.

Joe A. Oppenheimer is a professor in the department of government and politics at the University of Maryland and the associate director of the University of Maryland Collective Choice Center. His research interests include political economy, fairness in distribution, and public choice. He has published numerous articles and three books, the most recent one in 1992, co-authored with Norman Frohlich. Professors Oppenheimer and Frohlich have been collaborating on a wide range of research for over 20 years.

Nelson Phillips earned his PhD in organizational analysis at the University of Alberta and is currently an assistant professor in the Faculty of Management at McGill University. His current research interests include transitional economies, tourism as a cultural practice, the management of socialist enterprises, and the role of organizational collaboration in development.

Ronald Savitt is the John L. Beckley Professor of American Business at the University of Vermont. He earned his PhD at the University of Pennsylvania. His current research interests include managerial issues of privatization and the role of marketing in economic development and transformation.

Emeric Solymossy is associate director of the recently initiated Institute of International Entrepreneurship at the Weatherhead School of Management, Case Western Reserve University, where he is completing his PhD in strategy and policy, specializing in international entrepreneurship. He earned his MBA at Colorado State University. He has initiated seven entrepreneurial ventures in addition to being a consultant for small businesses and corporate turnarounds.

Nikolaus Uhlenbruck is an assistant professor of international management at California State University in San Marcos. As a German citizen, he has been involved in the transition of the East German and other Central European economies. His current research is on mergers in Eastern and Central Europe of privatized firms with companies from Western Europe and North America.

Vladimir I. Victorov is an associate professor in the department of management and social-economic systems at St. Petersburg Technical University in St. Petersburg, Russia. He received his PhD in psychology from Leningrad State University. He has served as a consultant in several joint ventures and Russian companies in the areas of motivation and supervisory training.

Richard M. Weiss is an associate professor in the department of business administration at the University of Delaware in Newark, Delaware. He currently is researching the influences of ideology and legitimacy on organizational structure and population dynamics. He has taught and conducted research in Bulgaria under the auspices of USAID.

Douglas P. Woodward earned his PhD in economics at the University of Texas at Austin. He is a research economist and associate professor of economics in the College of Business Administration at the University of South Carolina. His primary research interest is foreign direct investment, and he is currently investigating the locational determinants of foreign investment in Central and Eastern Europe.

Introduction

Alfred Lewis

This volume evolved from our close professional and personal ties to Europe. The immediate catalyst was the fifth Eastern Academy of Management international conference which in 1993 was held in Berlin, Germany, and had the transformation of Central and Eastern Europe as the conference theme. The location in the reunited city of Berlin was symbolic as were the obvious differences in the appearance of the two halves. In spite of formal unification of East and West, actual unification would take time. While the tangible signs of the past had disappeared, the Wall continued to exist in the heads of the Germans and, we might add, in the minds of the people throughout the region.

The title of this volume grew out of many discussions we had with colleagues as we were embarking on the project. For management scholars, "privatization" as a public policy issue is not the issue. Rather, since it encompasses legal and political considerations, it is a challenge to economists and politicians (e.g., Gomulka, 1993; Keating and Hoffman, 1991; Lewis, 1992; Rojec 1993; Rondinelli, 1991). They need to devise a policy that reflects the optimal mix of fast, "big-bang" privatization through the issue of vouchers and the much slower approach via auctions and sale of individual companies to domestic and foreign buyers (Ernst, Alexeev, and Marer, 1996). From a managerial perspective, however, the key problem is at the micro level–the transformation of these enterprises into viable entities that can participate in competition on a global platform irrespective of their legal form. Thus, from a managerial perspective, "privatization" entails not only the transfer of ownership as a way to address the agency problem at the institutional level but also the transformation of firm conduct.

Implicit in the title to our volume is the conviction that the path toward economy viability in the region entails both the transformation of the state-owned enterprises and the creation of many new firms. The top-heavy industry structure in these countries needs to be changed toward one that has many small firms as the foundation; a smaller number of mid-size companies above and an even smaller number of large firms at the top of the pyramid. Also, state-of-the-art management techniques need to be introduced in the hitherto state-owned centrally planned enterprises, in the emerging private sector and in government bureaucracies. Equally important, as a consequence of the transition to a market-based economy the role of the manager changes from that of a plan implementor to a plan formulator and implementor–activities that require initiative and decision making. This change of the decision space requires more than merely new management techniques–it mandates a new way of thinking. Several of the chapters in this volume address the complexities of the path toward a new managerial role and identity as we felt very strongly that it is at this level that more research was needed.

A number of contributions in this volume suggest that several other conditions need to be present for transforming existing enterprises and for creating new ones: An overall entrepreneurial climate is essential to transform the economies of Central and Eastern Europe both at the public policy and the enterprise levels. Here, we use the concept of entrepreneurship from a macro perspective. This includes not only the spirit of innovation and risk-taking about creating new business entities but also the ability of established enterprises to innovate and thereby renew their offerings and processes to compete successfully. Furthermore, peoples attitudes need to change in many fields, for example concerning the labor market.

We therefore decided to concentrate on the many facets of economic transformation from a managerial viewpoint. Given the fast pace of change in Central and Eastern Europe and the many difficulties in obtaining reliable data, we did not want to exclude valuable contributions by imposing a narrow thematic focus or methodological approach. We believe that our approach of methodological plurality conveys a certain richness to this volume. The contributions in this volume follow several different approaches, these include:

1. conceptual papers;
2. empirical papers along established principles of science; and
3. case studies based on field research used to illustrate dimensions of the transformation process and to convey a rich picture of the difficulties and challenges faced by managers.

We have arranged the twenty chapters in the volume into five sections based on common themes. Summaries of the contributions are provided in the following text.

Part I - Prerequisites for Management Transition

In Chapter 1, Norman Frohlich and Joe Oppenheimer discuss the ethical problems arising when moving from a centrally planned to a market-driven economy. The changes in the economies of Central and Eastern Europe have created a large class of losers and a small group of winners as previous state monopolies under central planning have been replaced with private firms. The authors propose that distributive justice issues need to be factored into the transition process and criticize the failure of policy relevant economic theory to do so.

In Chapter 2, Devi Jankowicz presents alternate approaches to the process by which language is used to create understanding—an issue that is at the core of Western efforts for assisting managers in Central and Eastern Europe. The first is language as a means of communication, and the second language as a means of encoding experiences. The author draws from his firsthand experience as a trainer of Polish managers to provide examples of possible miscommunications. Given the ambivalent nature of language, Jankowicz argues that it is hard to estimate the actual impact of the training effort due to the difficulties in assessing how the message being conveyed was understood by the Polish managers.

Michael Mauws and Nelson Phillips discuss the institutional requisites of capitalism in Chapter 3. They argue that any successful movement toward a Western style market economy will require significant social change in order to produce a system in which certain institutional and moral conditions can exist. Key features include individualism and new forms of regulation, all of which in the West have developed in a historically unique manner. The authors emphasize that to accomplish such a change will take a long time and, given the different history and cultures, may lead to a system dissimilar from that in the West.

In Chapter 4, John Kmetz reflects on the dearth of research about the dramatic changes taking place in Central and Eastern Europe with particular reference to studies on transformation and entrepreneurship. He attributes this to the difficulties Western researchers experience when conducting research under the prevailing conditions in these countries, and to the peculiar incentive structure surrounding instructors from Western universities who were primarily conduits for carrying out the training effort.

Part II - Management Challenges of Privatization

In Chapter 5, Douglas Bartley and Michael Minor provide firsthand insights gained from consulting assignments with 26 former state-owned enterprises in Central and Eastern Europe as well as the former Soviet

Union. The authors explore problems facing managers and first-line supervisors and provide a critical assessment of the level of managerial and supervisory skills in these enterprises.

In the subsequent chapter, Julio De Castro and Nikolaus Uhlenbruck offer a comparison of the privatization process in former communist, developing, and industrialized Western countries. They examine mergers and acquisitions as a means of privatization of state-owned firms. By studying the patterns of acquisitions in the three types of economies they are able to discern patterns. In particular, they assert that the need to acquire "know-how" and technology to be an important factor in the privatization of state-owned companies via acquisitions by foreign firms.

In Chapter 7, David Lutz and James Davis present a case study of a furniture manufacturer in one of the non-Russian former republics of the Soviet Union from the perspective of a Western consultant. The case deals with a single, seemingly basic and crucial accounting error for which there is a straightforward solution. Yet, the error–which is threatening the company's existence–is not corrected in spite of repeated efforts by the American consultant. The detailed account gives a vivid picture of the frustrations that Western consultants who are working in the region experience and of the politics that prevails within the state-owned enterprises attempting to transform themselves.

In Chapter 8, Karen Newman and Stanley Nollen discuss the managerial challenges during organizational re-creation. They use the case of a Czech firm to illustrate the challenges that managers face. The case study highlights the elements needed for a privatized company to re-create itself and to adapt to the new economic order, notably leadership and valuable capabilities.

In Chapter 9, Ronald Savitt examines Skala, one of Hungary's foremost retailers as it faces the challenges of Hungary's transition to a market economy. Skala, already under communism long recognized for its innovative marketing, was widely expected to maintain its superior performance in spite of the political-economic changes. However, the failure of Skala to respond adequately demonstrates the importance of corporate leadership for a successful transformation.

Part III - Management Challenges of Entrepreneurship

Frank Hefner and Douglas Woodward provide two Polish case studies in Chapter 10 to highlight the beneficial impact of foreign direct investment. They argue that there are widespread misconceptions about how managerial and entrepreneurial skills develop. It is true that firms remain hampered by the lack of managerial talent needed to survive in a competitive environment and thus are easy prey to the agile and experienced Western multinationals entering the region. The authors, however, demonstrate that the multinationals infuse these transforming economies with much-needed competitive practices and managerial skills by training the local partners in Western standards and methods to achieve them.

In Chapter 11, Robert Lynch and Valeri Makoukha discuss the emergence of entrepreneurs in post-communist Russia. This phenomenon is particularly noteworthy given that entrepreneurial activity as understood by the West was treated as a criminal activity in communist Russia. The authors trace the evolution of entrepreneurship in Russia since its inception in the late 1980s using a three-phase framework.

Patrick Marx focuses on the critical success factors for entrepreneurial ventures in Romania in Chapter 12. His detailed case study of a print shop, in whose development he actively participated, highlights that foreign direct investment can come from unexpected sources. It furthermore underscores how strong religious beliefs can form the basis for profound cultural change.

Part IV - Strategic and Operational Reorientation

In Chapter 13, Patrick Arens and Keith Brouthers discuss the factors that affect the strategic decision-making process in the Romanian banking industry. Findings from their research suggest that in spite of the transition of the economy, bank managers may not develop a competitive orientation as quickly as expected. The large number of customers during the transitionary stage of Romania's economy could signal to management that customer service is not important. Also, the pressure exerted by the banking regulators may impede competition between the banks.

In Chapter 14, Wade Danis, Andrew Gross, Robert Hisrich, and Emeric Solymossy present case histories of four Hungarian enterprises in different industries. The authors illustrate the variety of approaches employed by each company to reinvent itself and to redefine its market focus by deploying different product and market strategies commensurate with their position.

In Chapter 15, Scott Erickson discusses the importance of creating a suitable system of patent protection in Central and East European countries drawing upon lessons from the West. Typically, a patent system is designed to protect and disseminate technological information and to attract foreign direct investment. To modernize their respective economies, Erickson recommends a course for the Central and East European countries that combines elements of different systems existing in the West.

In Chapter 16, Lynn Miller and Richard Weiss compare the reactions of Bulgarian and U.S. employees to different organizational structures–a topic of interest to Western firms setting up operations in the region. They tested four hypotheses to determine the differences on measures such as job specificity, rule observation, participation in decision-making and hierarchy of authority. They found that employees from the United States reacted more positively to participation in the decision-making process than did the Bulgarians. Additionally, American employees reacted more negatively to constraints on their autonomy.

Fritz Kröger examines the survival potential of newly privatized companies in Chapter 17. He introduced the concept of dual restructuring as a means to assist both Western and Eastern companies. Dual restructuring is defined as dividing the value-added chain of a product between Western and Eastern companies in such a way that significant improvements in competitive advantages can be realized for both. The author views this strategy as a way for firms suffering from the high cost in Germany to regain a competitive edge while, at the same time, enables companies in the former CMEA countries access to Western knowledge and technology.

Part V - Employees and Consumers in a New Context

In Chapter 18, Jacob Chacko and Piotr Chelminski examine labor relations and policies in Hungary and Poland. They argue that one of the many implications of transitioning to a market-based economy is the introduction of competition into the labor market. The old full employment policy of the centrally planned economies has not prepared the labor force for the psychological dimension of employment practices prevailing in a market-based economy. Hence, Western firms need to adapt their human resource management practices correspondingly.

Jane Giacobbe-Miller, Daniel Miller, and Vladimir Victorov explore historical and current pay practices in state-owned and joint venture enterprises in Russia in Chapter 19. Their findings, drawn from three experiments of Russians' perceptions of pay equity and of different bases for determining pay is placed in the context of compensation systems design for joint ventures in Russia.

Chapter 20 by Christoph Melchers deals with the life and consumption styles in former East Germany after the collapse of the Berlin Wall. His findings suggest that it is a fallacy to assume a single type of the Eastern consumer. Also, the notion of people in the East wishing to become Westernized as soon as possible is incorrect. Rather, there are new types of lifestyles and consumer groups in the East that reflect past orientations and behaviors which persist in new forms given the different environment in unified Germany.

The volume concludes with a discussion by Arieh Ullmann regarding the many challenges facing managers and entrepreneurs involved in the transformation process. He speculates why empirical research indicates that only a fraction of the state-owned companies have actually re-created themselves as suggested by theory. He proposes that old, informal networks assume a new function in these transitioning economies. As a consequence, he foresees the development of a unique post-communiust mixed economy in the countries of Central and Eastern Europe.

REFERENCES

Ernst, M., Alexeev, M., and Marer, P. 1996. *Transforming the core. Restructuring industrial enterprises in Russia and Central Europe.* Boulder, CO: Westview Press.

Gomulka, S. 1993. Poland: Glass half full. In R. Portes, (Ed.), *Economic transformation in Central Europe: A progress report.* Brussels: Office for Official Publications of the European Community.

Keating, G. and Hoffman, J. 1991. Privatization theory: Hold back for a swift advance. *Central European*, April 1991, p.34.

Lewis, A. 1992. Political-economic restructuring of Eastern Europe. *International Review of Strategic Management*, 2(2): 109-118.

Rojec, M. 1993. Foreign direct investment and privatization in Central and Eastern Europe. Some facts and issues. *Second Annual Conference of Central and Eastern European Parliaments- Privatization and Foreign Direct Investment.* July 5-6, Warsaw, Poland, CEEPN.

Rondinelli, D.A. 1991. Developing private enterprise in the Czech and Slovak Federal Republics. *Columbia Journal of World Business*, 26(3): 26-36.

PART I:
PREREQUISITES
FOR MANAGEMENT TRANSITION

Chapter 1

Ethical Problems
When Moving to Markets:
Gaining Efficiency While Keeping
an Eye on Distributive Justice

Norman Frohlich
Joe A. Oppenheimer

For more than 40 years after World War II, almost half the world's population operated under autocratically governed command economies. In those countries the means of production were owned by the state, purportedly in the collective name of the people. As is well known, most of those political regimes suffered a rapid disintegration in the late 1980s and early 1990s. In the end, command economies were unable to keep their core promise: a minimally acceptable standard of living for all.

It is widely acknowledged that the socialist economies of Central and Eastern Europe in the 1980s were grossly inefficient. Western economists, secure in their theories, have advocated wide-scale privatization to increase efficiency. This chapter raises questions about the applicability of those models in the European context. Evidence of massive numbers of losers in the process of privatization leads us to raise two troubling issues. The first question is an epistemological one regarding the validity of applying a theoretical model when the antecedent conditions of the theory are wildly at variance with those that obtain in the domain of application. The second, which follows from the first, focuses on a normative aspect of the problem: How can a policymaker adjudicate between norms of distributive justice and promises of efficiency? If efficiency gains claimed for some future point are accompanied by decreasing social welfare in the

The authors thank John Guyton, Virginia Haufler, and Eric Uslaner for comments on early drafts.

present, and if there is no compensation for those who suffer net losses in the process, then it is impossible to make a decisive claim that social welfare has improved. Without that, one cannot even claim improvements under the traditional welfare economic definition of efficiency.

CAUSES OF ECONOMIC DECLINE

It is easy to understand what happened in the Central and Eastern European economies. The means of production were owned by the state. One of the main ideological justifications for state ownership was the state's commitment to use proceeds from the collectively owned goods to furnish economic entitlements–a welfare floor–to all. This manner of organizing production required that the productivity of the system was sufficient to generate the social welfare subsidies legitimating the governments. But the command form of organizing production and distribution, along with policies of setting prices according to social and political considerations, produced two damaging consequences:

1. Wages and benefits were divorced from individual productivity. This removed incentives for innovation and created conditions under which individuals could free ride. As a result, many feasible gains in productivity from labor were forgone.
2. The lack of market signals also led to the misallocation of other factors of production. This resulted in the further reduction of both productivity and the general welfare.

The first consequence rendered the entire command economy a giant "commons" problem.[1] The outputs of the command economies declined to a point where they were barely adequate to guarantee a minimally acceptable standard of living. They even threatened the supply of goods deemed to be inherent rights: food, medical care, and housing, components of the implicit social contract.

THE PRESCRIPTIONS
AND THE FIRST RETURNS FROM PRIVATIZATION

The classic suggestion for dealing with a commons problem is to introduce market signals through privatization (Hardin, 1968). Entitling the participants to specific portions of the resources, and giving them the rights to trade these entitlements, generates incentives to move to an efficient outcome. The same policy is usually presumed to be applicable to the general holdings in the command economies of Central and Eastern Europe. The prescribed solution for managers of the economy is to privatize and introduce markets for trading the newly privatized resources.

It was anticipated that such policies would be associated with some manageable short-term disruptions, and then with medium- and long-term overall economic improvements that would produce significant gains in output and welfare. That was the theory. The process that has been unfolding is somewhat different.

Privatization has shown some immediate positive effects, such as the availability of certain consumer goods, and the enrichment of successful entrepreneurs. At the same time, privatization has led to the impoverishment of a significant proportion of the population. While some of the welfare setbacks may be transitory, there are no theoretical guarantees about their duration, much less about their political impact. One commentator has noted: "The almost Dickensian division of Russia into two nations–the conspicuously rich and the desperately poor–threatens to become a source of major social tension that could push the government into reintroducing elements of the discredited communist system of centralized distribution" (Dobbs, 1992). And the hardships of the transition may not be strictly short-term. As a former Polish ambassador stated: "Liberty has its price and the price is high. We knew the poor would suffer but we thought it would be two or three years. Now it's beginning to look like 10 or 20" (Darnton, 1993).

The changes in the economies of Central and Eastern Europe have led to a small class of big winners and a large class of economic losers: some with radically lowered economic status and expectations. Competition has been far from perfect; often some state monopolies have been replaced with private ones. Given the gravity of the situation, a closer look at the reflexive support for the policy of unfettered privatization as social policy is in order. One is moved to ask: What are the implicit arguments underlying the prescriptions of privatization offered by Western economists? Are there some possible lacunae in those arguments that might account for the problems being encountered?

WHY ARE THERE PROBLEMS WITH PRIVATIZATION?

Economists are accustomed to thinking about free market systems in equilibrium: systems in which transactions are fluid and costless, and information is available and accurate. Under those circumstances, markets operate efficiently and lead to optimal results for the society. Identifying the assumptions of the traditional economic argument, and questioning their applicability in the Central and Eastern European context, can illuminate some of the problems of, and some of the normative premises implicit in, applying the arguments there.

From an economic point of view, the argument which justifies privatization is seemingly straightforward. It relies on exposing both labor and other factors of production to the rigors of the free market. Trades freely entered into can have no losers. Trading is the key liberal right that enables the system to overcome free-riding and inefficient allocation inherent in a command economy. People are free to enter and exit markets in accordance with their own desires: If a peasant enters a market with an endowment (say of millet), the argument goes, she cannot exit worse off than she was before she entered it. After all, the peasant need not accept any deal that does not improve her welfare. Similarly, buyers need not accept bad deals. Both buyer and seller are thereby given the potential only to improve by privatization and the existence of free markets.[2]

Privatization coupled with markets allows individuals to pursue trades until no more improving moves are possible. Typically, if one identifies the status quo welfare of all individuals at the start of the process, each move (trade) will be welfare-improving (a Pareto improvement) and the trades will cease only when no more welfare-improving trades are possible (on the Pareto frontier). When this has been achieved, the system is said to have reached an equilibrium at an optimal point. Given the standard assumptions of economics, as a solution to the problems of free-riding and inefficient allocation, market processes can be criticized only in terms of distributive criteria.[3]

But the arguments of the free market economist are usually framed in terms of what happens under perfect market conditions, not at the initiation of the market. It is assumed that there are many buyers and sellers, no barriers to entry, mobile labor and capital, and costless, perfect information about the availability and price of all factors. Given these assumptions, their theoretical conclusions are the inferences of valid arguments. If the premises of their model hold in any particular empirical situation, one would expect the conclusions to hold in that context as well. But economists fail to give adequate attention to the consequences of introducing trading of property in very imperfect markets—where the assumptions of their model do not hold. Note that it is the very imperfection of the markets in command economies that has led to the call for free market solutions. These imperfections mean, in reality and theory, that the models can guarantee neither that there will be no losers nor that the losses will be limited in time and scope.

Welfare economists agree that a particular new policy p is "an improvement" over the status quo, s, if everyone who is affected by p is at least as well off as under s, and at least one person is better off under p than under s. Assuming individuals prefer outcomes that make them better off, one would get unanimous agreement for shifts from s to p. Such changes are referred to as Paretian. They represent the easiest of all possible cases for the policymaker. These are the sorts of moves anticipated by the argument sketched above. And as long as we subscribe to some loose form of utilitarianism we should be supportive of such changes (see Arrow, 1963, Chapter 4).

Of course, there are still normative questions involved in policy choices here. Different Paretian policies will lead to different points on the welfare frontier, and have differing distributional outcomes. Many words have been written on the ethical questions of economic distribution. If we are primarily concerned with such issues as equality, or even relative well-being, there are many issues which the policy analyst must face.

Increasing evidence, both theoretical and empirical, shows that people place high normative valuations on general rules guaranteeing individuals some degree of economic safety. John Rawls (1971) argued that individuals have rights to the basic necessities of life—part of what he called primary goods. Focusing on societies which are at least *moderately* well off, Rawls argued that liberty, broadly defined, constituted the first requirement of any just society. Clearly the disestablishment of totalitarian rule was a prerequisite for the meeting of Rawls' first set of desiderata. Following that, however, Rawls argued that goods in society must be distributed so that those at the bottom of the economic ladder are as well off as possible (in terms of those primary goods).[4] So, for example, Rawlsians would not adopt Paretian policies if they didn't lead to a maximum improvement of the welfare of the worst off. While the evidence suggests that Rawls' description of what needs to be provided to the worst off is too generous, there are clear indications that a minimal safety net enjoys broad public support in most societies. Indeed, there is mounting evidence that virtually all individuals have normative social concerns regarding the setting of inviolable welfare floors (Frohlich and Oppenheimer, 1992).[5]

We have found that access to some minimum level of primary goods is generally viewed as a socially generated right in a broad range of societies (Frohlich and Oppenheimer, 1992; Jackson and Hill, 1995; Lissowski, Tyszka, and Okrasa, 1991; Saijo and Turnbull, 1994). Allowing an individual to receive less than that bundle of goods is morally unacceptable in those societies. Everyone is deemed to have the right to *some* acceptable level of food, water, shelter, medical care, etc. If privatization policies engender inequities that threaten this value, serious social tension over conflicts between efficiency and distributive justice are likely to result. The policy-makers and managers will be stuck with the task of resolving these tensions.

THE PROBLEMS STEMMING
FROM THE POSSIBILITY OF LOSERS

The perceptive reader might ask: "How can there be 'losers' under a policy of privatization when all trades are presumed to be welfare improving?" The answer lies in a close look at the real context of privatization.

Privatizing the rights to dispose of property does not create new property and an immediate gain in welfare. Rather, there is a distribution of property and an increase in the choices open to individuals to exchange property at market values, which fluctuate with market signals. Two problematic areas come to mind: first, the initial distribution of property bundles; and second, the changes in the value of the property over time.

Any reorganization which leads to a move from a suboptimal status quo *s* to a point *p* on the welfare frontier can be thought of as defining welfare *trajectories* for the members of the society. The points traced out over time as results of trades and economic activities constitute the trajectories (as well as the endpoints) of the process. They are the *outcomes over time* of the policies. They are experienced by the members of the society. Paths can be usefully distinguished as follows: (1) they can be Paretian (no one is made worse off), or not Paretian, where (2) some are made temporarily (or permanently) worse off, and if some are worse off, (3) they may fall temporarily (or permanently) below the socially acceptable welfare floor. If the paths are chosen with full information, only the Paretian paths are attainable via Pareto moves without compensatory redistribution. The other trajectories would require compensation to gain prior consent of those who will lose in the short or long run.

What factors would lead one to anticipate losers, i.e., individuals who fall below their status quo ante? To see how privatization under radically imperfect market conditions can create losses, even losses that threaten to drive some below a minimally acceptable floor, let us consider two phases of privatization. In phase 1, individuals receive a bundle of property and trading rights; in phase 2, they engage in trades. Seeing how an individual could suffer losses in the first stages of privatization is straightforward.

In the first place, losses could stem from misevaluations of the assigned bundles. After all, there are numerous imperfections, rigidities, and difficulties preventing an accurate estimation of the values of distributed assets absent market signals. Moreover, privileged segments of the population enjoy systematic and unfair advantages in parceling out the property and in early rounds of trading. Former party members and managers are likely to control vital information and key factors of production and thus often have the ability to enter into and monopolize certain forms of economic activity. Even if the policymakers try hard to be fair, the values of the privatized goods assigned to individuals are likely to be different than planned.

An additional loss of welfare could stem from a restriction on the ability to trade the privatized goods in the next phase. Information is highly restricted and concentrated and much of labor and capital are immobile. These inequalities can easily affect the subsequent value of any resources that may be distributed.

If the great bulk of individual entitlements is to stem from exchange, as it does in a pure market economy, the two sources for these entitlements will be the value of the allocated basket of newly privatized goods and the individual's earned income. Each of these sources of exchange entitlement is also a source of risk.[6] First, the basket of allocated privatized property is certain to fluctuate in value. Market values of goods change. That is the whole point. Hence, as the value of market-based exchanges shifts, gains, as well as losses, are produced. Entitlement to goods, including necessities in a pure market economy, are generated by the exchange value of each citizen's share of the privatized property plus her capacity to earn income.

As one moves to the new market economy, where market signals replace socially engineered prices, owners of different subsets of capital and labor will experience different fortunes. Those with greatest labor and asset mobility, and with rising valuation for their skills and other assets, are likely to prosper under privatization. Their new privileges are likely to allow them to invest in costly information, and to diversify their holdings sufficiently to avoid undue risks.

Their condition contrasts with that of the less fortunate citizen, whose allocation might include rights over immobile property, such as an apartment and shares in an enterprise of decreasing value in a dying industrial town, and whose low-skilled job with the marginal enterprise is not likely to continue to deliver its current pay. Such an individual may lack the exchangeable resources to maintain a steady flow of everyday necessities and would have the surplus funds neither to invest in information, nor to diversify her holdings, nor even to move where her skills are in greater demand. This is especially problematic where a great deal of the capital is geographically fixed. Further, supply constraints on such overhead capital as information networks, and severe housing shortages, can create additional hurdles to labor mobility.

Given the great inefficiencies in state industries, the market values of many of the newly private assets of individuals are sure to be limited. Industries which produce unwanted items are almost certain to shed employees, reducing the average value of labor in the short run. Trading under these conditions can clearly create the potential for significant losses, losses which can endure a long time, and which can lead to violations of any implicitly agreed upon welfare floor.

Of course, a broader perspective also helps to explain how any of the paths which place individuals at risk of falling below an acceptable floor might occur in practice. In adopting a policy of privatization, policymakers face a risky rather than a certain environment. Their choice is not likely to be between one path and another. Rather, it is likely that the only practical policy for economic improvement is associated with an *ex ante* probabilistic combination of all possible paths. After all, movement to a market economy implies the decentralization of decision making and the opening of choices to market players. Thus, the paths sketched could represent different combinations of independently made investment decisions as well as the unfolding of stochastic events, such as the weather, world trading conditions, etc., that will change the values of individuals' holdings over time. As bankrupt entrepreneurs in the West know, the market does not guarantee only winners. Indeed, it could well be that the *expected* value of the welfare of all individuals under a chosen policy was higher at all times (but not all contingencies) than both a welfare floor and the status quo. However, a bad roll of the dice, post hoc, could result in a society's following a policy which unfolds along a less desirable path, but still toward efficiency, so that the *actual* welfare of some individuals ends up lower than either the status quo ante or even the welfare floor.

How relevant and widespread are these conditions and concerns likely to be during the transition period from an inefficient nonmarket socialized system to a market base? A partial answer would require knowledge of the relative size of the groups of winners and losers, as well as information about how many of the losers are below an acceptable floor. We might also wonder who the venture capitalists are who win and who the losers are. Are they heads of households or single? Are they wealthier citizens (e.g., former Communist Party members with caches) or just common folk?

Gains in overall efficiency have no guarantee of spreading improvements to all, even in the long run, if some of the trades are made under conditions that disadvantage one subset of the parties. The result may be an unfair final distribution. Many possible alternative economic paths may contain significant losers. Those inequitable consequences, which the economists may dismiss as "merely distributional," could be severe and, we argue, have to be weighed against efficiency gained from unconstrained privatization.

Thus, the likelihood of long-term losers is a substantial negative consequence of creating new markets. It poses serious problems for policymakers who are considering the simple application of the economists' policy prescriptions; serious normative questions are raised. First, the possibility of losers means that alternative policy paths must be evaluated; the impacts of the policy alternatives on different classes of individuals must be considered. More specifically, the normative weight assigned to large numbers falling below an acceptable welfare floor must be compared to the weight given to possible gains of others.

Obviously, any evaluation of a proposed privatization policy must consider the effects of that policy on the aggregate welfare of society over the long run. Anticipated long-term improvements in aggregate welfare must weigh heavily in any evaluation. But that concern cannot stand alone as a criterion. The expected welfare conditions of the actual *individuals* as they unfold over time must also be considered. The near-past, the short-term, and the intermediate-term welfare conditions of individuals constitute the paths along which any society travels to the long-term future. Therefore, to assume these paths to be irrelevant to policy evaluation is to assume the evaluative independence of the future path from its origin. It is not at all clear how, and in what way, economists might justify such a discounting. Indeed, succinct arguments have been made against any such move (Nozick, 1974). For economists and other advocates of Paretian efficiency, alienability of property is desirable and unproblematic. Economists see the expansion of *tradable property rights* to be a potent prescription for achieving *efficiency*. But, as we have argued under slightly different conditions, alienability–especially of collectivized rights-poses problems.

WHAT IS TO BE DONE?

What, then, must policymakers consider in light of these problems of social justice which may be associated with privatization policies? Clearly, when welfare needs become widespread and are not addressed, moves toward Pareto efficiency can violate the norms of universal entitlement to a minimum level of support that is a component of implicit social contracts. Were significant numbers of individuals to fall below acceptable levels of subsistence as a result of alienable privatization policies, the new social policies, designed to achieve efficiency, could be identified as undercutting the insurance function of the social contract. Under such conditions, the policies, and even the social fabric underlying the policies, are unlikely to be stable.

But the problem is still more complex; there are additional considerations for the policymakers and managers. To stimulate optimal choices in the face of inherently risky investment decisions, and to ensure against risk-averse behavior that would produce suboptimal investment while also including a system of social supports, raises problems of moral hazard. At the same time, there will be constraints placed on the timing of the new social insurance policies. For when the state divests itself of its main assets, it limits, in the short to medium term, its ability to provide minimal levels of support to those who need it. Although in theory privatization is presumed to generate enough surplus value in the long run to compensate losers, how soon the long run comes, and whether those who, in that future, run the state will have the ability, *or political will*, to carry out the compensation, are questions which need to be addressed. How these policies should be designed and implemented constitute both the theoretical and practical core of the problem that both policymakers and free market economists need to address.

Potential conflicts between efficiency and distributive justice are often dismissed by economists as the products of fuzzy thinking. As Henry Simons wrote: "It is urgently necessary for us to quit confusing measures for regulating relative prices and wages with devices for diminishing inequality. One difference between competent economists and charlatans is that, at this point, the former discipline their sentimentality with a little reflection on the mechanics of an exchange economy" (1947: 83). In other words, because the two concerns can be divorced theoretically and institutionally, issues of fairness need not weigh on the policy advocate as she develops efficiency-improving proposals.

But from the words of Simons, and the observation that once property is distributed, it is very hard to redistribute, one can infer that any concern for fairness and distributive justice must be built into the development and initial distribution of property rights and endowments.

Compensation

Modern economics has had little to offer in terms of firm policy prescriptions when gains to efficiency are achieved by creating both winners and losers. Built on Paretian assumptions that states of individual welfare cannot be meaningfully compared, today's economics often declares social states of equal efficiency socially indifferent (see Sen, 1973, Chapter 1). With such constraints, policy analysts have come to use the Kaldor-Hicks criterion as the evaluative principle. The criterion holds that if, in comparing two social states (again call them p and s), p would lead to an increase in output so that all those who prefer s *could be* compensated to a point of indifference, while others would be left preferring (after the compensation) p, then p should be chosen. The criterion does not claim that the compensation need be made. It is not built upon *actually* making a trade-off between efficiency and other values, only on its hypothesized possibility. The problem with this notion is known: if compensation is not made, then the Kaldor-Hicks criterion is nothing more than a claim that the purportedly more efficient state should be chosen. When compensation is not made, the resulting claim regarding net improvements is on shaky ground.

But this small extension of economic reasoning, with its implicit disregard of distributive values, gains little and comes at a potentially high cost. When there is more than one commodity, the Kaldor-Hicks criterion serves as a very poor implicit measuring rod. It is known to deliver no firm foundation for social or policy choice. As Kenneth Arrow put it, "there is no meaning to total output independent of distribution" (1963: 40).[7] Or putting it differently: we may even have difficulty measuring improvements in efficiency (if implicitly understood as Paretian improvements) if we leave out the compensation. In other words, without compensation, not only can *efficiency* conflict with *fairness* in distribution, but one might have improperly identified *efficiency gains* accompanied by *welfare losses*.

In defending, albeit imperfectly, the Kaldor-Hicks criterion, economists have talked about the great difficulties of developing explicit compensatory schedules. In the absence of such schedules they, by default, opt for efficiency. But efficiency alone, measured without regard to achieved individual welfares, will make for neither a stable nor a desirable social order. Moreover, much support could be gained by actually making the compensation.[8]

One should not lose sight of the fact that collectively owned property is property that is owned nevertheless. Privatization of collective property constitutes appropriation of all but one person's property rights. From that perspective, security of property rights, and fair compensation for appropriating those rights, need to be taken seriously. Compensation for loss of property is a long established and valued part of virtually all legal and constitutional systems. Americans, in particular, need no reminder that arbitrary and uncompensated seizures of property by government can furnish the seeds from which sprout popular rebellion. The fact that the changes in Central and Eastern Europe affect rights to collectively owned property may even increase the force of the argument. In redistribution for collectivization, a leveling element of fairness is present. In privatization, the reverse may hold. And, as noted above, there is broad scope for foul play and illicit deals in the process. Compensation is necessary to legitimate a policy of appropriation for both private and public property rights.

Of course, paying compensation might be difficult, given the great costs which are involved. Decentralization of ownership reduces (at least in the short run) the resources available to the political system for compensatory purposes. When compensation is going to groups of citizens, it will be difficult to assess an aggregate value for the compensation needed to privatize an erstwhile shared asset. The government may have difficulty calculating an asset's proper privatization price so as to cover losses. But this response of impracticality should not be accepted too readily. Theoretically, any move toward Pareto optimality *implies* the existence of enough gained resources in the improvement so that everyone could be more than fully compensated for any losses they might suffer. But massive reallocations of property, coupled with change in the political system, place strains and limitations on both the political and economic managerial structures.

In addition, stochastic events can occur, which are quite beyond the ability of individuals and the system to predict. The consequences for the welfare of individuals of these stochastic events, as they impinge on entitlements for necessities, may be very severe. Thus, over a considerable period of time, the interrelationship between the political process and the choice of improvement policies may not allow for the ex post facto compensations necessary to secure the ex post facto approval of the relevant losers. In sum, we might expect that any move toward a radical restructuring of the economy is likely to lead to both the temporary violation of the floor and decreased compensated property losses for some of the citizens. What is essential is that long-term expectations are stabilized and the legitimacy of some sort of loss claims is established.

But even a carefully engineered, good faith, and popularly structured partial compensation effort may generate substantial needed support for a privatization policy. Such partial solutions should not be dismissed lightly, as they can help establish loyalty to the new institutions, springing from expectations that the institutions are fair and not designed to redistribute to a favored few. Such loyalty is requisite for any emergent political structures. After all, revenue for the government, in the absence of open sales of property, will stem from taxation. Changes in legitimacy of the state may even limit the state's ability to collect the taxes needed to function at all, much less to make compensatory payments.

Safety Nets

So the issue is not whether, but only how, to manage compensation. Carefully and endogenously developed compensatory schedules and schemes must be an integral part of any privatization policy. Compensation can be made either with shares in the current and future value of the privatized property, or with notes of long-term indebtedness of the government to its populace. Compensation should not be confused with the existence of a social safety net. To ensure that market incentives have the power necessary to mold behavior, one might have to ensure that income support levels are significantly below the market wage rates.[9]

Especially when the political institutions are weak and widely perceived as illegitimate, the potential impact of a class of significant losers needs to be thought about carefully, from the initial stages of policy design to the final stages of policy evaluation and implementation. Indeed, when the forces of the market are to be newly unleashed on the provision of necessities, predictable welfare injustices which might occur ought to be considered. In the designing of the market and of the privatized property rights, policymakers need to consider provision for a welfare floor, possibly even an *inalienable* entitlement.[10]

Both a compensatory scheme and a social safety net would need to be worked out with imagination and patient negotiation. To do so might be easiest were there legitimized representative bodies, so that both the private and the social values of the parties would be respected. But what to do when the representative bodies are not available, or are highly imperfect, must also be considered. For the development of policy supplements to any privatization scheme, a legitimate expression of social values is needed. In the absence of legitimate national political institutions, some structure must be produced for the discovery/definition of the values which are to serve as welfare constraints for the society in its pursuit of efficiency. Specifically, the content of the welfare floor (i.e., its height and its weight when in conflict with other values, such as those of just desserts, growth, etc.) must be discoverable. So must a scheme and schedule for compensation. In other words, mechanisms must be found which are capable of giving some legitimating, rebuttable, expression to the values of the group, and acceptable trade offs between these values. In the absence of more generally acceptable institutions, networks of focus groups dedicated to impartial consideration of alternatively formulated social insurance and compensatory policies could be used along the lines sketched in (Frohlich and Oppenheimer, 1992).

The Limitations on the Role of Outside Advisors

A policy which privatizes property rights carries with it the likelihood of failure of a socially accepted floor. The acceptable trade-offs between efficiency and justice must be determined by the internal social and political system and must be compatible with any privatization solutions proposed. The basis for the appropriate trade-offs should stem from the endogenous values of the society.

An outside policy advisor cannot identify what an acceptable support level is without conducting a careful analysis of the cultural values within the society. Nor can an outsider, without careful research, presume to understand when the consequences of alienable privatization are acceptable and when they are not. And the task is not only to identify a floor and a compensatory schema, but formulas for their variation with the capacity of the economy. This is a somewhat larger task, but one which is essential for the maintenance of the social fabric during the privatization period.

On the other hand, there may be some social or political factors which can help an advisor identify some of the content of an acceptable floor. Amartya Sen (1990) argues forcefully but indirectly that the nature of the floor may be determined primarily by the political processes of the society rather than by other cultural values. Democracies, he observes, do not generate famines. Rather, their political processes lead to policies to head off mass starvation. Thus, the policymakers, in a democracy, may have some sense of the sort of trade-offs which are to be considered in designing policy. To be precise, one must consider both the indigenous social values and the political processes which aggregate those values into social decisions. Only after weighing those factors can one discuss the trade-offs which are likely to be acceptable between efficiency and justice from the policies of alienable privatization of property rights.

We believe that market economies are generally more efficient than command economies, and we agree with the neoclassical economic conclusion that significant efficiency gains can be achieved by privatizing command economies. Increasing the net product of a society is the metaphoric equivalent of many new lunches. Theory to the contrary, however, practical experience teaches us that there are very few free lunches. We believe the costs of the economic reforms will include numerous effects that are unjust, disruptive, and destabilizing. It is necessary to keep attention fixed on some of the normative issues associated with that disruption and on some possible means for addressing those issues.

ENDNOTES

1. The well-known "Tragedy of the Commons" (originally defined by Hardin, 1968) identifies the inefficiencies that can occur when individuals are given unfettered access to a resource on a common basis. It is degraded; and so it was.

2. Of course there are conditions that lead to distortions of this argument, and others have written about them very well. For a relatively standard treatment see Lindblom (1977), Chapters 3 and 6.

3. This also requires leaving out a number of real-world characteristics, such as external effects, public goods, and bargaining.

4. Here, we consider the economic necessities of life as the fundamental index of this second, distributional, requirement for a just society. Here, we set aside such questions as *how much* of each primary good individuals are entitled to. It should also be noted that Rawls stated that his arguments should be viewed as applying to societies of "moderate scarcity." We believe the economies of Central and Eastern Europe fall within that ambit.

5. These results stem from experimental research in Canada and the United States (Frohlich and Oppenheimer, 1992), replicated in Poland (Lissowski, Okrasa, and Tyszka, 1991), Australia (Jackson and Hill, 1995), and Japan (Saijo and Turnbull, 1994). Other experiments and empirical studies have been performed, reinforcing the claim; see Konow (1994), Frohlich and Oppenheimer (1994), and Beck (1994).

6. The importance on individual survival of such shifts in exchange entitlements has been graphically underscored by Sen in his analysis of famines (Sen, 1981, especially Chapter 1 and its associated appendix). Also, see Frohlich and Oppenheimer, 1995.

7. Arrow also quotes Baumol as describing this criterion as "a measuring rod which bends, stretches, and ultimately falls to pieces in our hands" (Baumol, 1946-47: 46).

8. Clearly, generating the support of all is not foolproof. For example, some limitations may be needed to rule out compensation to those who have amassed illegitimate fortunes (collective or private, e.g., via coercion); but this is a matter which could be handled via adjudication. Also, it may be impossible to compensate fully those who are against the changes.

9. But free-riding in newly legitimated economic structures may not be as serious a problem as in older economies. Elsewhere (see Frohlich and Oppenheimer, 1992, Chapters 8 and 9) we report that in experimental contexts, when subjects discussed the ethical imperatives behind the provision of a guaranteed floor and subsequently chose and then worked under such agreed-upon provisions, productivity, rather than suffering, actually rose. Those who could have free ridden because their individual productivity was below the guaranteed floor actually doubled their effort and productivity. The same effect was *not* found in a control group that operated under a similar guarantee but did not discuss and agree to its implementation. Thus, participatory democratic decision making might be an additional factor needed to preclude a return to rampant free-rider behavior.

10. Indeed, many actual contracts that alienate rights to water (and gas, etc.) prioritize use during times of scarcity to maintain welfare floors. What would happen to an inalienable entitlement in the face of *extreme* scarcity (i.e., when resources are sufficiently scarce to make it impossible to guarantee everyone their entitlement)? This hard-choice question is left unanswered here.

REFERENCES

Arrow, K. (1963). *Social Choice and Individual Values*, 2nd ed. New Haven: Yale University Press.

Baumol, W. J. (1947-48). "Community Indifference." Review of Economic Studies, 14(1): 44-48.

Beck, J. H. (1994). "An Experimental Test of Preferences for the Distribution of Income and Individual Risk Aversion." *Eastern Economics Journal*, 20(2): 131-146.

Darnton, J. (1993). "A Polish Thesaurus: Free, Rich, Hungry" *The New York Times*, March 17, 1993, p. A1.

Dobbs, M. "Russian Reforms Impoverish Millions: Soaring Prices, Plunging Ruble Prove Calamitous for Middle Class." *The Washington Post*, October 1, 1992, pp. A1 and A20.

Frohlich, N., and Oppenheimer, J. A. (1992). *Choosing Justice: An Experimental Approach to Ethical Theory*. University of California Press: Berkeley.

Frohlich, N., and Oppenheimer, J. A. (1994). "Preferences for Income Distribution and Distributive Justice: A Window on the Problems of Using Experimental Data in Economics and Ethics." *Eastern Economics Journal*, 20(2): 149-155.

Frohlich, N., and Oppenheimer, J. A. (1995). "Alienable Privatization Policies: The Choice Between Inefficiency and Injustice." In: *Water Quantity/Quality Management and Conflict Resolution: Institutions, Processes and Economic Analysis*, pp. 131-142, Ariel Dinar and Edna Loehman, (Eds.). Praeger: Westport, CT.

Hardin, G. (1968). "The Tragedy of the Commons." *Science*, 162: 1243-1248.

Jackson, M., and Hill, P. (1995). "A Fair Share." *Journal of Theoretical Politics*, 7(2): 169-179.

Konow, J. (1994). "A Positive Theory of Economic Fairness," working paper 94081, Loyola Marymount University, Los Angeles.

Lindblom, C. (1977). *Politics and Markets: The World's Political-Economic Systems*. New York: Basic Books.

Lissowski, G., Tyszka, T., and Okrasa, W. (1991). "Principles of Distributive Justice: Experiments in Poland and America." *Journal of Conflict Resolution*, 35(1): 98-119.

Nozick, R. (1974). *Anarchy, State and Utopia*. New York: Basic Books.

Rawls, J. (1971). *A Theory of Justice*. Cambridge, MA: Harvard University.

Saijo, T., and Turnbull, S. (1994). Private communication of results from experiments piloted in the summer of 1994 with the authors.

Sen, A. K. (1973). *On Economic Inequality*. New York: Norton.

Sen, A. K. (1981). *Poverty and Famines: An Essay on Entitlement and Deprivation*. Oxford: Clarendon Press.

Sen, A. K. (1990). "Individual Freedom as a Social Commitment." *New York Review of Books* 37, pp. 49-54.

Simons, H. C. (1947). *Economic Policy for a Free Society*. Chicago: Chicago University Press.

Chapter 2

The Stories Hidden in the Words We Use: A Constructivist Analysis of Business Language as a Device for Cultural Encoding

Devi Jankowicz

> . . . words, and especially the figures of speech and figures of thought . . . mould thought as much as they express it. Linguistic and intellectual patterns are all the more important in determining what individuals take as worthy of being thought and what they think of it in that they operate outside all critical awareness. (Bourdieu, 1971: 195)

Some years ago, the Berlin Wall came down. We mounted our bulldozers and swept it away; in some places we used crowbars to dismantle it; here and there we tried to use our bare hands to dismantle it stone by stone. We stepped across that space from both directions, from East and from West, seeking to begin trade under a new set of rules—and, strangely, found our movements hampered by a different form of obstacle: a ghostly wall of incomprehension.

Some of the difficulties experienced in Germany in reestablishing a unified national economy have been reported in accounts of the work of the *Treuhandanstalt*, the trust body charged with the transformation of ownership in former East Germany (see e.g., Cuming, 1991). My own part in this journey has been an involvement in a project funded by the European TEMPUS-program to train Polish managers in the ideas and techniques needed in operating within a market-driven economy, as part of the general Western drive to provide assistance to Central and Eastern Europe as these countries make their transition from the centralized command economies toward a market-driven economy. At first sight, it would appear that our educational objectives have been achieved. Yet in actuality it is difficult to estimate the real success of these activities because, in the final analysis, it is difficult to assess how well our message has been understood.

LINGUISTIC SYMBOLISM

There are two complementary viewpoints to model the process of shared understanding, when two parties meet and exchange ideas. Each of these perspectives depends on how we focus on language use. The first viewpoint sees language as a communication system, the second as a system by which experience is represented and encoded.

Language as a Communication System

In the first viewpoint, understanding between two people arises when one person uses verbal or behavioral symbols to encode his or her intended meaning, and the second person shares enough of the symbols to be able to decode the meaning. According to this approach, any difficulties which one encounters in working across two cultures stem from the existence of two separate natural languages, neither of which transcribes sufficiently well into the other. As the person initiating communication, it is my responsibility to use competent language translation to create a situation which will allow my meaning to be conveyed, and it is the responsibility of my partner to do likewise when s/he responds in turn.

Messages pass between us like parcels, moving between the two railway stations of meaning somewhere in our separate heads (see Figure 2.1). Any difficulties encountered along the track can be resolved by finding words which can easily translate; for, clearly, some words do not. There are, for example, no words for "manager" or "marketing" in Polish that would convey the English meaning intended (see Figure 2.2).

Language as a System by Which Experience
Is Represented and Encoded

The alternative perspective focuses attention on the disparate meanings themselves. The function of language is to encode experience, an experience influenced by phenomena taking place within a particular cultural environment. The individual ascribes significance by actively selecting from the phenomenal flow a subset which s/he calls an event because, given

FIGURE 2.1. Language as a Communication System

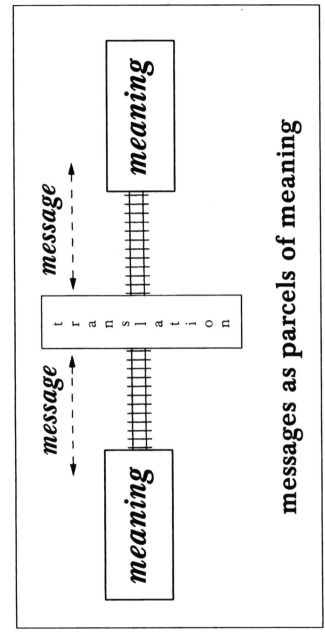

messages as parcels of meaning

FIGURE 2.2. "Manager" and "Marketing"

MANAGER

ENGLISH	POLISH
a manager	dyrektor
	kierownik

- handles
- organizes
- contrives
- succeeds
- copes
- controls
- administers
- takes charge

| directs |
| controls |
| governs |
| steers |
| commands |

- directs
- controls
- governs
- steers
- commands

different styles possible

dirigiste style

MARKETING

ENGLISH	POLISH
marketing	rynek
	targ

- segmenting
- targeting
- product strategy
- pricing, channel, distribution, promotion, advertising, selling
- research & control

- buying
- selling
- bargaining
- distributing

strategic and operational

operational

his/her previous experience within that culture, it is meaningful to do so. Meaning "arises" thereby (see Figure 2.3).

C. G. Jung has suggested a mechanism for the process involved:

> The creation of meaning is important in so far as the meaningful divides itself from the meaningless. When sense and nonsense are no longer identical, the force of chaos is weakened by their subtraction; sense is then endued with the force of meaning, and nonsense with the force of meaninglessness. In this way a new cosmos arises. (Jaffé, 1970: 146)

Only when pattern and structure are discernible can meaning be ascribed and implication become possible. Meaning cannot exist without some degree of interrelationship between representations.

Shared understanding occurs when two people collaborate in deciding on what seems sensible to them both, and what seems senseless. For this to happen, both must agree on the selection of a subset from the phenomenal flow which each recognizes and labels as an "event." Furthermore, the kinds of experience to which they attend, and the basis on which they typically ascribe meaning, must to some degree be common to both parties. According to this perspective, Western difficulties in working across two cultures stem only partly from differences in language, as language is seen as a set of rules available for encoding phenomenal flow into events. They stem preeminently from differences in experience and from differences in what Westerners and Easterners see as basically meaningful, that is, from *what they choose to give attention to* and therefore, from *what they are able to construe*. Rather than viewing this cross-cultural collaboration as a matter of messages which pass between two meaning centers, we focus on the way in which shared meaning arises as a function of the overlap between two sets of experiences and two construct systems, the boundaries of the overlap being specified by the encodings which are possible in the two languages being used. Clearly, some common symbolic ground is required in order to begin the process of sharing, and a knowledge of one another's language is convenient for communication, but this is not sufficient.

PRESENTATIONAL SYMBOLISM

Paradoxically, in some forms of collaboration a knowledge of the other's language may not even be essential, for it is also possible for mutual understanding to arise in nonlinguistic ways. Guthrie (1991) has drawn on the ideas of S. K. Langer to present ways in which it is possible for the

FIGURE 2.3. Language as a System for Encoding Experience

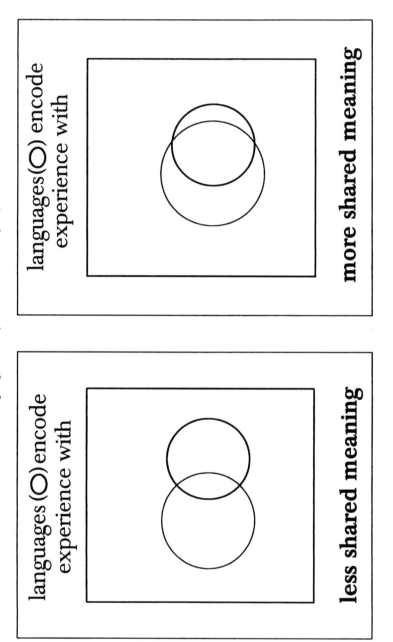

individual to abstract meaning from the phenomenal flow through presentational or nonlinguistic symbolization, through the personal recognition of perceptual invariants and the inner affective invariances to which these give rise. Feelings, emotions, and intuitions can then be articulated through nonlinguistic means such as ritual, myth, and music (to which one might add cultural history and values), an issue that is recognized in the various acculturation programs available to business executives preparing for service in overseas branches and subsidiaries of their employing organizations. Above all, mutual understanding arises through shared behavioral encounters: through the invariances formed as we interact with some degree of personal consistency with other people in situations as they recur, on foreign soil or on home territory.

When two individuals operate within two different cultures, then, they do so by drawing on the ways in which their language encodes experience in their own cultures, *and* by intuiting the nonverbal ways in which experience in both cultures is encoded. Using the terminology of Kelly's Personal Construct Theory (Kelly, 1955), we might speak of the existence of varying degrees of *cultural commonality*, and of the extent to which one culture encodes experience in ways which are similar to those of another culture.

In the moment when two individuals attempt to understand each other across those cultures, they seek to explore the similarities and differences in the ways in which the two cultures encode the phenomenal flow: which subsets are identified as events, what kinds of experiences are regarded as meaningful, and what the bases of meaning are in both cultures. The media in which they do so are, first, an understanding of the way in which language is being used in that moment. This is a metalevel analysis which asks "Am I being properly understood, and what does my interlocutor really mean and intend?" This has been pointed out by McNeill (1991), who advocates the use of two interpreters when doing business, one to handle the translation and the other to check on the success of the communication involved. The second medium consists of the developing knowledge of the rituals, myths, history, and values of the other culture. Third, and most important, are the behavioral invariances which occur as the two parties interact. Here one might draw on Kelly's notion of *sociality* and speak of *cultural sociality*, which emerges through mutual efforts to construe the construction processes of the other culture.

This analysis in terms of representation, rather than simple communication, provides a more useful way of looking at the problems of working between two cultures. It shifts our attention away from the point along a communication channel at which vocabularies are translated—issues of differing terminology—toward a consideration of differences in experience and differences in the construct systems developed by people raised in different cultures, as encoded in two separate languages and two distinct systems of behavioral invariance.

THE TRANSLATION OF LINGUISTIC SYMBOLS

Languages as used reflect differences in a number of respects:

Syntactical/formal requirements of orthography, vocabulary, terminology, and grammar, matters of how well-formed sentences should be constructed and articulated within a particular language to express a given meaning. For the moment, these are less interesting than idiom.

Idiom: In which phrases are used to convey meanings not deducible from the individual words themselves. The significance of idiom is that different languages have different idioms: either the same individual words when combined will express different meanings, or different individual words are combined to express the same meaning within the two languages. Any consideration of idiomatic differences across cultures must consider three meanings: the idiom used in one language, the idiom used in another, and the "common meaning" underlying both (see Figure 2.4).

Differences in history, values, and cultural tradition ensure that the idioms differ, and the importance and power of the cultural influence is reinforced when we remember that there are strong regional differences among users of the *same* language in the idioms they choose. These differences are charming–different games are being played in the phenomenal flow, much as children might splash around in a stream of running water–and only a little acquaintance with a *foreign* language is enough for the speaker to realize that fundamental differences in meaning are involved, and that the idiom used to express a given meaning is entirely arbitrary. Where there is no clue available from a previously learned syntactical/formal rule, each new idiom has to be learned individually each time. For example, one has to learn that one always addresses business acquaintances in the second-person plural in French and German, but that one uses the third-person singular in Polish, whereas for all these occasions English uses the second-person singular.

Etymology: The distinct origin of phrases and words, is more problematic. There can be little or no indication that a word as suggested by a dictionary or any other vocabulary source may evoke radically different meanings in the speaker's understanding of the word as used in the listen-

FIGURE 2.4. Differences in Idiom

I'm indifferent

DAS IST MIR ALLES WURST   SIX OF ONE, HALF
("It's all sausages to me")   A DOZEN OF THE
                                        OTHER

An annoying/inconvenient action

DANKE FÜR DIE BLUMEN   THANKS FOR NOTHING
("Thanks for the flowers")

You've done something stupid

DU HAST EINEN VOGEL   GONE A BIT "OUT TO
("You've a bird [in your head]")   LUNCH" or BATS IN
                                    THE BELFRY

I've had enough (too many) inconveniences

ICH HABE DIE NASE VOLL   gesture (hand under nose
("I've got a nose-full")   & words I'VE HAD IT UP
                                     TO HERE)

er's native language. Sometimes the existence of a third language shared by both speakers may provide a hint that the dictionary meaning does not express the full meaning involved, but, generally, one must simply have to learn something of the etymology of the foreign word in order to appreciate its meaning as uttered. Presumably this has to do with the fact that there are always several ways of expressing a particular idea, and, since meaning is (as we have seen) determined by association of ideas, the particular way chosen–the particular word used–will create one meaning, rather than another. Since the etymology of a word consists of a particular package or bundle of ideas, choosing one word rather than another will therefore convey different meanings and, in the case of speakers of two different native language, will require substantial collaboration before both can be assured that the intended meaning has been created.

Metaphor: The nonliteral encoding of phenomena for imaginative and rhetorical purposes, is particularly interesting in the ways in which meaning is conveyed within and across cultures. A literal translation of a metaphor from one language to another will often convey the point being made, even though some shade of meaning will be lost. For example, if I speak of "making a glaring error" in English, a Polish speaker will understand perfectly what I mean by "popełnić rażący błąd," even though this Polish term means "making a blinding/shocking error" and does not completely encode the further meaning of "glare," present in English but not in Polish, which conveys "an error so bad that it makes you as uncomfortable as an angry stare."

However, some words are in themselves *dormant* metaphors: they used to have a live metaphoric content, but this has disappeared over time, and only a knowledge of the etymology of the word will reveal the figurative meaning and its appeal to the imagination (Tsoukas, 1991). It is poignant to think that the metaphoric richness of so many words in any given language is no longer alive. We will all recognize that the word "manage," for example, has a classical origin in the Latin word for "hand," "*manus*": but what have hands got to do with it? We do not notice that its contemporary meaning in English, which includes the ideas of effective coping through negotiation and persuasion–ideas which the Eastern European words for "manage" lack–stems from the Renaissance Italian word "*maneggio*," a place where horses were trained into obedience through stroking, and the firm but gentle laying on of hands (Jankowicz, 1994b).

Of course we know all this in principle at some level, and yet we seem not to take it into account in our collaborative ventures across European borders. It is difficult to know the extent to which regional/cultural differences in meaning and experience have caused linguistic difficulties in the two Germanies, which use an identical language when language is seen as a communication system but not, one suspects, when one views it as a representational system (see Cuming, 1991; Geppert, 1994). But the issue is certainly present in West-East collaboration, being of vital importance to the success of cross-national collaboration with Central and Eastern Europe as we seek to develop a new understanding of what it means to trade in a global marketplace. This is especially pertinent in those instances in which we seek to develop joint ventures and other forms of strategic partnership.

A dramatic example of the importance of these factors in working across two cultures is given in Kelly (1962). Speaking of the Georgian understanding of the word "capitalist" in 1962, before changes in the socialist command economy made the issue particularly acute, Kelly gave examples of the etymological, historical, and experiential meanings of the word to a Georgian. The meanings actually had little to do with contemporary associations with the Western way, as opposed to the Marxist way, of doing business, and much with the historical usage of the word well before Marxism appeared on the scene. To the Georgian, whatever else a capitalist does when engaged in the activity of wealth creation and financial husbandry, he was also, in Georgian history, the local landlord and princeling who had the power to exercise droit du seigneur *(jus primae noctis)*[1] when the Georgian married, and to refuse access to education for the children of that marriage. The colossal arrogance evoked by such associations with respect to some rather central constructions about existence would, one imagines, overwhelm the dictionary meaning of the word "capitalist" to the extent that this etymology still persists, in any effort to teach Western approaches to the market economy to Georgians.

THE TRANSLATION
OF PRESENTATIONAL SYMBOLS

Turning to nonlinguistic symbolism and behavioral invariances, from the stories people tell to the stories they live (Mair, 1990), it is interesting to see how the same processes involved in formal requirements, idiom, etymology, and metaphor might operate across two cultures.

Formal requirements: Here we are asking about the orthography, vocabulary, terminology, and grammar of existing, being, and behaving in ways which are meaningful to oneself and to others. What constitutes a "well-formed" statement in the case of presentational symbolism?

---

1. The right of a feudal lord to share the wedding night of a vassal's bride.

Clearly, we are not concerned with intuitings or behavior that are merely *inappropriate* to the situation or to the individual's understanding of self, for inappropriate behavior can still be self-consistent and well-formed in itself. The indicators would seem to be in the realm of clinical psychology: understandings and behavior that are bizarre, florid, and fragmented in structure or discoordinated in their articulation, as that culture understands and expresses its meanings.

Idiom: A culture will express values and intuitions in behavior whose meanings are not discernible from the ways in which they are expressed. The same behavior in a different culture will express different meaning, or the same meaning will be conveyed by different forms of behavioral expression. These are the situations which are so difficult for the foreigner to understand that they will frequently lead to irritation and cultural arrogance.

Why does a Polish manager accede to a proposal with such obvious, attractive, and infectious enthusiasm, driving it onward with inspired and creative embellishment, only to behave the next day as if the subject had never ever been raised? It may not happen often, but when it does, it is enormously puzzling to the Western mentality. One thinks of Bismarck's exasperation with the Poles as "ungovernable, and unable to govern themselves," when it was not primarily rebelliousness which he had in mind. The Polish idiom conveys pleasure with life's possibilities and a trust in the proposer. It simply does not carry implications of commitment to action, and *none* of the inferences of unpredictability can be made by the foreigner that would be made in his or her own Anglo-Saxon culture. In their use of presentational symbols, Poles simply do not express meaning our way.

Having negotiated a contract, why does the Polish manager continue to look for a better deal from another potential partner and attempt to ignore the commitments entered into, even at the risks of legally enforceable financial penalties? The Polish idiom connotes that the future offers many possibilities, that there is a value in keeping options open, and that the contractual responsibilities, while acknowledged, will no doubt be managed with fluidity as just another of life's little tasks, to be tackled with concern, but also with flair. A contract is not a foreclosing of options, and to see that manager as irresponsible is to remain locked in the assumptions of one's own cultural idiom.

Conversely, the Polish manager will express the same meanings of commitment and responsibility familiar to the Anglo-Saxon by adopting an approach to supervision which in our culture would be seen as autocratic, dirigiste, and authoritarian (Maczynski, 1991). Again, a different idiom is at work, an idiom which we in the West have called "autocratic management style" while remaining blatantly ignorant that alternative idioms are possible which make this label inappropriate (with few exceptions: see Maruyama, 1982; Smith et al., 1989).

Etymology: Personal background and upbringing, history and custom, are to presentational symbolism what a study of etymology is to linguistic symbolism. In this sense, the need for etymological understanding is generally appreciated in cross-cultural collaboration over meaning. We realize the need to understand "where the person is coming from" when we deal directly–especially in negotiation over trade terms–with *individuals*, although in our laziness we may not exert sufficient efforts in familiarizing ourselves with the provenance of the whole *culture*, by studying the historical record which would illustrate the ways in which that culture has developed the norms and values which differ from our own.

Similarly, when we interact in collaboration to create meaning on a particular occasion, the history of that occasion–the significance and context of its commencement, the personal goals which we discern being served, and the multiple meanings of those goals which we discern in one another–are basic constituents in our search for interpersonal and intercultural sociality. As Eden and Sims (1979) have noted in addressing the issue of consultancy style in organizational development work, expert pronouncement and interpersonal empathy are poor substitutes for the effort to negotiate common visions of the subject involved, even though the expectation from the foreign participant might be for the simplicities of expert pronouncement. This has been the case in much of the management development work in Central and Eastern Europe, where quick and easy expert solutions to the problems of the post-command economy have been initially sought by the Eastern participants themselves (Holden and Cooper, 1994; Jankowicz, 1994a; Jankowicz and Pettitt, 1993). Part of the etymological work in self-presentation involves changing the content of the other's, and one's own, *expectations* of what is possible during and from that presentation.

Metaphor: As stated earlier in discussing linguistic symbolism, metaphor is the nonliteral encoding of meaning for imaginative and rhetorical purposes. What is it in the case of presentational symbolism? Here, we seem to be dealing with certain forms of *role-playing*: those forms in which behavioral and emotional styles characteristic of one kind of social position are adopted in expressing another. We speak of behavior associated with, e.g., paternal, nurturing, pastoral, or creative roles being utilized in the form of "paternalistic," "supportive," "pastoral caring," or "playful" behavior in situations in which the literal roles of "father," "provider," "priestly shepherd," and "child" do not particularly apply. We may construe life as *leela*, a joyful and playful encounter with phenomena, or at times as a battle in which we struggle against great odds; and so forth.

As in the case of linguistic symbolization, the difficulty is not with the live form of the metaphor, where the role-playing is deliberate and sufficiently publicly intentioned that the recipients of the role can recognize it and, by behavioral mirroring, amplify its expression (to take the Parsonian definition of role as behavior *expected of* a person in a given social position), whether within the culture or between cultures. All of the role examples quoted above would be recognized in all cultures, and the issue for the communication of meaning would simply be one of whether the metaphor is felt to be appropriate to the situation.

The difficulty arises when we give behavioral expression using dormant forms of metaphor: roles which our culture and upbringing have prepared for us and which we use without realizing we are doing so. A person from a different culture will certainly notice the metaphor, but it is unrealistic to expect that person to appreciate its function and power if, in our own culture, the metaphoric aspect of the behavior is dormant or dead.

There is sometimes suspicion and resentment in Poland of the successful trader who has personal access to capital funds, uses them well, and makes quick returns honestly. Could this stem less from the knowledge that some of the funds available for investment were gained by ex-communist managers from their state-owned enterprise during the 1980s period of "nomenclatural capitalism," and perhaps rather more so from the historical prejudice against the Jewish merchant who, in medieval times, was the only person legally entitled to charge interest and therefore make relatively speedy additions to capital? It may be that, in playing his role as capitalist, the successful Polish entrepreneur is giving expression to the dormant metaphor of the successful (Jewish) trader and evoking the anti-Semitic prejudices which this culture still holds.

The metaphor which underlies the role of teacher, or university lecturer, is that of the holder and caretaker of knowledge, dating back to the times in the nineteenth century when the country did not exist as a nation-state and in certain regions, like the Russian-administered east, the national language was forbidden in schools. It is easy for a *caretaker* to construe and be construed as an *owner*. These are the dormant metaphors which account for the meaning of the lecturer's role, which takes current expression in an authoritative, ex cathedra lecturing style.

Sometimes, the person who is the more active agent in an interaction across two cultures will remain blind to a metaphor which underlies his or her behavior, but which is nakedly obvious to the person with whom s/he is interacting. Kostera (1995a) has provided us with an excellent account of the religious metaphor which underlies Western attempts to train and to trade with Central and Eastern European partners "in the market-economy way," a metaphor which we westerners scarcely notice until it is drawn to our attention. Our use of such terms as "management guru", our reliance on charismatic examples of successful management in our use of the case study method in management education, our advocacy of the role of values in organizational development interventions, all suggest that a credo is being fostered as an essential aid to material salvation. Indeed, our preference for such English-language terms as "manager" and "marketing" in preference to the Central and Eastern European terms, so that our full meaning may be conveyed even when speaking in the local Central and Eastern European language, suggests an esoteric concern for forms and ritual to the partners with whom we deal. Polish has a phrase for unnecessarily confusing terminology, "*jak na tureckim kazaniu*" ("like listening to a Turkish sermon"), which reveals this metaphor of religious proselytization, hidden to us but perfectly plain to our Central and Eastern European partners.

CONCLUSIONS

Translations of linguistic and presentational symbols, then, are problematic. Misunderstanding when dealing with a different culture has something, but relatively little, to do with the simple translation of messages between two fixed points of meaning. It has much more to do with the difficulties that arise when two people, with different methods for abstracting meaning from the phenomenal flow, engage in the collaborative, negotiative activity that mutual understanding requires—the mutual generation of meaning from the phenomenal flow which they experience in the moment of their encounter.

The point is not that this flow differs for both people; rather, it is that the systems which they each utilize to identify events as meaningful embody cultural differences in the form of formal requirements, idiom, etymology, and metaphor, whether these are expressed in linguistic or presentational form. Why does this matter? Simply because cross-cultural work is done by people who are relatively ignorant of these differences in the foreign culture, and, in the case of dormant metaphors, likely to be ignorant by definition, and who, in the case of the "know-how" exporters seeking to assist Central and Eastern Europeans into a market economy, operate within a marked power differential. "If we seek to help, and they seek our help, we must know something they don't, and that means that they must listen to us, doesn't it?"

Moreover, the problems which ensue are persistent beyond the moment of encounter. Misunderstandings and arrogance on the part of an uninformed Westerner, where s/he attempts to create meaning by drawing solely on the linguistic and presentational symbolization of his or her own culture, continue as s/he becomes aware of the developing symbolizations within the other culture, as the media of that culture seek to interpret the imported ideas according to the recipient country's linguistic and presentational formal requirements, idiom, etymology, and metaphor. Kostera (1995b, 1995c) has described the imagery and metaphor used in the Polish press to describe the activities of Poland's new business entrepreneurs. This is a language of apparent triviality and fashion—it is sexy to be a *biznesmen*. It describes an endeavor in which all problems are soluble, provided the Poles follow the Western magic prescriptions, an endeavor, incidentally, in which the role poses threats to conventional Polish sex roles. For management is seen largely as a masculine activity, the reader is told, before being speedily reassured that where a woman engages in business, she does so with no threat to her "girlie"-role status, or her implied "real" fulfillment as a happy wife-and-mother-of-two. Reading this imagery in simple translation, the Westerner forms his or her reactions of dismay from the very different linguistic and presentational assumptions that his or her media value and espouse.

The resulting dangers we must seek to avoid are best expressed by Bourdieu (1971:198):

> Misunderstandings, borrowings removed from their context and reinterpreted, admiring initiation and disdainful aloofness—these are all signs familiar to specialists on the situations that arise when cultures meet . . . any action for the handing on of a culture necessarily implies an affirmation of the value of the culture imparted (and, correlatively, an implicit or explicit depreciation of other possible cultures).

REFERENCES

Bourdieu, P. 1971. Systems of education and systems of thought. In M. F. D. Young (Ed.), *Knowledge and control: New directions for the sociology of education*. London: Collier Macmillan.

Cuming, M. 1991. *The Treuhand: The instrument for transforming the economy of eastern Germany*. M.A. dissertation, Brunel University.

Eden, C., and Sims, D. 1979. On the nature of problems in consulting practice. *International Journal of Management Science*, 7: 119-127.

Geppert, M. 1994. The problems of intraorganisational change in East-German firms. *Journal of European Business Education*, 3: 20-28.

Guthrie, A. F. 1991. Intuiting the process of another: Symbolic, rational transformations of experience. *International Journal of Personal Construct Psychology*, 4: 273-279.

Holden, N., and Cooper, C. 1994. Russian managers as learners and receivers of Western know-how. *Management Learning*, 25: 503-522.

Jaffé, A. 1970. *The myth of meaning in the work of C. G. Jung* (trans. R. F. C. Hull). London: Hodder and Stoughton.

Jankowicz, A. D. 1994a. Holden and Cooper's "Russian managers as learners": A rejoinder. *Management Learning*, 25: 523-526.

Jankowicz, A. D. 1994b. The new journey to Jerusalem: Mission and meaning in the managerial crusade to eastern Europe. *Organization Studies*, 15: 479-507.

Jankowicz, A. D., and Pettitt, S. 1993. Worlds in collusion: an analysis of an eastern European management development initiative. *Management Education and Development*, 24: 93-104.

Kelly, G. A. 1955. *The psychology of personal constructs*. New York: Norton.

Kelly, G. A. 1962. Europe's matrix of decision. In Jones, M. R. (Ed.), *Nebraska symposium on motivation*, 83-123. Lincoln, NB: University of Nebraska Press.

Kostera, M. 1995a. The modern crusade: The missionaries of management come to Eastern Europe. *Management Learning*, 26: 331-352.

Kostera, M. 1995b. Organisational identity transfer: Enterprise and managers as depicted by the Polish post-1989 press. A paper given at the EMOT/Judge Institute Workshop on Managerial Learning in the Transformation of Eastern Europe, St. John's College, Cambridge, April.

Kostera, M. 1995c. *Postmodernizm w Zarzadzaniu (Postmodernism in Management)*. Warsaw: PWE Press.

Maczynski, J. 1991. *A cross-cultural comparison of decision participation based on the Vroom-Yetton model of leadership*. Report PRE23, Institute of Management, Technical University of Wroclaw.

Mair, M. 1990. Telling psychological tales. *International Journal of Personal Construct Psychology*, 3: 121-135.

Maruyama, M. 1982. New mindscapes for future business policy and management. *Technology Forecasting and Social Change*, 21: 53-76.

McNeill, I. 1991. The reality of doing business in Poland. *The Intelligent Enterprise*, 1: 9-16.

Smith, P. B., Misumi, J., Tayeb, M., Peterson, M., and Bond, M. 1989. On the generality of leadership style measures across cultures. *Journal of Occupational Psychology*, 62: 97-109.

Tsoukas, H. 1991. The missing link: A transformational view of metaphors in organizational science. *Academy of Management Review*, 16: 566-585.

Chapter 3

The Institutional Requisites
of Capitalism

Michael K. Mauws
Nelson Phillips

THE SOCIAL FOUNDATION OF CAPITALISM

The recent armed insurrection in Chechnya is further evidence of the rapid social, political, and economic changes occurring in what was, until recently, the Soviet Union and its satellite states. But despite the ongoing instability of the region, the movement toward a closer integration with the Western world seems irreversible, and Western businesses are increasingly looking toward Central and Eastern Europe for new opportunities. Nevertheless, although the general direction of social change in these new nations has been chosen, the path to be followed and the final destination remain in question. The challenge facing these new nations is significant: creating a workable economic system compatible with Western market economies from the ashes of a failed command economy. Meeting this challenge is a prerequisite to attracting and retaining Western investment.

But the problem is not solely economic, despite much of the rhetoric in the West: moving toward a market economy requires much more than simply changing government policy. A free market does not exist in a social vacuum but, rather, in a socially constructed environment in which the market is "extensively and continuously regulated" (Sayer, 1991: 28). As E. P. Thompson observed, the "social and cultural phenomena do not trail after the economic at some remove" but, rather, are constitutive of what we refer to as economic phenomena (Thompson, 1978: 84). Therefore, any successful movement toward a Western-style free market will require important and fundamental social change to produce a system in which certain institutional and moral conditions can exist. It is these social underpinnings of the Western market system—what we are calling the institutional requisites of capitalism—that will concern us below. The resulting theoretical framework is useful in understanding the requirements for reform in Central and Eastern Europe and other post-communist nations.

The remainder of this chapter is structured in four parts. In the first section, a brief introduction to institutional theory (e.g., Powell and DiMaggio, 1991) is presented along with a discussion of its applicability to the analysis of social systems. In the second section, some of the social structures underlying Western market systems are presented, as well as historical explanations for their current form. The social system which exists in Central and Eastern Europe is considered in the third section and compared to the requisites of capitalism presented in the second section. Finally, in the conclusion, the importance of these requisites for transnational business ventures is discussed.

INSTITUTIONAL THEORY:
A BRIEF INTRODUCTION

While there are several variants of institutional theory (see Powell and DiMaggio, 1991; Scott, 1987, 1995), most share a concern with social order and the taken-for-granted characteristics of social forms. Institutional theorists are interested in the matter-of-fact nature of social reality and the way in which social facts, such as particular organizational forms, are created, maintained, and communicated. Formal organizations such as corporations depend upon complex sets of practices and understandings which are deeply ingrained, so deeply that they appear natural and lawlike despite their socially constructed nature. As Meyer and Rowan explain:

> In modern societies, the elements of rationalized formal structure are deeply ingrained in, and reflect, widespread understandings of social reality. Many of the positions, policies, programs, and procedures of modern organizations are enforced by public opinion, by the views of important constituents, by knowledge legitimated through the educational system, by social prestige, by the laws, and by the definitions of negligence and prudence used in the courts. Such elements of formal structure are manifestations of powerful institutional rules which function as highly rationalized myths that are binding on particular organizations. (1977: 343)

In other words, the formal organizations which make up the economic system (the corporations, legal firms, accounting partnerships, stock exchanges, etc.), and the nature of the relations between these organizations, are all dependent upon a set of shared definitions of social reality which social actors use to create and interpret organizations. The existence of a formal organization of a particular type depends upon these rationalized myths and their acceptance by the individuals who interact to create and maintain the organization.

The process by which certain activities come to be labeled as activities of a particular type–the creation of a myth which both structures activity and makes it meaningful–is the process of institutionalization; i.e., "institutionalization occurs whenever there is a reciprocal typification of habitualized actions by types of actors" (Berger and Luckmann, 1967: 54). The process of institutionalization produces social reality in that "it is the process by which individual actors transmit what is socially defined as real" (Zucker, 1977: 728); it "involves the processes by which social processes, obligations, or actualities come to take on a rule-like status in social thought and action" (Meyer and Rowan, 1977: 341).

From this perspective, society is essentially a social construction growing out of the interaction of its members; social reality is produced through a set of shared typifications which have developed over a particular period of time (Berger and Luckmann, 1967). Institutions are products of these typifications; they cannot be created instantaneously nor can they be understood adequately without an understanding of their history (Berger and Luckmann, 1967: 54). The implication, then, is that all societies are a product of their history and their variety attests to the importance of historical difference in the formation of alternative institutional arrangements.

Seen in this way, capitalism is an economic system, but one based on particular social institutions. Capitalism requires an extensive array of social institutions and practices–free labor, private property, money, etc.–to function and, importantly, *these institutions are a product of a particular history.* Understanding capitalism and the changes required for the implementation of a free market in a previously noncapitalist country includes an understanding of these institutions as social constructs and the historical dialectics that produced them. In brief, implementing a free market requires much more than simply legislation: it requires a comprehensive institutional arena to supply the regulation which underlies the anarchy of capitalism.

INSTITUTIONAL REQUISITES
OF WESTERN MARKET SYSTEMS

Private property and the opportunity for profit–the most basic hallmarks of capitalism–can exist only as a result of the institutionalized arrangements upon which they have been constructed. For writers such as Giddens, the capitalist social order should, in fact, be defined in terms of its main "institutional alignments" (1990: 57). Capitalism, from a sociological standpoint, is considerably more than a means of economic exchange; it is also the outcome of a specific combination of institutionalized social behaviors. Durkheim's (1984) discussion of the institutional and moral bases of contracts, for example, illustrates that even laissez-faire economics requires a considerable degree of formal and informal regulation. Paraphrasing Sayer (1991: 28), the anarchy of the market is possible only within a socially constructed economic sphere. It is the nature of the institutions which make up this socially constructed economic sphere–the institutions which, through their alignment, *produce* the Western market system–that will be explored in this section.

Unfortunately for those wishing to emulate it, the Western economic order is the product of a very complicated, nonlinear, historical process which continues to develop in unpredictable ways. The development of a social system is a dialectical process in which the development of each institution is both constituted by and constitutive of other institutions (Ranson, Hinings, and Greenwood, 1980). The complexity of this process is further compounded by the fact that any knowledge gained through an analysis of the system is incorporated into the system itself–what is often referred to as reflexivity: "[t]he point is not that there is no stable social world to know, but that knowledge of that world contributes to its unstable or mutable character" (Giddens, 1990: 45). This serves to underscore the nonteleological character of the *progress* of the social order and the unpredictability of any attempt at emulating it.

This is not, however, to deny the possible benefit of learning from the experience of Western capitalism; rather, it merely discounts the possibility of its replication. Because the histories of the post-communist nations are distinct from those of Western nations, any form of economic order will have its own unique nuances in the same manner that there are differences among the market systems of the Western nations. In attempting to emulate a Western market system, the economic order of the West must be seen as effect rather than cause and policies aimed at emulation must reflect the institutional sources from which the Western systems emerged.

Individualism

An understanding of the role of individualism in the West is essential in attempting to understand the institutional foundations of the Western market system. The ethic of individualism provides a justification for the social inequalities that occur in a free market system: individuals are equal, at least in principle, and differential achievement is the matter-of-fact result of more or less successful negotiation in the market (Sayer, 1991). But individualism also provides autonomy and therefore produces an environment in which innovations can flourish and niches can develop. The diversity, change, and growth desired by the post-communist nations grows out of the individualism that permits and encourages each person to strive for whatever it is that he or she might desire. But individualism is not universal: its institutionalization in Western societies has been facilitated by specific institutional histories resulting, in large part, from the abstraction of the individual, the commodification of social relations, and the ethic of accumulation.

Abstraction of the Individual

The common Western notion that an individual's social standing is the result of personal effort and ability (or, perhaps, good luck), and therefore somehow separate from their "self," is a fairly recent invention (Taylor, 1989). As a result, in capitalist societies social positions are seen as accidental rather than fixed. As described by Marx (1989: 123), "[i]n the state . . . man is regarded as a species-being, he is the imaginary member of an illusory sovereignty, [he] is deprived of his individual life and endowed with an unreal universality." In contrast, within precapitalist societies individuals are engulfed by the social relations which defined them. As Sayer argues, "[t]heir subjectivities are inseparable from their social position" (Sayer, 1991: 18).

The institutionalization of the abstract individual, thus described, serves a twofold function in the Western market system. First, because each person effectively has two *identities*, the institutionalization of inequality is facilitated in that all are equal qua individuals despite their social inequality; i.e., *political egalitarianism sanctions economic inequality.* Second, it is the abstraction of the individual which makes possible the capitalist employment contract. Because the person who enters into the social relations necessary for employment can be differentiated from the person *as* an individual, the commodification of wage-labor is made possible and organizations are able to concern themselves only with those relations related to the employment contract as opposed to responsibility for the *whole* person, as is characteristic of precapitalist societies. Thus, for the Western free market system to function as it does, it is imperative that the individual be able to separate her- or himself *as* an individual from the social relations required for economic survival.

The Commodification of Social Relations

The roots of this transition can be found, in large part, in the commodification which accompanied the rise of capitalism. As individuals moved from the production of goods for personal consumption to the production of goods for exchange, their relationships were transformed from ones of personal dependence to relationships mediated by commodities.

> [I]t is one of the fundamental characteristics of an individualistic capitalistic economy that it is rationalized on the basis of rigorous calculation, directed with foresight and caution towards the economic success which is sought in sharp contrast to the hand-to-mouth existence of the peasant. (Weber, 1958: 76)

The logical end of this process was one in which production was directed at the acquisition of the means of exchange—money—rather than at a desired product or service. But money today, as a result of its historical and institutional development, acts as much more than a means of exchange (Simmel, 1978). Money, in a modern capitalist state, serves as a "means of bracketing time" (Giddens, 1990: 24). It is a means whereby social relations can be taken from the context in which they occur and transported to an alternative time or place. In this manner money facilitates accumulation (which will be discussed later) across generations and across national boundaries. It is because money represents the social relations necessary to produce it that Marx saw the modern man as carrying his social power "in his pocket" (Sayer, 1991: 67) and that transnational organizations are able to benefit from globalization.

So what has resulted from the commodification of social relations is, in fact, their objectification. And as commodification encroaches upon an increasing portion of people's activities, thus objectifying it, activities which in precapitalist societies would have contributed to an individual's identity are now abstracted away from the individual. Similarly, in the political sphere, the advancement of democracy served to produce the abstract individual as someone separate from the holder of office or citizen of nation-state. This further objectified social relations and "it is this objectification which enables power to be exercised by individuals *as* individuals rather than as personifications of a community" (Sayer, 1991: 67).

Ethic of Accumulation

In attempting to understand the development of individualism, one must also examine the ethic of accumulation and its historical roots in the

Protestant work ethic (Weber, 1958). In brief, it was the coincidence of technological progress and the advent of Calvinism that launched Western markets along the historical trajectory which characterizes them today. The Protestant philosophy of hard work and thrift was the ideal catalyst to foster the accumulation of capital necessary to finance the development of early capitalism. The provision of the initial concentrations of capital, combined with an ethic of work as a calling done for the glory of God, provided the impetus required to form a functioning capitalist system capable of providing an adequate standard of living for participants. The ethic of individualism was further strengthened by the notion that one received wealth in proportion to one's favor with God; i.e., economic inequality was divinely sanctioned.

Although the Protestant roots of capitalism have faded, they still remain, in Sayer's words, as "the ghosts in the machine" (1991: 133). Much of the ethic which propelled our society into the age of capitalism endures despite the demise of the metaphysical roots which gave it meaning. As Weber so aptly noted, "man is dominated by the making of money, by acquisition as the ultimate purpose of his life. Economic acquisition is no longer subordinated to man as the means for the satisfaction of his material needs" (1958: 53). However, it is not avarice which Weber wishes here to associate with capitalism, for the "impulse to acquisition, pursuit of gain, of money, of the greatest possible amount of money, has in itself nothing to do with capitalism." Instead, it is the pursuit of money as the means to more money which Weber sees as characterizing capitalism; ironically, "capitalism may even be identical with the restraint, or at least a rational tempering, of this irrational impulse" (1958: 17).

Regulation

There are four institutional mechanisms by which control is achieved within the capitalist state: the means of exchange, the institutionalization of knowledges, the nature of the employment contract, and the development of property rights. Because the ethic of individualism fosters an environment in which all are in competition with all, and because capitalism "has never allowed its aspirations to be determined by national boundaries" (Wallerstein, cited in Giddens, 1990: 69), it is necessary for these control mechanisms to be in place if the identity of the nation-state and social order are to be maintained. Contrary to what laissez-faire economics might have us believe, "the state's influence . . . is *always* present in the economy insofar as it provides an institutional and legal framework that influences the selection of different governance regimes and thereby permanently shapes the economy" (Campbell and Lindberg, 1990: 637). It is this institutional framework which must be understood in examining the functioning of a "free market" economy.

The Means of Exchange

The development of trust is a fundamental requirement for the smooth functioning of capitalism (Giddens, 1990). With respect to the means of exchange, those who are willing to accept money as payment do so with the confidence that they can purchase something elsewhere or at another time with the money they possess. If individuals' intentions were otherwise, it would be hard to imagine (other than for reasons of divisibility) why barter would not be sufficient. In referring to money as the "means of exchange," our temptation is to think of it as the vehicle by which we can exchange "two cows for a pig or three goats" when, instead, it should be seen as the means whereby we exchange our work *today* for consumption *tomorrow*. But in order for this to be possible, those who accept money must trust that it will serve this purpose.

We have already stated above that money is representative of the social relations necessary to produce it. As with all social relations, however, trust is something that is developed over time as a result of increasing confidence. Today, many people invest large sums of money in retirement savings plans and other financial instruments because our currency has proven its stability over time (inflation in no way alters this so long as it also remains relatively stable). However, this stability, and hence trust, is the outcome of many other institutional influences. It is because the government limits its production of currency, because the central banks of other nations are willing to cooperate, and because our economy is regulated, that we can have any degree of confidence in the value of a currency at any point in the future. Conversely, it is because we place our trust in the means of exchange and are willing to express all but our most intimate social relations in the form of money, that the state is able to maintain control. Through money, all social relations are quantifiable and thus easily expressible in the form of statistics. This provides the state with an incomparable means of surveillance and the necessary summation of social activity to facilitate policy formulation.

The Institutionalization of Knowledges

Much has been written about the epistemological foundations of knowledge. Recently this discussion has often occurred under the rubric of "modernism" versus "postmodernism." The discussion of these issues is not new; what is new, however, is their significance given the transition within the Western nations to a knowledge-based society. Lyotard, for example, notes that "the right to decide what is true is not independent of the right to decide what is just . . . the question of knowledge is now more than ever a question of government" (1984: 8-9). If knowledge "has no final legitimacy outside of serving the goals envisioned by the practical subject" and there "is no other proof that the [knowledge is] good than the consensus [of] the experts" (Lyotard, 1984: 36, 29), the role it serves within society is drastically altered.

Continuing with Lyotard's argument, knowledge "is and will be produced in order to be sold, it is and will be consumed in order to be valorized in a new production: in both cases, the goal is exchange. Knowledge ceases to be an end in itself, it loses its 'use-value' " (Lyotard, 1984: 5). With the commodification of knowledge–its translation into exchange-value–instead of deriving its value as truth, its value stems from the "guarantees" which are associated with it, thus facilitating the transference of social relations across space and time: "an expert system disembeds in the same way as [money], by providing 'guarantees' of expectations across distanciated space-time" (Giddens, 1990: 28). For example: it is consistency, rather than accurate representation, that explains the institutionalization of accounting within capitalism. With the institutionalization of knowledge bases comes their valorization, hence the tendency toward "professionalization" by psychologists, certified professional accountants (CPAs), and even tow-truck drivers. As with the means of exchange, however, the institutionalization of knowledges serves the twofold purpose of providing trust and facilitating state control: "supervision [in the modern state] may be direct, but more characteristically it is indirect and based upon the control of information" (Giddens, 1990: 58).

The Nature of the Employment Contract

That the "workers of the world" have failed to "unite" would seem to undermine the teleological view of economic history set out by Karl Marx in the 1800s. Yet Marx's seemingly accurate observation that "Nature does not produce on the one side owners of money or commodities, and on the other men possessing nothing but their own labour-power," (1989: 65) requires an explanation for why workers have failed to realize their disadvantaged position relative to the so-called "owners of money." One influence has undoubtedly been the institutionalization of standards of employment limiting what an employer can require of an employee and defining a basic set of rights to be possessed by all employees. The logic of competition is such that, in the absence of regulation, employees must be encouraged to work harder and for less money. The recognition of this tendency and its detrimental effects has brought about minimum wages, overtime wages, workers' compensation, etc., which have served to eliminate the threat of overthrow envisioned by Marx.

A second mitigating factor with respect to the control of employment has been the development of a general agreement that capitalism is the best possible economic system[1]–a capitalist hegemony (Gramsci, 1971). Given the performance orientation of capitalism, the fact that "administrative procedures should make individuals 'want' what the system needs in order to perform well" (Lyotard, 1984: 62) would verge on the axiomatic. In order for capitalism to sustain itself, it is necessary that it establish its self-evidence (Sayer, 1991). "The 'normal' functioning of a particular social order [must create] 'submission and intellectual subordination' among a population" (Alford and Friedland, 1985: 8) if its participants are to submit to its logic. Because the capitalist state, in theory, provides everyone with the possibility of success, and has the myths, folklore, and history to substantiate these claims, the drudgery of low-level employment is mitigated by the possibility of future riches as well as any threat to the system itself.

The Development of Property Rights

Because physical assets become capital only within certain relations (Sayer, 1991: 37), property rights at the most basic level are a prerequisite of capitalism. But property rights also "specify relations among people" and, as a result, "they also define the institutional basis of power relations in the processes of production, exchange, and accumulation" (Campbell and Lindberg, 1990: 635). Through their ability to define what is "possessable," governments wield considerable influence within the capitalist economy. In relation to the earlier discussion of knowledges, we might note how property rights have evolved to include intellectual property in addition to land, buildings, and machinery.

The evolution of property rights is, in itself, an expression of relations of power in the capitalist state since these relations often develop in an ad hoc manner rather than within a carefully planned structure (Campbell and Lindberg, 1990). The attitude of protectionism and its accompanying tools of tariffs and duties, the development of marketing boards, the granting of monopolies, and the approval of oligopolies are all expressions of property rights. Perhaps the most timely example of these rights would be with respect to environmental regulations. The determination of "how much"

---

1. See, for example, *The End of History and the Last Man* by Francis Fukuyama as an example of this sort of argument.

of the environment belongs to business and is thus considered "expendable" is an expression of how far ownership has developed in the capitalist state. That this is so is exemplified in the recent implementation in the United States of "environmental credits" which facilitate the "exchange of pollution" among market participants.

THE EASTERN BLOC:
INSTITUTIONAL OBSTACLES

The economic problems which faced the newly democratized states of Central and Eastern Europe and the former Soviet Union in the early 1990s were severe: inefficient industrial plants, mismanagement, and inadequate infrastructure plagued the economy; conflict, confusion, and uncertainty afflicted the political system; and social disintegration, doubt, and scarcity characterized the everyday experience of citizens. The result, not surprisingly, was a disintegrating empire providing a declining standard of living for its citizens. In 1990, for the first time in the postwar period, the Soviet government reported a fall in gross national product (2 percent), industrial production (1.2 percent), and agricultural production (2.3 percent). By 1991, the economy appeared to be worsening at an increasing rate, with gross national product estimated to have dropped by 10 percent in the first half of the year. In the same period, industrial output dropped by 6 percent while heavy industry declined 7 percent and the output of consumer-related goods declined 3 percent.

In response, many plans for economic reform—such as the 500-day Shatalin plan and the less radical Ryzhkov plan—were introduced (Hewitt, 1990). While each plan agreed on the necessity of moving toward a freer economy—the Presidential plan adopted by the Soviet Congress of People's Deputies on October 19, 1990, for example, stated that there "is no alternative to switching to a market" and that "the choice of switching to the market has been made, a choice of historic importance to the fate of the country" (Schroeder, 1991: 325)—each disagreed on the appropriate steps, on the speed of reform, and, even more important, on the actual nature of the goal.

The confusion in the government was reflected in the lack of agreement among its citizens: a lack of agreement on how free the market should be, on what the effects of the introduction of a free market system would be, at what speed liberalization should take place, and on the nature of a "market economy." While it appeared that externally both the final goal and the activities required to reach it were clear—the OECD (Organization for Economic Cooperation and Development), for example, was advocating "a radical approach" to reform "in order to achieve a successful trans-formation into a market oriented economy" (OECD, 1991)–internally both were (and still are) sources of confusion and conflict. While a poll in June 1990 found that two-thirds of the Russian population preferred a market economy, it was unclear as to what might constitute the market economy they were said to prefer.

It seems by market economy the respondents mean a system that prom-ises affluence, but not its shadows–social inequality and unemployment. The oxymoronic "regulated market" launched by the authorities corre-sponds to the wishes of the majority of the Soviet people who want the prosperity of capitalism as long as incomes remain roughly equal and jobs are guaranteed. A mere 28 percent approve of a free market in the true meaning of the word, three percent less than those who prefer a strictly centralized economy. The remaining 41 percent would have their cake and eat it too (Pipes, 1991: 80).

Reflecting on the discussion of the institutional requisites of capitalism, the degree of disagreement is troubling. If, as Weber points out, the devel-opment of capitalism depends not so much on the availability of capital or the level of technology but rather on "the development of the spirit of capitalism," then this deep lack of agreement reflected an equally deep lack of the spirit of capitalism (Weber, 1958: 68). As we have seen above, a free market requires a taken-for-granted acceptance of particular types of social relations and particular social practices; they must appear natural and law-like in order to provide a substantial basis for the free market. This natural and lawlike appearance depends on a taken-for-granted acceptance, hardly a result of deep divisions and even misunderstandings among the individuals who make up a particular society.

At the most functional level, we can see that the ethic of individualism which undergirds capitalism has no historical place in the post-communist states. The historical events which supported the development of capital-ism in the Western countries have no parallel in these countries. In fact, 80 years of communist rule has had the opposite effect, producing a country of citizens who look to the government for direction and who understand many functions which we associate with entrepreneurial activity as the purview of the state.

And yet the state is in no condition to provide leadership: "Although six years of perestroika have wrought considerable havoc on the economy, the real crisis in the Soviet Union . . . is one of governance" (Schroeder, 1991: 327). The governments are increasingly unstable and discredited, just as unable to set in motion the structures to support capitalism as they were to continue supporting the command economies of the communist regimes. The trust required to support a monetary system has long ago disappeared, but the governments have only limited amounts of information on the current state of their economies in any case; the system of surveillance required for effective public policy is very different from what is required to support a totalitarian state.

CONCLUSIONS AND IMPLICATIONS

In this chapter we have attempted to widen the discussion of transforming the economies in Central and Eastern Europe and the former Soviet Union into market-based systems to include some of the sociological aspects of capitalism. In particular, we have attempted to outline some of the institutional obstacles—e.g., the lack of an ethic of individualism—to the introduction of a free market in post-communist countries. The ramifications of these obstacles for the nature and potential of trade with these nations are important and lasting. In the remainder of this section we will summarize our argument.

1. Western capitalism is supported by a substrate of institutionalized beliefs and practices—the institutional requisites of capitalism—which provide a rationalized and regulated arena within which the anarchy of capitalism can thrive.

Capitalism can exist only in a highly regulated environment characterized by both legitimate social structures and institutionalized social practices. Understanding the nature of these institutions provides an important addition to a purely economic understanding of the problems encountered in moving from a command economy to a free market, and of the problems which will be encountered in doing business with these newly independent states.

2. These circumstances are a product of an historically contingent, culturally specific set of circumstances.

The process of institutionalization occurs over time, and institutionalized structures and practices are therefore historically contingent; they are the product of a complex dialectical process which has occurred over the history of a particular social group. Different cultures produce and sustain different economic systems: while both Japan and the United States are nominally free market systems, they are characterized by very different sets of social practices and understandings.

3. The unique history of the West has produced a particular institutional framework including an ethic of individualism, a stable and trusted monetary system, and a complex and well-developed system of governance.

In the West, the unique pattern of historical development has produced an economic system which grows out of particular social institutions and understandings: (1) an ethic of individualism which legitimates differential economic rewards on the basis of equal opportunity and efficient markets; (2) a system of commodified social relations mediated by money; and (3) a system of well-developed governance to support notions of private property, contracts, fair employment practices, and fair trading.

4. The unique histories of Central and Eastern Europe and of Russia have produced very different sets of institutionalized practices and beliefs, many of which preclude an economic system parallel to the Western market system.

The histories of Central and Eastern Europe, and of Russia in particular, differ greatly from that of the West. The cultural and technological constellation which produces capitalism in the West does not exist in these post-communist nations, and the effectiveness of trying to emulate our system is problematic at best. In fact, many of the social practices and cultural values—beliefs regarding the immorality of profit taking and economic inequality, for example—are in direct contradiction to the required institutionalized practices and beliefs.

5. These nations cannot simply adopt a Western market system parallel to one of the successful Western nations but must develop an economic system which conforms to and strengthens their social system.

As a result, the economic system appropriate for these new nations is certainly not a replica of any Western system, any more than the economic system of Japan can be considered a replica of that of Britain. The system must develop over time and grow out of the beliefs and practices which underlie their culture, not be based on some idea of a "correct" or "natural" economic system.

EPILOGUE

An understanding of the institutional requisites of capitalism, combined with a consideration of the economic and social disarray of the post-communist countries, provides several insights: (a) an understanding of the deep cultural differences which currently provide little support for private property, high levels of profit, and economic inequity; (b) an appreciation of the time required to develop a functioning economic system compatible with the West; and (c) the possible differences in the resulting economic system. Economic reform will be neither quick nor easy, but will require time to instill new social norms and to develop new social structures to support new economic processes. As Kennan points out:

> What is now emerging on the territory traditionally known as Russia will not be–cannot be–the Russia of the tsars. Nor can it be the Russia of the communists. It can only be something essentially new, the contours of which are still, for us and for the Russians themselves, obscure. . . . The tasks to be encompassed are immense. A workable system of humane representative government–something of which Russian history provides only the most rudimentary experience–will have to be devised and rendered acceptable to a people among whom the principle of reasonable compromise, essential to its success, is largely foreign. A new economic system, compatible with Russian traditions but not limited by them, will have to be devised. . . . And, finally, the immensely complex and dangerous process of political and institutional decentralization of the traditional Russian will have to be in some way managed. (1990: 184)

In brief, simply replicating the institutions of the West will not suffice to introduce a market system in these countries any more than wearing a baseball uniform makes one a baseball player. The patterns of interaction, the expectations, and the social structures to support the economic sphere must be developed concurrently with the development of new economic forms appropriate for the cultural foundation.

REFERENCES

Alford, R. R. and Friedland, R. 1985. *Powers of theory: Capitalism, the state and democracy*. Cambridge: Cambridge University Press.

Berger, P. and Luckmann, T. L. 1967. *The social construction of reality*. New York: Doubleday.

Campbell, J. and Lindberg, L. 1990. Property rights and the organization of economic activity by the state. *American Sociological Review*, 55: 634-647.

Durkheim, E. 1984. *The division of labour in society*. London: Allen and Unwin.

Giddens, A. 1990. *The consequences of modernity*. Stanford: Stanford University Press.

Gramsci, A. 1971. *Prison notebooks.* New York: International Publishers.

Hewitt, E. 1990. The new Soviet plan. *Foreign Affairs,* 146-167.

Kennan, G. 1990. Communism in Russian history. *Foreign Affairs,* 69(5): 168-186.

Lyotard, J. F. 1984. *The post-modern condition: A report on knowledge.* Minneapolis: University of Minnesota Press.

Marx, K. 1989. *Readings from Karl Marx.* D. Sayer (Ed.). London: Routledge.

Meyer, J. W. and Rowan, B. 1977. Institutionalized organizations: Formal structures as myth and ceremony. *American Journal of Sociology,* 83(2): 340-363.

OECD, 1991. Advertising insert. *Foreign Affairs,* 70(1).

Pipes, R. 1991. The Soviet Union adrift. *Foreign Affairs,* 70(1): 70-87.

Powell, W. W. and DiMaggio, P. J. 1991. *The new institutionalism in organizational analysis.* Chicago: University of Chicago Press.

Ranson, S., Hinings, C. R., and Greenwood, R. 1980. The structuring of organizational structures. *Administrative Science Quarterly,* 25(1): 1-17.

Sayer, D. 1991. *Capitalism and modernity: An excursus on Marx and Weber.* London: Routledge.

Schroeder, G. 1991. A critical time for perestroika. *Current History,* 90(10): 323-327.

Scott, W. R. 1987. The adolescence of institutional theory. *Administrative Science Quarterly,* 32(4): 493-511.

Scott, W. R. 1995. *Institutions and organizations.* Thousand Oaks, CA: Sage.

Simmel, G. 1978. *The Philosophy of Money.* Boston: Routledge.

Taylor, C. 1989. *Sources of the self.* Cambridge, MA: Harvard University Press.

Thompson, E. P. 1978. *The poverty of theory and other essays.* London: Merlin.

Weber, M. 1958. *The Protestant ethic and the spirit of capitalism.* New York: Charles Scribner's Sons.

Zucker, L. G. 1977. The role of institutionalization in cultural persistence. *American Sociological Review,* 42: 726-743.

Chapter 4

Where Is the Research from Central and Eastern Europe?

John L. Kmetz

INTRODUCTION

Following the sudden and unexpected collapse of the former Soviet-dominated bloc of Central and Eastern Europe in 1989, the United States and Western Europe quickly organized a variety of projects intended to assist these countries in the transition from central planning to a market system and democracy. My personal involvement in these programs began in the fall of 1990, when the University of Delaware was awarded a grant from the U.S. Agency for International Development (USAID) to provide training in management, economics, and English language to the Republic of Bulgaria. As the program director, I have been active in Central and Eastern Europe since that time.

This chapter draws on both my experience in this work as well as the published and unpublished experience of others. While my primary activity was in Bulgaria, I have maintained close contact with many others working in the region, at the University of Delaware and other U.S. and European universities, through several academic and practitioner organizations, and personal and professional interactions. I want to emphasize that the points I make in this chapter are based on both my experience and much information I have learned from others who have worked in these countries. Thus, while most of my examples are drawn from Bulgaria, I have selected them because they are similar to the experiences of others; where I do not feel that generalizability is warranted, I draw attention to that point. Most of this chapter, it should be noted, assumes the perspective of an educator from a Western market economy who is working in a transitional economy.

Among the many outcomes our university group expected when we started working in Bulgaria in 1991 was the creation of a large body of research into the transition process, and to see an outpouring of information on the transformation of the economy. We especially anticipated a large body of privatization and entrepreneurship research (PER). Five years later, it is apparent that far less of that research has materialized than we expected, and that perhaps little will. What has happened?

We argue that three interacting factors have prevented the development of a strong PER program from Central and Eastern Europe: (1) the well-documented difficulties of working in the context of such an enormous sociopolitical change; (2) the intended and unintended consequences of relying on universities as the primary source of training; and (3) the lack of strong paradigms to guide the work. These factors are related to one another in a systemic manner in that feedbacks and interactions between them are often as important as the individual factors themselves. Thus, some of the discussion is connected to the training and transition programs which were the vehicle by which researchers gained access to Central and Eastern Europe. In addition, much of what has been needed in Central and Eastern Europe is research which is useful rather than theoretical, and this has often been difficult to do under the best of circumstances (Kilmann et al., 1994).

THREE FACTORS LIMITING RESEARCH IN CENTRAL AND EASTERN EUROPE

Catastrophic, Chaotic Change

There is one overarching factor which has major consequences on the ability to conduct research in Central and Eastern Europe. This is that change in the entire region has been truly "catastrophic" and "chaotic" in both the mathematical sense as well as the more ordinary interpretations. No one who has followed events in the former CMEA (Council for Mutual Economic Assistance) countries, and the collapse of communism in the former Soviet Union in 1991, can be unaware of the obvious: the collapse of a social, political, and economic system of this magnitude, barring involvement of military force, disease, or disaster, is without precedent. Within the course of two years, between the summers of 1989 and 1991, the defining characteristics of the economic, political, and military world all changed. Euphoria replaced despair, offers for joint ventures replaced overt hostility, and people in regions of the world long difficult to gain access to became interested in the development of hard-currency tourism.

Rapid and discontinuous change processes are considered to be the primary characteristics of the catastrophe and chaos models of mathematics. Those features, exemplified by unstable political alignments, on-again, off-again privatization programs, civil war in the former Yugoslavia, massive inflation, institutional collapse, and all the other attendant consequences of change in Central and Eastern Europe, are the norm. Much of the basis of scientific research assumes some degree of orderliness of change, and therefore the ability to describe, measure, and predict phenomena over time. Little of that description matches events in Central and Eastern Europe and the Newly Independent States (NIS).

This property of change in Central and Eastern Europe has had two effects on PER and transition research in general. First, it has meant that the time usually needed for papers to go through the social science publication review and revision process renders research obsolete before it can be published. For example, concern has shifted rapidly from debate over appropriate macroeconomic models of change to issues of control of organized crime; from consolidation of democratic institutions to dealing with the reemergence of governments of former communists now elected to office, etc. This kind of change means that by the time an article has worked its way through the review process, it may well be irrelevant to the current situation. For that reason, much of the research that is appearing is being presented at conferences and specialized meetings, similar to the model of the exact sciences.

In the author's experience, it is clear that some research is emerging through specialized conferences and meetings of international scholars and others involved in the change process, but little of this research is being published elsewhere, particularly in the highly ranked journals of management. Some articles are appearing in the management literature, but few of these deal with privatization and entrepreneurship. Most of these are general commentaries on the transition of these economies, such as Clark, 1994; Hunter, 1993; King, 1994; Maruyama, 1990; Newman, 1992; and Shama, 1993.

It should be noted that an additional factor limiting the development of research is that many of our colleagues in Central and Eastern Europe, despite a deep interest in the change process, had not been trained in the dynamics and operation of market economies. While fully capable of conducting research, as is clear from the achievements of exact and physical scientists from the region, many researchers interested in PER are approaching the subjects with this disadvantage. Time will be needed for them to engage in PER research effectively.

Thus, it may be that the chaos in the region inhibits research from Central and Eastern Europe from finding its way into more "mainstream" academic outlets, rather than actually preventing it from being done. Yet several factors, which follow, emerge from this overarching chaos and appear to inhibit both the performance of PER and its wider publication.

The concept of "market." The gulf between the understanding of a "market" on the part of the people of Central and Eastern Europe and the Westerners who came to do business training was enormous. The "market" that had existed there was a much more highly structured, centrally planned entity than Westerners understood, even in the more liberal countries such as Poland, Hungary, and former Czechoslovakia. Much of the ordinary behavior of a market that is taken for granted in the West was considered to be criminal "speculation" in Central and Eastern Europe. Consequently, expectations of entrepreneurship ranged from anticipation of immediate wealth as a result of starting a company, to beliefs that one could buy insurance to prevent business loss, to beliefs that entrepreneurial behavior was illegal. Privatization was often surrounded by equally divergent and unrealistic expectations, even for those few state firms which had begun to prepare for actual private ownership. Attempts to do meaningful PER within this context were strongly inhibited by uncertainties over responses to research questions, wherein the researcher could never be sure that the respondents had really understood research questions in terms Westerners intended.

"Information" and "information sharing." A related problem in PER research surrounds the value of information and the meaning of information sharing. In the economies of scarcity of Central and Eastern Europe (Shama, 1993), "information" was a commodity of great value, to be used for bargaining. Western-style information sharing never happened, and if information was shared, it was never without a quid pro quo. Widely available information implied a market much more efficient than the planned one in which people made their livelihoods. And so readily available information was often viewed with suspicion: If it is so easy to get, what can it be worth? To simply have a questionnaire answered by a group of potential training or research beneficiaries frequently raises questions as to motives and intentions on the part of the researcher, and concerns over who will see the responses.

This problem is very deeply rooted, as two brief examples will show. In one case, the author worked with a growing, successful small Bulgarian firm to write a business plan to secure a short-term loan for acquisition of a winery. None of the plan writing required anything more than a fax machine and a word processor, and the owners needed to do little except send the raw data from Bulgaria to me in the United States. But the owners were simply unwilling to disclose all the information needed, and so I traveled to Bulgaria to complete the plan. It never was completed—the owners simply could not bring themselves to openly disclose internal business affairs, as is taken for granted in the West, and so the company never approached a lending organization. For many of the organizations in Central and Eastern Europe trying to place loans and investments, this gap in understanding of business practice has been equally intractable and frustrating as it has for those seeking capital. In another example, our University of Delaware group was charged with forming a coalition of business, educational, and community leaders in Bulgaria as part of our USAID work. A colleague in an associated Bulgarian university was disturbed by the relatively open admission of people to the coalition, and strongly suggested that he should be the gatekeeper, since he believed he knew far better than we who should be part of this process, and further, felt that not everyone in Bulgaria needed to know what we were doing.

Language and translation difficulties. It is very difficult to conduct research in countries where the language of market-economy business has not been widely used; this makes accurate mapping of business terms and concepts from other languages even more difficult than it ordinarily is. This is a major problem, even for those prepared for it. Except for specialists trained to deal with Western businesspeople, much of the language of trade and business in everyday use in market economies is still new to entrepreneurs and managers in the region. For example, in one early experience working with a Ukrainian group, I found that I had confused my audience by using the term "wholesaler." Wholesaling is widely understood in the West; in the Ukraine, legitimate wholesalers as we know them did not exist until very recently.

This problem is further complicated by the fact that much of the English used in Central and Eastern Europe is of British origin. For North American researchers, there is constant need to be sure what has been understood when the word "stocks" is used, for example. This phenomenon is an outcome of the Cold War, wherein English instruction in the U.K., or from teachers trained in the U.K., was often more available than from Americans, whose travel and work in Central and Eastern Europe was more restricted. The amount of time and the cost of getting translations of research questionnaires is a significant deterrent to PER. Translators, of course, add an additional filter in any language.

Time. As is true in much of the world, outside the United States most things take longer to accomplish. There are many cultural and other reasons for this, but these problems are compounded in much of Central and Eastern Europe by poor communications and infrastructure. A frequent frustration for many Americans is to find that they have scheduled themselves very tightly for a teaching or consulting trip to Central and Eastern

Europe and then to learn that their schedule and objectives are simply impossible.

Lack of clear models for change. One of the hard realities that most of those who work in Central and Eastern Europe had to accept is that we really have little by way of clear models for change to guide us. This is partially due to the novelty and magnitude of the changes in the region. However, it is also the case that we have little by way of strong models to guide us (see below). For example, the debate over the merits of "shock therapy" versus "go slow" models of macroeconomic change continues without resolution. The kindest thing to say about this debate is that it has been overcome by events. Much the same is true for models of management—we have few strong paradigms (Pfeffer, 1993), and it is highly questionable whether the American model of organization behavior has much relevance outside of the United States (Hofstede, 1993).

The consequence of this lack of strong models meant that everyone had to "write the book as they went along"; while this is not unusual in new ventures, it has had some additional, and unintended, consequences. First, despite early U.S. Department of State guidance specifying immediate, hands-on, highly applicable training for bidders on Central and Eastern European contracts, there was little by way of a clear model to guide such efforts. (With the passage of the Support for Emerging European Democracies Act, the U.S. Department of State published guidance information intended to inform bidders on these contracts what services the U.S. government was seeking; this is ordinary practice for all new U.S. government programs, so that all bidders have equal access to relevant information to prepare their proposals.) Indeed, how to effect immediate change in American organizations is a difficult problem. Second, grantor organizations had few criteria to guide them for program evaluation, and since nearly every government assistance program is subject to review, it was and is far from clear what those criteria should be. Since the contractors for these programs were predominantly universities, the grantors used university criteria. These criteria often resulted in avoidance of the risky and uncertain outcomes involved in privatization and entrepreneurship, and therefore limited research into them.

Unintended Consequences of the Academic Model

Selecting universities as prime contractors for delivery of much of the training given to Central and Eastern Europe certainly made excellent sense from the perspective of gaining access to professional educators. However, relying on universities as the principal providers of training also had unintended consequences, several of which detracted from their ability to train effectively and to do PER.

"*Academic overshoot.*" One of the first unintended problems to emerge was the tendency to model Central and Eastern European training programs after the U.S. model, especially the Master of Business Administration (MBA) degree. In reality, few Central and Eastern Europeans were prepared to deal with the conceptual model of business embedded in MBA-level programs. In fact, many were having difficulty with such fundamental concepts as that of "price." True, in several countries where a more liberalized market had been established, particularly the Czech Republic, Poland, and Hungary, these programs fared better. This overshoot carried over into the conduct of PER and other transition research, where respondents frequently could not fully understand the questions asked of them, let alone provide meaningful answers. For example, in one interview with the CEO of a major electronics manufacturer which was scheduled for privatization, I asked whether he could accurately calculate the cost of goods sold for his product line. His reply was that he could, but only for units produced after the date when he had been given new manufacturing equipment. When I tried to clarify his response, it became clear he did not understand the idea of fixed costs or depreciation. I had intended to use this company as part of a study on privatization, but had to give up the project when it became clear that the responses received from this firm and others would never be based on a consistent interpretation of the questions or underlying business concepts.

The lack of adequately tailoring programs to the needs and understanding of the audiences was compounded by the practice of many universities to assign faculty to a training program for only a short time. The expectation of many faculty was that they could quickly obtain data on a subject which could be analyzed after return to their home countries. This seldom happened. When it became apparent that the complexity of the issues involved would not permit research to be carried out quickly, many instructors became disenchanted with research projects in Central and Eastern Europe. Since time pressures to publish are always great, many faculty who went to the region simply found it unproductive to attempt to conduct PER.

In most cases, attempts to work with local scholars have been made difficult by these same factors. While there are scholars in these countries who have had Western academic training, the large majority of faculty transitioning into business schools, or with scientific academies and organizations, have been trained in the economics of the former centrally planned system. While extremely bright and hardworking as a group, and usually quite progressive, these individuals are still working with the disadvantages of their own background and training, as well as limited access to Western publications, and are often hard-pressed to deal with the transitional problems facing their own institutions. Budgetary difficulties, for example, prevent many Central and Eastern European scholars from participating in conferences and programs with Western colleagues. Along with the infrastructure limitations–particularly poor telecommunications–in many of these countries, these factors are strong inhibitors of either local research or joint work with colleagues elsewhere, although research activity is slowly increasing.

A final component of the academic overshoot problem, although perhaps the most significant, is that most of the training needed in Central and Eastern Europe is extremely basic, and that the primary issues to be dealt with in any manner are equally basic. As a result, Central and Eastern Europe is, in many ways, a poor site for research since one of the criteria for publication in the West, and particularly in the United States, is whether the work is academically and theoretically "impressive." Much of what is needed to support privatization and entrepreneurship in the region simply does not lend itself to theoretically or methodologically "impressive" research activity.

Somewhat more research and commentary on business in these countries is appearing in popular business magazines and trade journals. Magazines such as *The Economist, Business Central Europe*, and *Business Week* and all major business newspapers regularly feature information on the general progress of economic transition. While not necessarily scholarly or scientific, these publications are the best sources of information on the region at present, and in my view, academic research could profit from including more of it.

Suspicion regarding relationships with Central and Eastern European institutions. Many Western universities quite naturally entered into relationships with their counterparts and other institutions in Central and Eastern Europe. Unfortunately, many in the nascent business community in Central and Eastern Europe perceived the universities as being too closely affiliated with the former governments. This was surprising in many respects, since the universities were often the principal sources of opposition to their former communist governments. Nevertheless, many businesspeople in the East perceived the relationships between Western institutions and local universities as indicative of being too close to the "old guard" to really be a reliable source of assistance. While academies of science are generally well regarded as scholarly institutions, the business community found them largely irrelevant to business. Also, the relationship between the academies and Western business trainers was perceived as questionable. The effect has been that in many countries the students now enrolled in formal management courses are frequently not entrepreneurs or managers of privatizing or privatized state firms.

As an example, our attempt to form a coalition in Bulgaria barely survived its own birth. At our first joint meeting, many of those who were invited wondered why they had been asked to attend an event with individuals they would never choose to associate with. In fact, most never returned to subsequent meetings. The only major company to join the coalition did so only because I asked them to, and they left after my departure as program director. The coalition barely survived two meetings, and was effectively dead within six months.

Grantor disavowal of state firms. Partly in order to minimize the appearance of assisting former communist government bodies, many grantor organizations strongly discouraged training or any other involvement with the managers of former state companies and organizations. This had obvious negative consequences for doing PER, but in addition made it more likely that university programs would become isolated from many of the more experienced members of the transitioning economy.

The inversion of equity. Many grantor organizations found their programs being objected to because they were assisting some private firms but not others. Being discouraged from establishing relationships between the North American university and representatives of former state firms, Western faculty now found themselves also being discouraged from forming close working relationships with newly created companies. The consequences of this practice were an "inversion of equity," wherein attempts to be completely fair to everyone resulted in being of little benefit to anyone. This also negatively affected those attempting to do PER and learn more about successful transitions.

Inadequate involvement of the private sector. Unfortunately, from the outset of these programs, little systematic involvement of the Western private sector was included (Behrman, 1994). While universities organized faculties and training programs, little was done to seek advice or gain support for training in the region from private businesspeople from the West. A number of private-sector volunteer programs were established, but very little programmatic work resulted. Consequently, programs of hands-on, highly applicable content often were structured like courses in degree programs. While the education gained from these courses is certainly beneficial, the most urgent need was for assistance in solving immediate, practical business problems—a need that still remains. This has also limited PER studies, in that better and more relevant questions could have been formulated early in the transition process.

The perception of tawdriness. Finally, there is a seldom recognized, but important, issue that affects PER within both the Eastern and Western academic communities and many of the countries of Central and Eastern Europe as well. This is the problem that I term "tawdriness"–the image of tarnished old state companies and their managers on the one hand, and, on the other hand, of entrepreneurs who see enormous potential in common things like pizza, or who may have been black marketeers and definitional criminals in the former regimes. None of these individuals appear as the leaders for multibillion-dollar national refinancing concerns, or for restructuring of national economic frameworks, and yet they are. At the same time, none of these individuals seem to be the building blocks on which great theories of management transition are based, and yet they are. These transitional leaders, in my view, deserve attention and study early in the process, simply because they are leading the way toward change.

The Lack of Strong Models

A final inhibitor of PER in Central and Eastern Europe has been the lack of strong models in several disciplines to guide research, and to a considerable extent, to guide much of the other training done there. This problem is more specific to broader disciplines such as economics, management, and organization theory, and less applicable to more focused disciplines, such as accounting. But even for focused disciplines the job is difficult. We know the techniques and conventions of accounting; teaching Western accounting practices to countries in need of good financial reporting is relatively simple. However, teaching people why they need to disclose information is more difficult, and accounting training alone cannot overcome that problem. It may be more accurate to say that what we lack is models with prescriptive value, and not necessarily the models themselves. For example, there is no shortage of economic models in the West, but there is a great shortage of agreement about what works (Colander, 1991). Nevertheless, all PER and training done in the region has been made more difficult than it might have been by the lack of strong models and paradigms.

Surely the most fundamental problem is the one mentioned in the beginning of this chapter: We simply have no models to deal with chaotic change of the magnitude now under way in Central and Eastern Europe. While the factors discussed above have contributed significantly to this problem, there is another major contributor within the academic research model itself, and that is the immaturity of organizational and management science. This is a subject which cannot be discussed in great detail here, but several of the more important factors can be summarized. These include the lack of systematic or programmatic research, an absence of standardized definitions and terminology, and editorial practices which reward novelty and the appearance of originality rather than the replication of research findings. As a consequence of these practices, we are unable to cumulate research and consolidate gains over time (Cummings and Frost, 1985; Kilmann et al., 1994). These problems are compounded and exacerbated by the most important weakness of the social science model, the mistaken attribution of meaning to statistical significance.

The latter problem is probably the most crucial one, since it allows for virtually any result taken from a large sample to be statistically significant, and therefore offered as "support" for a "theory." What actually needs to be examined in theory testing is effect size–the magnitude of an association or of a difference between measures. When a difference is "big enough," or an association "strong enough," an effect has some importance. The difficulty is that there are no unambiguous criteria for an effect to be meaningful, and virtually every scholar who has discussed the mistaken interpretation of statistical significance emphasizes that the researcher must make that call. Since such a judgment is never beyond challenge, it is likely that the persistent misinterpretation of statistical significance is partly due to the desire to find an unambiguous criterion for meaning, but there is none.

This has probably been explained best by Carver (1978: 384-385) through his black-humor example of incorrectly interpreting "the probability of obtaining a dead person (label this part D) given that the person was hanged (label this part H); in symbol form, what is p(D|H)?" as "the probability that a person has been hanged (H) given that the person is dead (D); that is, what is p(H|D)?" As he points out, the probability referred to by the *p* level in significance testing is the probability of getting the data we did under the conditions of the null hypothesis, or p(D|H). It is not the probability of the hypothesis given the data p(H|D)–this is the incorrect, but typical, interpretation Carver refers to. In spite of decades of commentary on this mistaken belief (Bakan, 1966; Berkson, 1942; Campbell, 1967: Carver, 1978; Cohen, 1962, 1990, 1994; Dunnette, 1966; Greenwald, 1975; Hays, 1963; Meehl, 1978, 1986, 1990; Rosnow and Rosenthal, 1988, 1989; Rozeboom, 1960; Sedlmeier and Gigerenzer, 1989), it still persists. The consequence has been to draw conclusions only marginally supported by actual effect sizes, and therefore to seriously impede development of strong paradigms to guide us in PER in Central and Eastern Europe or any other research. The incorrect interpretation of statistical significance in Western research literature further inhibits PER, since "statistical significance" is virtually impossible to attain with small samples (while it is certain with large ones; see Meehl, 1978, 1986). Since transitions occur in small increments, Western academic editors tend to dismiss these potentially valuable studies as unimportant "small-sample" studies, made especially difficult by the absence of statistical significance (Rosenthal, 1979). The opportunity to learn is lost.

Suggestions have been made that might help to correct this problem in PER and more broadly in the study of management. These include publication of research based on review of the design alone (Kupfersmid, 1988), to suggestions that a "covenant" be drawn between editors and researchers wherein designs will be published with a guarantee that replications of the study will be performed, and all results, supportive or nonsupportive, will also be published (Kmetz, 1992). While these might help in the future, they cannot compensate for the lack of strong paradigms to guide PER at present.

THREE CONCLUDING THOUGHTS

In examining all of the factors accounting for the relative paucity of research from Central and Eastern Europe, which outwardly would appear to be an unprecedented "living laboratory," it appears that they form a complex and interdependent web of inhibitors. Some of these are derivatives of the social, political, and economic environment there, and some are derivatives of the academic research enterprise itself. All of these interact with one another to limit creation of new knowledge about the sweeping range of privatization and the creation of new economic entities occurring throughout the region. Three recommendations are offered here to stimulate more research and bring it into public view. They are of greatest utility for near-term editorial policy on the part of journal editors who want to take immediate steps to increase research output. Reduction of inhibitory pressures more broadly will need longer-term editorial and reward-system practices within the many institutions and disciplines comprising the economic and organization sciences.

First, there is need to conceptualize change and PER using systems thinking (Senge and Sterman, 1992). Conceptualization of PER and other transition research as part of a larger system will result in better models and better integration of "normal science" research into a meaningful whole. Normal, reductionist models of science can be complemented very effectively by systems models which enable the smaller pieces of individual-company research to be placed within a more meaningful and dynamic context. This is helpful to both the research practitioner for formulating research questions, and to the research consumer in interpreting what has been done. It is also useful to editors and publishers, since different models of publication may be better adapted to highly changeable environments than to those more commonly encountered in the West. Thus, publication of research designs or program designs in anticipation of findings may be better suited to circumstances in Central and Eastern Europe.

Second, there is need for increased use and consumption of "applied" research in the academic world. There is much to be learned from observation of radical changes in thought and activity at the microcosmic level which has value for understanding processes at higher levels of the system. Research which may not satisfy the criteria of "impressiveness" on individual merits may be seen as part of a much larger program when evaluated within a systems framework. "Applied" research is often the best test of theory when considered this way; the test of a change of conceptual frameworks on the part of a new population of managers and entrepreneurs may be their willingness to engage in seemingly mundane behaviors which are a departure from past patterns. Certainly, such changes are required to successfully develop the market economies of this region (Hunter, 1993).

Finally, there is need for new methods of dissemination which are more responsive to the rate of change of the system under observation-a lesson learned about how we learn our lessons. Electronic exchange, electronic publication, and the development of more specialized publication outlets tailored to the changes in Central and Eastern Europe, may be necessary simply to accommodate the rate of change. There is much to be learned from the transitions of these countries which can be beneficial to other transitional and emerging economies, and it would be most unfortunate to miss the opportunity to gain such knowledge.

REFERENCES

Bakan, D. 1966. The test of significance in psychological research. *Psychological Bulletin*, 66: 423.

Behrman, J. N. 1994. Assisting private sector transformation in Russia. *Business & the Contemporary World*, 6(1): 84-101.

Berkson, J. 1942. Tests of significance considered as evidence. *Journal of the American Statistical Association*, 37: 325-335.

Campbell, J. 1967. Editorial: Some remarks from the outgoing editor. *Journal of Applied Psychology*, 6(6): 691-700.

Carver, R. P. 1978. The case against statistical significance testing. *Harvard Educational Review*, 48: 378-399.

Clark, T. 1994. Moving mountains to market: Reflections on restructuring the Russian economy. *Business Horizons*, 37(2): 16-21.

Cohen, J. 1962. The statistical power of abnormal-social psychological research: A review. *Journal of Abnormal and Social Psychology*, 65(3): 145-153.

Cohen, J. 1990. Things I have learned (so far). *American Psychologist*, 45(12): 1304-1312.

Cohen, J. 1994. The earth is round (p < .05). *American Psychologist*, 49(12): 997-1003.

Colander, D. C. 1991. *Why aren't economists as important as garbagemen?* Armonk, NY: M. E. Sharpe.

Cummings, L. L., and Frost, P. J. 1985. *Publishing in the organizational sciences.* Homewood, IL: R. D. Irwin.

Dunnette, M. D. 1966. Fads, fashions, and folderol in psychology. *American Psychologist*, 21: 343-352.

Greenwald, A. 1975. Consequences of prejudice against the null hypothesis. *Psychological Bulletin*, 82: 1-20.

Hays, W. L. 1963. *Statistics.* New York: Holt, Rinehart and Winston.

Hofstede, G. 1993. Cultural constraints in management theories. *Academy of Management Executive*, 7: 81-94.

Hunter, W. C. 1993. Banking reform and the transition to a market economy in Bulgaria: Problems and prospects. *Federal Reserve Bank of Atlanta Economic Review*, 12: 15-22.

Kilmann, R. W., Thomas, K. W., Slevin, D. P., Nath, R., and Jerrell, S. L. (Eds.). 1994. *Producing useful knowledge for organizations.* San Francisco: Jossey-Bass.

King, M. T. R. 1994. The challenge to accounting in Eastern Europe. *Business & the Contemporary World*, 6 (1): 112-121.

Kmetz, J. L. 1992. Proposals to improve the science of organization. Paper presented at the annual meeting of the Academy of Management, Las Vegas, NV.

Kupfersmid, J. 1988. Improving what is published: A model in search of an editor. *American Psychologist*, 43: 635-642.

Maruyama, M. 1990. Some management considerations in the economic reorganization of Eastern Europe. *Academy of Management Executive*, 4(2): 86-89.

Meehl, P. 1978. Theoretical risk and tabular asterisk: Sir Karl, Sir Ronald, and the slow progress of soft psychology. *Journal of Consulting and Clinical Psychology*, 46: 806-834.

Meehl, Paul E. 1986. What social scientists don't understand. In Fiske, Donald W., and Shweder, Richard A. (Eds.): 315-338, *Metatheory in Social Science.* Chicago: University of Chicago Press.

Meehl, P. E. 1990. Why summaries of research on psychological theories are often uninterpretable. *Psychological Reports*, 66: 195-244. Monograph supplement 1-V66.

Newman, W. H. 1992. Focused joint ventures in transforming economies. *Academy of Management Executive*, 6(1): 67-75.

Pfeffer, J. 1993. Barriers to the advance of organizational science: Paradigm development as a dependent variable. *Academy of Management Review*, 18: 599-620.

Rosenthal, R. 1979. The "file drawer problem" and tolerance for null results. *Psychological Bulletin*, 85: 185-193.

Rosnow, R. L., and Rosenthal, R. 1988. Focused tests of significance and effect size estimation in counseling psychology. *Journal of Counseling Psychology*, 38 (3): 203-208.

Rosnow, R. L., and Rosenthal, R. 1989. Statistical procedures and the justification of knowledge in psychological science. *American Psychologist*, 44: 1276-1284.

Rozeboom, W. 1960. The fallacy of the null-hypothesis significance test. *Psychological Bulletin*, 57: 416-428.

Sedlmeier, P., and Gigerenzer, G. 1989. Do studies of statistical power have an effect on the power of studies? *Psychological Bulletin*, 105(2): 309-316.

Senge, P. M., and Sterman, J. D. 1992. Systems thinking and organizational learning: Acting locally and thinking globally in the organization of the future. In Kochan, T. A., and Useem, M. (Eds.), *Transforming organizations*. New York: Oxford.

Shama, A. 1993. Management under fire: The transformation of managers in the Soviet Union and Eastern Europe. *Academy of Management Executive*, 7(1): 22-35.

PART II:
MANAGEMENT CHALLENGES
OF PRIVATIZATION

Chapter 5

Managerial Implications of the Transition from Public to Private Ownership in Central and Eastern Europe: Are Managers Equipped to Compete?

Douglas L. Bartley
Michael S. Minor

One of the major shifts in economic activity across the globe in the last decade has been the transition from state-owned enterprises (SOEs) to private enterprises. No region has felt the effects of this transition more acutely than the nations of Central and Eastern Europe and the former Soviet Union.

Since the fall of the communist governments, initiatives were started to privatize most of the SOEs (Chubais, 1993; Kornai, 1992; Minor, 1993, 1994; Sachs, 1992; World Bank, 1992). The speed of this transition has varied by country and by industry. Generally speaking, privatization implied a transfer of ownership of productive assets from the state to private parties. "The effect of this move was expected to be a transition from one idealized state of affairs to another: from the 'command' to a 'market' economy" (Frydman and Rapaczynski, 1994: 169).

One major problematic element of the transition "from one idealized state to another" is management experience needed in a market economy at various levels of the enterprise.

MANAGERS

Under the command system, decision making was carried out through the "Bermuda triangle" of ministry, workers' council, and trade union

The authors thank Jason B. MacDonald for sharing his experiences in Poland.

council (Bilsen, 1994); even operating decisions were made in government offices and transmitted to those responsible for day-to-day operations. Besides the dependence on ministerial directives, the major operational problem was obtaining inputs. Product quality or financial performance were minor concerns.

Now decision making is being transferred to plant level management. Are these managers prepared to make effective decisions in a timely fashion? Most companies lack data to aid their decision making and have only the vaguest notions of whether products meet customer needs, at what price, in what volume, and at what location. Coupled with this lack of information is the inexperience of the general management of the new enterprise, especially with regard to decision making. "Nothing so much frightens people in former Communist countries, visitors report, as to be asked to make a decision. They are paralyzed by fear of making a mistake" (Dumitriu and Nicolaescu, 1994: 153).

Planning and Goal Setting

Formulating of goals is part of the planning process. Goals outline activities that are necessary to achieve the objectives of the company (Mintzberg, 1987). They provide direction, focus the company's efforts, guide decision making, and assist in evaluating the progress being made. Decisions should be evaluated in terms of how they will affect the firm's ability to meet established objectives (Jones, 1995). Under the command system, goal setting was performed by the central administration and had two objectives: to ensure full employment and to maximize production. Customer needs were ignored when it came to product, production volume, and product quality. Enterprise level managers were not exposed to setting objectives or to formulating marketing strategy. Inkpen and Choudhury (1995) have recently argued that attention needed to be given to firms with no strategy: Eastern Europe, in effect, provides a virtual laboratory for research into this phenomenon.

Costing and Budgeting

In order to measure performance a company must be able to compare actual performance with standards (budgets). The preparation of the budget is a planning function; its administration is a controlling function.

In the early 1990s, enterprises in Central and Eastern Europe are inadequately prepared to create and use budgeting effectively, mainly because management is mentally not prepared for properly recording critical processes:

- One company in Slovakia produced approximately 50 different products, but was not able to determine the manufacturing cost for each product.
- It is reported that Polish Telecom payroll employees propped their old ledgers on top of new 80486 computers, since the computers were in the way.
- A Hungarian food processor could not process all of the fresh crop during the regular harvest period. It had to store part of the harvest in five-gallon containers and later reprocess it into smaller jars which could be sold to consumers. When establishing a price the company could either include the double-handling cost in the price of all the jars sold or it could establish two price levels, one for the fresh pack and a higher price for the off-season pack. Instead, the company priced all of its finished product at the fresh pack price–and lost money (Bartley and Minor, 1994a).
- Another company in Hungary had two factories which it treated as one. The two plants made different products. One plant was very old and should have been totally depreciated; the other had a modern, very expensive can-manufacturing line. Instead of allocating depreciation costs for the equipment used in each department, the company used an average depreciation rate for the entire company. Thus, the older plant was charged depreciation costs against its products when none should have been charged, and the can-making costs were lower than they should have been. Using the average depreciation cost for all equipment distorted the manufacturing cost for each variety produced. This error also affected the selling price and profitability of the various products manufactured.
- A company in Slovakia had computerized its accounting, but still tracked costs as it did under the command system. One cost-allocating error uncovered was that the cost of water was allocated equally to all products being manufactured each month. In actuality, one of the products used 75 percent of the water, while the other eight products used the remaining 25 percent (Bartley and Minor, 1994b).

These examples show that the thought process of managers must be changed. Preparing a budget will train them to use their accounting system to ferret out information enabling them to make better managerial decisions.

Staffing

Under the command system, the objective of state officials was full employment for the people of the region where the SOE was located. Cost did not matter since year-end subsidies made up any loss the company might have sustained because of overemployment. In 1995, one plant in Hungary had 2,300 hourly and 700 salaried employees. If properly scheduled, the tasks probably could have been done with 600 hourly and 70 salaried employees.

Little attention was given to job assignments, employee training, or job-related experience. During the time the first author was reviewing the work at a plant, he learned that a new college graduate had been placed on the payroll and assigned the job of operating the fax machine. How could this job motivate a college graduate? Under the old system, employee motivation was not a factor. In a market economy, motivation is a key management tool.

Under the old system, marketing was an unknown managerial function (Pendergast, 1995). When companies were privatized they needed marketers, who were hard to find. One response to this problem, albeit a short-term solution, was to recruit foreigners or expatriates who had the needed expertise. However, recruiting such individuals to fill available positions usually succeeds if the plant is located in an attractive city, but is problematic if the company is in a small town or village. A food-processing company in Nagyatad (Hungary) attempted to recruit a foreigner to fill a position in the company. No good housing was available and it turned out to be impossible to entice a foreigner to move to Nagyatad to take the job.

Motivating

Central and Eastern European managers are barely acquainted with the task of motivating their subordinates. Marxist theory assumed that, as owners of the productive means, workers were automatically motivated. Disagreements exist in market economies as to the efficacy of wages as a motivator compared to other approaches. In Central and Eastern Europe the workers presently have very little disposable income, and barely subsist from one payday to the next. Therefore, the primary motivation approach used in newly privatized firms–to pay higher wages than those being paid by SOEs–may be sufficient for now. However, sole reliance of monetary rewards may create motivational problems as wages increase and job opportunities multiply. Very few of the managers are aware of Maslow's hierarchy of needs (Maslow, 1954), Herzberg's (1987) two-factor theory, expectancy theory (Vroom, 1964), or other approaches used in the West to achieve increased productivity.

In sum, as indicated by Table 5.1, which reflects our experience with 26 newly privatized companies, managers were poorly prepared for their

TABLE 5.1. Evaluation of Senior Management of 26 Companies in the Czech Republic, Hungary, Kazakhstan, Latvia, Poland, Russia, Slovakia, and on Factors Involving Experience Affecting Decision Making

FACTOR	No experience		Fair experience		Good experience	
	1	2	3	4	5	6
Setting objectives for the company	X					
Planning work	X					
Conceptual skills		X				
Organizing the company	X					
Directing the workforce		X				
Use of motivation factors	X					
Proper staffing	X					
Use of accounting data (budgeting)	X					
Willingness to delegate	X					
Technical knowledge					X	
Materials procurement		X				
Supplies procurement	X					
Improving methods of operation		X				

1 = low, 3 = fair, 6 = high

tasks in a drastically changed environment. Technical knowledge is the only factor on which managers rate well.

FIRST LINE SUPERVISORS

Many of the comments pertaining to the managerial skills of managers are also applicable to first line supervisors working in these companies.

Directing the Workforce

Several basic problems existed under the command system.

Supervisors were not allowed freedom to operate their department. Detailed instructions were communicated from above and the supervisor merely followed through by seeing that the directions were implemented. Very little attention was given to how the instructions were transmitted.

No attempt was made to explain to the hourly employees why a change was taking place or how a change would affect them in their jobs.

Hourly employees paid little attention to the work being performed. They believed that if they did not complete the task, one of their co-workers would, since others in the department were doing the same work. No job descriptions existed in most of the companies in Central and Eastern Europe, and employees did not know exactly what they were supposed to do. Supervisors seldom investigated whether instructions were properly implemented.

Job descriptions would help, but would not entirely solve the problem of inadequate direction of employees. The techniques of setting work standards, monitoring performance, and correcting for deviations from the standard were not being used in directing the workforce in these newly privatized companies. A few examples may illustrate this:

- Quality control is still practically unknown. In one factory in Latvia, the supervisor of the processing department had over 25 years of experience. The product being processed was apple juice, manufactured as follows. The employees would place a 48″ × 48″ wooden rack in the processing unit, line the rack with a burlap cloth, place 60 pounds of diced apples onto the cloth, and fold the ends of the cloth over the apples. They placed a second rack over the first, filled it, etc. After ten racks were in place, a pressing machine would press out the juice. Juice would overflow the racks, and more important, after the spent pulp was taken out, the racks were placed on the concrete floor, inviting contamination. A solution was obvious. Workers placed two wooden beams (two-by-fours) spaced a foot apart on the floor and placed the racks on top. This also allowed the racks to be hosed off between uses.
- Another unsolved mystery in the same factory was the cloudiness of the apple juice. The solution was to give employees paring knives so they could cut rotten spots out of the apples before they were diced and pressed. Although the supervisor in charge of this procedure in the plant had many years of experience, apparently little time had been devoted to innovative problem solving.
- In a fish factory in Tembruk, Russia, eight employees filled tin cans with fish, and two employees monitored the weight of the cans. In a way reminiscent of slapstick movies where conveyer belt speeds exceeded employees' abilities and products were hidden in any available area, cooked fish was stored willy-nilly in every nook and cranny, while the cooking department merrily produced the same quantity of cooked fish, totally oblivious to what was going on further down the

production line. In the sterilizing department, cans zipped off the conveyer belt to tumble haphazardly into iron baskets for sterilization. Not only were more sterilization operations needed, because 25 to 30 percent more cans could have been sterilized in a single run had they been stacked neatly, but cans were damaged in the process as well.

Clearly, each of these problems could have been resolved by supervisors who understood their function.

Table 5.2 provides an evaluation of factors concerning their tasks as supervisors of a department or a section of a department.

TABLE 5.2. Responsibilities of Supervisors: An Evaluation of Supervisors in the Czech Republic, Hungary, Kazakhstan, Latvia, Russia, and Slovakia.

FACTOR	No experience		Fair experience		Good experience	
	1	2	3	4	5	6
Equipment maintenance		X-	-X			
Maintaining discipline		X				
Obtaining good productivity	X					
Operating safely	X					
Teaching safety	X					
Indoctrination of new employees	X					
Employee training	X					
Employee appraisal	X					
Maintaining good housekeeping	X					
Maintaining proper quality	X					
Maintaining proper cost control	X					
Evaluation of the department's work		X				
Evaluation of work flow	X					
Cooperation with other departments		X-	-X			
Adherence to state laws			X			
Proper scheduling of overtime	X					
Representing management to employees		X-	-X			
Representing employees to management	X					

1 = low, 3 = fair, 6 = high

CONCLUSION

It is obvious that a company cannot be successful if the individuals holding key management and supervisory positions are not competent. Based on our recent experience in 26 companies located in the Czech Republic, Hungary, Kazakhstan, Latvia, Poland, Russia, and Slovakia, this is largely the case for most recently privatized firms (see Tables 5.1 and 5.2).

One reason for the relatively poor skill levels of supervisors and managers may be rooted in the traditional wage structure. Supervisors and managers are grossly underpaid compared to their responsibilities. In some cases hourly employees continue to earn more than their supervisors.

- In one company in the Czech Republic, the top manager earned less than several of his hourly employees.
- In the summer of 1995, we discovered that medical doctors in Latvia earned an average of about U.S. $185 per month. Factory workers earned monthly wages of about U.S. $130. Similarly, in Tuldy Kurgon (Kazakhstan) a worker shoveling sunflower husks into a stove was found to earn more than a PhD working in the university in the same city.

This lack of wage differentials creates little incentive to become better educated. Also, it fuels an entrepreneurial drive to start a small business, since this is the only method of dramatically increasing incomes as long as the old wage structure remains in place.

Much training of this class of employees needs to be done before these new companies can expect to be really successful (Kasperson and Dobrzynski, 1995).

In companies privatized through a joint venture with a foreign firm, management needs to make dramatic changes in how the new plant will operate. Unfortunately, there are few qualified managers available in the present workforce to make these changes (Ullmann, 1995).

Fortunately, managerial and supervisory skill levels are improving thanks to the influx of managers brought into the country when joint ventures were made with foreign firms. All of these experiences are helping to make the transitional period more rewarding and less painful.

Is There Hope?

At the bottom of recent advertisements for sell-offs of SOEs, the Hungarian government has been using the phrase "privatization goes on."

This sentiment applies to much of Central and Eastern Europe. For example, privatization "goes on" in Romania, which has passed the Law on the Acceleration of Privatization (*Romania Economic Newsletter*, 1995), and in the Czech Republic, where shares of enterprises sold in the second wave of mass voucher privatization have doubled the size of the stock market (*Finance East Europe*, 1995b). In spite of setbacks and delays, privatization continues and ways are found to surmount the resulting difficulties.

An equally large challenge is to create a transition in the minds and hearts of workers, supervisors, and managers as they struggle with the new realities. Several avenues to acquire the new skills present themselves.

A first one, clearly, is learning by doing. As Western management practices are important now that communication lines to the former Eastern bloc are open, on-the-job learning and copying are the most obvious paths toward acquiring new skills. A second route is joint ventures with and acquisition by Western firms, which through a variety of ways will upgrade the skills of their Central and Eastern European partners (see the chapter by Hefner and Woodward in this volume or Welfens and Jasinski, 1994). A third option is expatriates, who can bring with them much-needed expertise. A fourth route, finally, is formal education programs. In recent years many such programs have been initiated by Western governmental agencies such as the U.S. Information Agency, supranational bodies such as the European Union and the United Nations, and by private organizations (see the chapter by Marx in this volume). In addition, local universities have been rapidly changing their curricula and course offerings, sometimes with support from the West, to help train current and future managers and supervisors to successfully work in an emerging market system.

REFERENCES

Bartley, D. L. and Minor, M. S. 1994a. Privatizing canneries in Hungary. *Cross-Cultural Management: An International Journal*, 1(2): 34-39.

Bartley, D. L. and Minor, M. S. 1994b. Why would a company want to enter a joint venture in the former Soviet Union or Eastern Europe? *Journal of Product and Brand Management*, 3(2): 28-36.

Bilsen, V. 1994. Privatization, company management and performance: A comparative study of privatization methods in the Czech Republic, Hungary, Poland, and Slovakia. In M. Jackson and V. Bilsen (Eds.), *Company management and capital market development in the transition*. 35-56. Aldershot, UK: Avebury.

Chubais, A. 1993. Russia: Birth of an entrepreneurial nation. *The Wall Street Journal*, June 16: A12.

Dumitriu, I. and Nicolaescu, T. 1994. Delayed privatization, financial development and management in Romania during the transition. In M. Jackson and V. Bilsen (Eds.), *Company management and capital market development in the transition*. 145-184. Aldershot, UK: Avebury.

Finance East Europe. 1995b. Second wave shares come to market. February 24: 11-12.

Frydman, R. and Rapaczynski, A. 1994. *Privatization in Eastern Europe: Is the state withering away?* Budapest: Central European University Press.

Herzberg, F. 1987. One more time: How do you motivate employees? *Harvard Business Review*, 65: 109-120.

Inkpen, A. and Choudhury, N. 1995. The seeking of strategy where it is not: Towards a theory of strategy absence. *Strategic Management Journal*, 16: 313-323.

Jones, G. R. 1995. *Organizational theory*. Reading, MA: Addison Wesley.

Kasperson, C. J. and Dobrzynski, M. 1995. Training and development for a market economy. In R. Culpan and B. N. Kumar (Eds.), *Transformation management in postcommunist countries*: 119-137. Westport, CT: Quorum Books.

Kornai, J. 1992. The postsocialist transition and the state: Reflections in the light of Hungarian fiscal reforms. *American Economic Review*, 82 (May): 1-21.

Maslow, A. H. 1954. *Motivation and personality*. New York: Harper and Row.

Minor, M. S. 1993. *Privatization: A worldwide summary*. Prepared for the Transnational Corporations and Management Division, New York: United Nations.

Minor, M. S. 1994. The demise of expropriation as an instrument of LDC policy, 1980-1992. *Journal of International Business Studies*, 25(1): 177-188.

Mintzberg, H. 1987. Crafting strategy. *Harvard Business Review*, 65: 66-75.

Pendergast, W. R. 1995. Transforming management in Central Europe. In R. Culpan and B. N. Kumar (Eds.), *Transformation management in postcommunist countries*: 217-233. Westport, CT: Quorum Books.

Romania Economic Newsletter. 1995. Parliament passes law to accelerate privatization, April-June: 1.

Sachs, J. D. 1992. Privatization in Russia: Some lessons from Eastern Europe. *American Economic Review*, 82 (May): 43-48.

Ullmann, A. A. 1995. TeMAFL: Teaching management as a foreign language. In R. Culpan and B. N. Kumar (Eds.), *Transformation management in postcommunist countries*: 139-149. Westport, CT: Quorum Books.

Vroom, Victor. 1964. *Work and motivation*. New York: Wiley.

Welfens, P. J. J. and Jasinski, P. 1994. *Privatization and foreign direct investment in transforming economies*. Aldershot, U.K.: Dartmouth.

World Bank. 1992. *Privatization: The lessons of experience*. Washington, DC: World Bank.

Chapter 6

Comparing Privatization Characteristics in Former Communist, Developing, and Developed Countries

Julio O. De Castro
Nikolaus Uhlenbruck

Privatization of state-owned enterprises (SOEs) has become an important tool of economic policy, especially in the economic advancement of developing and former communist countries (Nankani, 1990).

Most research on privatization has dealt with public policy issues focusing on the societal benefits of privatization (Donahue, 1989; Ramamurti, 1992). For example, methods of privatizing SOEs (e.g., the voucher system, liquidation) are widely discussed in the economics and finance literature (Frydman and Rapaczynski, 1992; Vickers and Yarrow, 1988). The emphasis of privatization research in the tradition of the public policy perspective leaves firms interested in acquiring SOEs without specific guidelines as to under which conditions privatization is likely to be more effective, given the competitive characteristics of the firm and country.

Further, theory suggests that reductions in government ownership not only should improve a country's economy, but also that competitive environments and capital-market discipline lead to increased efficiency of privatized SOEs (Aharoni, 1986; Goodman and Loveman, 1991). Empirical research on this point, however, has yielded conflicting results (Cook and Kirkpatrick, 1988; Hutchinson, 1991; Parker and Hartley, 1991). One reason for these discrepancies might be the lack of examination in extant research of firm-level variables of the privatization process, such as deal terms stipulated by the selling government or the fit between the privatized firm and its acquirer (De Castro and Uhlenbruck, 1993).

While most privatization deals during the 1980s attracted local investors, the recent privatization wave, centered mostly in developing and former communist countries, has drawn significant amounts of foreign direct investment (*The Economist*, 1993). For the investing firms, the cross-border acquisition of SOEs represents an opportunity to enter emerging markets (Freudenberg and Bird, 1991). Research on international acquisitions, however, indicates that home and host country conditions, for instance taxes or foreign exchange convertibility, influence the performance of cross-border mergers (Lessard, 1973; Datta and Puia, 1993; Markides and Ittner, 1994). Thus, privatization deals are likely to be affected by merger variables as well as cross-border issues, and influenced by the government as seller of the SOE and as economic policymaker.

The effective outcome of privatization deals depends, among other things, on the conditions of the privatization process and the host country. Murtha and Lenway state that "public and private choices interact to influence whether and where multinational corporations invest in firm-specific intangible assets and where and when they commit capital to product-specific assets that preempt competitors" (1994: 114). The same argument should apply in the context of privatization. Host-country characteristics and characteristics of the privatization process should help determine the choices firms make when acquiring privatized SOEs. Even when considering only developing countries, there are significant differences in market and firm conditions among the countries that have privatized extensively (Nankani, 1990). In some developing countries, such as Mexico and Chile, privatization has been aided by relatively developed capital markets, while the lack of any established markets has been a significant problem in many other privatizing nations (Ramanadham, 1993). At the same time, these conditions should affect the strategy of firms acquiring an SOE from the government (Lenway and Murtha, 1994). Privatization characteristics vary across countries, and privatization experiences may not translate across borders.

This chapter examines whether there are differences in diversification strategy depending on the type of country in which the investor acquires a privatized SOE, and whether the approach governments take to privatization with respect to investors varies by country. This study utilizes a mergers and acquisitions (M&A) framework to examine whether there are differences in the characteristics of privatization in developed, developing, and former communist countries. Four areas are examined in particular, reflecting acquisition strategy and privatization policies:

- degree of relatedness of acquiring and acquired firms;
- local vs. cross-border acquisitions;
- type of acquisition (i.e., partial or full ownership); and
- government requirements with respect to the future operation of the privatized SOE by the acquirer.

Our findings indicate that when investing in privatized SOEs firms' acquisition strategies are influenced by the type of country where investment takes place. The results also highlight the importance of governmental policies for firm strategy, as recently stressed by Murtha and Lenway (1994), and their effects on the privatization process. Further, the results indicate that privatization policies vary significantly across different types of host countries, in fact highlighting the fallacy that advice in privatization cases is applicable across different countries and firms. Finally, the results suggest that host-country conditions affect the acquisition method utilized when acquiring an SOE.

PRIOR PRIVATIZATION RESEARCH ON FORMER COMMUNIST, DEVELOPING, AND DEVELOPED COUNTRIES

In the past, research on privatization has examined the process of privatization in individual countries or regions. From these individualized examinations, attempts were made to draw generalizable conclusions about the characteristics of privatization processes. Although the results of most of these studies favor privatization, no unequivocal conclusions can be drawn from them about the benefits of privatization.

- Why do governments in developing countries privatize? Ramamurti (1992) identifies large budget deficits, high foreign public debt, and dependence on international agencies such as the World Bank as the main reasons. Other research has examined performance differences between privatized and nonprivatized firms. For example, Walters (1987) found that privately owned firms were more cost-effective than SOEs while delivering equivalent services. Longitudinal research by Young (1987) in Bangladesh found that privatized textile mills had shown significant performance improvements. Research by the World Bank shows net gains in shareholder wealth for 11 out of 12 firms (*The Economist*, 1993). Cook and Kirkpatrick (1988), however, failed to find superior productive efficiency in privatized vs. state-owned firms.
- Research in Central and Eastern Europe finds positive but quite tenuous links between privatization and firm performance (*DIW Wochenbericht*, 1994; Pfohl et al., 1992). Much other work is prescriptive with respect to governments' privatization policy or management issues or describes privatization as part of the economic transition in the region while neglecting firm-level aspects (e.g., Berger, 1991; Targetti, 1992; Rondinelli, 1994).

- Studies pertaining to developed countries have tended to focus on the economic benefits. Studies based on data from the U.K. also provide conflicting results. While Caves (1990b) argues that the British privatization strategy was a success in that it increased the efficiency of formerly state-owned enterprises while still providing allocative efficiency, Hutchinson (1991) found that privatization had a negative effect on labor productivity. Parker and Hartley (1991) found no overall increases in firm productivity as a result of moving firms away from government control.

REEXAMINING PRIVATIZATION: A MERGERS AND ACQUISITIONS APPROACH

The arguments in the prior section indicate that research on privatization (1) has failed to identify a consistent link between privatization and performance, (2) has relied on the use of small samples drawn from particular nations and attempted to generalize its findings, and (3) has failed to examine the characteristics of privatization across different types of countries. The last two problems might be a reason why prior research has provided inconsistent results with regard to the benefits of privatization programs.

The literature on mergers and acquisitions provides a useful framework for examining the question of privatization from the perspective of the firm. Research on strategic intent and synergistic effects in mergers (Chatterjee, 1986; Chatterjee and Wernerfelt, 1991; Pablo, 1994; Shirvastava, 1986), on the characteristics of the transaction and its outcomes (Chatterjee et al., 1994; Lubatkin, 1983; Napier, 1989), on cross-border acquisitions (Bleeke and Ernst, 1991; Datta and Puia, 1993; Markides and Ittner, 1994), and on the acquisition process (Haspeslagh and Jemison, 1991; Jemison and Sitkin, 1989; Schweiger and DeNisi, 1991; Pablo, 1994) provides important theoretical backing for the study of privatization.

Relatedness and Privatization

In privatization deals, is the decision to undertake related or unrelated acquisitions affected by characteristics of the host country? Prior research in M&A has examined the question of relatedness in mergers and acquisitions, in particular with regard to possible synergies between merging firms (Chatterjee, 1986; Napier, 1989) and the strategic intent of the acquirer (Haspeslagh and Jemison, 1991; Lubatkin, 1983). International M&A work indicates that characteristics of the host country have a significant effect on the choice of relatedness in acquisitions (Hisey and Caves, 1985). Bleeke and Ernst (1991) find that related cross-border acquisitions have higher success rates than unrelated acquisitions. Datta and Puia (1993) show that shareholder wealth effects are greater for related international acquisitions, and that smaller shareholder wealth effects occur when cultural differences and country-specific risks are high. Finally, Chatterjee et al. (1992) find that in related mergers there is an inverse relationship between perceptions of cultural differences and shareholder value. The greater the perceived differences in culture, the smaller the realized shareholder value in the acquisition.

The above argument points toward a relationship between the degree of uncertainty in acquisitions, influenced by differences in organizational and national culture, and acquisition relatedness. As the level of uncertainty increases, the acquirer is more likely to engage in related acquisitions. This level of uncertainty will conceivably be higher in privatization deals because of the differences in organizational culture and operations between the private acquirer and the government-run target firm (Aharoni, 1986), and because of the changes in government policies inherent in privatization.

Particularly in the case of former communist countries, there will be a perception of high uncertainty by potential acquirers. In addition to concerns relating to acquiring a government-run organization, there will probably also be uncertainty with respect to the legal and regulatory framework. Given the lack of marketlike environments and because of political problems in the large-scale transition to market economies (Ramanadham, 1993), the degree of uncertainty for acquirers in former communist countries should be higher than in either developed or developing countries, and thus acquirers should be more likely to engage in related acquisitions in those countries. To reduce uncertainty, therefore, the acquirer in privatization deals in former communist countries would be expected to focus more on related acquisitions compared to privatization deals in developing or developed countries.

Local vs. Cross-Border Acquisitions and Privatization

Are acquirers of privatized SOEs likely to be local or foreign firms? In view of the politicized environment within which privatization occurs (Ramanadham, 1993), the acquiring firm's country of origin is an important variable. On the one hand, governments in developing and former communist countries seek foreign acquirers to attract capital and technological and management skill (Ramamurti, 1992). On the other hand, the citizens of these countries may blame governments for selling the country's assets to foreigners (Sobell, 1993).

Possible resentment toward foreign firms may be amplified by the arguments of some economists who argue that cross-border acquisitions may allow firms to exploit inefficiencies in the market for corporate control (Adler and Dumas, 1975; Fatemi, 1984). These market imperfections may conceivably occur more often if the government sells SOEs directly to private acquirers, which is more common in developing and former communist countries, than if SOEs are sold via the stock market, as is typical for privatization in developed nations. In many cases, capital markets in developing and former communist countries are still in a nascent stage. Large-scale privatization in these markets therefore appears problematic (Rondinelli, 1994).

The characteristics of the privatizing country should have significant effects on the choice of local vs. cross-border privatization acquisitions, based on the interests of both the government and private investors. Because of the need for foreign expertise and capital, there tend to be more foreign acquisitions in privatization deals in developing and former communist countries than in developed economies. Because of the extent of privatization and their new, probably imperfect capital markets, former communist countries should have the strongest involvement of foreign investors in privatization deals. Following this logic, privatization deals in former communist countries are more likely to be cross-border acquisitions than privatization deals in developing and developed countries.

Type of Deals and Privatization

Scholars of strategy and international business have examined the characteristics of total vs. partial international acquisitions, and the conditions under which each type may be most efficient. Markides and Ittner (1994) and Kitching (1973) have argued that partial acquisitions of international targets may allow the U.S. firm to experience a "getting-acquainted" period, and result in lower integration costs for the acquirer than full acquisition. Markides and Ittner (1994) also restate Caves' (1990a) barrier argument and posit that partial acquisitions could be a less expensive way for oligopolistic firms to prevent their competitors from acquiring the target firm. Their results seem to confirm this argument since partial acquisitions were only significant in their model when combined in an interaction with the degree of industry concentration.

However, we argue that uncertainty in the transition period to a market economy in former communist countries would support whole acquisitions. Given inadequate legal and regulatory frameworks and weak market institutions, once the decision has been made to acquire a firm in a former communist country, controlling the whole venture would reduce the acquiring firms' uncertainty of the process. Therefore, privatization deals in former communist countries should be more likely to be total acquisitions than privatization deals in developing or developed countries.

Post-Privatization Requirements

Are there differences in the post-privatization requirements imposed on acquirers between developed, developing, and former communist countries? The presence of post-privatization requirements is important because they may limit the activities of the acquirer to integrate and renew the target organization, with significant implications for post-privatization performance (Donahue, 1989). The issue of post-privatization requirements could be one of the most consequential differences between the acquisition of an SOE and typical mergers and acquisitions deals (De Castro and Uhlenbruck, 1993).

Lessard (1973) and Cooke (1988) discuss the economic and political environment in the context of international mergers and acquisitions. Important conditions in the context of international mergers involve labor laws, including restrictions on termination of employees, political pressures, social costs, and even direct government control of the economy. All these conditions should also affect privatization deals. Lessard (1973, 1976) also argues that the ability to arbitrage tax regimes is an important reason for cross-border acquisitions. Prahalad and Doz's (1987) discussion of host-government demands for local responsiveness also addresses the issue of post-privatization conditions.

Lenway and Murtha (1994) highlight a number of reasons why there may be significant differences in post-privatization conditions in developed, developing, and former communist countries: differences in domestic policymaking capability and the role of authority vs. markets, the role of individualism vs. communitarianism, emphasis on security vs. prosperity, and, in particular, an interest in equity vs. efficiency, all of which would cause governments to try to control the range of possibilities available to acquirers in privatization deals and to impose post-privatization conditions. Because of established markets, relatively high individualism, prosperity, and efficiency, governments in developed countries will stipulate fewer post-privatization requirements than elsewhere. By contrast, both in developing and former communist countries, the political process and the scale of privatization, in combination with popular values opposite to those in developed countries, may result in more post-privatization requirements.

However, the conditions in developing and former communist countries are not necessarily equal. Often, the political process in developing countries emphasizes nationalism and a need to maintain political coalitions, whereas former communist countries need to jump-start their stalled economies (Ramanadham, 1993). These differences would indicate that developing countries are more open to imposing post-privatization requirements than former communist countries which may have to grant investors a higher degree of freedom. The prior arguments imply that (1) privatization deals in former communist and developing countries should be more likely to include post-privatization conditions than privatization deals in developed countries, and (2) privatization deals in less developed countries tend to include more post-privatization requirements than privatizations in former communist countries.

THE EMPIRICAL EVIDENCE

Description of Research Data and Statistical Methods

The data for this study come from 467 privatization deals completed worldwide between 1989 and 1992 and collected in the Investment Dealers' Digest, Inc. (IDD) mergers and acquisitions database. IDD compiles worldwide data on M&A, including information on industry and Standard Industrial Classification (SIC) codes, type of ownership and type of transaction, deal terms, dates, financial information, advisor information, and stock and premium information, for both the acquiring and target firm. From the database, we selected all 467 cases in which the target firm was owned by the government. The average size of the target firm was 940 employees, with the smallest target firm having eight employees and the largest 18,400. Thus the sample represents both large and small privatization transactions.

Three analytical methods were utilized to examine the above predictions: Chi-square, Spearman rank correlation, and Kruskall Wallis tests. These methods have the advantage of confidently testing differences between groups using categorical variables (Freund and Walpole, 1980). In combination, these tests ensure that the results are not due to an inherent mathematical bias within one statistical technique (Woodcock, Beamish, and Makino, 1994).

Countries of acquiring and target firms were classified into three groups: developed, developing, and former communist countries. Organization for Economic Cooperation and Development (OECD) member countries were classified as developed countries, and of the remaining countries, the former communist nations of Central and Eastern Europe were extracted, while the remaining countries were classified as less-developed. Table 6.1 shows the country groups representing both the acquiring and target firms in the sample.

TABLE 6.1. Acquiring and Target Firms

Acquiring Firm Country	Target Firm Country		
	Developed	Former communist	Developing
Developed	80	331	11
Former communist		16	
Developing		6	12

The information used from the database for the present study relates to the following subject matters: (1) industry information (SIC codes and business description) for both acquirer and target firm, (2) home country of both the acquirer and target firm, (3) percentage shares of the target purchased by the acquirer from the government, and (4) deal terms affecting the post-privatization operations of the SOE negotiated between the government and the acquirer, such as maintaining a specified number of employees at the target, investing certain amounts of money into the target, maintaining a specified percentage of local shareholders or managers from the home country of the target firm, meeting financial targets, building distribution systems, receiving financial support from the government, etc. We tested if there were differences between type of country for each of the above conditions individually as well as for an aggregate measure which indicated if one or several of the post-privatization conditions were specified in the deal terms.

Results

The comparison of the 467 privatization cases across developed, developing, and former communist countries supports for the most part the predictions made above. Somewhat uncertain are the results with respect to the industry relatedness between acquirer and target firm. Two of the three statistical methods applied suggest that in Central and Eastern Europe more privatization deals involve acquirers and target firms that operate in the same or similar industries. However, not all statistics support this finding.

With respect to the other predictions made above, the empirical evidence is quite strong. The analysis indicates that indeed privatization deals in Central and Eastern Europe are more likely to be cross-border acquisitions than privatization deals in developing and developed countries. Also, the results show that privatization deals in former communist countries are more likely to be total acquisitions compared to privatization cases in developed and developing countries where taking equity stakes is more prevalent.

As expected, there are significantly more conditions associated with privatization transactions in former communist and developing countries than in developed countries. Their OLC governments often demand that acquirers of SOEs agree to maintain a specified number of employees at the former SOE and invest a certain amount of capital. Nevertheless, the data are inconclusive here with respect to the other government requirements listed above.

Finally, we had expected that there are more post-privatization conditions set forth in the transaction terms in developing countries compared to former communist countries. The data, however, provides no evidence for this hypothesis. Apparently, Central and Eastern European governments intend to control the operations of an acquired SOE after privatization to a degree similar to that of governments in the developing world.

CONCLUSIONS AND IMPLICATIONS

Although there has been a significant increase in privatization research in the last decade, research on privatization from a firm-level perspective as opposed to a macro level, public policy view is still lacking. We believe that this exploratory study contributes to our understanding of the privatization process by using a firm-level perspective to analyze a large cross-section of privatization cases. As such, it should fill a significant void in our understanding of privatization and the determinants of privatization effectiveness.

The study highlights several points of the process of privatization that have implications from both macro and micro perspectives. First, the study clearly indicates that there are differences in the ways and means of privatization between these three types of countries. Clear evidence of these differences is the role that privatization programs play in acquiring know-how and technology. For example, as earlier research has indicated, governments in both developing and former communist Central and Eastern Europe are using privatization as a tool to attract capital and technological know-how. This form of international technology transfer is achieved best through related acquisitions where the acquirer can transfer technology. The significantly higher incidence of cross-border acquisitions in former communist countries, even when compared to developing countries, can also be interpreted in the context of their need to acquire know-how and technology.

Although the results on relatedness are not as strong as the results on the other variables, it seems that, overlapping with the interest of governments in obtaining know-how and technology, foreign acquirers of SOEs have reduced uncertainty by relying on related acquisitions in developing and former communist countries. In this case, as Lenway and Murtha (1994) have argued, the strategies of the firms are affected by the policies of the countries, and the need to have new technology and processes translates into related acquisitions. This suggests that managers of firms interested in entering Central and Eastern European markets via acquisition of privatized enterprises should target related firms to improve their chances for a successful bid while at the same time reducing the risk of the investment.

The findings of this study identify overall differences with respect to privatization conditions in developed compared to developing and former communist countries. This is consistent with the argument that, while developed countries score high on both market orientation and private property rights allocations, former communist and developing countries score low to medium on these dimensions (Murtha and Lenway, 1994). This appears to result in more government guidance, control of the privatization process, and post-privatization requirements in both types of countries. Acquirers interested in acquisitions in former communist or developing countries should expect more privatization conditions than acquirers targeting SOEs in developed countries.

The large number of acquisitions of privatized SOEs in which the terms specify limits to the freedom of the acquirer highlights the governments' concerns. These terms also highlight the political nature of the decision that accompanies the privatization process. They also suggest the limits of using a mergers and acquisitions framework when studying privatization acquisitions. In order to effectively study these transactions, mergers-and-acquisitions-based research should also encompass the political process and the implications of government ownership of the firms.

Government needs are also important in the context of partial or total acquisitions. Clearly, keeping partial ownership affords the government continued control over the firm. This, however, may not be in the acquirer's interest. Recent economic policy in the developed world suggests that market regulation rather than firm ownership by governments encourages productive as well as allocative efficiency (Caves, 1990b). Therefore, privatizing governments in Central and Eastern Europe should cede ownership to private investors and use indirect measures to ensure economic goals rather than maintaining direct control through partial privatization. This will likely attract more investors as well as improve the efficiency of former SOEs.

REFERENCES

Adler, M. and B. Dumas. 1975. Optimal international acquisitions. *Journal of Finance*, 30: 1-20.

Aharoni, Y. 1986. *The evolution and management of state-owned enterprises.* Cambridge, MA: Ballinger.

Berger, R. 1991. Unternehmerische Aufgaben und Perspektiven bei der Restrukturierung der ostdeutschen Wirtschaft. *Betriebswirtschaftliche Forschung und Praxis*, 43(2): 104-120.

Bleeke, J. and D. Ernst. 1991. The way to win in cross-border alliances. *Harvard Business Review*, 69(6): 127-135.

Caves, R. E. 1990a. Corporate mergers in international economic integration. Presented at CEPR/Instituto Mobiliare Italiano Conference on European Financial Integration, Rome, Italy.

Caves, R. E. 1990b. Lessons from privatization in Britain: State enterprise behavior, public choice, and corporate governance. *Journal of Economic Behavior and Organization*, 13: 145-169.

Chatterjee, S. 1986. Types of synergy and economic value: The impact of acquisitions on merging and rival firms. *Strategic Management Journal*, 7: 119-139.

Chatterjee, S., M. Lubatkin, D. M. Schweiger, and Y. Weber. 1992. Cultural differences and shareholder value in related mergers: Linking equity and human capital. *Strategic Management Journal*, 13: 319-332.

Chatterjee, S. and B. Wernerfelt. 1991. The link between resources and type of diversification: Theory and evidence. *Strategic Management Journal*, 12: 33-48.

Cook, P. and C. Kirkpatrick. 1988. Privatization in developing countries: An overview. In P. Cook and C. Kirkpatrick (Eds.), *Privatization in developing countries.* 3-44. New York: St. Martin's Press.

Cooke, T. E., in association with Arthur Young. 1988. *International mergers and acquisitions.* Oxford, UK: Blackwell.

Datta, D. K. and G. Puia. 1993. Cross-border acquisitions: An examination of the impact of cultural difference, country risk and relatedness on the wealth effects of U.S. acquiring firms. Presented at the Academy of Management National Meetings, Atlanta, GA.

De Castro, J. and N. Uhlenbruck. 1993. The privatization process in developing countries: A strategic model from the perspective of the acquiring firm. Presented at the Academy of Management National Meetings, Atlanta, GA.

DIW Wochenbericht, 1994. Gesamtwirtschaftliche und unternehmerische Anpassungsfortschritte in Ostdeutschland. Deutsches Institut für Wirtschaftsforschung, Berlin, 61(15): 209-227.

Donahue, J. D. 1989. *The privatization decision*. New York: Basic Books.

The Economist, 1993. Selling the state. August 21: 18-20.

Fatemi, A. M. 1984. Shareholder benefits from corporate international diversification. *Journal of Finance*. 34: 1325-1384.

Freudenberg, T. and A. Bird. 1991. An outsider's primer on East German investment. *Mergers & Acquisitions*, 25(5): 50-53.

Freund, J. E. and R. E. Walpole. 1980. *Mathematical statistics*. 3rd edition. Englewood Cliffs. NJ: Prentice Hall.

Frydman, R. and A. Rapaczynski. 1992. Mass privatization proposals in Eastern Europe: Ownership and the structure of control. In Ferdinando Targetti (Ed.), *Privatization in Europe: West and East experiences*. 75-88. Brookfield, VT: Dartmouth Publishing Company.

Goodman, J. B. and G. W. Loveman. 1991. Does privatization serve the public interest? *Harvard Business Review*, 69(6): 26-38.

Haspeslagh, P. C. and D. B. Jemison. 1991. *Managing acquisitions: Creating value through corporate renewal*. New York: The Free Press.

Hisey, K. B. and R. E. Caves. 1985. Diversification strategy and choice of country: Diversifying acquisitions abroad by U.S. multinationals, 1978-1980. *Journal of International Business Studies*, 16 (Summer): 51-64.

Hutchinson, G. 1991. Efficiency gains through privatization of UK industries. In A. F. Ott and K. Hartley (Eds.), *Privatization and economic efficiency*. 87-107. Hants, U.K.: Edward Elgar.

Jemison, D. B. and S. B. Sitkin. 1986. Corporate acquisitions: A process perspective. *Academy of Management Review*, 11: 145-163.

Kitching, J. 1973. *Acquisitions in Europe: Causes of corporate success and failures*. Geneva: Business International S.A.

Lenway, S. A. and T. P. Murtha. 1994. The state as a strategist in international business research. *Journal of International Business Studies*, 25: 513-536.

Lessard, D. R. 1973. International portfolio diversification: A multivariate analysis for a group of Latin American countries. *Journal of Finance*, 28: 610-633.

Lessard, D. R. 1976. World, country, and industry relationships in equity returns: Implications for risk reductions through international diversification. *Financial Analysis Journal*, 32 (January-February): 32-37.

Lubatkin, M. 1983. Mergers and the performance of the acquiring firm. *Academy of Management Review*, 8: 218-225.

Markides, C. C. and C. D. Ittner. 1994. Shareholder benefits from corporate international diversification: Evidence from U.S. international acquisitions. *Journal of International Business Studies*, 25: 343-366.

Murtha, T. P. and S. A. Lenway. 1994. Country capabilities and the strategic state: How national political institutions affect multinational corporations' strategies. *Strategic Management Journal*, 15 (Summer): 113-130.

Nankani, H. B., 1990. Lessons of privatization in developing countries. *Finance and Development*, 27 (March): 43-45.

Napier, N. K. 1989. Mergers and acquisitions, human resource issues and outcomes: A review and suggested typology. *Journal of Management Studies*, 26: 271-289.

Pablo, A. L. 1994. Determinants of acquisition integration level: A decision-making perspective. *Academy of Management Journal*, 37: 803-836.

Parker, D. and K. Hartley. 1991. Do changes in organizational status affect financial performance? *Strategic Management Journal*, 12: 631-641.

Pfohl, H. C., F. Trethon, S. L. Freichel, M. Hegedues, and V. Schultz. 1992. Joint Ventures in Ungarn. *Die Betriebswirtschaft*, 52: 655-673.

Prahalad, C. K. and Y. Doz. 1987. *The multinational mission: Balancing local demands and global vision*. New York: The Free Press.

Ramamurti, R. 1992. Why are developing countries privatizing? *Journal of International Business Studies*, 23: 225-249.

Ramanadham, V. V. 1993. Concluding review. In V. V. Ramanadham (Ed.), *Privatization: A global perspective*: 526-591. London, U.K.: Routledge.

Rondinelli, D. A. 1994. Privatization and economic reform in Central Europe: Experience of the early transition period. In D. A. Rondinelli (Ed.), *Privatization and economic reform in Central Europe: The changing business climate*. 1-40. Westport, CT: Quorum Books.

Schweiger, D. M. and A. S. DeNisi. 1991. Communication with employees following a merger: A longitudinal field experiment. *Academy of Management Journal*, 34, 110-135.

Shrivastava, P. 1986. Postmerger Integration. *Journal of Business Strategy*, 7(1): 65-76.

Sobell, V. 1993. Privatisation in Central and Eastern Europe. *European Trends*, 2(2): 71-87.

Targetti, F. 1992. The privatization of industry with particular regard to economies in transition. In F. Targetti (Ed.), *Privatization in Europe: West and East experiences*. 1-29. Brookfield, VT: Dartmouth Publishing Company.

Vickers, J. and G. Yarrow. 1988. *Privatization: An economic analysis*. Cambridge, MA: MIT Press.

Walters, A. A., 1987. Ownership and efficiency in urban buses. In S. H. Hanke (Ed.), *Prospects for privatization*: 83-92. New York: Academy of Political Science.

Young, P. 1987. Privatization around the world. In S. H. Hanke (Ed.), *Prospects for privatization*: 190-206. New York: Academy of Political Science.

Chapter 7

First-Rate Furniture Firm

David W. Lutz
with
James H. Davis

THE ASSIGNMENT

In the spring of 1994, during my final semester in a U.S. MBA program, my capstone-course professor assigned teams of four students to various companies, so we could analyze and propose solutions to real-world problems. My group worked with a furniture-manufacturing company in one of the non-Russian former republics of the Soviet Union. To conceal the identity of the firm, I will call it "First-Rate Furniture Firm," or "FFF."

My professor had visited FFF briefly a few weeks earlier, en route to other companies, in Russia, and had learned that its transition from operating within a command economy to operating profitably in the global marketplace was proving to be difficult. He was not, however, able to spend enough time with the company to learn the full nature and scope of its problems. Through my professor FFF extended an invitation to an MBA to spend six weeks helping the company during the summer of 1994, but said it could only provide a free room in a company-owned apartment building and free lunch in the company cafeteria as compensation for the work. I was the only group member interested in continuing the relationship with the company beyond graduation.

Our professor told us what he knew about FFF, and gave us its Chief Executive Officer's business card and photographs of some of its products. He said that freedom from central planning had cost FFF most of its customers. For decades FFF had sold most of its products within the Soviet Union, in quantities and at prices determined by the government. But with the declining level of economic activity that followed the collapse of the Soviet Union, few of its former citizens could afford to buy new furniture. The company's survival required selling furniture to the West; its CEO hoped to export furniture to the United States.

ESTABLISHING CONTACT

Our professor also told us that while some of FFF's 700 employees spoke Russian or German, in addition to their native tongue, extremely few spoke even rudimentary English. Because I speak some German, but no Russian, I decided to introduce my group to FFF in English by letter. I wrote a one-page letter to FFF's CEO ("General Director") and requested as much information as possible about FFF's product line. We offered to do what we could to identify American customers for the company and to help in whatever other ways conceivable.

After several unsuccessful attempts to fax the letter at various hours of the day and night, I sent it by airmail. After waiting three weeks without a reply, I wrote a second letter, addressed to the CEO "or any other member of FFF," explaining that we were well into our semester, and that if we did not receive a response immediately, our professor would have no choice but to assign us to a different company.

When I was also unable to fax this letter, I contacted my long-distance telephone company, and learned that it had previously given me an incorrect country code. I was then able to fax the letter. I waited two hours, in the middle of the night, for a response and then, for the first time, telephoned FFF. The CEO's secretary answered the phone, and told me in a halting combination of English and German that she had received my letter, but that her boss had not yet read it. It struck me that while she obviously could not reply to the letter herself, she could have communicated on her own initiative the fact that it had been received, without waiting for the CEO to read it. I then reported to my professor that we had finally established communication with FFF, and therefore did not need to be assigned to a new company. As my MBA group waited for FFF to give us detailed information about its products, we studied the global furniture market and the economy of FFF's country.

To shorten a long story: After mailing and faxing several more letters to FFF, FFF finally replied nine weeks after the CEO's secretary had told me that they had received my fax, and twelve weeks after I first mailed a letter. This message was signed by one of FFF's engineers, who, as I later found out, was the only FFF member fluent in English. Because nearly all of FFF's international communication was transmitted in English, he was the firm's primary interpreter, translator, and communicator, in addition to his full-time responsibilities as the chief engineer of the largest division of the factory.

FIRST IMPRESSIONS

In the final weeks of the semester, I made arrangements to visit FFF during the month of June 1994, to spend the next five weeks touring Europe, and then to return for an additional two weeks in August. I departed for Europe without having received either a catalog or a price list from FFF. Because I knew the company could produce more furniture than it was selling, that it had minimal distribution channels outside the former Soviet Union, and that it paid its workers far less than Western workers, I thought the greatest service I could provide was to identify one or more U.S. firms for which FFF could become a high-volume, low-cost producer. I took with me the names and addresses of several dozen U.S. furniture firms, and planned to send each of them a packet of information with a letter in English signed by FFF's CEO.

Once I arrived at FFF, the responsibilities of the engineer who had written to me were increased to include becoming my host. He was the only employee of FFF with whom I could conduct a conversation. He (and his wife) went above and beyond the call of duty in attending to my needs, even though this was in addition to what was already more than a full-time job.

ACCOUNTING FOR BANKRUPTCY

I soon learned that there were no catalogs, brochures, or price lists to send to U.S. firms, or to any other potential buyer. But I also soon learned that finding companies which would buy its furniture was not FFF's greatest problem. Western European and North American would-be customers were standing in line to buy FFF's furniture, but either were receiving no response or were being turned away.

The day after I arrived at FFF, my host guided me on a tour of the company. We spent most of the time walking through the various buildings of a large factory containing many pieces of Western European production equipment–some of it idle. My guide also took me through the office area, including the computer room. I was surprised to find state-of-the-art Italian hardware and American word-processing and spreadsheet software. I was told that only a few years earlier FFF's financial calculations were made by abacus; and there was still an abacus serving as a cash register in the company cafeteria.

An employee identified to me as a "technologist" was working in the computer room that afternoon. My host briefly explained the calculations the technologist was making. I almost immediately saw a problem more serious than any I had previously anticipated, and yet so simple that I thought we would solve it immediately, and then move to more formidable challenges.

Because Western firms knew that the cost of labor in the former Soviet Union was extremely low, FFF had numerous offers from the West. In most cases these were not inquiries for FFF's products, but rather offers for subcontracts for a certain quantity of a new product conforming to the customer's design and specifications. Since most of this correspondence was in English, it first went to the English-speaking engineer for translation. Depending upon his workload at the time, it could be a matter of days, weeks, or even months before he found the time to translate the letters. In some cases his burden was compounded by the letter-writers' own poor command of the English language. Several weeks after I arrived, my host gave me a half-dozen letters that he was unable to translate. All were several months old, and all but one were from potential customers.

Once a letter was translated, FFF would decide whether to accept the offer or to reject it as unprofitable. The decision-making process began with revenue and cost data from the recent past. Table 7.1 provides this data (converted to U.S. dollars) for the largest division of the company for the period January 1 to June 30, 1994.

Cost of materials was primarily for lumber. Transportation cost included both the transportation of raw timber from one of the company's sawmills to the factory and transportation of finished furniture from the factory to the point at which the buyer assumed the cost of transportation. Most of the workers on the factory floor were paid piece-rate wages, except for the quality-control inspectors, who were paid an hourly wage.

Most of "other costs" were the salaries of personnel in the division's headquarters and the division's share of salaries at corporate headquarters. Then a variety of lesser costs followed. After comparing Total Cost to total revenue and calculating profit and profitability, FFF determined one additional number: the ratio of other costs to piece-rate wages which at the time, was 5.12.

With this historical data on hand, FFF estimated the cost of materials, transportation, and piece-rate wages for a potential customer's order. These estimates were made with a high degree of precision. The order's share of other costs was then determined by multiplying its Piece-Rate Wages cost by the historical ratio of other costs to piece-rate wages (5.12 in this case). FFF then added these costs, plus 10 percent profit, to determine its price. It accepted an order if and only if its price was lower than the price offered by the customer. In most cases, FFF's price was higher than the customer's, and the order was rejected as unprofitable.

TABLE 7.1. First-Rate Furniture Firm's Largest Division's Income Statement: January 1 to June 30, 1994 (U.S. $1,000)

Revenue		853.1
Cost		
	Materials	415.9
	Transportation	20.8
	Piece-Rate Wages	64.9
	Other Costs	
	Corporate Headquarters	55.5
	Division Salaries	172.0
	Equipment Repairs	1.3
	Parts	22.0
	Business Trips	4.3
	Visas	0.8
	Customs	6.1
	Insurance	3.5
	Amortization	47.0
	Heating Fuel	14.9
	Electricity	12.9
	Water	0.8
	Miscellaneous	0.5
	Work in Process	(9.1)
	Total Other Costs	332.5
Total Cost		834.1
Profit		19.0
Profitability		2.3%
Total Other Costs/Piece-Rate Wages		5.12

The problem, of course, was that this decision-making rule failed to recognize the distinction between and the nature of fixed and variable costs. If the factory had been operating at or near full capacity, this method might have worked well. But for a company in FFF's position, it was a prescription for bankruptcy.

THE DOWNWARD SPIRAL

Because FFF lost most of its market when it gained freedom from central planning, its level of production, and consequently its variable cost of production, fell sharply. As the factory went from two shifts to one, many workers lost their jobs. Subsequently the amount of work further decreased for the employees who remained. While this was happening, the number of salaried personnel was lowered only slightly, not in proportion to the decline in production. The company was, therefore, in a state of disequilibrium as the ratio of fixed costs to variable costs increased dramatically. FFF never calculated this ratio; but since piece-rate wages were highly correlated to total variable cost, and since most other costs were fixed, the ratio FFF did calculate was a good proxy for the ratio of fixed costs to variable costs.

Obviously, a company in FFF's situation of operating at a low or, at best, minimal profitability with plenty of excess capacity should have accepted every order with a price higher than its variable cost. But by requiring each order also to pay its share of other costs, plus 10 percent profit, it had been for several years rejecting as unprofitable many orders that in fact would have been quite profitable.

As fewer orders were accepted, the ratio of other costs to piece-rate wages grew steadily larger. And as this ratio increased, fewer and fewer potential orders were able to overcome the hurdle and pay their share of other costs. But as more orders were rejected, this key ratio grew even larger, and still *more* orders were rejected. FFF was in a downward spiral on its way to bankruptcy.

All of this I learned during my first full day with the company. Incredible as it may seem, I left FFF more than 11 weeks later without seeing a change in its method of deciding which orders to accept and which to reject.

ATTEMPTS TO SOLVE THE PROBLEM

I began my attempt to persuade FFF to change its managerial accounting procedures by offering a fictional example with small, round numbers (see Table 7.2).

From this point onward, I was handicapped by my inability to speak the native language. I spent several days with FFF before I had an opportunity to explain the problem to my host. I suggested to him that we should explain it to the managers as soon as possible. We went to several offices, and my host described the "new method" in his native tongue. This invariably led to long, emotional exchanges, of which I understood not a word. Eventually my host would turn to me and ask in English for further clarification. Although I did the best I could, these conversations always ended with the managers remaining not persuaded, but with no clear explanation why this was so.

TABLE 7.2. Two Alternative Decision Methods

Two methods of deciding whether an order would be profitable provide contradictory guidance when applied in a simple example. First, some equations are needed:

Profit = Revenue − Total Cost
Total Cost = Variable Cost + Fixed Cost
Profit = Revenue − Variable Cost − Fixed Cost

Now assume that these are the company's revenue, cost, and profit data for an average month:

Revenue   = 950
Variable Cost = 600
Fixed Cost   = 300
Total Cost   = 900
Profit   = 50

Next, assume that a potential customer offers to pay 140, but no more than that, for an order with a variable cost of 100. Should FFF accept or reject this order?

Method A

Price = Variable Cost + Share of Fixed Cost + 10% Profit

Share of Fixed Cost = (300/600)(Variable Cost) = (0.5)(Variable Cost)

Price = 100 + (0.5)(100) + Profit = 100 + 50 + 15 = 165

Since 165 > 140, reject the order.

Method B

If we reject the order		If we accept the order
950	Revenue	1090
900	Total Cost	1000
50	Profit	90

Since 90 > 50, accept the order.

For a company with excess production capacity and low profitability, Method B is the appropriate method.

Next, I presented the same argument with the numbers of actual proposals from U.S. firms that either were being evaluated or had recently been rejected as unprofitable. These attempts were equally unsuccessful.

Two weeks after my arrival at FFF, I was invited to meet the CEO for the first time, in the conference room next to his office. He talked at some length with my host serving as interpreter about the history and organization of the company, said he was glad to have me working with FFF, and asked whether I would give him a written report at the end of the summer. I said that I would, and then attempted to tell him the importance of the cost-accounting mistake. He replied that this was only an opportunity to get acquainted, and that we could talk later about specific issues. My only subsequent opportunity to explain the problem to him came more than two months later.

The hours and days that I could not spend talking with anyone, because my interpreter was meeting his other responsibilities, I spent helping him by making long-distance telephone calls and drafting replies in English to reduce the backlog of inquiries from abroad. But then FFF hired, for the duration of the summer, a student studying English at a nearby university who, in fact, spoke the language better than most Americans. As she assumed the responsibility of communicating with the outside world–which she could do better than I, because she could also communicate with everyone in FFF–and as I prepared to leave the company for five weeks, I made yet another attempt to explain as clearly as I could, with spreadsheet software and real customer orders, the accounting problem. I then asked the student to translate the document into the native language. As she prepared the translation, my discussions with her assured me that she understood the issues at stake and accurately translated what I had written. I then gave the translated document to seven key persons in the company, so that when I returned five weeks later, the problem would be solved.

Soon after I returned in August for my final two weeks with FFF, my host suggested that I prepare a presentation for the managers of the company about business in the United States. I replied that I would oblige, but that since the topic was so large, it would be helpful to know more specifically what they were interested in hearing. Several days later, he reported that the CEO wanted me to talk about the "new method" of determining whether to accept a customer order. So I prepared myself once again, this time with an overhead projector and an interpreter in a roomful of people. While I was getting ready, the manager of FFF's largest division came to me to ask a simple question about the document he had received more than a month earlier. It was obvious that he was looking at it for the first time.

After I completed my oral presentation, everyone waited for the CEO's response. Although my primary focus was on the accounting problem, I also emphasized the need to create a marketing department, staffed by persons able to communicate fluently in English and, ideally, in other Western European languages as well. The CEO then stood up and graciously thanked me for spending half of the summer with FFF, and for "giving us something interesting to think about."

STATIC MANAGEMENT
IN A DYNAMIC ENVIRONMENT

FFF arrived at the brink of bankruptcy because a chief executive who may have been competent in one context was incompetent in another. As a manager of FFF within the Soviet system, his responsibilities did not include determining which customer orders to accept and which to reject, because those decisions were made by the government. In contrast, he had human resource management responsibilities far broader than those of most Western managers. For example, FFF's employees and their families lived in apartment buildings owned by the company, and the CEO was responsible for maintaining order and discipline within those buildings. If someone's after-working-hours drinking problem disturbed the peace, the company's management was responsible for dealing with the problem. And even though my two exchanges with FFF's CEO required interpreters, it was clear that he was a skilled communicator.

Thus, this executive had achieved success as a command-obeyer, not as a decision maker. His career depended upon doing well what he was ordered to do, not upon deciding at the level of business strategy what to do. The careers of his subordinates depended upon how well they followed his commands. During the Soviet period, all of FFF's managers were members of the Communist Party. That does not mean they believed in communism, but it implies that they decided to play by the rules. And Marxist-Leninist theory notwithstanding, those who obeyed received greater economic rewards than those who did not.

But with the collapse of the Soviet Union, one game ended and a new game, with new rules, began. The CEO no longer received commands from a central planning bureaucracy. Instead, the decision-making responsibilities of his position expanded greatly. Moreover, decisions had to be made more quickly than they were within a centrally planned economy.

Although the abacus was replaced by the computer, no one in the company understood how to think about the difference between fixed and variable costs. Also, it may be difficult for someone who has competed and succeeded for years with one set of rules to admit that he is being defeated by another set.

I find it difficult to believe that none of the managers to whom I explained the accounting problem, albeit through an interpreter or translator, understood the problem and my explanations. Some had earned university degrees in engineering, and therefore had mastered mathematical and technical concepts far more complex than simple managerial accounting. My hypothesis is that they did indeed understand, but pretended not to, because they feared the consequences of doing things differently, without a directive from above.

On several occasions during my time with FFF, someone was instructed to report to the CEO's office. Although I never witnessed any of these sessions, I came to understand that they were not pleasant. And while the CEO criticized his subordinates both for making bad decisions and for failing to make decisions, they were clearly more afraid of the former than of the latter. I believe FFF's middle managers faked a lack of understanding of a simple concept for an entire summer, so that they could avoid admitting to me that they understood my point, but feared the consequence of doing things differently without explicit orders from the CEO.

Within a company whose managers have been trained to follow orders, to maintain discipline, and to avoid incurring the wrath of the boss, there is a high degree of reluctance to take the initiative. In the past, success or failure of FFF or any other Soviet company did not depend on strategic decisions made by its CEO, and the pace of decision making was glacial and remained so even though the environment had changed drastically. After acknowledging that something was wrong, after requesting help from the West, and after receiving an offer of free assistance from a team of four American MBAs, FFF took three months to reply. And after an MBA reported the discovery of a problem with the potential to bankrupt the company, the CEO waited two months to listen to the explanation.

Near the end of my stay with FFF, I learned that the CEO had postponed his retirement in order to remain at the helm until the privatization of the company. Also, several of FFF's best managers had left the company since the collapse of the Soviet Union for other companies or to start new ones, but might be persuaded to return after the CEO's retirement. It remains to be seen whether there will still be anything to return to after the CEO retires.

CONCLUSIONS

Although my experience with FFF does not provide a sufficient basis for drawing conclusions about management in Central and Eastern Europe in general, it seems likely that other companies in the region encountered similar problems during the period of transition following the breakup of the Soviet Union. The comments of one unidentified observer of the situation describes quite accurately the state of FFF when I arrived at its door in June 1994. In an article titled "Retraining Eastern Europe," Robert O'Connor reported:

> A London economist says the need for skills training in the Eastern [European] countries extends "all across the board, especially in things like accounting and finance. They know more or less how to run an assembly line. But in terms of calculating or properly ascribing costs and doing research on what would sell, what wouldn't, and how it would be priced, they just really haven't got a clue." (1992: 41)

As I understand the factors responsible for FFF's precarious condition, the root of the problem is not an inability to think clearly about cost accounting, but rather an atmosphere in which managers are afraid to change existing business practices, created by a chief executive who is still managing as if he were in the USSR. It seems highly probable that this situation is far from unique to this particular company.

The strongest evidence that FFF's CEO was successful during the Soviet period is the simple fact that he retained his position for many years. Within the Soviet context, executives who were not successful, as success was defined within that context, were removed from their positions. Therefore, there were probably many other successful chief executives in the Soviet Union with similar management styles. But since the management style of FFF's General Director proved to be hopelessly inadequate during the period of transition, the same is probably true of other executives who remained in office, but failed to keep up with the pace of change.

There is some empirical support for the hypothesis that "the habits of thought engendered by decades of Communism" (Penrice, 1995: 14) have handicapped many firms in addition to FFF. In a 1994 survey conducted by the Central and Eastern European Teachers Program, 231 managers in Bulgaria, the Czech Republic, the former East Germany, Hungary, Poland, Romania, Russia, Slovakia, Slovenia, and Ukraine reported on 431 instances of "recent or ongoing efforts to change managerial practices or policies in their companies." When asked to classify barriers to attempted change as either internal to the company or present in the external business environment, the managers classified 54 percent of the barriers as internal. Furthermore, "among those internal barriers, the managers identified two factors as having overwhelming significance: 'unfavorable attitudes' among both managers and workers (accounting for 43 percent of internal barriers cited and 23 percent of all barriers) and 'lack of skills and knowledge' on the part of managers themselves (41 percent of internal barriers cited and 22 percent of all barriers). 'Unfavorable attitudes' were said to range from a reluctance to take initiative, responsibility, and risks to ideologically based suspicions of such fundamentals as private ownership" (Penrice, 1995: 14).

During a period of such rapid change in the business environment as that following the breakup of the Soviet Union, the management of individual firms must also change, either by a change in the prevailing practices or by a change of leadership (Datta and Guthrie, 1994; Schwartz and Menon, 1985; Virany, Tushman, and Romanelli, 1992). FFF had state-of-the-art production equipment, computer hardware and software, and intelligent middle managers, but this was insufficient to ensure success, because the CEO did not adapt to the new situation. When the CEO, of this firm or of any other firm in a similar situation, fails to adapt, the survival of the firm requires that he be replaced by someone willing and able to do so. With a CEO who has been at the helm for many years, and identifies his personal success with that of the firm which he has guided for so long, the best approach is probably to offer a retirement package that he cannot refuse, and to allow him to step down without being humiliated.

REFERENCES

Datta, D.K. and J.P. Guthrie. 1994. Executive succession: Organizational antecedents of CEO characteristics. *Strategic Management Journal*. 15: 569-577.

O'Connor, R. 1992. Retraining Eastern Europe. *Training: The magazine of human resource development*. 29(11): 40-45.

Penrice, D. 1995. The post-communist world: The obstacles to change. *Harvard Business Review*. 73(1): 14.

Schwartz, K.B. and K. Menon. 1985. Executive succession in failing firms. *Academy of Management Journal*. 10: 680-686.

Virany, B., M.L. Tushman, and E. Romanelli. 1992. Executive succession and organizational outcomes in turbulent environments: An organizational learning approach. *Organization Science*. 3(1): 72-91.

Chapter 8

Managerial Challenges During Organizational Re-Creation: Industrial Companies in the Czech Republic

Karen L. Newman
Stanley D. Nollen

DISCONTINUOUS CHANGE

The Velvet Revolution of 1989 brought unprecedented change to virtually all companies in the Czech Republic. Almost overnight, the central planning system of the communist regime was replaced with a market-based system and a massive privatization effort that would yield a market economy.

If we examine the pace, timing, and type of change experienced by organizations, we observe long periods of relative stability in which change is incremental, punctuated by short periods of fundamental, discontinuous change (Gersick, 1991; Romanelli and Tushman, 1994; Tushman and Romanelli, 1985). During periods of incremental change, minor adjustments are made to bring the organization into alignment with its product environment and bring internal systems into alignment and consistency with each other. This type of change is analogous to learning by exploitation (March, 1991), first-order learning (Lant and Mezias, 1992), or single-loop learning (Argyris and Schön, 1978), in which changes serve to make existing patterns of behavior more stable, predictable, and efficient. Changes in structure, decision-making authority, or control mecha-

---

All quoted statements in this chapter were obtained from interviews conducted at KPS in Brno, Czech Republic, in March 1993, December 1993, and July 1994.

nisms are incremental changes. Reorganizing, decentralizing, or starting a new reporting system are minor organizational adjustments made in the context of a relatively constant environment. Paradoxically, as organizations succeed with incremental, convergent change, inertial forces are created inside the firm that have the effect of decreasing the organization's ability to make more fundamental, discontinuous change (Hannan and Freeman, 1984).

The stimulus for discontinuous change normally comes from outside the firm (Romanelli and Tushman, 1994). It is of such a great magnitude that existing systems, structures, strategies, and core values in the firm cannot adapt to it. Discontinuous change becomes necessary when the firm's performance falls below (or threatens to fall below) a threshold level of performance believed to be desirable (Lant and Mezias, 1992) or necessary for survival. Gersick (1991) illustrates the difference between incremental and discontinuous change:

> During [periods of incremental change] systems maintain and carry out the choices of their deep structure. Systems make adjustments that preserve the deep structure against internal and external perturbations, and move incrementally along paths built into the deep structure. . . . [Periods of discontinuous change] are relatively brief . . . when a system's deep structure comes apart, leaving it in disarray until the period ends, with the "choices" around which a new deep structure forms. [Discontinuous] outcomes, based on interactions of systems' historical resources with current events, are not predictable; they may or may not leave a system better off. (pp. 17, 20)

Examples of discontinuous change include introduction of competency-killing technologies (Tushman and Anderson, 1986), as experienced in the computer industry when personal computers were invented or as experienced in the buggy whip industry when the internal combustion engine was invented. Discontinuous change can also come from market upheavals such as airline deregulation in the United States in the 1970s and 1980s, or the breakup and deregulation of the U.S. telecommunications industry. In these cases, it is not enough for firms to introduce a new product, decentralize, or institute a quality control system. Discontinuous change requires fundamental change in the core values of the firm, the businesses in which it competes, and the way in which it competes. Underlying assumptions about how business should be conducted, and the corporate core values that accompany those assumptions, are all modified during discontinuous change (Figure 8.1).

FIGURE 8.1. A Framework for Discontinuous Change

Type of change	Change includes	Magnitude of change	Outcome	Example
Incremental	Structures Systems	Small	Convergence, better alignment, and more inertia	Reorganizations Performance appraisal systems
Reorientation	Structures Systems Strategy	Moderate	Discontinuous change with respect to products or markets	Breakthrough technological change Change in regulatory environment
Re-Creation	Structures Systems Strategy Core Values	Large	Discontinuous change with respect to products, markets, internal systems, and core values	Firms in Central Europe

Adapted from Tushman and Romanelli, 1985.

BUSINESS BEFORE THE VELVET REVOLUTION

The political, social, and economic changes that took place in the Czech Republic after late 1989 created the need for discontinuous change in firms. The Velvet Revolution occurred in late November and early December of 1989 in Czechoslovakia, within weeks after the fall of the Berlin Wall. The name "Velvet Revolution" comes from the fact that the existing communist government resigned without bloodshed after massive peaceful demonstrations in Prague, giving way to a democracy almost overnight. The first post-communist government was led by Vaclav Havel, a playwright who had been imprisoned under the former regime for his political views. Havel, though inexperienced in government, was a strong symbol of the moral underpinnings of the Velvet Revolution and the future for Czechoslovakia. One of the first orders of business was rapid transformation of the economy (one of the ten largest in the world between World Wars I and II) from the most state-owned of all Soviet-bloc economies to a market economy based on private ownership of property.

Under central planning, the objectives of the enterprises were to produce output to meet a plan and to provide paid employment for local citizens. Production functions were well developed and tended to dominate the firms. There was no need for more than rudimentary bookkeeping because the main concern about cash was that there be enough to pay employees on payday. There was no need for a finance function because capital budgeting and financing decisions were made and financed by central planners. Sales and marketing were not necessary functions because firms produced to a centrally derived plan, not to market demands, and delivered their product to separate distribution enterprises.

Firms within industries were highly specialized and interdependent. Monopolies or near-monopolies were usual at all points in the value chain to obtain scale economies in production and to reduce transactions for central planning administration. A typical enterprise faced sole suppliers of components and sole distributors of its output.

Managers under central planning were adept at "making do." Distortions and shortages were present in centrally planned economies. To make the annual plan, managers had to be skillful negotiators for supplies from nonconventional sources, had to know which supplies to stockpile, and had to be skilled negotiators with central planners. The annual plan was a matter for negotiation and the ease with which a plan was met every year was partly a function of how challenging the plan was. It was in both sides' interests for plans to be achieved. At the same time, political pressure for ambitious plans was brought to bear in some industries, which created differences in interests between the central planners and company managers. Even when annual and five-year plans were not challenging, negotiations continued regarding the allocation of capital resources necessary to achieve the plans.

Firms were structured as social entities as well as production entities. A wide range of social services were provided by enterprises, including housing, health care, and leisure time opportunities. The enterprise was the locus of the worker's life and the State's instrument for providing employment for everyone. Workers were highly educated (99 percent literacy among mentally capable adults in the Czech Republic), but not motivated to work hard or well in the Western sense.

AFTER THE VELVET REVOLUTION

Under central planning, alignment for firms meant producing to a plan created outside the firm, producing a product line determined by central planners, producing for customers who were content to receive any product that functioned, without much concern for perfection, and producing for delivery to a separate distribution organization. Because of the comprehensiveness of central planning and the vast difference between a centrally planned economy and a market economy, organizations in Central Europe that were well adapted for operation under central planning were not necessarily suited to a market economy and were likely to find it difficult to change to meet the demands of a competitive, open economy. The organizational competencies developed under central planning did not fit with the demands of the market economy.

The political and economic changes brought on by the Velvet Revolution called for much more than incremental change within firms. The underlying premise of economic activity was changed. Overnight, profit was good, not bad. Individual initiative was good, not bad. Strategic planning was required. Capital budgeting was relocated to the firm from the State. Suddenly some of the skills necessary for success in centrally planned firms were considered useless, especially skills associated with meeting production quotas regardless of quality. Though technology had not changed overnight, the changes were analogous to competence-killing changes in technology (Tushman and Anderson, 1986). The new business environment required skills not present and previously not valued in Central European firms. This was the stimulus for re-creation change, requiring a fundamental shift of internal structures and controls, but also requiring a change in business strategy and in the underlying core values of the firm.

How do firms get through discontinuous change successfully? Radical change in a firm's environment may signal the need for discontinuous change internally, but does not necessarily cause it. The firm must react to the external stimulus appropriately. One common response to radical external change is for firms to depend upon their existing routines, systems, and structures ever more strongly (Greenhalgh, 1983). This response is likely to create more difficulty for them. For appropriate discontinuous change to occur internally, the firm must stop doing things the old way and begin doing things in fundamentally new ways. But this still does not say *how* firms get through discontinuous change successfully. Apart from the importance of new leadership (March, 1991; Romanelli and Tushman, 1994; Virany, Tushman, and Romanelli, 1992), very little work has been done to identify organizational characteristics likely to contribute to successful discontinuous change.

We use the case of Královopolská to illustrate the change process at the firm level. Based on the experiences of Královopolská and on other firms' experiences, we will identify organizational factors that appear to contribute to change. The result of this discussion will be a framework for a better understanding of the managerial challenges facing company managers in transition economies.

KRÁLOVOPOLSKÁ

Královopolská (KPS) is a medium-sized producer of a range of industrial products, including water treatment systems, storage facilities, gantry cranes, chemical plant equipment, and woodworking apparatus. It was founded in 1889 in the city of Brno. Located in southeast Moravia, Brno is the second largest city in the Czech Republic. KPS was nationalized in 1945 and enlarged in 1948 when six facilities were combined with the original plant.

Between 1958 and 1988, KPS status as an independent enterprise changed as it became part of CHEPOS, an organization of firms in the chemical and food-processing machinery business. From 1958 to 1964, KPS was the centerpiece of CHEPOS. This meant that KPS coordinated the efforts of five other enterprises in the industry, including two research and development institutes. During the 1958-1968 period, KPS developed the capability to deliver turnkey projects–to engineer, produce, and construct entire water treatment facilities and chemical processing in cooperation with other CHEPOS enterprises.

Between 1965 and 1988, KPS lost its independent legal status and its status of CHEPOS centerpiece. When KPS regained its independence from CHEPOS in 1988, it lost most of its turnkey project business, becoming instead a producer of parts for other engineering firms. Nevertheless, a small turnkey business, later known as the RIA (Realization of Investment Activities) Division, survived.

Exports grew rapidly during the 1960s and 1970s for KPS, especially as it added machinery for the nuclear power plant industry to its product line. KPS exported this equipment predominantly to the USSR and was a major supplier in Czechoslovakia. One KPS manager noted, "Královopolská may have been favored by the central planners because we produced products of great importance to the Soviet Union and we produced hard currency in some of our export activities."

The Situation in 1989

Manufacture for the chemical industry dominated at KPS during the 1980s. Roughly two-thirds of its production volume was targeted for the chemical industry. KPS had a reputation as a reliable supplier of serviceable products, winning medals at industry fairs in Brno despite the fact that no significant investment had been made in technology or equipment for 20 years.

KPS was a monopoly supplier in some of its markets, like other Czech firms. It had a domestic monopoly in heavy chemical equipment—its largest business—and cranes, and a domestic monopoly in water treatment facilities that was precarious because such equipment was readily available outside then-Czechoslovakia and easily imported.

Like most other Czech companies, KPS did not own its own distribution channels. It exported through one state trading company, Technoexport. It also distributed as a subcontractor via the engineering firms actually building power plants, chemical plants, or water treatment facilities.

KPS was less reliant on sole source supplier relationships than many other Czech companies. It had about 40 main suppliers and another 2,500 small ones in 1990. Some of its relationships were sole source, but not all.

Like most large enterprises during the communist era, KPS provided a wide assortment of social services to employees. Královopolská had 579 flats for workers, a "staff quarters building" with 478 beds (later to become the company hotel), four recreation centers, a youth pioneer camp, a heated swimming pool near the factory which was open to townspeople as well, three kindergartens and one nursery, a clinic located within the plant area, staffed by seven full-time general practitioners, six full-time specialists, and five part-time specialists, and two kitchens that prepared hot meals for all three shifts, served in ten dining rooms on the grounds.

Approximately 5,400 people were employed by KPS at the time of the Velvet Revolution.

Effects of the Velvet Revolution

The COMECON (Council for Mutual Economic Assistance) market in Central and Eastern Europe accounted for 63 percent of Czechoslovak exports in 1989 (Economist Intelligence Unit, 1995). Czechoslovak manufacturers developed their technologies to produce large volumes of standard quality products for COMECON markets, especially for the former USSR. After the COMECON market broke down, the demand for most Czech products in the COMECON markets dropped substantially. In 1991, exports from Czechoslovakia to former COMECON countries decreased by 31 percent (in real terms) from 1990, mainly because exports to the former USSR decreased by 39 percent. Exports to well-developed market economies increased by 10 percent (Economist Intelligence Unit, 1995).

KPS was more dependent on exports than the average Czech firm. In 1989, KPS exported 74 percent of its production. About three-quarters of its exports went to COMECON countries, most of it to the former USSR. Exports dropped to 67 percemt of production in 1990 and to 9 percent of production in 1991 (Table 8.1), mainly due to the breakup of the USSR and to the Gulf War (Iraq was a large non-COMECON customer). KPS was relatively well off with respect to its exports of equipment for oil refineries in the USSR. It was able to extract payment for machinery in U.S. dollars from Russia because Russia needed the equipment to produce its main hard currency export product, oil.

Královopolská was also affected positively by the new government's increased emphasis on reducing environmental pollution and improving water quality. During the previous 40 years, municipal water systems had not received adequate government investment. Water treatment and sewage treatment facilities were in disrepair. The new government quickly began investing in water improvement and sewage treatment facilities, effectively expanding one of Královopolská's key markets (Table 8.2). As a consequence, the RIA Division grew between 1992 and 1993, from sales of 641 million kčs to sales of 2.3 billion kčs.

Královopolská was partly privatized in 1992 during the first wave of large enterprise privatization in the Czech Republic. Its status changed again in 1994 when new shares were issued and again in 1995 when an arrangement was made for a controlling interest to be acquired by a private sector buyer. The fact that it was initially privatized in the first wave was the result of aggressive management that wanted to establish new owner-

TABLE 8.1. Selected Financial Results for KPS, 1988-1993

	1988	1989	1990	1991	1992	1993
No. of employees	5500	5469	5142	4682	4000	3700
Net sales* (mil. kčs)	1753	1820	1737	1560	1915	2430
% revenue from exports	75%	74%	67%	9%	13%	16%
Profit before taxes (mil. kčs)	−50	98	112	206	190	−88**
Accounts receivable (mil. kčs)	459	485	781	717	1008	796
Accounts payable (mil. kčs)	413	133	456	940	1048	799

Source: KPS *Annual Reports* 1991-1993.

* Net sales, as defined in the 1991, 1992, and 1993 annual reports from KPS, includes all goods and services that had been sold and invoiced to external customers.

** Loss is due primarily to changes in accounting rules in 1993 that required recognition of depreciation for the first time.

TABLE 8.2. Financial Results by Business for Královopolská (KPS), 1991-1993

Division	1991 Revenues (mil. kčs)	1992 Revenues (mil. kčs)	1993 Revenues (mil. kčs)	1992 Return on Sales (%)
Water, Wood, and Light Chemical	341	487	414	17.8
Heavy Chemical	172	325	430	1.6
Special Chemical (Nuclear)	330	416	354	68.0
Cranes and Steel Construction	301	377	408	3.7
Metallurgy	229	96	100	22.9
RIA (turnkey)	920	641	2332	6.1

Source: KPS *Annual Reports* 1992-1993. Gross revenue reported, including internal sales.

ship as soon as possible and government ministries that believed Královopolská had the financial strength to privatize early. Structurally, Královopolská was organized by function prior to 1989, as were most Czech companies. As early as 1991, Královopolská had reorganized by business unit. Between 1991 and December 1994 it went through several reorganizations to rationalize product divisions. Top management was keen to create strategic business units and measure financial performance at the Strategic Business Unit (SBU) level as soon as possible. Pre-1989 and 1992 organization charts are shown in Figures 8.2 and 8.3.

Financial results for Královopolská were better than those of many companies in 1991 and 1992 (Table 8.1), though in 1993 Královopolská lost money, largely due to changes in the accounting system. As shown in Table 8.2, in 1994 Královopolská had six main businesses, varying considerably in size and profitability. Reorganizations and changes in reporting methods made growth trends difficult to discern within each product group, but it is safe to say that the RIA Division had experienced considerable growth and financial success after the Revolution. This division provided complete plant systems design, engineering, manufacturing, and installation services. According to top management, turnkey operations such as those undertaken in the RIA Division were the future for Královopolská. One manager went as far as saying that Královopolská may become an engineering company in the future, forgoing production entirely.

As with many Czech manufacturers, Královopolská was a relatively low-cost producer because of its low labor wages. At the same time, it had a reputation as a quality manufacturer. This combination gave Královopolská an advantage in international markets as it could undersell producers in the West and market products for developing countries that were affordable in those economies. Barriers to new customers in the West arose because of preexisting technical specifications rather than cost. Problems arose in developing countries because of the countries' unstable economies.

Strategic Actions Taken by Top Management

Following the Revolution, top management took as its main task to determine "a clear strategy of development for the company with the objective of creating an added value very close to the value usual in the prosperous companies in the developed European countries" (*Královopolská 1992*, [company document]). Working with people from the Consulting Institute of the Prague School of Economics, the following questions and issues were addressed by management in 1992:

- objectives of the company
- expected profit and turnover
- product quality and activity analysis
- effectiveness of management and organizational structure
- home and foreign market share
- company image for the future
- personnel policy

Action steps from the study included:

- set up a marketing information system to enable market research
- contact present and former partners in all markets to ensure customer satisfaction
- track and reduce costs so as to become price-competitive
- set up network of after-sales service
- manufacture only high-margin products
- acquire advanced processing technology
- improve efficiency
- pay debts and collect receivables
- privatize the company, intending to acquire capital, new markets, and technologies
- improve employee commitment to the company
- train employees for market-oriented activities
- introduce quality control systems in line with International Standard Organization (ISO) standards
- improve discipline

These action steps were the driving force behind strategic change in Královopolská after the middle of 1992. All of this research was done without the help of Western consultants, a consistent theme in Královopolská. Top management believed that Western consultants were too interested in the consultants' way of doing things and not familiar enough with Czech business practices, circumstances, and culture to be of much use. One bad experience with a German consulting firm that delivered a product for DM38,000 that was little more than copies of publicly available documents supported their point of view. "Consultants," said the General Manager, "don't respect Czech management. They forget that we did not just jump down from the trees. We think, therefore we are." His allusion to the philosopher Descartes was a way of emphasizing the cultural sophistication and intellect of Czech managers.

FIGURE 8.2. Inferred Organizational Structure Prior to the Velvet Revolution

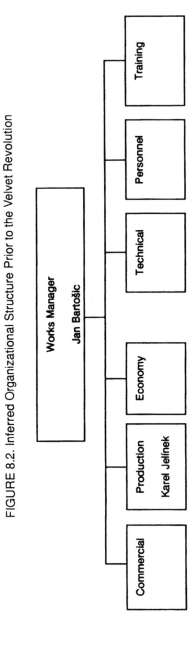

Source: Královopolská Strojírna Brno (100-year anniversary book) and company documents.

FIGURE 8.3. Organizational Structure in 1992

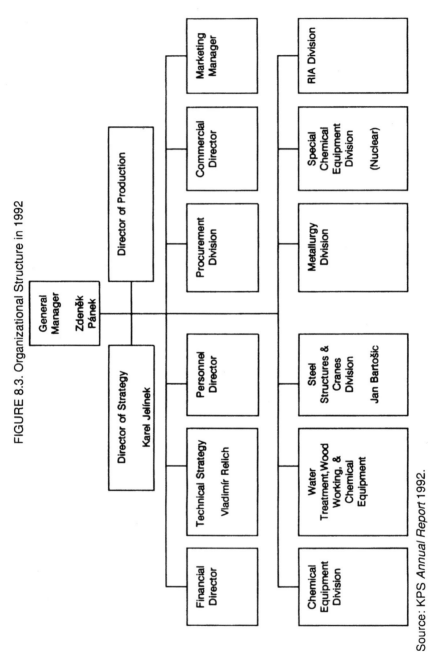

Source: KPS *Annual Report* 1992.

Quality Initiatives

Quality, customer orientation, and competitiveness became the mantras of top management in 1992. A company-wide quality assurance program was undertaken in 1992. ISO 9000 certification and other relevant certifications were obtained by the end of 1994. The company produced glossy brochures with eye-catching graphics that illustrated Královopolská's commitment to quality and meeting customers' needs, including language about the firm's trust in its own employees to demonstrate Královopolská's commitment to quality in every interaction with customers.

An international competitive analysis of every Královopolská product was conducted in 1993 and 1994, covering the products' technical specifications, quality, price, and perceptions of customer service. The competitive analysis yielded six categories of products, those that were excellent (7 percent), competitive (44 percent), needed innovation (11 percent), needed a price decrease (21 percent), needed marketing support (7 percent), and were not competitive (11 percent). The competitive analysis served as an important guide for investment and divestment decisions during 1994 and 1995.

People

Královopolská had a young top management team in place after the Velvet Revolution. The General Director, Zdeněk Pánek, was about 40 years old in 1994. He assumed the top position in mid-1992. Pánek was unusual because he was not trained as an engineer but, rather, in economics (the pre-Revolution preparation for commerce). His background was in the RIA Division, where his job was similar to that of a Western-style field sales engineer before heading the division. This was significant, because the RIA Division was the only division that had extensive customer contact and focused on delivering a product to customer specifications.

Pánek had no Western-style management training, nor did he speak German or English. However, he did provide management training to employees and mandated that all top managers learn English in company-provided classes. Pánek had a very keen sense of the importance of customers' needs and of the need to change the corporate culture to one that rewards quality, customer orientation, financial performance, and initiative rather than longevity or Party membership.

The next layer of management was mostly composed of engineers who devoted their whole working life to Královopolská. Vladimír Relich was typical. He was educated at Brno Technical University in engineering. He started at Královopolská as a designer, then became head of a department (chemical equipment), then head of all design, then head of Central Product Development, and finally Director of Technical Strategy. The quality assurance program and the competitive analysis were both conducted by Relich.

One persistent challenge identified by Královopolská managers was the company culture. The history of the firm favored manufacturing. "Production was king," said one manager. "Management tries now to put sales on top and production next," he went on. "We are still learning to make what the customer wants."

Speaking in 1994, Karel Jelínek, Chairman of the Board, discussed the difficulty Královopolská was having in changing the corporate culture from one that focused on following orders to one that focused on the customer, quality, and initiative.

> We are trying to change the corporate culture, and have been trying hard for three years. The easy thing is to write it down. The hardest is to persuade the people so that they are convinced about the company. We want our customers to feel the corporate culture from every employee. This is the basis of a market-based approach. We introduced a motivation system. It is too early to show results. People don't like to take responsibility for their own decisions. They expect other signatures on decisions [an attitude left over from the Communist era]. We are trying to find people who are not afraid of big decisions. I like people who make me lose sleep because of the potential negative outcomes associated with their decisions. I prefer these people to those who wait for my approval.

Královopolská was attempting to create a new corporate culture in several ways. In addition to public statements such as these by the General Director and the Chairman of the Board, Královopolská used management training, competitive analyses, merit-based performance appraisal, and incentive pay—with "disappointing results so far," said one manager in 1994—to create a more customer-, quality-, and performance-oriented climate. In addition, the firm was organized into SBUs with considerable individual identity and autonomy to foster product-level identification and to decentralize profit responsibility. Finally, Královopolská created a company bank to create competition among divisions for corporate resources.

Královopolská steadily reduced its employment during the five years after the Velvet Revolution, from 5,469 in 1989 to about 3,700 at the end of 1994. Still, according to top management, employment needed to be reduced by about 400 people per year for the next few years. When asked about the future, one manager said,

Královopolská is among the top third of all Czech companies. The future is relatively good for us, but the next two years are important for us. It is necessary to change people's minds. The highest level people have changed but it is necessary to go to the lowest level. We will change the base of our business. We want to become an engineering company. We used to build whole plants when we were in the CHEPOS trust [in the 1960s]. Results from turnkey projects will be two times higher in five years. We will start to buy parts from outside Královopolská. The result will be a more competitive environment within our own divisions.

SUCCESSFUL RE-CREATION

In a business landscape populated with companies in trouble, Královopolská stood out as a relative success story. Like other formerly state-owned enterprises, Královopolská faced extraordinary change in its business environment over which it had no control. Yet after four years of transition, prospects for Královopolská were reasonably bright. Company managers appeared to understand what types of strategic decisions were necessary and began to implement solutions. Financial results were mixed by Western standards, but Královopolská was a survivor and had made it through the rough patch defined by the first half of the 1990s. What explains the ability of a company to successfully re-create itself?

To understand why some companies are able to achieve re-creational change successfully while others are not, we suggest a four-factor framework. Based on the experience of Královopolská, the experience of other firms, and existing research, we suggest firms will be able to successfully re-create themselves to the extent that they

1. can cope with ambiguity and uncertainty;
2. are diversified;
3. have generalizable core competencies and skills; and
4. have access to transformational leadership.

Coping with Ambiguity and Uncertainty

Firms that face extraordinary change in their environments, whether changes in government, regulation, or technology, are more likely to survive if they have the capability internally to deal with a new external environment that is less certain and more varied than in the past (Tushman and Anderson, 1986). Two characteristics of firms are particularly important: flexibility and connectedness.

By *flexibility* we mean the ability of firms to move quickly. Normally younger, smaller firms are more flexible than older, larger firms because smaller firms are likely to have fewer costs of coordination (Blau, 1970) and younger firms are likely to have less history and tradition that can inhibit change.

As noted in the opening section, firms tend to implement incremental change in order to bring their internal systems and structures into closer alignment with each other and with the demands of their environment. Over time, and under stable environmental conditions, this alignment is likely to become quite tight. Firms that were not in tight alignment before the Revolution are therefore more likely to be able to change because there is less inertial energy reinforcing the old way of operation.

In addition, firms that are more decentralized are likely to be more flexible because their autonomous subunits can respond to change independently of each other and relatively independent of centralized top management. Finally, firms with a team-based structure are likely to be more flexible as they form and reform task teams to solve particular problems rather than invest in more rigid structural approaches to solving problems.

While Královopolská was not decentralized at the time of the Velvet Revolution, it did reorganize and decentralize within about two years after the Revolution, earlier than many other Czech companies. Further, Královopolská restructured itself in such a way that its units were relatively autonomous, increasing the likelihood that each of them could respond to its markets appropriately, with less need for internal coordination. The type of reorganization and decentralization pursued by Královopolská was appropriate, given that it operated in five different markets, each exhibiting differences in magnitude and type of change.

By *connectedness* we mean relationships in which the firm might be engaged, whether with other firms or with nonbusiness entities. Firms with existing strategic alliances may be able to depend upon these relationships for survival and learning during periods of extraordinary change. Firms with good connections with suppliers, customers, or government officials may also be advantaged.

Královopolská is in a favorable position in this regard, as it has a history of working directly with end users through the RIA Division. Královopolská is one of the few large industrial concerns in the Czech Republic with direct, relevant, and recent experience working with the ultimate customer. However, Královopolská did not have particularly strong connections with Western firms or strategic partners prior to the Revolution.

Zetor, the Czech tractor manufacturer, is a good example of a firm advantaged by its historic relationship with a Western company, John Deere (Newman and Nollen, 1995). The relationship between Zetor and Deere goes back to the mid-1960s, when Zetor won an international competition to produce tractors for Deere's Latin American markets. History intervened—the crackdown following the Prague Spring of 1968—to prevent the relationship from progressing. However, at the time of the Velvet Revolution, the people involved in the terminated relationship in the 1960s were still working in Zetor and Deere, and were able to resume the relationship. Zetor began producing tractors for Deere's Latin American markets in 1994.

The importance of connectedness is illustrated in another way by the Zetor-Deere relationship. Zetor needs to learn how to produce a product to exacting customer standards in a timely way. Its previous knowledge had been toward producing a reliable tractor in the context of constant shortages. Thus, Zetor had a very "make do" corporate culture. Technology and production were paramount. Making the quota was the most important task. Technology was used to find substitutes for missing parts or for jury-rigging a solution to a technical problem when resources were scarce. Customers under the old system were not very demanding. They were content to get any tractor at all. Thus Zetor's culture had adapted well to the task environment in which it operated.

After 1989, Zetor's customers became much more demanding, particularly new customers in the West. The firm's employees had the technical know-how and intelligence to produce high-quality products in a timely way. What they lacked was the mind-set that valued quality and timeliness. In contrast, one of John Deere's core competencies was its strong customer service orientation and dedication to top-quality products. Zetor managers and employees learned this quality mind-set by working side by side with advisors from John Deere.

New knowledge in this case is not textbook, technical know-how. Instead, it is mind-sets, attitudes, and orientations toward products, customers, quality, and technology. New mind-sets are not easily learned from a textbook. They are deeply held habits, values, and norms. As such, they are slow to change, and do so best in the presence of respected others demonstrating their value in concrete, day-to-day work settings. Zetor was learning by working side by side with Westerners. Královopolská was learning by having top leadership from a formerly small and unusual division. In both cases new skills were articulated, modeled, and rewarded by respected leaders.

Diversification

Firms with diversified product lines may be better able to cope with radical change and more likely to re-create themselves than nondiversified firms, though diversified firms under conditions of relative stability are often less profitable than more focused firms (Porter, 1987). Diversified firms have the benefit of several businesses operating simultaneously beneath a corporate umbrella. When the environment changes radically, the firm may lose some of its markets or may experience a competence-killing change in technology in one or several of its businesses, but rarely in all of them. One of the benefits of diversification, apart from risk sharing, is that a relatively small, unimportant part of the business can become the centerpiece in the firm's future because the firm has had the opportunity to develop and hone a broad set of skills and competencies.

Diversification in suppliers and distributors is also important. All firms are dependent to some degree on their environment for inputs and customers. Firms in transition economies faced these types of dependencies to an extraordinary degree. Because of central planning, many firms were specialized to produce a very narrow product range, distribution and selling were handled by separate companies, and firms relied on sole source suppliers who themselves made but a small number of products and sold to a very small number of customers. These arrangements might have made sense under central planning, but they created a network of extreme interdependencies in a market economy when each firm in the network was privatized separately. If one firm in the network failed, all firms in the network were endangered. Therefore, to the extent that a firm was only loosely connected to such webs and to the extent a firm had multiple sources of supply and access to multiple channels of distribution, the firm was more likely to survive in the new environment.

Královopolská certainly benefitted from product diversification. Prior to the Revolution it was a supplier to five distinct markets, water treatment plants, petrochemical manufacturing, nuclear power generation, woodworking, and construction cranes. Prior to the Revolution the petrochemical market was by far its biggest, accounting for over two-thirds of production. After the Revolution, Královopolská benefitted from the new government's emphasis on investment in water improvement and sewage treatment. Although the chemical manufacturing industry in the Czech Republic was in deep recession, Královopolská was able to compensate for one set of losses with gains in other areas.

In addition, prior to the Revolution, Královopolská operated the small RIA Division that had been in the turnkey water treatment plant business for 35 years, since the time of the CHEPOS cooperation during the 1960s.

Even though it was only a small part of the business prior to the Revolution, the RIA Division was able to meet new demand in the environment and in a way that was profitable for Královopolská. Top managers believed that the RIA Division is the model for the future of Královopolská.

Generalizable Core Competence

Firms that have narrow, specialized core competencies risk extinction just as animals and plants that can survive only under limited environmental conditions. Firms with more generalizable core competencies are more robust, able to survive under many circumstances. Moreover, firms that know what their core competence is and are able to see how it can be adapted to new businesses are more likely to change effectively.

One indicator of a generalizable core competence is a large cadre of technically trained specialists in several different areas. The combination of more than one critical mass of technical expertise and cadres of professionals who have connections with similarly trained professionals outside the firm provides firms with a better chance to be able to adapt their technologies to new demands in the marketplace.

Královopolská, at its core, makes three products: tanks, cranes, and woodworking machines. However, Královopolská also has engineering expertise. Therefore, in addition to being able to manufacture three rather different groups of products, Královopolská has a core group of technically trained professionals who also know how to design entire systems. The RIA Division is, again, an example of a general core competence that can be applied to any number of end products. Královopolská did not define its core competence as tank making. Instead, Královopolská leveraged its competence in turnkey projects to create higher value-added, more engineering-intensive products for a growing market.

Transformational Leadership

The importance of top leadership during a re-creation change effort is critical. Whether we are discussing discontinuous change as posited in the punctuated equilibrium model (Romanelli and Tushman, 1994) or building internal capability for change (Ulrich and Lake, 1990), the importance of leadership is obvious. Firms that have access to new, transformational leadership are more likely to successfully re-create themselves than firms relying on internal, transactional leadership (Greiner and Bhambri, 1989; Romanelli and Tushman, 1994; Tushman, Newman, and Romanelli, 1986; Virany, Tushman, and Romanelli, 1992). By transformational leadership, we mean leadership that emphasizes vision, change, the future, and a break from the past rather than one that emphasizes existing relationships and incremental improvement (Kuhnert and Lewis, 1987).

Re-creational change is more likely to be successful if led by new top management from outside the firm (Romanelli and Tushman, 1994), even though there is long-term benefit to an outside team, led by an insider (Virany, Tushman, and Romanelli, 1992). A critical task for re-creational change is to successfully break from the past before establishing the new. Internal leadership is less likely to be able to effect such a radical internal change because they are often creators of the current system and therefore biased by existing inertial forces. As Ansoff notes, "A manager with a record of success in his historical environment is a pathological case with respect to new environmental turbulence" (1982: 5).

New leadership in Czech companies is unlikely to come from outside the firm because of a culture and history of low labor mobility and lifelong employment in one firm. However, after the Revolution, leadership is almost surely to come from among younger managers who before were not part of the ruling elite, most of whom left their firms after the Revolution because their membership in the Communist Party was no longer an asset. Younger managers, those who had not been part of the Party apparatus, and those with a background different from the norm were likely to help their firms get through the transition period.

Královopolská did not appoint new leadership from outside the firm. However, because Pánek was from the RIA Division, in a way Královopolská is benefitting from "outsider" leadership. As a former sales engineer who worked directly with customers in the field, Pánek brought to top management a clear and unequivocal emphasis on quality and the customer. Unhampered by the old assumptions and values in the production divisions, Pánek acted like an outsider with a mission. After taking the top position in July of 1992, he immediately developed a comprehensive strategic plan for the company and relentlessly pursued a course that stressed the primacy of customers and quality.

Jelínek, the Chairman of the Board, was a company insider, but also young. He was Director of Production at the time of the Revolution in 1989. He then became Technical Director and Chairman of the Board. By 1994 he was still Chairman of the Board and was listed as Director of Strategy on the organization chart–a subordinate of Pánek's. In fact, the two were a team and of one mind about how the company should be managed.

After 1989, Královopolská as a whole benefitted from the fact that it had always been a relatively apolitical organization. It was known during the Communist era as a place where technical know-how was more important than Party membership for success, unlike many other Czech firms. This was one factor that allowed Královopolská to re-create itself with internal leadership, perhaps more successfully than other Czech firms.

CONCLUSIONS

We described a process of discontinuous change for Czech firms that is built on Western notions of re-creational change. Surely, the changes in the economic climate in the region are more extreme than anything faced in the West since the industrial revolution. Yet, concepts useful in the West are also useful for examining and understanding how firms in the Czech Republic are adapting.

Královopolská took a comprehensive approach to re-creational change, as summarized in Figure 8.4. Preexisting organizational characteristics (flexibility, connectedness, diversification, and generalizable core competence), combined with transformational leadership, gave them multiple avenues with which to effect change in their systems, structures, strategies, and core values.

Perhaps the most important asset at Královopolská was the RIA Division, which helped Královopolská learn to become an engineering company with a strong customer focus because this division had always had customer contact. RIA led the way for Královopolská to become an engineering company as well as or instead of a production company. Moreover, because RIA bought its materials from the most cost-effective source, Královopolská production divisions were encouraged to become more efficient and quality-oriented. Finally, the RIA Division produced Královopolská's top leadership that understood the way in which Královopolská would have to change to become competitive in open markets.

Královopolská appeared to have relatively bright prospects for the future. It suffered a drastic decline in export business, but found new businesses domestically in which it could excel. It had top management that understood the importance of product quality and a customer orientation. It also had top management that was coming to understand that it was easy to say the right words but hard to change the behaviors of employees. The re-creation under way in this firm was not completed overnight.

The lessons from Královopolská's experiences may be applicable to more than one company in a single country. Dramatic changes in the economic environment are not limited to a specific region or historical moment. Transformational leadership, generalizable core competencies,

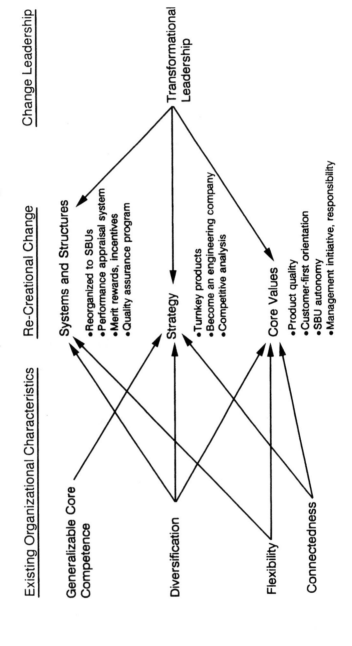

FIGURE 8.4. Královopolská's Re-Creational Change Effort

and customer focus surely can assist other firms to succeed in accomplishing re-creational change under a wide variety of circumstances.

EPILOGUE

In 1995, the privatization of KPS was completed. A group of the company's top managers, including the president, Zdenek Panek, bought a majority stake. The leveraged buyout brought with it a new urgency to generate cash flow to meet debt repayments, and it focused top management's attention more sharply on the company's strategic direction.

However, KPS's progress through the transition to a market economy remained incomplete. The company suffered a second year of losses in 1994 on the heels of declining sales of its main products and services, even as the Czech economy began to grow again. The company's plan to concentrate on turnkey business for its RIA Division was slow to develop, especially in the growing Czech and Slovak water treatment market. Domestic competitors, also newly privatized, arose. An engineering group in the RIA Division was established to promote the sale of professional services, but it was small. KPS needed new technology to make its business fully competitive with Western standards, and it needed capital for plant improvement. Explorations with foreign companies about some type of strategic alliance or joint venture had not succeeded yet.

KPS managers expected that 1995 would see a return to profitability, and the future still looked bright. The company's strategic decisions were not in question. The company's flexibility, connectedness (except with Western firms), and diversification continued to serve it well. Yet now its needs for new business, new technology, and new capital have become more apparent, and the management buyout made solutions more critical.

REFERENCES

Ansoff, H.I. 1982. Managing discontinuous strategic change: The learning-action approach. In H.I. Ansoff, A. Bosman, and P.M. Storm (Eds.), *Understanding and managing strategic change:* 5-31. New York: North-Holland Publishing Co.

Argyris, C. and Schön, D. 1978. *Organizational learning.* Reading, MA: Addison-Wesley.

Blau, P.M. 1970. A formal theory of differentiation in organizations. *American Sociological Review*, 35: 201-218.

Economist Intelligence Unit 1995. *Country Reports—Czech and Slovak Republics*, First Quarter. London: EIU.

Gersick, C.J.G. 1991. Revolutionary change theories: A multilevel exploration of the punctuated equilibrium paradigm. *Academy of Management Review*, 16: 10-36.

Greenhalgh, L. 1983. Organization decline. *Research in the sociology of organizations*, 2: 231-276. Greenwich, CT: JAI Press.

Greiner, L. and Bhambri, A. 1989. New CEO intervention and dynamics of deliberate strategic change. *Strategic Management Journal*, 10: 67-86.

Hannan, M.T. and Freeman, J. 1984. Structural inertia and organizational change. *American Sociological Review*, 49: 149-164.

Králavopolská Annual Reports 1991-1993: 100-year anniversary book–1992 company brochure.

Kuhnert, K.W. and Lewis, P. 1987. Transactional and transformational leadership: A constructive/developmental analysis. *Academy of Management Review*, 12: 648-657.

Lant, T.K. and Mezias, S.J. 1992. An organizational learning model of convergence and reorientation. *Organization Science*, 3: 47-71.

March, J.G. 1991. Exploring and exploitation in organizational learning. *Organization Science*, 2: 71-87.

Newman, K.L. and Nollen, S.D. 1995. Zetor Tractors (A) and (B). *Case Research Journal*, 15: 10-33.

Porter, M.E. 1987. From competitive advantage to corporate strategy. *Harvard Business Review*, May-June: 43-59.

Romanelli, E. and Tushman, M.L. 1994. Organizational transformation as punctuated equilibrium: An empirical test. *Academy of Management Journal*, 37: 1141-1166.

Tushman, M.L. and Anderson, P. 1986. Technological discontinuities and organizational environments. *Administrative Science Quarterly*, 31: 439-465.

Tushman, M.L., Newman, W.H., and Romanelli, E. 1986. Convergence and upheaval: Managing the unsteady pace of organizational evolution. *California Management Review*, 29: 29-44.

Tushman, M.L. and Romanelli, E. 1985. Organizational evolution: A metamorphosis model of convergence and reorientation. In L.L. Cummings and B.M. Staw (Eds.), *Research in Organization Behavior*, 7: 171-222.

Ulrich, D. and Lake, D. 1990. *Organizational Capability*. New York: Wiley.

Virany, B., Tushman, M.L., and Romanelli, E. 1992. Executive succession and organization outcomes in turbulent environments: An organization learning approach. *Organization Science*, 3: 72-91.

Chapter 9

Transformation and Marketing Developments in Skala of Hungary

Ronald Savitt

INTRODUCTION

Over the past six years, the transformation of the Central and Eastern European economies has received considerable attention. The focus has been primarily on economic and social issues. The managerial challenges affecting individual enterprises–be they newly created privately owned firms, state-owned firms moving toward privatization, or the remaining state enterprises–have received less consideration. This perspective is understandable because the efforts of Western nations have been directed toward helping these countries to shed their socialist past and move toward market economies. The accompanying effects, such as high unemployment, inflation, shortages of goods and services, and holes in the safety net, required immediate attention. Little is known about the effects of transformation on individual enterprises, especially with regard to specific management functions.

Privatization as one of the major elements of the transition implies a great deal more than replacing "passive public ownership with active private ownership" (Ellerman, Vahic, and Petrin, 1992: 130). Of great importance is the development of a market-oriented strategy at the enterprise level. All too often this has not been fully appreciated. In Hungary, where privatization began earlier than in other economies of the region, the demands of the new economic environment have not always been part of the process. Frequently, the old managers became the new managers or

Support for this research came from a Business in Eastern Europe Fellowship from the Center for Russian Studies and East European Studies, University of Pittsburgh, and from the John L. Beckley Endowment to the University of Vermont.

owners, yet they did not adapt to the changed conditions (Hoch, 1991; Pasztor, 1991).

In this chapter we examine Skala, one of Hungary's most important retailers, as it faced the challenges of transformation. The analysis focuses on the disruptions brought to a historically successful marketing program as a result of dramatic changes in the environment. Given the track record of nearly 15 years of innovative marketing under socialism, Skala was expected to adapt with ease to the evolving market economy. However, this did not happen in the early period of transformation, 1991 to 1993. Seemingly because of past success, Skala's management failed to recognize the extent and revolutionary character of the changes and hence did not protect itself from the threats arising nor seize on the opportunities that presented themselves in the transitionary stage.

A BRIEF HISTORY OF SKALA

Original Strategy

Skala was created in 1976 by the decision of the directors of over 200 consumer cooperatives in order to take advantage of the Hungarian economic reforms, a practice which Skala's management continued throughout most of the enterprise's history (see Tables 9.1 and 9.2).[1] The new retail enterprise was indirectly owned by some 3 million Hungarians, nearly one-third of the population. The first store opened in 1976. It was a marketing revolution for Hungary. Skala was air-conditioned; it offered hairdressing and dry cleaning services; and it was the first retailer to engage in advertising and special promotions. Perhaps the most important strategy consisted in abandoning the large, inefficient Hungarian wholesale system, with its strong heritage of central planning. Skala also replaced traditional domestic products with a variety of foreign goods, including electrical appliances, fresh fruit, Italian shoes, and Japanese stereos, whose store display was accompanied by piped-in music (Colitt, 1987: 22).

At the time, Skala was led by Sandor Demján, a manager of one of the participating cooperatives and head of Budapest's Communist Party. Demján, aged 43 at the time, introduced a completely new management philosophy to Skala. "When we started, I told my people either we take risks or we closed. We had to establish an aggressive competitive situation

---

1. Some of the materials in this discussion are based on in-depth personal interviews in 1993 and written responses to questions mailed in 1994. Participants are listed in References.

TABLE 9.1. Selected Economic Reforms in Hungary

Period	Policy Changes and Measures Taken	Managerial Opportunities
1968-1972	*New Economic Mechanism*[1] Eliminated central planning and administrative rationing	Allowed for quantity and quality decisions
	Start of price liberalization Start of enterprise with a few investments	Emergence of market competition, emergence of independent small business
1979-1980	*Return to Price Reform*[2] Sought to link prices of domestically produced goods to those of foreign	Increased competition
	Single forint exchange rate	Forced real cost analysis
	Single Ministry of Industry to regulate, set plans, and control	Extended independence of decision making to firms' "regulated" decision making
1980-1985	*Small Business Reform of 1982* Enterprise management reforms of 1985	Provided for small private firms with great competitive freedom Introduced entrepreneurial organizations with "near market" freedom in production and marketing
1989	*Hungarian Law on Association*[3] Facilitated emergence of flexible economic organizations	Enabled individual initiative in state and private enterprises, development of corporate governance, protection of property rights, allowed joint ventures, allowed conversion of state companies
1990-1992	*Privatization Legislation*[4] Defined property rights, and forms of business organizations	Created market-based discretion with regard to most business decisions including marketing, production, investment, and employment

Sources: 1. Chavance, 1994; 2. Frydman, Rapaczynski, and Earle, 1993; 3. Lamm, 1990; 4. Naor, 1993.

143

TABLE 9.2. Major Marketing Developments in Skala of Hungary, 1976-1993

DEVELOPMENT	YEAR
Founded	1976
Entered Wholesaling for Public and Private Stores	1979
Introduced Franchising (First Time in Hungary)	1980
First Discount Supermarket Expanded into Boutique Stores	1981
Expanded into Leisure-Activity Stores	1982
Received License to Trade Internationally	1983
Opened Drive-In Discount Department Store (First in Hungary)[1]	1984
Received Permission to Provide Advertising Agency Services[2]	1984
Attempts to Issue Credit Card[3]	1985
Skala in Joint Venture with ITT to Produce TVs and VCRs[4]	1987
Full Ownership by Cooperatives[5]	1988
Remington in Joint Venture to Operate Electrical Product Departments[6]	1989
Young and Rubicam Create "Skala Angel"[7]	1992
Tegelmann Takes 50.1 Percent Control[8]	1993

Sources: 1. "Discount Store . . ." 1980; 2. Naor, 1993 (includes items 1-3 and 5-8); 3. British Broadcasting Corporation, 1985; 4. Colitt, 1987; 5. Blitz, 1988; 6. "Kiam sold . . .", 1989; 7. Bobinski et al., 1992; 8. "Tegelman nübernimmt . . ." 1993.

that until that time was unimaginable in socialist conditions" ("Hungary's western . . ." 1986: D10).

Under Demján's guidance, Skala pursued a number of radical marketing programs (Table 9.2). In 1979 it developed its own wholesale operations. Subsequently it introduced a franchise system that eventually included 66 other retailers. New policies were also initiated in purchasing. Skala gave exclusive contracts to producers if they met specific quality standards. It also began to trade merchandise with department stores in other socialist countries, and eventually developed cooperative agreements in Western Europe as well. As a result of the economic reforms, Skala entered a joint venture with Standard Elektrik Lorenz, then a West German subsidiary of ITT, to assemble television sets and video recorders for their own sale as well as for export to Western nations (Colitt, 1987: 14). Internally, Skala adopted Western management practices to stimulate and reward employees. Salaries were 25 percent higher than the wages in state retail enterprises. Each employee was carefully selected, and promotions were based primarily on merit. On the one hand Skala adopted a practice of hiring young people, paying them well, and promoting them quickly, and on the other hand it discharged those who were unwilling to work ("Hungary . . .": op. cit.).

The immediate and short-term results were nothing less than amazing. In the first year, Skala recorded twice the average sales per square foot of its nearest state competitors. Within three years, Skala began a major expansion aimed at taking market share from the state-controlled retail sector. By 1985, Skala's six department stores and franchise operation stores accounted for 46 percent of the department store market in Hungary. The Skala-owned stores were financially and managerially independent although common policies existed concerning wages, amortization, and the introduction of technology (Colitt, 1985: 22).

Skala's aggressive marketing program continually tested the limits of the state's economic reforms. For example, in 1985 Skala attempted to introduce credit cards. Its purpose went beyond making shopping more convenient for customers; a second objective was to use the payments as a "cash float." This would have provided Skala with access to funds well below the established interest rates (Colitt: ibid.). The plan was rejected by the Ministry of Finance which saw the scheme for what it was–a means for circumventing the Ministry's authority with regard to how enterprises could raise funds. Skala had gone well beyond the limits of the reform program.

A series of joint ventures were consummated with several Western firms. These gave Skala access to management skills, merchandise technology, and access to Western markets. One with Remington provided in-store boutiques for the sale of electric razors and associated products, a program that became a model for other relationships ("Kiam sold . . ." 1989: 2B).

By the end of the 1980s Skala was the undisputed marketing leader in Hungary. It had developed and implemented a number of marketing and business programs that compared favorably with those of many Western retailers and that put it far ahead of other Hungarian retailers. Marketing programs tested new ideas and practices for Skala and most of them were very successful in increasing Skala's market position.

SKALA IN THE NEW ENVIRONMENT

A Different Environment

As a result of transformation, significant changes occurred in the Hungarian economy in five areas:

1. trade liberalization, including the reduction of export and import barriers;

2. market-based pricing;
3. creation of a convertible currency;
4. promotion of direct foreign investments (Köves and Marer, 1991: 15); and
5. continuation and expansion of the privatization of old state enterprises and the encouragement for new entrepreneurial ventures (Brada, Singh, and Török, 1994: 14-15).

These changes were quickly felt in retailing. High inflation and increasing levels of unemployment, both of which were virtually unknown under socialism, greatly affected consumer purchasing power. The government eliminated or reduced price controls on a broad variety of goods and services. Competition increased as newly privatized firms, entrepreneurial ventures, and foreign competitors entered the market ("Western discount . . ." 1993: 1). For example, Julius Meinl of Austria purchased many Hungarian grocery stores and began to introduce new products, to offer new in-store services, and to engage in aggressive promotional programs. By 1993, the Ministry of Trade estimated that as much as 50 percent of the Budapest retail food trade was controlled by foreign firms (Dobos, 1993: personal interview). Consumers were confused by the dramatic changes in the marketplace. While the selection of products and stores expanded, they had less money to spend. Well-established shopping patterns needed change but, given the almost daily changes in the market, consumers were not certain how to change. Consumers had to learn "how to shop in the new environment" (Savitt, 1992: 124). Gone was the familiar market stability characterized by the traditional, stodgy conduct of state-owned retailers on the one hand and the radical behavior of Skala on the other hand.

To compound the challenges, Skala's leadership had changed, too. Sandor Demján had left Skala in 1988 to pursue a career in banking. His loss was critical for Skala because he was the innovator and the radical. What he left was a legacy of success. However, he did not create an organization that could move ahead without his crucial leadership. His contributions continued to provide historical reference points, but there was no one who could match his creativity or was prepared for the changes which were on Skala's doorstep.

Skala's Response

With the onset of transformation in 1991, Skala made no major changes in its marketing activities. Marketing managers continued to remain focused on the reforms of the past without recognizing that the new ones were substantially different. They believed that the events of 1991 were no different than previous reforms.

Some changes in the overall organization structure were implemented, however. The cooperatives—the owners—sought foreign help in restructuring Skala's financial obligations so that tradeable shares could be issued to establish Skala as a private stock company. In 1992, Skala owners allowed Tegelmann of Germany to take control of a regional store as part of their developing equity position in Hungary. Although new marketing practices, especially in-store promotions and an expansion of foreign merchandise, were introduced in that store, little of what happened there spread to other company-owned stores. They continued to operate under different organizational structures, and store managers coordinated few marketing activities.

The one exception was in the area of advertising and promotion, where the relationship with Young and Rubicam led Skala to a comprehensive advertising program that built on the store logo and reintroduced Skala's Christmas Angel of the pretransformation period. The new campaign relied on print and electronic media, especially television, which had been the mainstay of Skala's advertising over the years. Flyers and handbills were distributed in the stores' neighborhoods as a means of informing consumers about special promotions. As part of the advertising efforts, marketing research was initiated. The emphasis was on developing an understanding of local neighborhood demographics. Much of the information came from secondary sources, although some in-store interviews were conducted. Offsetting this approach was the limited coordination of marketing policies. Merchandise which was featured in the promotional material was not always available at each of the stores. Store managers chose to feature specific items over which they had purchasing discretion in contrast to those selected for the advertising campaigns. These practices and the absence of central coordination or locally, among the store managers in Budapest, added an internally generated element to the general confusion and the turmoil in the retail market.

The advertising program itself was poorly defined and explained to the individual store managers. Its purpose was to stimulate sales and to develop consumer patronage using familiar themes from the past. Most important, the campaign failed to understand and cope with the turmoil in consumer markets. Skala continued to view itself as the "marketing innovator" in a period when consumers needed some stability and/or innovations that were in tune with the changing market conditions (Illes, 1993: personal interview). In contrast to Skala Centrum, the state-owned retailer chose to develop a marketing program that directly addressed the challenges faced by consumers who were lost in the turmoil. Centrum's program was based on Western concepts; the marketing strategy was not much different than what a Western firm would do. Management reduced prices, especially on food and clothing, and promoted as many Hungarian products as possible in an attempt to position itself as "the store for Hungarians" (Santa, 1993: personal interview). In other words, Centrum reacted aggressively to both reform and transformation. It is interesting to note that the state planning mechanism prevailing in Centrum was able to respond to market conditions more skillfully than Skala in spite of its past.

Explanations

What might explain Skala's conduct? Two reasons explain their lack of attention to the challenges and opportunities created by transformation in the Hungarian economy in the 1991-1992 period.

First, Skala's management did recognize the dramatic and substantive nature of the changes in the economy. However, they saw transformation as a part of the continual evolutionary process which had been well institutionalized in their operations. It seems that management had become too confident about their abilities, and their success clouded their vision about what the critical issues were. While markets were changing, past experience suggested that only tactical changes in marketing were required. Instead of developing new marketing programs to build consumer loyalty, as they had in the early days, Skala responded with more of the same, basically a series of attention-catching promotions that, unlike those of the past, failed to increase sales or market share. Skala continued to innovate following its own tradition in an environment in which direct adjustment of marketing programs to the changes in the consumer market would have been more important (Illes, 1993: personal interview).

Second, past marketing successes had come to dominate Skala's strategy. What really had held the organization together was the commitment to be an innovative force in the Hungarian economy. Skala's strategy and marketing plans were greatly influenced by the reforms that prevailed under Hungary's peculiar form of communism rather than coming from an effort to understand what information is required to formulate and manage such programs. The innovative organizational culture had partially stripped away the formal planning and operating structures that once had existed. During Demján's tenure there was strong central control. In many ways he took "the mantle of an innovator" (Dobos, 1993: personal interview). Operations were characterized by narrow specialization and top-down operations although these were not as strong as in most state-owned enterprises. While initiatives were encouraged and rewarded in Skala, managers still depended on superiors for direction in many matters, some of which are trivial from the perspective of Western firms. When Demján, the visionary leader, left, his legacy promoted a "business as usual attitude," the net result of which was that Skala managers adopted a short-term, inwardly directed outlook.

WHAT CAN WE LEARN FROM SKALA?

Evolutionary Change and Punctuated Equilibrium

Two highly interrelated concepts, evolutionary economics and punctuated equilibrium, provide a framework for viewing Skala's history in the new economic environment in Hungary. Evolutionary economics offers a framework for tracing an organization's movements through time by focusing on "*selection* mechanisms and *learning* mechanisms" (Silverberg, Dosi, and Orsenigo, 1988). Selection describes the philosophy or orientation that is used to make strategic decisions; learning describes the methods that the organization develops over time to ensure success for its strategy. Skala selected a radical marketing program standard, and then learned how to carry it out for most of its first 15 years by working just within the limits of the evolving economic reforms. Evolution was highly successful because Skala's management understood the limits of the reform measures and rarely went beyond them. Demján expressed this succinctly when he stated that "there must a historic compromise between communism and social democracy" (Diehl, 1988: A15).

Skala's evolution and equilibrium were punctuated by the leap toward transformation and the breakdown in the evolution of economic reforms. The Hungarian economy experienced a short, dramatic burst of change that disrupted "established activity patterns and installed the basis for new equilibrium periods" (Romanelli and Tushman, 1994: 1141). The process has been more vividly described as "something akin to the letting go of one trapeze in mid-air before a new one swings into view. . . . Unlike transitional change, the new state is usually unknown until it begins to take off . . ." (Ackerman, 1986: 2).

What happened to Skala is that over the years its concentration on learning how to make the best out of economic reforms as a way to maintain its innovative marketing programs limited the organization's ability to recognize that other types of change were possible. Managers were surprised much like the driver of a car who suddenly discovers that the smooth pavement of a four-lane highway has turned into the rough surface of a dirt track. It is easy and somewhat unfair to be critical and condemn management for not anticipating this type of change. Yet management does bear the responsibility for evaluating potential and existing changes in the environment. One would expect Skala to flourish in the transition phase given its competence developed over many years to react to the opportunities created by economic reforms. Instead, it seems that exactly this skill has desensitized Skala's management to the true nature of the changes in the early 1990s to which they responded with "business as usual."

Further, it may also be somewhat unfair to criticize the marketing managers since by the very nature of the Skala organization, their function was to develop and implement innovative marketing programs, although in retrospect these looked more like gimmicks rather than well thought-out action plans. They failed to understand marketing as an integrated process that requires the combination of several functions and elements. Skala did not have an all encompassing strategic process. Unlike their Western counterparts, marketing managers were not responsible for monitoring trends in the environment. Their responsibilities were narrowly defined, and they performed them with great skill honed over many years. They were asked to do innovative things, to create marketing programs that tested the economic system, but not to evaluate the system, and forecast its future. Senior management should have been responsible for mapping out the future, but they were not. In part they too were caught up in the long established successful patterns of behavior. Further, at a moment when their attention was needed, they were preoccupied with moving Skala through privatization. Also, the intensive negotiations between Skala, on the one hand, and Tegelmann, on the other, strained managerial resources that otherwise might have been directed toward developing a comprehensive strategy and toward developing an integrated marketing plan in tune with the changes in the marketplace.

Only in 1993, did Skala begin to bring focus to its marketing activities and thereby perhaps prepare for establishing a new equilibrium period. The managers, attuned to the pace of the previous period, were asked to develop a marketing strategy facing a chaotic environment. They were ill prepared for the challenges and had to learn how to use methods they did not fully understand. It took several years for them to acknowledge that dramatic changes had taken place and that many of their past successes could not be used as a paradigm for the future. Skala's position was compromised internally by the lack of formal planning, and externally by the success of state-owned Centrum, the aggressive marketing of foreign competitors and of new private firms which often were supported by Western suppliers.

EPILOGUE

It comes as no surprise that in December 1993 Tegelmann secured 50 percent percent control of Skala ("Tegelmann übernimmt . . .," 1993) which brought it under outside control. In the simplest sense, Skala's experience reinforces the well-known point that change is difficult, even under the best of all conditions. Undoubtedly, any outside observer would have agreed that Skala, on paper, was better prepared than most firms to weather the storm of transition: It had a successful history as an innovator; its Western linkages provided essential management expertise; it had managed to decouple itself from the arduous state-planning regime. Part of the difficulties arose from Skala's successful history under a leader who had no successor when one of his caliber was badly needed. What Demján taught the organization was to exploit evolutionary change to the fullest in a slowly changing environment. Some of the success undoubtedly is also due to the market protection that Skala enjoyed under the old regime.

It is clear that Hungary's strong commitment to transformation beginning in 1991 combined with the dramatic events occurring throughout Central and Eastern Europe should have been viewed as a fundamental change as described by punctuated equilibrium (Romanelli and Tushman, 1994:1145). Unfortunately it was not. In 1994, Skala was still grappling to find a new equilibrium period based on a new strategic thrust supported by new procedures.

REFERENCES

Ackerman, L. 1986. "Development, transition, or transformation: The question of change in organizations," *OD Practitioner*, (December), 1-8.

Blitz, D. 1988. "Hungary steps out along a capitalist path," *The Financial Times*, (October 28), 2.

Bobinski, C., V. Boland, R. Corizine, N. Denton and V. Marsh. 1992. "Santa rises in the East," *The Financial Times*, (December 17), p. 13.

Brada, J.C., I. Singh, and A. Török. 1994. *Firms afloat and firms adrift: Hungarian industry and the economic transition.* Armonk, NY: M.E. Sharpe.

British Broadcasting Corporation. 1985. "Is what is good for Skala good for Hungary?" *Summary of World Broadcasts*, (October 28) Lexis-Nexis.

Chavance, B. 1994. *The transformation of communist systems: Economic reforms since the 1950s.* Boulder: Westview Press.

Colitt, L. 1985. "Department store sets the pace," *The Financial Times*, (May 14), 22.

Colitt, L. 1987. "Hungary 2," *The Financial Times*, (September 11), 14.

Diehl, J. 1988. "Hungary's economists seek reform," *The Washington Post*, (July 8), A15.

"Discount store excites shoppers in Budapest." 1980. *The New York Times,* (November 2) Section 1, Part 1, 11.

Dobos, F.S. General Director, Ministry of Industry and Trade, Government of Hungary, May 22, 1993, personal interview.

Ellerman, D.P., A. Vahic, and T. Petrin. 1992. "Privatization controversies in the East and West," in M.P. Claudon and T. L. Gutner, (Eds.). *Comrades go private: Strategies for Eastern European privatization.* New York: New York University Press, 117-146.

Frydman, R., A. Rapaczynski, and J.S. Earle. 1993. *The privatization process in central Europe, Volume 1.* Budapest: Central European University Press.

Halasz, J. Direktor, Fehervar Warenhaus, AG Skala Trade, May 24, 1993, personal interview; follow up correspondence; June 12, 1994.

Hoch, P. 1991. "Changing formation and privatization," *Acta Oeconomica,* 43(3-4), 263-280.

"Hungary's Western-style retail group." 1986. *The New York Times,* (February 3), D10.

Illes, G. Marketing Director, Skala Trade, May 20, 1993, personal interview; follow up correspondence, May 25, 1994.

"Kiam sold on Hungary" 1989. *USA Today,* (July 13), 2B.

Kornai, J. (1992). *The socialist system: The political economy of communism.* Princeton: Princeton University Press.

Köves, A. and P. Marer. 1991. "Economic liberalization in Eastern Europe and in market economies," in A. Köves and P. Marer, (Eds.). *Foreign economic liberalization: Transformation in socialist and market economies.* Boulder, CO: Westview Press, pp. 15-36.

Lamm, V. 1990. *New tendencies in the Hungarian economy: Studies on Hungarian state and law.* Budapest: Akademiac Kiado.

Naor, J. 1993. "Can the Hungarian reform experience provide an alternative approach to current reform in the East?" Working paper, College of Business Administration, University of Maine at Orono.

Pasztor, S. 1991. "Being hidden (The privatization of APISZ)," *Acta Oeconomica,* 43(3/4), 297-314.

Romanelli, E. and M.L. Tushman. 1994. Organizational transformation as punctuated equilibrium. *Academy of Management Journal,* 37: 1141-1166.

Santa, L. Director of Trade, Centrum, May 25, 1993, personal interview.

Savitt, R. 1992. "Privatization and the consumer," *The New Hungarian Review,* 33 (Winter), 121-124.

Silverberg, G., G. Dosi, and L. Orsenigo. 1988. "Innovation, diversity and diffusion: a self-organization model," *Economic Journal,* 98 (December), 1032-1054.

"Tegelmann übernimmt Mehrheit in Skala-Coop," (July 22, 1993), Gesellschaft für betriebswirtschaftliche Information GmbH, FITT (Wirtschaftspressein-dex), Lexis-Nexis.

"Western discount supermarket chains target Hungary," (December 21, 1993), Euromarketing, Reuters' Textline, Lexis-Nexis.

PART III:
MANAGEMENT CHALLENGES
OF ENTREPRENEURSHIP

Chapter 10

Foreign Direct Investment Linkages and Entrepreneurial Development in Poland: Two Case Studies

Frank L. Hefner
Douglas P. Woodward

Half a decade into the economic transition of Central and Eastern Europe, there appear to be some widespread misconceptions about how managerial and entrepreneurial skills develop. Many indigenous businesses remain hampered by lack of managerial talent–at least the kind necessary to advance into modern, competitive enterprises. Since most local experience still stems from managing quota-driven state enterprises, many firms do not understand, let alone meet, the standards of modern competition.

At the microeconomic level, real reform of Central and Eastern Europe requires exposure to the operations of modern business enterprise. Through foreign direct investment (FDI), emerging private industry in Central and Eastern Europe has opened to the rigors of global capitalism for the first time in decades. Yet some observers view the new competition from Western business (and to a lesser extent from Japan) as standing in conflict with local entrepreneurial development. A small business consultant in Warsaw argued, "Poland has not fought a war of liberation from

The authors wish to thank the Society of International Business Fellows for support and advice. In particular, we are indebted to Peter Dean, President, SIBF Foundation, Inc., P. D. Robbins, Operations Manager of British Sugar, and Zygmunt Gasowski, SugarPol, in Torun, Poland; Marek Kalus, Vice President, Bielskie Zalady Graficzne, and Adam Kalus, Director, Baupol Consulting, in Bielsko-Biala, Poland, who graciously agreed to be interviewed and gave us tours of their facilities.

155

Moscow just to be absorbed by multinational corporations. They will have to develop an entrepreneurial class with home-grown solutions, and this is where Poland is very short" (quoted in Milbank, 1995).

This chapter suggests that local entrepreneurial development and multinational enterprise in Central and Eastern Europe can be compatible. What is often overlooked is that multinational companies infuse these economies with globally competitive practices and managerial skills, hiring and training locals with little previous experience. They also indirectly foster managerial skills through their linkages with the rest of the economy, helping local firms meet global standards of efficiency. There is no doubt, however, that some state enterprises attempting to operate in the market economy will find the adjustment process arduous.

In 1994, we interviewed upper management of and analyzed two companies that exemplify some of the managerial and entrepreneurial issues raised by the Polish economic transition. The first company, British Sugar, provides an example of a foreign firm entering an established domestic industry: sugar refining. In Poland, sugar refining remains viable, but highly inefficient. Our analysis of British Sugar uncovered some far-reaching and surprising impacts of FDI on local entrepreneurial development in transitional economies.

In the second case, we interviewed the management of a state-owned printing company, Bielskie Zaklady Graficzne, in the process of becoming privatized. The problems of this company illustrate some of the firm-level problems encountered during a transition from a planned to a market-oriented economy.

Both of these analyses were part of a larger case study of the economic impact of Coca-Cola's investment and operations in Poland. The results of that case study may be found in Woodward et al. (1995). The two firms described in this chapter were suppliers to Coca-Cola. British Sugar is an example of FDI in Poland and is connected to the operations of another multinational. The printing company supplies to Coca-Cola, a multinational, and is in competition with another Polish printing company which has received a major infusion of foreign capital.

FDI AND ENTREPRENEURIAL
DEVELOPMENT IN POLAND

There has been an explosion of entrepreneurial development in Poland since 1989. It has been estimated that two million entrepreneurs have started businesses since the fall of communism. According to recent estimates, small business is growing at a rate of 10 percent a year (Milbank, 1995).

FDI in Poland has also grown since 1989, although at a slower pace. While FDI throughout Central and Eastern Europe has been modest in the first four years of the transition, Poland was the third largest recipient of direct investment, behind the Czech Republic and Hungary. Poland received about $2 billion, or 16 percent of the total FDI stock in Central and Eastern Europe in 1992 (United Nations, 1994). According to figures from the Polish State Agency for Foreign Investment (PAIZ), from 1991 through 1993, 162 FDI projects were initiated in Poland, many of them related to the privatization of state enterprise. FDI took off following the liberalization course set in 1990 by Leszek Balcerowsicz, Poland's first non-Communist finance leader.

Poland had some experience with foreign investment before the liberalization in 1990. Appearing in the 1970s, these "Polonian" companies, mostly subsidized by ethnic Poles living abroad, served as the only real link to efficient global business practices employed outside the Communist bloc. Some achieved quality standards to meet demands of foreign buyers (Ciechocinska, 1994). The Polonian companies led the way for the opening to FDI in the early 1990s.

Inward foreign investment promised to introduce modern managerial expertise and technology, key elements of microeconomic reform, as the economic "shock therapy" program attempted to transform Poland's macroeconomy. Still, it could be argued that FDI has been too small in the first decade of reform to have made a real difference. The slow progress of Polish privatization has discouraged some foreign investment in the 1990s. In fact, the Polish economy received only a modest amount of direct investment.

Therefore, early entrants took on a special significance–offering the only demonstration of how capitalism operated at the microeconomic level. Most of the early FDI came from Western consumer goods multinational companies; for example, Procter & Gamble, Unilever, Nestle, Pepsi, Fiat, Phillip Morris, Gillette, and Gerber. It appears that most early investments in transitional economies were market-oriented, not using the region as an export platform (see Welfens and Jasinski, 1994). Because foreign firms seek to compete in the local market (rather than export), they typically engage in direct competition with emerging local enterprise–the source of most controversy.

Previous research indicates that Polish citizens, many witnessing FDI for the first time, are divided about the relative benefits and costs of foreign production. According to one series of interviews conducted in Poland, some government officials, enterprise managers, and others understood that foreign investment was not a cost-free benefit (Stoever,

1995). Others saw FDI as "a panacea . . . that could solve their problems of resource scarcity, managerial inefficiency and technological backwardness if only enough of it could be enticed into the country" (Stoever, 1995: 107). The study also found a prevalent view that foreign investment contributes little to economic development because of its low level of domestic input sourcing, or local content.

Over the past 30 years in the West, a broad consensus has formed regarding the host country impacts of FDI. Dunning (1994: 39) encapsulated the effects of multinational enterprise on the local economy in four categories:[1]

- The development of backward (supply) and forward (marketing) linkages.
- The introduction of complementary assets: technology, management, and organizational competence.
- The raising of product quality of indigenous competitors and of consumer expectations.
- Stimulating local entrepreneurship and domestic rivalry.

In Woodward et al. (1995) we discussed how Dunning's four categories applied to the investment and operations of Coca-Cola. British Sugar, by supplying all of the sugar demanded by Coca-Cola bottlers, provides forward linkages in the Polish economy. By exerting a demand on beet growers, it also has backward linkages in the economy. The printing company is a supplier to Coca-Cola and must meet Coca-Cola's rigid quality standards and requirements for almost just-in-time delivery; both features were uncommon business practices in the old regime. We will show that British Sugar, as an example of FDI, has encouraged local entrepreneurship, raised standards of product quality, and has introduced Western-style business practices to the production of sugar and the planting of sugar beets. The printing company, by way of supplying to Coca-Cola, has been required to rise to higher standards of quality and be responsive to short lead times on orders. In the next section we present our analysis of these two cases with emphasis on how FDI has effected their operations in the transitional economy.

REVIVING SUGAR REFINING AND FARMING

Poland's farmers have played a special role in the country's history of private enterprise. They were once recognized for technical expertise in agricultural management. Even under communist rule, most farms were left in private hands. Unfortunately, the land was parceled into small plots, and agriculture deteriorated relative to Western efficiency. Today, private agriculture employs over four million, the largest number of persons in the private sector (Warsaw School of Economics, 1993).

Sugar beets provide a case in point. Poland was once a leading sugar beet exporter, but at the end of the communist era, its beet farmers and refineries were not capable of producing high quality sugar on a competitive basis. Exposed to global standards, the sugar beet industry (farming and refining) could not survive without fundamental reform.

Seeking to expand, British Sugar Overseas entered into negotiations in 1989 to form a joint venture with two Polish sugar beet factories, Unislaw and Ostrowite. On October 9, 1989, the agreement for the joint venture was signed and the company, SugarPol (based in Torun), was formed. This joint venture consists of three partners: Cukrownie Torunskie (a state company: 45 percent), Rolimpex (a Polish state import/export agency: 4 percent), and British Sugar Overseas, now owned by Associated British Foods (51 percent).

British Sugar entered the Polish market with the expectation of exporting sugar and in anticipation of the large consumer market that would be developed with economic liberalization. In 1989, exporting sugar was a feasible idea. However, since then, the cost of production in Poland has risen higher than the world price.

Poland's sugar refining industry suffered from mismanagement as a state-owned industry and was inefficient compared to the Western European sugar industry. In Poland, 78 sugar factories produce about 1.5 to 1.6 million tons of sugar each year. The beet is grown by approximately 350,000 growers on 360,000 hectares of land. In contrast, in the United Kingdom, ten beet sugar factories produce 1.4 million tons of sugar from 170,000 hectares of beet grown by 10,200 growers. In other words, the sugar industry in the United Kingdom produces about the same tonnage of sugar with fewer factories, about half of the land, and with less than three percent of the growers.

With respect to the refineries SugarPol operates, British Sugar managers identified several key areas of underperformance compared with Western refineries: low agricultural yields, poor factory sugar extraction, poor quality products, poor financial control and inadequate investment. In an effort to become profitable under adverse conditions, British Sugar introduced a number of innovations in the Polish sugar beet industry. Starting with the grower, British Sugar has a continuous program of education and demonstration. The company provides the services of an agronomist to assist growers in improving yield. However, it has been noted, "In an atmosphere where changes in husbandry practice have not been normal for many years, suggestions which challenge traditional practice are treated with suspicion until proven" (Farrow, Robbins, and Warnes, 1993: 256).

British Sugar educates by demonstration. For example, each year a number of field-scale crops have been planted to teach improved crop production techniques. The company has also introduced soil analysis and improved fertilizer usage to the growers. In addition, British Sugar provides subsidized, low-interest loans to select growers to purchase precision drills. Since the small size of many farms precludes such modern machinery, British Sugar has encouraged these growers to operate as contractors and offer drilling services to other growers. In this manner, British Sugar is introducing modern entrepreneurial techniques to what could be characterized as a very outdated farm industry. Through these sorts of activities, British Sugar also demonstrates that it is committed to Poland for the long-term.

Since 1989, British Sugar has initiated a program of capital investments, operational changes, and training to enhance the productivity of the sugar factories. Polish factories in general were found using more antiquated technology than was realized in the West. Factories were also often constructed at inappropriate locations. An overseas manager for British Sugar, P. D. Robbins, noted an example of the kinds of inefficiencies that were common in the centrally planned system: two sugar factories were built in an area where no beets were located, thus increasing transportation costs.

Many state-owned factories continue to operate inefficiently. Typically they pay above average wages, have a bloated workforce, and operate under large debt. State-owned factories also put their capital in the wrong places. As Robbins stated, "They wouldn't dream of investing to cut costs."(See also the following case study in this chapter.)

British Sugar, on the other hand, reinvested its profits to make capital improvements. The company has also initiated Western-style financial planning and accounting. Under the previous regime, the goals of financial reporting were substantially different from those of a profit center. As Farrow, Robbins, and Warnes (1993: 257) noted, "In a centrally planned economy all the systems and reports were designed to give the central organization what they [*the firm*] thought they [*the central organization*] wanted."

British Sugar has also introduced Western-style marketing. The basic concepts of marketing as well as providing a service and the products that the customer requires are all new concepts. Previously, the supplier was "king." British Sugar has been active in educating the business community to a system where the consumer is "king." While consumer sovereignty is a well-established principle in capitalist economies, it is still a foreign concept in transitional economies. As we were told by P.D. Robbins, "the introduction of new technology is straightforward, but to exploit these new techniques, one needs to also change the thinking and culture. British Sugar uses the same Polish workers that were in place before the formation of the joint venture and is making strides educating workers in new attitudes and technologies."

British Sugar is closely related to other FDI in Poland, primarily to Coca-Cola, which began investing heavily in Poland in 1991 and achieved market dominance by 1993. Coca-Cola demands high-quality sugar, what is known as EC2 quality (sometimes referred to as "Coke-Quality" in Poland). Coca-Cola requires much higher purity than other local beverage makers and food processors. Yet high-quality refined sugar is very expensive to produce.

From British Sugar's perspective, Coca-Cola provided the market demand to justify producing high-grade sugar for the first time in over 40 years. Without British Sugar's investment, Coca-Cola (and other Western bottlers) would have to import high-grade sugar. Thus, with Coca-Cola, there has been an increase in the standards of product quality in sugar (Woodward et al., 1995). With British Sugar investments, Poland now has a producer that can deliver the required quality at a competitive price, which in this case is slightly lower than the world price plus import duties. Through the backward linkages extending from Coca-Cola bottling and SugarPol, Woodward et al. (1995) found that some 6,400 jobs are supported in the private agricultural sector through the production of high-grade sugar for Coca-Cola. In order to produce high-grade sugar at a competitive price, British Sugar has had to transfer its expertise and competitive style of operations "upstream" to the sugar beet growers.[2]

REVITALIZING POLISH PRINTING

Bielskie Zaklady Graficzne is a printing firm in Bielsko-Biala, Poland. At the time of our visit (October 1994), the company was state-owned but was in the process of becoming privatized. The management team consisted of a consulting firm that was working to take the company private.

As in many state-owned firms, efficiency and profits were alien concepts. In 1992 the company operated at a loss with an inflated workforce. Management had not done any analysis of the business in order to determine costs and profitability. When Baupol (the consulting firm taking the printing company private) took over, they reduced employment levels to lower costs. Maintaining labor surpluses within the firm was part of the inherent inefficiency of the old system. Reducing employment in order to become more competitive is a recurring theme in the modernization process for Poland and throughout Central and Eastern Europe.

Treating labor as a variable rather than a fixed cost is a relatively new concept in Poland. To some extent the privatization process has been made inefficient by restrictions placed by the Ministry of Privatization. Baupol, at the time of our visit, anticipated that complete privatization would take place within two months. Up until privatization was completed, Baupol was permitted to reduce employment, within constraints set by the Ministry. However, the management contract prohibited dismissal of any employee for two years after the firm is privatized. We presume that the Ministry desired to prevent any wholesale restructuring of firms once the Ministry lost the ability to supervise any restructuring. From the employees perspective, this guaranteed job security. From the perspective of a newly privatized firm, the agreement locks in potential inefficiencies and prevents the firm from responding appropriately to changing market conditions.

In the meantime, the firm is having difficulty making profits and improving quality. The management team would like to make capital improvements by purchasing new printing presses. These would improve the quality of printing and reduce the number of employees needed. The firm is burdened with outdated equipment–a legacy of state ownership. Even though the printing machines were outdated, the previous company managers decided to spend limited capital to add to the office building. Thus, the firm has excess office space, redundant workers, and inefficient equipment.

The printing company now supplies labels to Coca-Cola bottlers that require strict adherence to quality control guidelines. Using outdated equipment and methods, Baupol is finding it difficult to deliver the quality demanded by Coca-Cola in a cost-effective manner. For example, we saw one production run of labels that was not up to standard and had to be discarded. These mistakes drive up the costs of production and reduce profits. New equipment is part of the solution. In the meantime, a competing printing company has received a major infusion of U.S. capital and has bought state-of-the-art printing presses. These presses are capable of producing multicolored labels with a high degree of uniformity. Thus, the competitor has been able to win most of the Coca-Cola printing orders. FDI in this case has had the effect of raising standard-of-product quality. By demanding higher quality, Coca-Cola has motivated Polish firms to seek ways to deliver higher quality products. In the case of Baupol, unfortunately one of their competitors has received an infusion of capital that has allowed it to produce the quality demanded by Coca-Cola at a competitive price.

The transition from a quota-driven to a market-driven economy has put Bielskie Zaklady Graficzne in the position of having antiquated equipment and yet having to satisfy the stringent quality requirements of a major multinational company. Further, the firm's ability to generate profits has been hamstrung by an inflated work force and by the requirement that employees cannot be laid off for two years. This put the firm at a disadvantage when competing for capital investment. Confronted with uncertain profitability, potential investors may shy away from this company. Thus, the inherited inefficiencies and the institutional requirements imposed by the Ministry of Privatization provide what may be insurmountable barriers to a successful transition for a modern competitive printing company–despite efforts to bring in better management. In the meantime, the demands of a competitive marketplace, spurred mostly by FDI, have forced management to find innovative ways to cut costs, increase productivity, and raise quality–all within a very constricting institutional framework.

At the time of our interview, the managing director planned to have the firm completely privatized within two months. There was no trade union involved initially. By October 1994, the employees decided to unionize. Twenty percent of the ownership in the privatized company was earmarked for the employees.

Having privatized over 25 companies in Poland, Baupol has had a successful track record of turning state-owned enterprises private. One of the directors of Baupol had worked in the United States. His experience could be construed as a form of FDI, if one considers human capital an investment and if we consider training abroad as an importable capital good.[3] Given Baupol's track record we believe they will be successful in this case also. The real question is whether the privatized company will be able to continue to provide high-quality products to a very discriminating Western consumer goods company, namely Coca-Cola, and whether it will be able to survive domestic competition without an infusion of foreign capital. It is too early to draw conclusions, but none of these questions would have been raised before the transition. The ebb and flow of business success and failure is still a relatively new concept to the Polish economy. However, the realization, although new, that failure (i.e., bankruptcy and the eventual termination) of an enterprise is a possibility, is beginning to take hold. Clearly, the management team of Baupol understands this. However, it was not clear that the employees did. This realization is part of the adjustment process to a capitalist economy that needs to take place.

CONCLUSION

When the old regime collapsed, macroeconomic stabilization was the primary concern of policymakers. Research tended to focus on stabilizing the rate of inflation, creating viable financial institutions, formulating privatization laws, and other macro policies. Five years into the transition process, many of these problems in Poland have been resolved, or at least stabilized to a point where massive uncertainty is not the norm. The problems we see now are more related to microeconomic stabilization. It seems unlikely that FDI will play a major macroeconomic role in the transition. Recent analyses of Central and Eastern European economies have sounded increasingly pessimistic about the extent to which FDI can affect the transition process (McMillan, 1993). However, the demonstration effect of early FDI is integral to the successful reentry of these countries into the global marketplace. If there is one fundamental advantage that multinational corporations bring to transitional economies, it is that production now traces back to consumers, and economic activity will rise and fall with market demand, not quotas set by planners. In both cases presented in this chapter, FDI was instrumental in establishing market-oriented, customer-driven production linkages. Previously, sugar beet growers, state-owned refineries, and printing companies knew only command systems where managers were not concerned with customers or marketing. Efficiency, regular delivery, and consistent quality were equally unknown. The old relations that had bound industries and agriculture broke apart in 1990, and even the remaining state-run industries had to search for customers. For the first time in decades, intermediate goods suppliers needed customers who, in turn, needed customers in the final demand sector. Production linkages now emanate from final markets.

Multinational corporations bring efficiency, which may conflict with attempts to maximize or maintain levels of employment. As we noted in the case of Bielskie Zaklady Graficzne, the drive to reduce costs in order to be competitive has resulted in a reduction in force at the printing plant. Using only employment as a metric, governments could easily be disillusioned about the true benefits of FDI and market reform, especially in the early phase of transition. Lower employment per unit of output is one of the results common to any process of industrial restructuring. We were not surprised to find that restructuring lowers the job count in particular sectors. In former communist countries, it is important to realize that state-owned enterprise figures represent a bloated benchmark.

In the case of British Sugar, FDI represents efficiency gains through technology transfer, in a broad sense. Technology here refers to managerial, production, agricultural, and entrepreneurial techniques. In the case of

Bielskie Zaklady Graficzne, FDI has imposed higher production standards, reduced lead times in production, and cost cutting. The requirement of profitability has imposed the bulk of the cost-cutting requirements. Both cases provide insight into the micro transitions taking place with the advent of marketplace reform and FDI in Poland.

ENDNOTES

1. Dunning's review is based on extensive work beginning with analysis of the impact of FDI in the United Kingdom in the 1950s, and draws on the well-known case study research by Michael Porter. The list has been modified slightly to include forward as well as backward linkages in the first category.

2. As an interesting side note, we discovered that British Sugar pays its growers in cash, which was not the norm for state-owned refineries. All too often, the state-owned enterprises pay the growers in kind, sometimes with the refined sugar itself.

3. We found in the course of our case study of Coca-Cola that other Polish plant managers that are finding success within the transitional economy have had foreign work experience. The entire concept of treating human capital as a form of FDI is fascinating but beyond the scope of this study.

REFERENCES

Ciechocinska, M. 1994. Development of the Private Sector in Poland During 1989-1990: The Early Phase of Structural Transformation. In Dennis A. Rondinelli, ed., *Privatization and Economic Reform in Central Europe: The Changing Business Climate*. Westport, CT: Quorum Books: 209-225.

Dunning, J.H. 1994. Re-evaluating the Benefits of Foreign Direct Investment. *Transnational Corporations*, 3(1): 23-50.

Farrow, B., Robbins, P.D., and Warnes, A.J.N. 1993. SugarPol (Torun) Sp. Z o.o., British Sugar's Joint Venture in Poland. *International Sugar Journal*, 95(1): 255-292.

McMillan, C.H. 1993. The Role of Foreign Direct Investment in the Transition from Planned to Market Economies. *Transnational Corporations*, 2 (3): 97-119.

Milbank, D. 1995. Polish Entrepreneurs Revitalize Economy But Battle Huge Odds. *The Wall Street Journal*, March 30: 1A.

Stoever, W. 1995. The Role of Foreign Investment in Poland's Economic Restructuring: Some Polish Views. *Journal of East-West Business*, 1(1): 97-115.

United Nations Conference on Trade and Development. 1994. *World Investment Report 1994: Transnational Corporations, Employment and the Workplace*. New York: United Nations.

Warsaw School of Economics. 1993. *Transforming the Polish Economy*. Warsaw: World Economy Research Institute.

Welfens, P.J.J. and Jasinski, P. 1994. *Privatization and Foreign Direct Investment in Transforming Economies*. Brookfield, CT: Dartmouth.

Woodward, D.P., Hefner, F.L., Arpan, J.S., Kuhlman, J.A., and Folks, W.R. 1995. *Foreign Direct Investment in Transitional Economies: The Coca-Cola System in Poland and Romania*. Unpublished monograph: The University of South Carolina, Columbia, SC.

Chapter 11

Entrepreneurs in Post-Communist Russia

Robert D. Lynch
Valeri V. Makoukha

After more than 70 years of communist orthodoxy, phenomena described as "Russian entrepreneurship" and "Russian entrepreneurs" seem out of place. Nevertheless, they have emerged, almost from nowhere. In 1993, studies estimated the number of new entrepreneurs in Russia at 4 percent of the population, equal to about six million people (*Biznesmeni Rossii*, 1994). This has to be regarded as unprecedented growth, since ten years earlier there were no entrepreneurs in Russia, in the traditional Western understanding of the term. Any private entrepreneurial activity was considered criminal.

What is Russian entrepreneurship? Is it an economic phantom that emerged from the ruins of totalitarian economics; or is it, as some people think, another "grandiose humbug" the hard-line Communists use to retain power against historical odds? There are precedents in recent Soviet history: for example, when under Lenin's New Economic Policy an entrepreneurial class was allowed to develop only to be mercilessly stamped out by Stalin.

Is this new class a true economic and political force able to change the course of Russian history and establish Russia as a free market democracy? Or have entrepreneurs always existed in Russia, as Hisrich and Grachev contend (1993)?

These questions have more than just theoretical value. Given its size, immense natural and human wealth, and military power, the course Russia will follow is bound to affect the stability and prosperity of the world community. We are convinced that Russia's new entrepreneurial class is destined to play a very important, maybe crucial, role in the future course of Russian history.

THE NEW RUSSIAN ENTREPRENEUR:
A SOCIOLOGICAL PROFILE

A tradition among economists to underestimate the role of the entrepreneur in the economy dates back, perhaps, to Adam Smith and his concept of the "invisible hand." Max Weber made it clear that modern capitalist expansion is not an exclusive function of financial resources, but rather a function of developing a "capitalist spirit." Where it emerges and develops, it finds the necessary resources and not vice versa (Weber, 1976). Marxism developed the traditional disdain for the entrepreneur to its logical end: the entrepreneur became a persona non grata in a future communist society. In communist Russia entrepreneurs were banned, jailed, and sometimes murdered under Stalin's rule.

According to several researchers, factors such as gender, age, educational level, professional background, family, and social environment play an important role in the genesis and sociological profile of entrepreneurs (Ronstadt, 1983a; Ronstadt, 1983b; Hisrich and Brush, 1986; Gasse, 1977).

Gender

Traditionally, males have dominated the entrepreneurial class in European countries as well as in North America. Recent Western research indicates clearly that, in some respects, female entrepreneurs possess very different motivations (greater need for achievement), business skills levels (better interpersonal skills), occupational backgrounds (administrative and service-related compared to specific line of work), and personality characteristics (more flexible and tolerant) than their male counterparts (Hisrich and Brush, 1986). Furthermore, some contend that changing business and social environments may lead to an increasing demand for female management qualities. Women in the United States and some other Western countries are now starting new ventures at three times the rate of men (Carsrud and Olm, 1986).

This is not true in Russia's initial stages of entrepreneurship. Success in business goes mostly to male entrepreneurs with a strong, and even aggressive, psychological core. A survey conducted by the Public Opinion Fund showed that the share of men among Russian entrepreneurs was 83 percent. Another poll of 110 big and small business-owners discovered only four female entrepreneurs, who, by their own account, "possess a hard, male character" (*Biznesmeni Rossii*, 1994: 384).

However, women have been developing entrepreneurial activities in their homes by focusing on specific household needs. In some instances, they are moving into the production of fashion goods. Small business skills may be lacking, but courses in small business are being offered by the Women's Union of Russia and the Alliance of American and Russian Women. On average, women are better educated than men in Russia and dominate fields such as economics, medicine, law, and education (Fong, 1993). In some cases they have been quite successful in business enterprises in male-dominated fields (Hamilton, 1993).

Age

There are no significant differences in the age of new entrepreneurs in Russia compared to the West. In developed market economies, men usually start their own business between the ages of 30 and 35, and women at around age 35. In Russia the average age of entrepreneurs is 36. The age distribution of Russian entrepreneurs confirms the prevailing view that people are inclined to start entrepreneurial careers when they already have a family and some life experience.

The under-40 age group has been described as being flexible, multilingual, of high energy level, and better educated than their parents. Max Agari, president of ABB Russia Ltd., is quoted as saying, "In five years, the young workers in Russia will have the same attitudes and work habits as those in the West" (Krantz, 1994: 24). Illia Baskin, one of Russia's newest and most successful entrepreneurs, stated in reference to the $24 billion aid package lobbied for by Yeltsin, "The best investments are not in the Russian economy, but in the Russian young people–the young generation" (Sheridan, 1992: 36).

Education

Educational characteristics of Russian entrepreneurs correspond with the general education level of the Russian population. Yves Sarrazin, director of Central and Eastern European operations for Digital Equipment Corporation, stated:

> The level of education is remarkable. It's surprising to see the number of people who have engineering degrees . . . the level of education will allow them to move very rapidly into reconstructing the environment in terms of infrastructures, services, manufacturing, and so on. They have many of the skills they need. (*Industry Week*, 1992: 38)

Many surveys agree that the educational level of Russian entrepreneurs may be one of the highest in the world. According to the Public Opinion Fund, the percentage of those with college or university degrees exceeds 80 percent, and by other accounts it reaches 95 percent (*Biznesmeni Rossii,* 1994). One survey found that among 60 highly successful entrepreneurs, 23 (or 38 percent) had "candidate of science" (equivalent to PhD) degrees, and seven started their businesses having attained MA degrees. The same study found that among these 60 entrepreneurs interviewed, 93.4 percent had college and universities degrees, and out of 50 small business owners only 2 percent had not attained a higher level of education (*Biznesmeni Rossii,* 1994).

Judging by these figures, it appears that better education provides an obvious competitive advantage in the emerging Russian market. Paradoxically, this phenomenon contradicts some basic concepts of entrepreneurship theory. For example, Joseph Schumpeter wrote that "solid preparation and business knowledge, intellectual depth and ability for logical analysis may become, in some circumstances, a source of a failure" (1982: 181). One possible explanation is that the Russian market is still in its early-growth stage. It lacks traditions and established practices encoded in laws, procedures, accepted patterns of behavior, etc., forcing entrepreneurs to manage their businesses in an ad hoc style. As a result they continuously look for innovative and original decisions in order to survive and make their venture a success. Understandably, this sort of environment is bound to require, among other things, a good educational background. Another explanation of the unusually high educational level of Russian entrepreneurs may be that most of them come from an intellectual environment–the so-called "intelligentsia." No more than 15 percent of entrepreneurs come from working class and peasant families, while the overwhelming majority (71 percent) can be considered second generation intellectuals. Indeed, as many surveys indicate, the fathers of most entrepreneurs are managers, specialists, and white-collar workers (*Biznesmeni Rossii,* 1994).

Family

As previously stated, many researchers posit that family environment may be very important for the development of future entrepreneurs, especially when parents are able to serve as entrepreneurial role models. For understandable reasons, until recently Russian parents could not serve as role models to their children in this regard. However, important entrepreneurial personality characteristics such as independence, individuality, and initiative-taking are also forged in the family. According to Russian sociologists, during the 1980s in Russia, the number of the so-called "democratic" families–that is families who encourage intellectual independence, individual responsibility and decision making in children–began to outnumber the "authoritarian" families, i.e., those who discourage the above-mentioned qualities (Mironow, 1989). This shift in family quality is an important factor for a society in which the traditional patriarchal peasant culture retained its influence even during the Soviet period. Besides, as has been stated previously, most Russian entrepreneurs come from educated families, and many researchers have been arguing that there is a direct correlation between educational level in a family and the desire of children to start entrepreneurial careers (Bowen and Hisrich, 1986).

An additional reason that explains a strong drive of the Russian educated class to become entrepreneurs is, paradoxically, the marginal social status that the educated have in the Russian establishment: a blue-collar worker often earns a better income than a highly qualified engineer or a university professor. Humble material status coupled with the total lack of opportunities for free intellectual and political expression has bred a desire to break out of the depressing circle of Soviet life and to take better control of one's own life. Gorbachev's Perestroika and Yeltsin's market reforms offered new career paths for the disgruntled intelligentsia: either to enter politics or to take up entrepreneurship. Those who had a passion for public service joined the Democratic Movement and some became legislators and government officials. Others, more pragmatic and action-oriented, started their private ventures in the years 1987 to 1990.

Nationality of Entrepreneurs

As a sociological characteristic, the nationality of entrepreneurs is a specific feature of the Russian situation. Although such phenomena as "minority business" or "immigrant business" are not uncommon for the United States and other Western economies, the problem of national identity of entrepreneurs is viewed quite differently in Russia. There is a widespread belief among the majority of the population that minority entrepreneurs operating in the Russian market abuse their rights. They are believed to stand a good chance to seize the leading positions in the economy and to dislodge entrepreneurs of Russian nationality. Such forecasts are often supported by the argument of an alleged "inability of the Russian bear to conduct business" (*Nezavisimaya Gazeta*, 1991). This popular belief has all the makings of myth and is used by Russian nationalists in political and ideological discussions.

In fact, many surveys indicate that these contentions are incorrect. First, they are not corroborated by statistical data. Entrepreneurs of Russian nationality make up 84 percent of all owners of small and medium-sized businesses, and 63 percent of the owners of large businesses. Second, among the entrepreneurs, the national minorities do not create any "national business enclaves," but display, in their behavior, cosmopolitan features common in free markets. By the accounts of minority entrepreneurs themselves, they tend to identify with the Russian people, if not "by blood," then through the common language they use and the shared cultural environment (Radaev, 1993). Finally, the myth about the "Russian Bear" being unable to succeed in business is refuted by many Western businessmen, who have been conducting business with Russians (Galuszka, Kranz, and Reed, 1994; Stevenson, 1994). Certainly, Russian entrepreneurs still have a long way to go in terms of business knowledge. However, the rapid development of business practices and technology, and their growing sense of self-confidence holds promise for the future (Warner, 1994).

THREE STAGES OF RUSSIAN ENTREPRENEURSHIP DEVELOPMENT

Since its inception in the late 1980s, entrepreneurship in Russia developed through three stages.

Stage One: Maverick Entrepreneurs

Historically, the cause of capitalism in most countries was initially supported by groups that found themselves outside the "establishment," but who possessed, using the term of Max Weber, a "capitalist spirit." Max Weber identified the entrepreneur as an outsider:

> . . . establishment of the entrepreneur in the society was not, by any means, a peaceful process. Supporters of new social ideas were always facing a sea of distrust, sometimes hatred, and, above all, moral indignation. We know of many instances when real legends about dark spots in the entrepreneur's past were created. (Weber 1976: 88)

Thus, the suspicion and hostility with which the new Russian entrepreneurs have been confronted in their short existence are not unique to Russia.

The first generation of Russian entrepreneurs, which started to emerge in 1987 after the Law on Individual Enterprise had been passed in the former Soviet Union, possessed all the makings of psychological outsiders. Starting an entrepreneurial career placed an individual at the periphery of the social structure, deprived him or her of social stability. Even in 1992, more than half of all entrepreneurs surveyed were convinced that in the eyes of the population they were crooks and thieves. Such attitudes were inevitably reinforced by the differences of an entrepreneur's psychological makeup compared to the mainstream Soviet citizen: a person almost totally dependent on the benevolent state for his or her income and whose career drive and material aspirations were limited to a slow process of rising along the hierarchical ladder within the organization.

Another distinctive feature of the first entrepreneurs was their ability to start life anew. This trait makes Russian entrepreneurs similar to their American counterparts. According to the U.S. Department of Labor, between 800,000 and 900,000 small businesses are created every year, and between 700,000 and 800,000 small companies go out of business every year. Unlike the majority of the population, the Russian entrepreneur displayed a number of features not common in Soviet society. These included social and psychological mobility and a passion for learning and innovation. Those entrepreneurs of the first generation who survived and succeeded were different from later entrepreneurs in other ways also. They, as a rule, were more goal-oriented, persevering, and strongly driven by a desire to expand their ventures. According to Max Weber, two types of entrepreneurs need to be distinguished: (1) "adventurers," motivated above all by the desire of personal enrichment; and (2) proper "capitalists" who put the interests of a business above their own (Weber, 1990). There is some evidence that within Russia now, the capitalists have begun to displace adventurers.

Second Stage: Bosses Are Coming

The second stage of entrepreneurship in Russia took place between 1989 and 1991. Its distinctive feature was that the ranks of Russian entrepreneurs were replenished with big and small bosses abandoning the state sector. Until 1989, the state-run economy seemed to be stable and secure, but after that year it began to collapse, and many managers started to migrate to the private sector. Sometimes this process took on peculiar Soviet features, when a transfer of managers from the state sector was carried out with the authorization and under control of the state. One survey estimates the number of the former "big bosses" among the present-day entrepreneurs at 8 percent and that of "small bosses" at roughly 45 percent (*Biznesmeni Rossii*, 1994). Among entrepreneurs of this second stage were many academics, engineers, and research personnel who were disenchanted with the pin money that the state paid them.

To some extent the new cohorts changed the dominant psychological profile of Russian entrepreneurs. Although the main psychological trait–a self-made person, starting his or her venture from scratch–remained in place, the motivations of the newcomers were often different. If among the first entrepreneurs there were many "adventurers" and mavericks, the second-stage types were looking mostly for opportunities of self-fulfillment in business, often disregarding economic efficiency and material returns. Some researchers even called them "idealistic entrepreneurs."

Third Stage: Mass Entrepreneurs

One of the consequences of the collapse of the Communist Party after the August 1991 putsch and the resulting political and economic changes was a growing drive of many people to start an entrepreneurial career. In early 1992, the Russian Information Agency (Novosti) reported that over 80,000 "new economic structures" had been registered (Sheridan, 1992).

The driving force behind this entrepreneurial activity was not only a natural desire to change one's life for the better–materially as well as spiritually–but also a sheer economic necessity that can also be found in the West (Hisrich and Peters, 1992). In many cases people were forced to start a venture to earn some living, even if they did not intend to become entrepreneurs. For example, research personnel were often forced to start some kind of business because of government cutbacks in financing research activities; army officers had to turn to entrepreneurship because they were discharged from the army without guaranteed job placement

THE NEW RUSSIAN ENTREPRENEURS: LIFESTYLE, MOTIVATIONS, AND NEW VALUES

The different social strata from which new entrepreneurs come determine the different lifestyles they practice. An extensive survey conducted by the All-Russian Institute for Studies of Public Opinion gives a detailed picture of personal life patterns of the new class (Mamardashvili and Levinson, 1993). The survey identified three categories of Russian capitalists: puritans, Westernizers, and merchants ("kupchiki").

Puritans

The "puritans" come mostly from academic, engineering, or research backgrounds. They are deliberately modest in their everyday life, place high value on rational calculation, and practice dedication and respect for their new occupations, including the financial rewards they provide. They regard the capital they own as the accumulated labor of many people who entrust it to their management, and therefore they see their mission as serving society. Some of them display an almost aesthetical attitude toward business operations. For example, they would like their own financial transactions to be as elegant as solutions of mathematical problems.

In the context of business strategy, these principles prompt them to place investment over consumption. They hate to see their capital lying idle and are reluctant to take money out of the business, even at the expense of the living standards of their families. In many respects, the lifestyle of this type of entrepreneur typifies the Protestant ethics described by Max Weber (1990).

Westernizer

The second type of entrepreneur is the "Westernizer." The term "new Russians" (Smith, 1990) refers primarily to this type of Russian entrepreneur who tries to imitate the life of the Western upper-middle class. Many Westernizers, for instance, have two homes: one in Moscow and the other in Madrid, London, or Haifa. They have gone through periods of adaptation and social conversion and participate as peers in the international business life.

Although these people are far removed from the problems and material hardships of the majority of Russians, they still identify their personal goals and interests with those of Russia. The "New Russians" are optimistic and believe in a better future for Russia. Their main goal is to help make Russia a more prosperous country.

Merchants

The third group of entrepreneurs are the "merchants" who frequently are called the new rich. This group displays all the signs of conspicuous consumption: luxury and lack of good taste and culture, excessiveness in everything from food and drink to fancy limousines. Because of their often exorbitant lifestyles, this group is the most hated by the population. Mistakenly, their behavior is often ascribed to all Russian entrepreneurs.

Motivations of a New Class: A Russian Touch

The motivations of Russian entrepreneurs initially centered around three basic elements: (1) to earn a better income; (2) to change life in order to ensure a better environment for self-fulfillment; and (3) to gain independence. The first motivator applied mostly to the small business entrepreneurs, and the second to the larger business entrepreneurs, many of whom may have been relatively well-off when they started their entrepreneurial career. Finally, the third motivator was common among all entrepreneurs, who were tired of the hard work and poor pay, abhorred being bossed around all the time, and felt a strong urge to reach independence.

Many entrepreneurs quickly attained a level of income at which its marginal value became insignificant, giving rise to a new motivational mechanism. In some important respects this mechanism is distinct from that of entrepreneurs in developed market economies. According to the findings of the Russian sociologist Michael Urnov, for Russian entrepreneurs, free enterprise turned into a sport they used to fulfill their urge for "battle royal," an urge to become a winner, a desire to prove to themselves their superiority over others. They have no patience for the rules of the game nor any forms of hierarchical subordination. The power motive is very prominent in their value system (*Biznesmeni Rossii*, 1994). In contrast, the same study suggests that motivations of British entrepreneurs are determined mostly by a drive for professional improvement, pride for being able to solve creative problems, and a desire to reach a balance between work and family life.

There may be additional reasons for the Russian type of entrepreneurial behavior. One further explanation may lie in the peculiarities of national character, which, according to many scholars and observers, tends to be rather spontaneous, emotionally charged, and prone to psychological extremes and intellectual exaggerations. "The Russian is more than just a democrat; in his heart of hearts, he is an anarchist" (Kohan, 1992: 66).

From a Western perspective, another explanation for this unusual pattern of entrepreneurial motivation may be a certain backlash on the part of the people, who for decades have been deprived of any means of free expression. According to Michael Novak, "The successful entrepreneurs speedily recognize that they are smarter and more able than generals and commissars" (1994: A16). Another motivational factor is creativity, a drive to solve new and innovative problems.

Social concerns have become increasingly important motivators of Russian entrepreneurs. Many of them voice a desire to make Russia a "normal country," which implies a strong and prosperous nation. They are convinced that only entrepreneurship is capable of reviving the country. They believe that the entrepreneurial class can prevent Russia from sliding back to a communist regime, or turning into a criminal Mafia-style society, or giving way to nationalistic and fascist forces.

New Values: Has the Blame Game Come to an End?

Other new values, which the emerging Russian entrepreneurial class is forging in society, include the principles of individualism, equality of opportunities, and a belief in the creative potential of every individual. This outlook is in stark contrast to the Soviet values of the omnipotent state that provides cradle-to-grave meager subsistence to its subjects.

The principle of individual responsibility for one's life, one's successes, and one's failures is the opposite of the one prevailing in Soviet society where, until recently, there was no place for any individual expression. Russians have always been prone to the "blame game" in which there is a vague, amorphous "they" responsible for any personal failures. The "they" includes selfish relatives, greedy capitalists, corrupt bureaucrats, and the government. This trait may predate the Soviet period and perhaps is rooted in the Russian Orthodox Church which, in contrast to Western Christianity, places little emphasis on the concept of personal guilt.

Another crucial new value being forged is that of equality of opportunity. Russians have a very specific understanding of the concept of social equality that stands in contrast to that in Western countries. It is not equality of opportunity that presumes inequality of material reward in accordance with personal ability and achievement, but rather equality in distribution of wealth independently of personal effort and achievement. However, this peculiar Russian perception was not a novel idea of the Russian Communists. They simply used an age-old Russian tradition of egalitarian mentality in their ideological indoctrination, which dates back centuries and is rooted, probably, in the social order of the Russian egalitarian peasants communes.

The new Russian entrepreneurs are convinced that this type of "equality" leads only to misery and dooms Russian society. There is encouraging evidence that the public at large has begun to accept new values. Surveys testify that 58 percent of the respondents agree that "incentives for efficient work exist only when the accompanying rewards in terms of income are sufficiently different in size" (12 percent of the respondents object to this). The same percentage of respondents has nothing against high incomes for entrepreneurs while only 19 percent objected. Overall only about 25 percent of those surveyed supported the concept of egalitarian income distribution (*Interzentr-VZIOM*, 1993).

At the same time the Russian population appears to be more tolerant of income inequality. The number of those who are fully tolerant of very rich people ("millionaires") exceeds the staunch opponents (58 percent and 35 percent respectively). Mass conscience, however, accepts the new rich only if their wealth has been acquired by "honest labor." Wealth, by itself, is not necessarily regarded as a result of personal effort and ability: More than 70 percent of those surveyed are inclined to ascribe the reasons for some people being able to earn high incomes to their connections with useful people, dishonesty, volatile economic situations, and other external factors (*Interzentr-VZIOM*, 1993).

In short, it may be argued that, compared to a few years ago, the public attitude toward new market values is changing favorably. However, the contradictions of the Russian-Soviet character still remain pervasive:

1. Many Russians want a free market but with heavy state regulation (of prices, for example).
2. Russians crave for the prosperity that market relations bring but are not inclined to exert personal effort to gain this prosperity and are reluctant to give up sloppy work habits.

In short, they want free enterprise and the opportunities that it provides, but hate to bear personal responsibility inherent in them. It may require two or three generations in order to overcome such mentality.

REFERENCES

Biznesmeni Rossii. 1994. Moscow, Ao Oko.

Bower, D. D. and Hisrich, R. D. 1986. The Female Entrepreneur: A career development perspective. *Academy of Management Review*, 11: 393-407.

Carsrud, A. L. and Olm, K. W. 1986. The success of male and female entrepreneurs: A comparative analysis. In R. Smilor and R. Kuhns (Eds.), *Managing take-off in fast growth firms*. New York: Praeger Publishers, 147-162.

Fong, M. S. 1993. *The role of women in rebuilding the Russian economy*. Washington, DC: The World Bank.

Galuszka, P., Kranz, P., and Reed, S. 1994. Russia's new Capitalism. *Business Week*. October 10: 68-80.

Gasse, Y. 1977. *Entrepreneurial characteristics and practices*. Sherbrooke, Quebec: Rene Prumer Imprimeur, Inc.

Hamilton, P. W. 1993. Russian revolution. *D & B reports*. July/August: 34-37.

Hisrich, R. D. and Brush, C. G. 1986. *The woman entrepreneur: Starting, financing, and managing new business*. Lexington, MA: Lexington Books.

Hisrich, R. D. and Grachev, M. V. 1993. The Russian entrepreneur. *Journal of Business Venturing*, 8: 487-489.

Hisrich, R. D. and Peters, M. P. 1992. *Entrepreneurship: Starting, developing, and managing a new enterprise*. 2nd ed. Homewood, IL: Irwin.

Industry Week. 1992. Starting small. August 17: 38.

Interzentr-VZIOM. 1993. Ekonomicheskie i sozialnie peremeni: Monitoring obschestvennogo mnenia. August (39): 7.

Kohan, J. 1992. A mind of their own. *Time*. December 7: 66.

Krantz, P. 1994. The young and ambitious. *Business Week*. November 18: 128.

Mamardashvili, E. and Levison, A. 1993. Gospoda-tovarischi kapitalisti. *Moscovskie Novosti*, 52: 11.

Mironow, B. 1989. *V. chelovecheskom izmerenii*. Moscow.

Nezavisimaya Gazeta. 1991. September 10.

Novak, M. 1994. Democracy, capitalism and morality. *The Wall Street Journal*. December 27: A16.

Radaev, V. 1993. Etnicheskoye redprinimeteljstvo: mirovoy opit i Rossia. *POLIS*, 5: 86.

Ronstadt, R. C. 1983a. The decision not to become an entrepreneur. *Proceedings, 1983 Conference on Entrepreneurship*. April: 192-212.

Ronstadt, R. C. 1983b. Initial venture goals, age and the decision to start an entrepreneurial career. *Proceedings of the 43rd Annual Meeting of the Academy of Management*. August: 472.

Schumpeter, J. 1982. *Teoriya economicheskogo razvitiya*. Moscow: Progress. (A Russian edition of his theory of economic development.)

Sheridan, J. 1992. Russia's entrepreneurs: Pioneering the new economy. *Industry Week*. August 17: 36.

Smith, H. 1990. *The New Russians*. New York: Random House, Inc.

Stevenson, R. W. 1994. Foreign capitalist brush risks aside to invest in Russia. *The New York Times*. October 11: 1.

Warner, M. 1994. How Russian managers learn. *Journal of General Management*, 19(4): 69-88.

Weber, M. 1976. *The Protestant ethic and the spirit of capitalism*. London: George Allen Unwin Ltd.

Chapter 12

Critical Success Factors
for Entrepreneurial Ventures

Patrick J. Marx

The Revolution of 1989 brought unparalleled change to the business environment in Romania. The central planning system began to collapse and the void was gradually being filled by a market-based economy. Private enterprises formed and foreign direct investment was encouraged. In this chapter, I use the case of one print shop, Multimedia International, to illustrate the critical factors of success, and demonstrate how one company is successfully managing it's challenging start-up phase and adapting to the new business conditions in Eastern Europe. I was the financial director for Multimedia International (MI) for one and a half years. Based on the experience with MI, I then analyze a similar print shop that is on the verge of collapse, Editura Traian Dorz, and make recommendations in context of the framework of critical success factors.

MULTIMEDIA INTERNATIONAL

From Idea to Concept

Multimedia International (MI) is a medium-sized print shop in Romania that prints paperback books, tracts, Sunday school materials, and more, for evangelical Christian organizations in Eastern Europe as well as forms, advertisements, high quality color work, and most general printing needs for private and state companies. It was founded in the spring of 1992 in Arad, a city of 200,000 in the northwestern part of Romania, by the Evangelical Baptist Mission (EBM) of Kokomo, Indiana.

During the 1980s the Mission Board of EBM desired to start a print shop in Romania but was prevented from doing so by the oppressive

Ceausescu regime. The Revolution in 1989 opened the door to both missionaries and private business ventures.

In 1990 and early 1991, Dave Howard, the owner of a print shop in Kokomo and EBM affiliate, traveled to Romania on two occasions to assess the feasibility of starting a print shop. There, two men, Mircea Aioanei and Traian Deznan, were selected to manage the project. EBM arranged for a three-month training for Aioanei and Deznan at the Howard Print Shop from December 1991 to February 1992. Aioanei was trained in typesetting, computer graphics, and photo/imaging, and Deznan in platemaking, printing, and bindery operations.

EBM received used printing equipment and supplies from donors and print shop liquidators interested in the project. In March 1992, a container with the equipment, supplies, and a 20' × 34' disassembled prefabricated building for production, valued at $120,000, was sent to Romania.

Deznan and Aioanei were expected to begin operations soon after the building was set up, which only took five days. There was at least one piece of equipment for all of the core operations of a basic print shop: typesetting, photo/imaging, platemaking, printing, folding, and cutting. However, most of the donated equipment was at least 20 years old, in poor condition, and missing many parts. Only a few pieces of equipment could be repaired and put in working condition. The task ahead was daunting, all the more so since it was rumored that in nearby Timisoara, a city of 400,000, only 5 of 41 print shops started after the 1989 Revolution remained in operation in 1992.

Deznan's priorities were to prepare the facilities and equipment for production operations and to obtain all of the government approvals necessary to operate a private production company. The cost to start a private enterprise was about the equivalent of one year's salary. The process was time consuming as it involved numerous agencies and multiple forms, and the laws governing private enterprises were frequently changing.

Actions Taken by the Sponsors

During the summer of 1992, Richard Yeargain and this author, Pat Marx, of Romanian Christian Enterprises (RCE) visited Romania to explore potential business development projects. RCE is a non-profit organization whose mission is to equip and empower Romanians to emerge from their economic crisis; to proclaim the Gospel; and to infuse Romanian society with a God-given perspective on the dignity of work, vocation, and an enthusiastic affirmation of individual responsibility, initiative, and creativity. Despite the large investment by EBM and the three-month training of the Romanian managers, MI was making no visible progress and was headed toward an expensive failure. It had excellent prospects but clearly needed technical and management skills as well as capital for repairs and operation. EBM agreed to allow RCE to provide business and financial expertise, capital, and desktop publishing equipment to help get the project started. EBM also planned to send an American printing specialist, Bruce Howard.

In February 1993, Richard Yeargain, Pat Marx, and Bruce Howard arrived in Romania. Each individual raised his own financial support through their mission groups. The primary goal was to develop the project into a financially self-sufficient print shop within two to three years.

The Management Team

•Traian Deznan (42): The Director of MI, Deznan had spent eight years in the Romanian army and then worked for CET, the state electric company. There, his responsibilities grew until he reached the position of Chief of Boiler Operations in 1991. He left his high-profile, high-salaried position for a very insecure one paying only 50 percent of his former salary. He was highly respected in his church and the Arad community.

•Mircea Aioanei (28): He was the co-founder of MI with Deznan and the manager of typesetting and computer graphics. He was trained as an electrical technician and worked for four years in this profession. Aioanei was the lead Sunday school teacher at a large church, Sega Baptist, that worked closely with the project.

•Bruce Howard (32): Howard was a printing specialist who served as the production manager for MI. He had worked in small print shops since the age of ten and was highly skilled in the critical areas of a print shop: printing, photo/imaging, bindery, and machinery maintenance.

•Patrick Marx (26): Marx was trained in finance and worked for two years as a financial analyst with a venture capital firm in the oil and gas industry in Washington, DC. He was the project director for Romanian Christian Enterprises and served as the financial director for MI.

•Richard Yeargain, Executive Vice President of Field Operations for RCE (42): Yeargain served as an advisor to MI. As an experienced entrepreneur he was one of five founders of a high tech firm in the United States. In Romania, he started an apple juice company, a private adoption program, taught business classes at Arad University, and advised other businesses and ministries.

•John Fuller and Mike Hockett: As devoted Christian businessmen in Indiana, they donated most of the financial support for MI.

Adjusting to the Romanian Culture

At first the Americans found it very difficult to adjust to the Romanian culture. Neither Marx nor Howard had any training in the Romanian language prior to moving to Romania. The language impediment was not a significant problem for Howard as most of his work was mechanically oriented. He could train people by demonstrating the task and many of the Romanians knew enough English to understand his instructions. However, for Marx, the language barrier was more complicated. Many simple financial, managerial, and general business terms were not directly translatable or even had different definitions in Romanian given its usage in a command economy. Therefore, it was very important for Marx to learn the language and culture as quickly as possible in order to effectively communicate the management and financial principles to be used in managing a free enterprise. The fact that he was single and lived with a Romanian family for ten months significantly aided in learning the language and understanding the culture.

Establishing a Succinct Corporate Culture

Multimedia wanted to create a corporate culture based on Christian beliefs. Many of the basic commitments that were made are as follows:

- In Every Transaction (Bible reference): Honesty (Proverbs 11:20); Honor Others (Philippians 2:3-4); Be Dependable (Proverbs 22:1).
- Being an Example: Be Fair (Proverbs 21:3); Be Patient (Proverbs 29:11); Be Consistent (Proverbs 17:17); Be Self-Disciplined (II Timothy 1:7).
- Demonstrate Integrity: Provide Value (Proverbs 22:29).
- Treat Employees Fairly: Give Employees Honor, Honesty, Fairness (Proverbs 28:16).
- Treat Creditor's Fairly: Pay promptly (Proverbs 3:27); Absolute Repayment (Psalms 37:21).
- Treat Customers Fairly: Demonstrate Honesty, Quality, and Dependability (Deuteronomy 25:13); (Burkett, 1990).

The prevailing Romanian culture was largely a product of the collectivist mentality which deemphasized individual responsibility and accountability. Romanians in general were well educated and had good technical skills. However, individuals were not motivated to work hard or well, in the Western sense. Businesses had serious problems with pervasive unethical practices. Employees routinely stole from their employers because tools, food, and many other items were not generally available for public purchase. This was so prevalent that it became an accepted practice. Improvement in these areas was a very important focus of management, who decided that the best way to lead was by example.

Crafting a Strategy

A number of basic issues and questions were addressed by management in March and April 1993, which led to a series of action steps (Table 12.1). Based on an analysis of the competition and an assessment of its own capabilities the following product strategy was targeted:

1. Simple forms for state and private companies	30-50% of Revenues	
2. Stitched and paperback books	20-40%	"
3. Quality spot and four-color printing	10-20%	"
4. Labels for products	10-15%	"
5. Other	10-15%	"

The primary competition in Arad consisted of two large state print shops and another private Christian print shop named Easy Print. The state shops employed 50 to 75 people each, had very old equipment, focused on printing low quality government forms, had very low prices, but provided very poor service. It was not uncommon to have an order lost or have a simple order take two months. In 1994, the state shops received several 486 computers and excellent desktop publishing software, but they were slow in utilizing them. Easy Print was started by a Dutch mission group in 1990 and had equipment similar to MI. It produced good quality materials at competitive prices and frequently printed jobs for its sponsor that were destined for Holland. It only printed for Christian customers.

Successful Start-Up

The operations began as Multimedia, which was 50 percent owned by Deznan and 50 percent by Aioanei. However, EBM was concerned about using donor money to create a business that would be owned by private individuals and produce profits for private individuals. A second issue was the lingering stigma of private ownership. Therefore, shortly after the start-up all of Multimedia's assets were transferred to a new company, Multimedia International, of which the nonprofit mission, EBM of Roma-

TABLE 12.1. Initial Issues, Problems, and Action Steps

---

(1) Issues, Problems:

Objectives of the company

Company image

Managerial and organizational structure

Primary markets and customers

Product capability and future specialization

Financial resources and needs

(2) Action Steps:

Managerial/Organizational Structure:
Find honest, hard-working Christians to be trained in all functional areas
Train employees to be disciplined and customer-oriented
Form a private company authorized for import/export to be owned by
  EBM of Romania
Slowly implement merit-based pay

Marketing:
Develop a list of competitors, their production capabilities and pricing
  levels
Develop a list of potential customers and begin contacting them
Differentiate MI by quality and integrity

Production:
Repair machines as fast as possible
Determine product capabilities; focus on simple products first, improve
  quality, and then develop specialties
Develop a list of equipment, parts, and supplies needed
Develop a list of suppliers for all supplies
Improve discipline and quality in all areas

Financial:
Borrow $2,100 at 0% from RCE for Romanian paper supply and printing
  supplies from Hungary
Track all transactions
Develop a computerized pricing model
Develop an inventory of equipment and supplies
Develop a production schedule/customer database
Develop a simple double-entry accounting system

nia, retained 100 percent ownership. The managers of MI, Deznan and Aioanei, were both paid salaries and had no ownership positions in MI. MI was set up with a legal structure that permitted import/export capabilities and a waiver of income taxes for five years. An employee stock ownership plan was envisaged for some future date. Multimedia would be developed in the future as a separate publishing company.

In May, the third month of operations, MI took on its first book project while its multidirectional, mechanical folder was completely in pieces. The printing technician and an electrician rewired the folder and designed the parts that were missing. Howard gradually repaired all of the equipment and began training at least one skilled person in each area.

In July, several serious problems developed that threatened to halt the print shop: paper prices rose almost 75 percent, the invaluable cutter had mechanical problems that Howard could not solve, RCE announced plans to remove its computer resources that MI was using for desktop publishing, the government ordered state companies to buy only from state print shops, and a Value Added Tax of 18 percent was imposed. Marx created a comprehensive list of equipment and supply needs that totaled almost $65,000 and faxed it to EBM in the United States.

On Monday, August 2, production was halted and a company-wide prayer meeting was held to petition God in the name of Jesus Christ for help. On Thursday, August 5, the sponsors notified the print shop that the entire list of items, including $15,000 worth of high grade paper, would be shipped in a container in October and that advanced desktop publishing equipment should be arriving the very next day in Budapest in nearby Hungary. The following week Howard was finally able to repair the cutter. In late August, due to MI's superior quality and service, state companies slowly became customers again. We were amazed at the sudden turn of events and continued the practice of gathering for prayers every Monday.

MI ended 1993 with sales of $16,000 and a profit of $150 on 350 jobs. Including the two Americans, the company employed 12 people. Due largely to the use of the negative plate process and the computer graphics capabilities, MI gained a reputation as the highest quality print shop in Arad.

In 1994, the efforts for quality and financial discipline were paying off. MI began receiving orders from outside Romania and more state companies became customers. The president of the Arad branch of the National Bank of Romania said that MI was his favorite customer because it was the only company that did not bounce checks.

In March 1994, the best press, a Heidelberg GTO 46, had serious mechanical problems and the water system was sent back with missionaries to be repaired in the United States. In the fall of 1994, a used cutter and a van for transporting supplies from neighboring countries were bought in Germany with $20,000 provided by the sponsors. MI sales were mostly in lei and it was very difficult to get U.S. dollars legally. However, MI was not even close to being able to afford Western prices for equipment. A second shift on the presses and in the bindery was slowly being implemented and an adjoining lot was purchased for future expansion, which cost $25,000.

To comply with the government reporting requirements and in order to have useful, accurate financial information, the company kept two sets of books. One was kept manually by a Romanian accountant and met the government reporting requirements. The other set was kept on the computer and maintained by Marx. He trained replacements to maintain the production schedule, customer database, customized pricing models, and the use of computer spreadsheets for simple tasks. However, MI was unable to find someone with sufficient accounting skills to be trained to maintain the double-entry accounting system.

In April 1994, Marx returned to America. In March 1995, the printing technician returned to the United States. He had successfully trained at least one skilled person in each of the key areas of the production operations. The print shop employed 16 individuals at this time. In two years, significant progress had been made. Working side by side with Americans had several important influences on the Romanians. It created a strong, disciplined work ethic. It gave them exposure to new technology and to novel, proactive ways to solve problems, and developed a commitment to quality, timeliness, and the customer. However, MI had not yet become financially self-sufficient as it was not yet able to pay for expensive repairs or significant capital improvements.

REQUIREMENTS
FOR A SUCCESSFUL START-UP

In the Romanian business environment that is dominated by failed ventures and collapsing state companies, Multimedia International stands out as a success story. The company overcame extraordinary challenges and rapidly climbed learning curves in developing the business. MI was gradually becoming financially self-sufficient, it had survived the difficult start-up period, and was in the early growth stage.

To develop an understanding of why some companies succeed and others fail in the start-up and early growth phases in Eastern and Central Europe, I suggest five critical factors for success. Based on the experience of MI, in other firms, and additional research, I posit that firms will successfully manage through the start-up and early growth phase if the following characteristics are present in the management/ownership team:

1. Biblical ethics in managing the business;
2. Strong managerial and technical experience in a similar field;
3. Innovative approaches to improving its product and service;
4. Will to make the personal and financial commitment to long-term growth;
5. Commitment to improving financial discipline and controls.

1. Biblical Ethics

It is the personal conviction of the author that start-up companies which are guided by a management team that applies Biblical ethics are more likely to lead their companies successfully through the tremendous uncertainty and risks of starting a venture. Operating a company according to Biblical principles may cost money in the short term, but in the long run it will generally lead to a productive and prosperous venture. The three important areas affected by biblical ethics are the development of a sound corporate image and culture; the creation of a strong, honest work ethic; and the infusement of trust in a company's relationships with its employees, customers, suppliers, investors, and the community.

Given that the entrepreneur is intensively involved in the early development of a new venture, the presence of an ethical entrepreneurial team is the first step in building the company's image and in shaping individual behavior. At this stage, a company has no track record, yet potential partners, investors, or customers tend to rely on individuals' track records which underscores the need to build mutual trust as the fundamental prerequisite for building the company's future (Dubini, 1990).

MI developed a corporate culture based on integrity, honesty, diligence, quality, and compassion based on the example set by the management team. In a business environment characterized by dishonesty and poor work habits, MI made commitments in the following areas: fulfill all business commitments, be honest in the use of all company resources, and work hard and well and help others do the same. In a short time, MI distinguished itself by the quality of its products, the promptness in paying suppliers and in completing orders, a disciplined and clean work environment, and its commitment to encouraging its employees to do their best. Led by Deznan, the team strove to serve the employees in uncommon ways. For example, when a pressman experienced severe water damage in his apartment, Deznan and several employees helped repair the damage and cover the expenses.

The success of American capitalism itself was largely a result of the Protestant work ethic (Weber, 1930).

> The orderliness and industriousness of conservative Protestants, along with their severe restrictions on lifestyle that limited the opportunities for spending, led to their substantial accumulation of capital. Evangelicals are noted for their emphasis on self-discipline, hard work, thrift, and delayed gratification. It is important to recognize that such behavior reflects a pattern that has influenced the very history of American progress. (Nash, 1994, p. 18)

Weber further argued that conservative Protestantism supported a way of life that was industrious, frugal, punctual, and equitable in all its dealings. Good treatment of customers or employees was a must–not just because it made business sense but because anything else was a forgetfulness of duty (Weber, 1930).

2. Strong Managerial and Technical Expertise

Firms that have a management team with strong managerial and technical expertise in a related field are best equipped to lead a company through the start-up and early growth phases. These skills are particularly important in training the employees, developing a corporate culture and image, and focusing on quality and customer needs.

Because of the vast differences between a centrally planned economy and a market economy, the new business environment requires skills not present and previously not valued in Romanian firms. The lack of expertise in equipment repair and printing was the primary reason MI made little visible progress the first year. If the management of a new venture first demonstrates managerial and technical expertise, investors are much more likely to invest the capital that start-up ventures always need.

Though only 32 years old, Howard had almost 20 years of experience in a small shop where he was forced to become skilled at all sorts of tasks. Marx was skilled in accounting and the use of computers to enhance the productivity of many aspects of a business. Deznan, the Director, was an experienced team-builder who had a vision of creating a corporate culture based on diligence, integrity, and quality. Trained in electronics and skilled in editing, Aioanei was well prepared to take on the responsibilities of typesetting and advanced desktop publishing. The Romanians provided invaluable skills needed to operate a business in the Romanian culture, and the Americans provided specific skills that were required to develop a print shop in a market economy.

Creating a new corporate culture requires the development of a new mind-set. In this area, the roles played by the two Americans, Howard and Marx, were very significant, for they were regarded as experts in their fields and had experience working in cultures similar to what MI was trying to create. New mind-sets are not easily learned from a textbook. They are deeply held habits, values, and norms. As such, they are slow to change, and change best in the presence of respected others demonstrating their value in concrete day-to-day work settings (see Newman and Nollen in this volume). Working side by side with Westerners, the Romanians were able to witness and learn new skills in the operations of a print shop and the hard to teach attitudes of quality, timeliness, a strong work ethic, discipline, and innovation.

3. Innovation in Product and Service

Innovation is a necessary prerequisite for creating a competitive advantage in most industries. Essentially, innovativeness becomes a core value of the company and a key element of its mission. In general terms, the more innovative a company, the more uncertainties arise during the development of the business idea. Therefore, innovative companies need to be characterized by an outstanding learning ability (Dubini, 1990). Innovation is particularly important for start-ups in mature industries as they may be able to radically change the rules of the game and become very successful (Dubini, 1990).

The Romanian printing industry was in a petrified, backward stage. While most Western shops had switched to the higher quality negative plate process 20 years before, almost all shops were still using the positive plate process. MI had a significant technological edge even considering that most of its equipment was outdated by Western standards. Its computer graphics capabilities enabled it to provide a broad variety of customized products and high quality camera-ready materials in a timely fashion. The use of computer resources improved financial management, production efficiency, and overall productivity of the company.

In order to survive the rapid changes overtaking Central and Eastern European countries, companies had to switch from a production mindset to a customer focus. A continuous learning process allows a new company to grow and to adapt to the changes occurring within the environment (Dubini, 1990). The Romanian managers, Deznan and Aioanei, both of whom dealt directly with the customers, quickly adapted from a production mind-set to a customer-driven mind-set. They also rapidly learned the printing industry.

The continual process of quality improvement was lead by Howard in production and Aioanei in computer graphics and imaging. Howard strongly valued quality and timeliness; he led the production team in constantly trying to find new ways to improve both. Aioanei focused on understanding and exploiting the full capabilities of the desktop publishing equipment and software. At the same time, Howard and Marx focused on educating the donors about the best-suited equipment and software for Romania in order to overcome the company's equipment-related constraints. The Americans were invaluable in this respect because they were familiar with Western technology and knew what to request.

4. Commitment to Long-Term Growth

For a new company to survive it must be willing to commit the personal effort and sacrifices and the financial resources to pursue a strategy of long-term growth and not just short-term survival. Investment in technologies and processes that will produce a competitive edge is the foundation for long-term growth. A company that does not commit the financial resources to growth will soon find its product or service obsolete.

All members of MI's management team were deeply committed to the long-term growth of MI:

- The Romanians had left their positions in state companies and felt that this was their one chance to develop a company of their own. It was a unique opportunity for them and they demonstrated their commitment daily.
- The Americans were motivated by the desire to equip Romanians to develop their own businesses, to build a strong print shop that would provide jobs and also print Christian literature that shared the truth about the Gospel message of Jesus Christ.
- The American sponsors demonstrated their commitment to long-term growth on several occasions. The initial $120,000 investment represented a commitment for an independent print shop that could operate at a higher level of technology than what existed in Romania at that time. Shortly after the start-up of the project, the sponsors provided additional capital. Without this commitment to growth, perhaps the project would have survived and slowly made progress, but the commitment stimulated the people directly involved in the project and enabled it to progress rapidly.

5. Financial Discipline and Controls

The extent to which a business is able to accurately track its financial performance and plan for growth is frequently a major factor in small business failures. The old adage, "If you don't know where you are, how can you tell where you are going or how to get there?" is very important for the management of company finances.

Under central planning, there was no need for more than rudimentary bookkeeping because the main concern about cash was that there be enough to pay employees on pay day. There was no need for a finance function because capital budgeting and financing decisions were made and financed by central planners (see Newman and Nollen, Chapter 8). The new system required that new financial leadership must come from a market-driven financial system. A few of the important steps that Marx took to develop financial discipline were to create a simple PC-based customer/production scheduling database, a double-entry bookkeeping system, and a customized pricing model and an inventory management system on a spreadsheet. These tools enabled the company to track all sales and expenses, accurately price products and thereby take advantage of competitors' inefficient pricing, effectively schedule production, plan for capital and large supply expenditures, and adjust to constantly changing business conditions such as hyper-inflation.

EDITURA TRAIAN DORZ

Editura Traian Dorz was a print shop begun by the Lord's Army in Romania. The Lord's Army was formed within the Romanian Orthodox Church as an evangelical revival movement in 1923 by a priest named Josef Trifa and suffered considerably during the communist regime. After the Revolution of 1989, it enjoyed greater freedom to get the Bible into the hands of the people and to spread its message. Traian Dorz, a powerful leader of the Lord's Army and a prolific writer, died in 1989 and entrusted his writings to three men, Gheorghe Gogan, Ioan Beg, and Ionatan Ille.

In summer 1992, Eastern European Missions (EEM) located in The Netherlands donated an assortment of printing equipment to these three men of the Lord's Army and thus Editura Traian Dorz (ETD) was formed. The primary purpose of ETD was to stimulate the spiritual revival in Romania by printing the writings of Traian Dorz, Josef Trifa, the Lord's Army's monthly newspaper, and other Christian literature. The company was privately owned by Gheorghe Gogan, Ioan Beg, Ionatan Ille, and Valer Irinca.

The Management Team

ETD relied on three key individuals.

•Ionatan Ille (42): The talented chief editor previously had been the chief editor of another Lord's Army newspaper, Jesus the Victor. He lived and worked as a horticulturist in Simbateni, a small village located 150 km from the print shop. He was a talented leader and well respected as a man of integrity.

•Gheorghe Gogan (41): A priest and member of the Lord's Army, he was an economist and the accountant for the Orthodox Church in Arad and Deva; he worked as accountant for ETD on a part-time basis.

•Samuel Oprean (32): Trained in the telecommunications field and responsible for all printing operations, he was bright, hard working, and innovative.

The company was located in Simeria, a small town about 20 km from Deva, a city of 200,000. ETD was housed in a small, single story building; the printing equipment was at least 10 to 15 years old and most pieces were in poor, but workable condition. ETD was missing several key machines necessary for an independent print shop. Larger jobs were sub-contracted to a Christian print shop in Sibiu or the local state shop. Cutting and folding were major bottlenecks and therefore production on the presses was operating at about 20 to 30 percent of capacity.

Samuel Oprean did all of the printing, camera work, cutting, machine repair, and most of the bindery work. On at least two occasions, EEM sent printing technicians for two to three weeks at a time to train him in many basic printing operations. When a particularly large job was in the shop, like the monthly newspaper or a book, Oprean was assisted with the bindery and administrative duties by other members of the large Oprean family and of the Lord's Army. Samuel Oprean and the typesetter, Betty Oprean, were the only full-time salaried employees. There were three part-time employees that helped with the bindery and administrative work: Christina and Stefan Oprean and Gicu Gogan.

The typesetting for the newspaper, small books, and pamphlets was done by Betty Oprean. Betty lived near the print shop in Simeria, and traveled 150 km once or twice each month to complete the typesetting at Ille's house in Simbateni. The typesetting and editing were done in Simbateni because Ille was the editor and his wife was a skilled proofreader. The monthly newspaper typically required seven days of preparation and the typesetting for the other jobs was sporadic.

The newspaper, *Oastea Domnului* (*The Lord's Army*), had been published monthly since November 1992. The 16 page, two-color publication was sold in churches and on a subscription basis to 4,000 subscribers, down from 10,000 previously. Several small paperbacks and stitched books and numerous pamphlets had been printed as well. Those printed for sale by ETD, such as books by Josef Trifa or Traian Dorz, were sold through the churches and a couple of Christian bookstores in other cities. The company did a limited amount of printing for customers.

ETD was the only print shop in Simeria. In nearby Deva there were several state and one or two privately owned print shops. ETD's primary competition was not in the printing but in the publishing business because of a strong downward pressure on book prices. This was a result of the state companies printing a large quantity of mediocre-quality paperback books at very low prices.

One of ETD's most pressing problems was cash flow. The time between the cash payment for supplies and the receipt of cash from book and newspaper sales was very long: between one and six months. Payments for the monthly newspaper varied: prepayment and monthly payment for the subscriptions and monthly sales at the churches. Particularly for the printing and distribution of books, the annual inflation of 30 to 50 percent quickly eroded the value of the cash to be reinvested in working capital.

During summer 1995, the financial situation worsened. ETD had yet to have a profitable year. Every three to six months ETD received donated paper and supplies from EEM in Holland and was highly dependent on these for its survival. The company was concerned about a Romanian law that stated that if a company did not show a profit in any of the first five years of business, the government would revoke its license to do business.

In short, Editura Traian Dorz was in a similar situation to Multimedia International's in 1992 before the printing technician and financial manager arrived. EEM was disappointed with the current levels of production and cash flow. The progress made did not seem to warrant further investment and the sponsors were concerned about the apparent lack of a plan for EDT to become financially self-sufficient. The question posed to the sponsors was whether the project could be turned around, and, if so, what steps had to be taken.

ANALYSIS IN CONTEXT OF THE CRITICAL FACTORS OF SUCCESS

The situation of ETD can be analyzed by using the framework of five critical success factors that became evident during Multimedia International's experience (Table 12.2).

TABLE 12.2. Framework of Critical Success Factors and Implications: Comparison of Two Print Shops

	Multimedia International	**Editura Traian Dorz**
Biblical Ethics	Created a plan to shape image and culture based on Biblical principles	Ionatan Ille and Gheorghe Gogan are highly respected in their communities and are known as men of integrity.
	Made commitments to honesty, pay debts promptly, treat employees with honor and respect, provide a quality product, etc.	It is not known how Biblical principles are applied.
Expertise in Field and Culture	Romanian management skills—Deznan	Editing—Ionatan Ille
	Electronics—Aioanei	Electronics—Samuel Oprean
	Printing technician—Howard (American)	Accountant—Gheorghe Gogan
	Business/financial/computer specialist—Marx (American)	Needs a resident printing specialist for 2-3 years
		Needs a business/fin./computer spec. from west for 1-2 yrs.
Innovation	Initial investment in equipment provided technical competitive advantages	Innovative solutions to deal with a significant lack of critical resources—no electric cutter or folder
	Investment in advanced desktop publishing computers and software	Innovation is focussed on survival and not the creation of competitive advantages
	Investment in van and excellent used cutter from Germany	
	Leadership by Howard in production and Aioanei in desktop publishing	

Personal and Financial Commitment to LT Growth	Deznan and Aioanei rapidly learned the printing industry and adapted to the high-pressure of free-market business conditions	Initial investment lacked several key pieces of equipment and demonstrated a strategy of survival, not LT Growth
	Initial investments in prefabricated bldg., complete chain of used equipment and supplies shows commitment to growth	High personal commitment shown by friends and family working for free to help the project survive
	Follow-up investments in a van, excellent used cutter, and the purchase of an adjoining lot for expansion	Recommended that sponsors develop an LT plan that includes investments in people, equipment, facility, and supplies
	Investment in a printing technician and fin./computer specialist for 1-2 years	
Financial Discipline and Control	Computerized pricing model, production scheduling/customer database, and spreadsheets to facilitate record keeping	Accounting done manually by a part-time accountant using many unproductive principles from a command economy
	Needs a double-entry accounting system based on free-market principles	Needs a double-entry accounting system based on free-market principles

1. Biblical Principles

It was not known whether or not, and if so how, ETD applied Biblical principles in its day-to-day operations. However, it was clear that the circumstances prevented ETD from developing a coherent culture: Living three to four hours away from the shop Ille, could not exert the same kind of leadership as someone present on a daily basis. Also, Gogan was only working in ETD on a part-time basis.

2. Strong Managerial and Technical Expertise

Two of the key managers, Ille, the editor, and Gogan, the accountant, had full-time jobs that diverted their attention from the print shop. The current management team lacked skills in several important areas: operations in a market economy, computer-based accounting and production, and the skills that come from many years of experience in all areas of a print shop. The chief editor, Ille, a man of integrity and with previous experience in publishing, had only a limited role in the day-to-day operations because he lived 150 km from the print shop without a phone at his house.

Samuel Oprean, the pressman, did not have a background in printing and only had the benefit of a few short-term visits by printing technicians from Holland. He proved to be adept at learning the printing trade largely on his own. However, as MI's experience demonstrated, there was a tremendous amount of knowledge and insight to be gained by working with a highly disciplined, experienced technician.

In summary, the lack of resources within ETD and the limited amount provided by its sponsor, limited ETD to doing things the way they were done under the command economy in the areas of accounting, the levels of technology used, and common printing practices.

3. Innovation in Product and Service

The management of ETD, in particular Samuel Oprean in production and those involved in the typesetting, displayed creativity and innovativeness in their attempts to overcome ETD's significant lack of adequate resources. The lack of resources, however, suggested that the sponsors employed a survival strategy and not one of growth. The lack of an electric cutter and folder significantly limited ETD's production capability.

4. Personal and Financial Commitment to Long-Term Growth

The owners and employees of ETD and other members of the Lord's Army had demonstrated a strong personal commitment to the company as evidenced by their long hours of work and many other personal sacrifices. However, this commitment was slowly weakening as the company continued to struggle with inadequate resources. The lack of critical equipment and insufficient training prevented the development of competitive advantages that would ensure survival and lead to long-term growth.

Recall that in 1992, after it was clear that the initial resources were inadequate for MI, the sponsors responded by sending a printing technician and a financial manager to train workers and to determine the additional needs. The sponsors then met those additional equipment and supply needs. This demonstrated a commitment to long-term growth and an understanding that starting a print shop in an economy transforming from state planning to a market-based system involved a long-term plan of financial support and training. ETD's sponsors had yet to display the same commitment toward long-term growth.

5. Commitment to Financial Controls and Discipline

ETD's accounting was kept manually to meet government reporting requirements. Essentially, the role of the accounting and finance function in ETD remained at the rudimentary level that prevailed under central planning. There was no effort underway to develop accurate information for pricing, scheduling, tracking sales and customers, inventory management and so forth.

CONCLUSIONS

I have proposed a framework of critical success factors for entrepreneurial ventures in Central and Eastern Europe. In a country where economic failure is rampant, Multimedia International is one company that has good prospects for the future. After the difficulties experienced in the first phase of the venture, the sponsors of MI learned that starting a successful print shop in a country recovering from central planning required a long-range plan of investment. MI then took a comprehensive approach to developing the business that demonstrated five critical success factors: application of Biblical ethics, development of a management team skilled in the culture and in the business, a commitment to innovation in its product and service, a personal and financial commitment to long-term growth, and a diligent focus on financial management.

This plan of investment included a complete chain of equipment, one to two years of training in printing, finance, and the development of competitive advantages in the product, service, and organizational management. Although an ultimate purpose of the print shop was to include the printing of Christian literature, the sponsors and management knew they first had to focus on mastering the business of printing.

Adapting to the nascent market economy and to new technologies required a rapid learning process and a change in mind-sets for the Romanians. Given their nature, mind-sets are slow to change, and change best in the presence of respected others demonstrating their values in concrete, day-to-day settings. Romanian employees of MI successfully learned by working side by side with Western specialists in printing and finance. In this case new skills were articulated, modeled, and rewarded by respected leaders (see Newman and Nollen, 1996).

Editura Traian Dorz was in a situation similar to that which MI faced after the first phase of the start-up. For the project to be turned around, the sponsors and management need to reformulate their strategy in view of the critical factors of success. I suggest that the turnaround will be successful to the extent that the factors identified above are sufficiently addressed and incorporated in ETD's revised strategy.

The economic situation in Central and Eastern Europe poses challenges to entrepreneurs that are either unknown or are not of the same magnitude as in the West. The lack of capital, the scarcity of resources, and the lack of skills necessary to compete in a market economy increases the importance of strong relationships with business partners in the West or special arrangements with the state. I worked with seven successful companies, and the critical factor in each one's survival was a relationship that had been developed with a Western partner. The scarcity of resources dictates that an entrepreneur develop a network of contacts in state and private companies merely to obtain resources that are readily available in most Western countries. While an entrepreneur in the West is usually entering a market with existing competitors and is under great pressure to provide a significant improvement in quality, price, or innovation, the entrepreneur in Romania often encounters little competition initially but must focus instead on overcoming all of the systemic inefficiencies that exist because the infrastructure that supports productive businesses simply does not exist yet.

The government and its banking system also pose significant obstacles. The inefficiencies of the banks and the restrictions on the use of hard currencies force entrepreneurs to devise creative financing solutions that are often "technically" illegal. The legal framework is gradually reflecting free-market principles, but still contains countless impediments that continue to serve to concentrate the power in the hands of the state and frustrate the efforts of entrepreneurs to develop private businesses. Dealing with laws that are obscure and frequently changing is a constant struggle. Despite the government's rhetoric about being open to free enterprise, the entrepreneur in Romania is usually plagued with paranoia about the state's desire and power to destroy private businesses. Overcoming this mind-set and focusing instead on creative solutions to all of the business problems, is often the difference between a successful and an unsuccessful entrepreneur in Romania. The obstacles, both real and perceived, to entrepreneurial activity in Romania are indeed significant and require a tenacity, flexibility, and creativity that may exceed that required to succeed in the West.

REFERENCES

Burkett, L. 1990. *Business by the Book*. Nashville, TN. Thomas Nelson, Inc., Publishers.

Dubini, P. 1990. Assessing new ventures success. In S. Birley (Ed.) *Building European Ventures*. Amsterdam: Elsevier: 179-195.

Nash, L. 1994. *Believers in Business*. Nashville, TN. Thomas Nelson, Inc., Publishers.

Newman, K. and Nollen, D. 1996. "Managerial Challenges During Organizational Re-Creation: Industrial Companies in the Czech Republic," in this volume.

Weber, M. 1930. *The Protestant Ethic and the Spirit of Capitalism*. Trans. Talcott Parsons. London: Unwin Paperbacks, 1930.

PART IV:
STRATEGIC AND OPERATIONAL REORIENTATION

Chapter 13

Influences on Strategic Decision Making in the Romanian Banking Industry

Patrick Arens
Keith D. Brouthers

In developing a market economy the tasks of banks are extremely important. Proper functioning of the financial system is crucial for the success of the transition toward a new economic system (Westlake, 1992). In Central and Eastern Europe, banks traditionally played an administrative role restricted to collecting and distributing funds. Strategic decisions regarding products offered and markets served were made by government representatives, not bank managers (OECD, 1992a). Since the reforms of 1989, banks are faced with the task of making strategic decisions that will dramatically affect their future.

Strategic decisions are in various ways influenced by the external environment, characteristics of managers, and rational analyses based on objective variables (Fredrickson and Iaquinto, 1989; Hitt and Tyler, 1991; Lawless and Finch, 1989; Neu, 1992; Schwenk, 1988). Research indicates that in highly turbulent environments, the influence from the external environment is most important (Dean and Sharfman, 1993; Fredrickson and Iaquinto, 1989; Schoemaker, 1993). Although the rate of change varies across countries it is clear that all firms operating in these newly opened economies face a highly turbulent business environment. For this reason it is important for firms located in Central and Eastern Europe to be aware of their strategic options.

In this chapter we explore the strategic decision-making processes in the Romanian banking industry with the help of a framework for understanding firms' decisions in highly turbulent environments (Oliver, 1991).

We attempt to (1) identify which institutions in the banks' environment are trying to influence the banks; (2) investigate what types of strategies these external institutions are trying to get the banks to follow; and (3) determine what the response is of the newly independent bank managers.

THE ROMANIAN BANKING INDUSTRY

Romania concluded a period of dictatorial rule in December 1989. Since then, the Romanian economy experienced high inflation and a decline in production which was at least in part due to the misallocation of resources during the era of the planned economy. Living standards deteriorated and the abolishment of subsidies on food articles caused further pain and social unrest (Ionescu, 1993a, 1993b; Shafir and Ionescu, 1993).

In this volatile environment banks have to transform themselves to become efficient, profit-oriented organizations. However, the banks' efforts are impeded by severe obstacles. First, the banks have substantial amounts of bad debt that cannot be written off because they lack capital. Thus they remain dependent on large, loss-making state enterprises for continued cash flow which implies continued misallocations of financial resources (OECD, 1992b; Sandu, 1993a, 1993b). The banks are also confronted with material constraints (Roşca 1993), an inadequate legal infrastructure (Popescu, 1993; Sandu, 1993a), obsolete payment systems, and rudimentary capital and money markets (OECD, 1992a; Sandu, 1993a, 1993b). Management and employees lack adequate training, skills, and for-profit experience (OECD, 1992b; Westlake, 1992). To conclude, Romanian banks find themselves in a turbulent, unstable environment for which they are poorly prepared.

Historically, the Romanian banking industry consisted of the national bank that functioned as a central bank and also provided commercial services. Additionally, the industry included an investment bank that financed long-term projects, an agriculture bank, a savings bank, and a foreign trade bank (Severa, 1979). With the introduction of a market economy, a new two-tier banking system was established. The national bank was transformed into a Western-style central bank. Its commercial activities have been assumed by the commercial bank. The investment bank was converted into the development bank which has subsequently diversified toward a universal bank, as have the agriculture bank and the bank for foreign trade (Georgescu, 1993). Private banks have also been established.

Romanian banks need modern technology, capital, skilled staff, and an adequate legal infrastructure. In the early 1990s, international organizations such as the European Community, the International Monetary Fund (IMF), the European Bank for Reconstruction and Development (EBRD), and the World Bank were starting to support the Romanian banks (Pântea, 1993; Roşca 1993).

STRATEGIC DECISION MAKING

Strategic decisions are commitments of large amounts of resources and have important effects on the long-term performance of the firm (Fredrickson, 1985; Schwenk, 1988; Shrivastava and Grant, 1985). Scholars have proposed various ways to explain and predict how managers make strategic decisions (Eisenhardt and Zbaracki, 1992; Hitt and Tyler, 1991; Schwenk, 1988). Proponents of the *strategic choice* framework believe that strategic decisions and processes are predominantly influenced by characteristics of managers (Bantel and Jackson, 1989; Barnes, 1984; Mintzberg and Waters, 1985). When managers are confronted with ill-structured, complex, and uncertain strategic questions they use heuristics to simplify the decision-making process. Since these vary from person to person, these heuristics may create systematic biases and consequently influence strategic decision making (Barnes, 1984; Hitt and Tyler, 1991; Schwenk, 1988). In the view of these researchers, ". . . human factors in the executive ranks greatly affect what happens to companies" (Hambrick, 1989: 5).

A second group of researchers which adheres to the *rational normative model* believes that an optimal strategic decision can be determined on the basis of a comprehensive analysis of the external and internal environments (Ansoff and Sullivan, 1993; Porter, 1991; Schwenk, 1988). Management biases, filtering, internal politics, etc., are assumed not to exist, or at best to have only a minimal effect on the strategic decision-making process. A third group of researchers emphasizes the role of the external environment on strategic decision making. External forces may influence the firm in two broad ways. First, firms are not independent and have to be responsive to demands from the external environment. This limits the options that are open to the firm (Pfeffer and Salancik, 1978). Second, institutional isomorphism theory stresses the role of powerful forces in the environment (institutions) that induce the firm to resemble other firms in the same industry (Dimaggio and Powell, 1983). These two views are part of the field of strategic decision making called *environmental determinism.*

In highly turbulent environments it is believed that *environmental determinism* is the most important predictor of strategic decision making (Dean and Sharfman, 1993; Fredrickson and Iaquinto, 1989; Schoemaker, 1993). Under such conditions, rational and synoptic planning systems may prove to be too slow. Characteristics of managers also may be of less importance when the firm is confronted with an environment that constrains its strategic choices to the utmost.

METHODOLOGY

Data Source

The main source of data for this study was the Banca Român ă pentru Dezvoltare S.A. (BRD). The BRD is the successor of what, under the previous system, was the investment bank. During the central planning era it financed long-term projects in a broad range of industries and conducted comprehensive audits of state enterprises. Since the reforms BRD has acquired clients among all kinds of industries including from the private sector and now provides services to individuals as well. It is connected to the international payment system, and serves as an agent for loans from international financial organizations such as the EBRD, the World Bank, and the IMF. The BRD is the only bank that is authorized to distribute shares and to conduct other activities related to the privatization of Romanian enterprises.

BRD's Board of Directors is responsible for the bank's strategy, structure, and organizational capabilities. Representatives from the Central Bank, the Ministry of Economy and Finance, and the Ministry of Industry all serve on the board which is supposed to represent its shareholders. At the time of this study the bank's equity capital (about U.S. $30 million) was totally provided by the state. The BRD's Board of Directors delegates the day-to-day operations of the bank to the managing committee which is chaired by the chairman of the board.

The BRD has about 40 branches in Romania. At the branch level, functional departments report to their parent departments at headquarters as well as to the branch manager, who in turn is responsible to one of the headquarter's vice presidents. In cooperation with their deputies, the branch managers take care of the most important customers. The branches have to file extensive formal reports with the head office, and must request approval for important investments, for credits beyond a certain limit, and for hiring and laying off of personnel.

Survey Instrument

Oliver (1991) uses institutional and resource dependency theories to explain how organizations respond to outside pressures. She identifies five distinct types of institutional and environmental characteristics that influence a firm's strategic choice. One extreme of the range of responses a firm can take is acquiescence, or unqualified conformity to the demands of the outside interest groups. This suggests a situation where management feels that not conforming would have severe consequences for the firm. At the other extreme is a manipulative response. It is used when a firm feels it can avoid compliance with outside demands, and attempts to change these to pursue what management considers to be the appropriate strategy.

Based on this framework we developed a questionnaire in order to measure (1) the differing perceptions of prevailing institutional pressures on the Romanian banking system and on BRD specifically; (2) the strategies the banks and BRD specifically should adopt according to the outside influential organizations; and (3) the strategies the BRD should adapt according to BRD management.

Respondents

The respondents were selected based on three criteria. First, they had to be abreast of the developments in the banking industry in Romania. Second, they had to be involved in dealings with BRD. Third, the respondents should have a management position within their respective organization.

The internal group of respondents consisted of managers of the BRD. Three members of the management team of the BRD branch in Braşov, as well as a vice president, two executive managers, and one subdirector at the head office of the BRD were included in this internal response group. The external group of respondents consisted of representatives from various external interest groups (Dimaggio and Powell, 1983; Pfeffer and Salancik, 1978). Input was obtained from a wide variety of external groups including competitors; state-owned enterprises as well as private customers; government organizations such as the Central Bank, the Ministry of Finance, the National Privatization Agency, the City Council of Braşov; the Chamber of Commerce; the main opposition party in the Romanian parliament; and the media.

Variables

The questions were originally written in English, translated into Romanian, and then translated back into English, etc., until the translations corresponded (Sullivan and Bauerschmitt, 1990).

- *Operationalizing Oliver's Predictors:* Oliver (1991) suggests five pairs of environmental relationships: (1) reasons for institutional pressures; (2) degree of conflict among constituents' expectations; (3) consistency of pressure with firm's goals; (4) form of external pressure; (5) level of environmental uncertainty. These relationships were captured in a series of questions.
- *Determination of Influence Groups and Level of Influence:* Following a recommendation by Pfeffer and Salancik (1978) each respondent was requested to rate 27 external interest groups according to their influence on the BRD's strategic decision-making process.
- *Choice of Strategy:* In order to determine BRD's preferred short-term strategy (two years maximum) the respondents were requested to rate 12 different bank strategies based on a previous banking study (Jaja, 1989).
- *Measurement of Environmental Turbulence:* Based on a survey of current literature we assumed the level of environmental turbulence in the emerging economies of Central and Eastern Europe to be very high. To ascertain this we included a set of questions for measuring the level of environmental turbulence (Ansoff and Sullivan, 1993). Respondents were asked to give their opinion as to the speed of changes, their complexity, recency, and their predictability in six domains of the Romanian economy: (1) the banking industry; (2) industry competition; (3) economic trends and events; (4) technical developments; (5) regulatory constraints; and (6) customer behavior.

FINDINGS

Table 13.1 shows the breakdown of respondents. Customers make up the largest portion. Seven competitors–five Romanian banks and two of foreign origin–represent the second largest group. Then follow public interest and media groups, and finally BRD managers and government agencies.

Influential Institutions

Table 13.2 indicates that external organizations consider the Central Bank and the Ministry of Finance as the two most influential groups, followed by the World Bank, IMF, Western banks, the EBRD, and the government (both national and local). In contrast, BRD managers perceive

TABLE 13.1. The Respondents to the Questionnaire

Respondent type	Number of respondents	Percentage of total respondents
Head office management	4	6%
Branch management	3	5%
Competitors	7	11%
'State' customers	28	42%
Private customers	12	18%
Public interest groups	4	6%
Media	6	9%
Central Bank	2	3%
	66	100%

the World Bank and Central Bank as the most influential followed by the IMF, training institutions, and Western consulting firms. Overall, outsiders attribute competitors a higher level of influence than organizational insiders, although competitive pressures are not regarded that significant by either group.

It is interesting to note that, with three exceptions, the bank managers rated the external institutions' influence levels lower than did the organizations themselves. They did not think these outside organizations had as much influence on the strategic decision-making process as the organizations themselves believed to have.

Preferred Strategies

Both managers of the BRD and representatives of the outside organizations were asked to provide their perceptions of the importance of 12 possible strategies the BRD could pursue. Recall that Oliver (1991) hypothesized that in a highly turbulent environment, as the pressure exerted from external constituents increased, the strategic responses available to the firm would become more limited until the firm would be restricted to one strategy only—to comply fully with external pressures.

Bank managers considered maximizing product improvement (average score 6.71), followed by technology implementation and deposit growth (each 6.57), competitive leadership (6.42), regulatory compliance (6.28),

TABLE 13.2. Mean Ratings of Outside Influence Groups

Interest group	Amount of influence Managers	Outsiders
1. Central Bank	4.71	5.80
2. Ministry of Finance	3.57	5.69*
3. World Bank	4.86	4.73
4. International Monetary Fund	4.43	4.66
5. Western banks	3.00	4.32
6. European Bank for Reconstruction and Development	3.57	4.10
7. Government / townships (as customers)	3.43	4.00
8. Training institutions	4.17	3.83
9. Consultancy firms	4.43	3.73
10. State companies	2.86	3.86
11. Private companies	1.71	3.51*
12. National Privatization Agency	3.14	3.61
13. Foreign Trade Bank (competitor)	1.71	3.74*
14. Media	3.00	3.47
15. Regii autonome (enterprises that will not be privatized)	2.57	3.24
16. Ministry of Industry	2.57	3.14
17. CEC (savings bank)	1.86	3.19*
18. Chamber of Commerce	2.14	2.95
19. Commercial Bank (competitor)	1.71	2.95*
20. Individual customers	1.57	2.73*
21. Banca de Agricole (competitor)	1.71	2.59
22. Universities	2.00	2.34
23. ASIROM S.A. (insurance)	1.57	2.46*
24. Coop Bank (competitor)	1.43	2.25*
25. Dacia Felix (competitor)	1.43	2.22*
26. Post Bank (competitor)	1.43	2.14
27. Mind Bank (competitor)	1.43	1.98

Notes:
   Scales range from 1 (no influence) to 7 (most influence).
   * Significant differences at $P < .05$.

and marketing effectiveness (6.16) as being the most important strategies. Taken together, managers expect a combination of ways to improve the bank's internal operations and growth as being the most viable path toward competitive leadership. Some strategies conflict with the efficiency emphasis, for example, maximizing deposit growth. The rationale behind this strategy is fairly clear. At present the banks rely on the state for capital and most have extended credit to former state-owned firms that are in default. Thus one good source of capital would be increased deposits. However, an emphasis on deposit growth would require the banks to pursue an aggressive expansion which may be risky as long as resources are scarce, skill levels low, and operating systems old.

Outside interest groups perceive achieving competitive leadership as being the bank's most important strategy (6.10), followed by product improvement (6.03), pursuit of growth and profitability (5.98), regulatory compliance (5.78), and new business development and technology implementation (each 5.76). External constituents therefore advocate the bank a posture focused on improving products and operations as well as introducing new types of services.

Statistical analysis indicates significant differences in the assessment for only three out of 12 strategies between insiders and outsiders: product improvement, deposit growth, and regulatory compliance. Each of these was rated higher by managers (Table 13.3).

Environment turbulence received a score of 4.48 out of a possible maximum of 5. Thus, both groups viewed the conditions under which BRD operated as very turbulent.

Environmental Constraints on Strategic Choice

Oliver (1991) posits that as external pressures rise, so should agreement between the bank managers and outside organizations regarding the importance of strategies options and vice versa. Table 13.4 shows the perceived levels of institutional pressures arising from different sources in the environment.

We found that six of the ten institutional pressures were perceived as high by both groups. Also, statistical analysis indicates a relatively high level of agreement between the two groups: significant differences existed for two of the ten sources of external pressure. Only in the case where both parties perceived the pressures to comply with the demands of the external institutions as high, should we find acquiescent behavior on the part of the BRD. If BRD management perceives the pressures as low then the bank would be relatively free in its strategic choice. The form of compliance and noncompliance would be apparent from the similarity in the assessment of strategic options. Since only six of the ten properties of institutional pressures were considered high we would not expect total agreement on all strategies; in fact, we would expect significant differences in strategic priorities between bank management and the outside interest groups as confirmed by the results summarized in Table 13.3.

TABLE 13.3. Student's T-test for Mean Differences in the Perceived Importance of Strategy Types Between Managers and Outside Interests

Variable	n	Mean	S.D.	p
Maximizing growth and profitability				
Management	7	6.1429	1.069	.747
Outsiders	56	5.9828	1.249	
Maximizing product improvement intensity				
Management	7	6.7143	.288	.012**
Outsiders	59	6.0339	1.203	
Maximizing marketing effectiveness				
Management	6	6.1667	1.169	.362
Outsiders	59	5.6610	1.295	
Maximizing market share				
Management	7	5.5714	1.134	.761
Outsiders	59	5.4237	1.511	
Maximizing return on investment				
Management	6	5.6667	1.211	.420
Outsiders	59	5.32034	1.700	
Maximizing new business development				
Management	7	5.5714	1.718	.756
Outsiders	59	5.7627	1.512	
Maximizing technology implementation				
Management	7	6.5714	.535	.207
Outsiders	59	5.7627	1.512	
Maximizing product innovation				
Management	7	6.1429	1.069	.136
Outsiders	59	4.4068	1.533	
Maximizing deposit growth				
Management	7	6.5714	.787	.064*
Outsiders	59	5.3729	1.649	
Maximizing lending growth				
Management	7	4.8571	1.069	.309
Outsiders	59	5.3390	1.469	
Maximizing competitive leadership				
Management	7	6.4286	.535	.217
Outsiders	59	6.1017	1.170	
Maximizing compliance with regulatory requirements				
Management	7	6.2857	.488	.077*
Outsiders	59	5.7797	1.565	

Note: The scales range from 1 (no importance) to 7 (very important).
* denotes significant differences at $p < 0.10$.
** denotes significant differences at $p < 0.05$.

TABLE 13.4. Student's T-test of Mean Differences in the Perceived Level of Institutional Pressures Between Managers and Outside Interests

Variable	n	Mean	S.D.	p
1. Pressure for social legitimacy				
Management	6	5.5000	1.643	.818
Outsiders	59	5.6780	1.805	
2. Pressure to become efficient				
Management	6	6.1667	1.329	.272
Outsiders	59	5.4576	1.897	
3. Multiplicity of constituents				
Management	6	2.6667	1.506	.358
Outsiders	59	2.0339	1.129	
4. Dependency on constituents				
Management	6	2.6667	1.506	.000**
Outsiders	59	5.4746	1.695	
5. Consistency with own goals				
Management	6	5.8333	1.169	.399
Outsiders	59	5.3559	1.885	
6. Less decision-making ability				
Management	6	5.0000	1.897	.579
Outsiders	59	4.4576	2.299	
7. Pressure by legal coercion				
Management	6	5.1667	.983	.158
Outsiders	58	6.0000	1.389	
8. Voluntary commitment				
Management	6	5.5000	1.871	.617
Outsiders	59	5.9153	1.381	
9. Environmental uncertainty				
Management	7	3.1429	1.215	.094*
Outsiders	57	4.2632	1.685	
10. Interconnectedness				
Management	7	3.8571	1.574	.845
Outsiders	59	4.0000	1.838	

Note: The scales range from 1 (low pressure for conformity) to 7 (high pressure for conformity), except line 3 where the scale ranges from 1 (few) to 5 (many).

* denotes significant differences at $p < 0.10$.
** denotes significant differences at $p < 0.05$.

DISCUSSION AND CONCLUSIONS

There are a number of organizations attempting to influence the course of banking activity in Romania. Among them, the Central Bank and the Ministry of Finance are perceived as having the most influence on the strategic decision-making process of BRD and, most likely, other banks as well. This is a logical result given the fact that most banks are owned by the state, which also has seats on the banks' board of directors. Moreover, these two state agencies have the power to regulate the Romanian banking industry. It is therefore important for Romanian banks to meet the demands of these authorities. Other influential external organizations include international financial institutions such as the IMF, the World Bank, and the EBRD which is also not surprising given their support to the banking industry. Other Western organizations, such as banks, consulting firms, and training institutions are also perceived to have a relatively strong influence on BRD's strategic decision making. The experience, skills, and capital of these organizations are important resources for the further development of Romanian banks.

In contrast to what may be expected in a developed market economy, relatively low levels of influence are attributed to competitors suggesting low levels of competition. Two reasons may account for this. First, the large number of new customers during this transitionary stage of Romania economy may cause management to think that competitors do not matter given that the banks are experiencing difficulties serving the current number of customers well. Second, the strong pressure exerted by the regulatory authorities may impede competition between the banks. However, this could be only a short-lived phenomenon. There are signs that the Central Bank will stimulate competition (Sandu, 1993a). Moreover, the rise in new customers may only be temporary.

The range of external constituencies affecting BRD's conduct seems to be fairly typical of most emerging countries in Central and Eastern Europe: A high level of dependence on state agencies on the one hand and on Western institutions providing support on the other hand. Competition still seems to be at a nascent stage. We can assume that these external influence groups are likely to transform the BRD and other Romanian banks to upgrade their level of performance and to become properly functioning banks.

Our findings related to the importance of the 12 strategy choices confirm the fact that management and the outside interests do not fully agree on the importance of the strategies the banks should pursue. Most strikingly, the importance of rivalry is viewed rather differently by managers and outside constituents. Both agree, however, on the importance of upgrading operations and product offerings.

REFERENCES

Ansoff, H.I. and Sullivan, P.A. 1993. Empirical proof of a paradigmic theory of strategic success behaviors of environment serving organizations. In D.E. Hussey (Ed.) *International Review of Strategic Management*, 4: 173-203. New York: John Wiley & Sons.

Bantel, K.A. and Jackson, S.E. 1989. Top management and innovations in banking: Does the composition of the top team make a difference? *Strategic Management Journal*, 10: 107-124.

Barnes, J.H., Jr. 1984. Cognitive biases and their impact on strategic planning. *Strategic Management Journal*, 5: 129-137.

Dean, J.W., Jr. and Sharfman, M.P. 1993. Procedural rationality in the strategic decision-making process. *Journal of Management Studies*, 30(4): 587-610.

Dimaggio, P.J. and Powell, W.W. 1983. The iron cage revisited: Institutional isomorphism and collective rationality in organizational fields. *American Sociological Review*, 48: 147-160.

Eisenhardt, K.M. and Zbaracki, M.J. 1992. Strategic decision making. *Strategic Management Journal*, 13: 17-37.

Fredrickson, J.W. 1985. Effects of decision motive and organizational performance level on strategic decision processes. *Academy of Management Journal*, 28(4): 821-843.

Fredrickson, J.W. and Iaquinto, A.L. 1989. Inertia and creeping rationality in strategic decision processes. *Academy of Management Journal*, 32(3): 516-542.

Georgescu, I. 1993. Instituţiile economiei de piaţă îşi diversifică oferta. *Capital* (Supliment Financiar Bancar), 2(1): III.

Hambrick, D.C. 1989. Guest editor's introduction: Putting top managers back in the strategy picture. *Strategic Management Journal*, 10: 5-15.

Hitt, M.A. and Tyler, B.B. 1991. Strategic decision models: Integrating different perspectives. *Strategic Management Journal*, 12: 327-351.

Ionescu, D. 1993a. Romania's cabinet in search of an economic strategy. *RFE/RL Research Report*, 2(4): 45-49.

Ionescu, D. 1993b. Wave of workers' protests in Romania. *RFE/RL Research Report* (News Briefs), 2(17): 12.

Jaja, R.M. 1989. *Technology and banking: The implications of technological change on the financial performance of commercial banks*. Unpublished doctoral dissertation, United States International University, San Diego, California.

Lawless, M.W. and Finch, L.K. 1989. Choice and determinism: A test of Hrebiniak and Joyce's framework on strategy-environment fit. *Strategic Management Journal*, 10: 351-365.

Mintzberg, H. and Waters, J.A. 1985. Of strategies, deliberate and emergent. *Strategic Management Journal*, 6: 257-272.

Neu, D. 1992. The social construction of positive choices. *Accounting, Organizations and Society*, 17(3/4): 223-237.

OECD. 1992a. Bank restructuring in central and eastern Europe: Issues and strategies. *Financial Market Trends*, 51: 15-30.

OECD. 1992b. *Reforming the economies of central and eastern Europe*. Paris: OECD.

Oliver, C. 1991. Strategic responses to institutional processes. *Academy of Management Review*, 16(1): 145-179.

Pântea, M. 1993. Banca Mondială susţine reforma în ţările sărace. *Capital*, 2(6): 13.

Pfeffer J. and Salancik, G.R. 1978. *The external control of organizations*. New York: Harper & Row Publishers Inc.

Popescu, I. 1993. Secretul bancar, secretul lui polichinelle? *Capital*, 2(11): 7.

Porter, M.E. 1991. Towards a dynamic theory of strategy. *Strategic Management Journal*, 12: 95-117.

Roşca, A. 1993. Odiseea conturilor bancare. *Capital*, 2(12): 13.

Sandu, T. 1993a. Mugur Isărescu: Rezervele Ţării Scad Dramatic. *Capital*, 2(11): 13.

Sandu, T. 1993b. Eugen Rădulescu: Acum Trebuie Ruptă Pisica. *Capital*, 2(16): 11.

Schoemaker, P.J.H. 1993. Strategic decisions in organizations: Rational and behavioral views. *Journal of Management Studies*, 30(1): 107-129.

Schwenk, C.R. 1988. *The essence of strategic decision making*. Lexington, MA: Lexington Books.

Severa, D. 1979. Das Bankwesen in Rumänien. *Die Bank*, 12: 602-607.

Shafir, M. and Ionescu, D. 1993. Romania: Political change and economic malaise. *RFE/RL Research Report*, 2(1): 108-112.

Shrivastava, P. and Grant, J.H. 1985. Empirically derived models of strategic decision making processes. *Strategic Management Journal*, 6: 97-113.

Sullivan, D. and Bauerschmitt, A. 1990. Incremental internalization: A test of Johanson and Vahlne's thesis. *Management International Review*, 30(1): 19-30.

Westlake, M. 1992. Can the banks fly? *The Banker*, (September): 20-26.

Chapter 14

Hungarian Enterprises: Marketing in Transition

Wade Danis
Andrew Gross
Robert D. Hisrich
Emeric Solymossy

INTRODUCTION

Since 1989, Hungary as one of the former Council for Mutual Economic Assistance (CMEA) countries has been experiencing economic and
political transformation. For the most part, these changes occurred in the
absence of changes in underlying cultural values or managerial attitudes.
This has impacted various functional business areas, including marketing.

This chapter focuses on four Hungarian enterprises in four distinct
industrial sectors to illustrate the course of action each company has taken
to "reinvent" itself. They need to redefine their marketing activities as
companies are wrestling with identifying their markets and satisfying both
old and new customers with their marketing efforts in the process of
evolution.

The four enterprises are: (1) Tungsram, a formerly state-owned enterprise with a 100-year tradition of making lamps and lighting devices that
has become a majority-owned subsidiary of General Electric company;
(2) Videoton, a 50-year-old manufacturer of industrial and consumer electronics; (3) Peko Steel Works, a new, small steelmaker trying to rise from
the ashes of an old, large one; and (4) Graphisoft, a small, new enterprise,
offering computer-assisted drafting software for architects.

Each firm is grappling with some basic concepts: Where are our markets and how can they best be approached? What are our strengths and
weaknesses? What opportunities and threats exist in executing the marketing concept?

With the traditional markets disrupted by the dissolution of the centrally planned economies of the CMEA companies in Hungary have been thrust into the international competitive market system. This has forced Hungarian companies to concurrently seek alternative (generally Western) markets and enhance production efficiency within a market-oriented context.

The official economic dogma of the socialist-communist countries maintained that private enterprise and its marketing functions were inefficient for achieving the objectives of social equality. The old and new thinking is succinctly captured in the annual report of Fotex, a major Hungarian enterprise.

> Marxist economics had a strange way of measuring economic activity: Output was the sum of the inputs plus the labor applied to them. Physical production (tonnes of steel, cubic meters of concrete) was all that mattered. What was left out of the equation were such questions as, "does anyone want to buy these goods at *any* price?", "Are the goods in the right place at the right time?" Not surprisingly, distribution and retail systems were grossly under-developed in socialist economies. The state owned shops were simply places where goods were stored until people bothered to buy them. The issue of consumer choice was easily dealt with: no-one asked the public how they would like to be governed, let alone what they would like to buy. (Fotex, 1993)

The antithesis of the old thinking is the so-called market concept which entails focusing the activities of the firm on the satisfaction of the firm's stockholders. Each firm recognizes that the most effective means to attain competitive advantage and achieve the firm's objectives is planning and coordinating all the company activities around the primary goal of satisfying customer needs. Under the market concept, the consumer becomes the dominant focal point of the firm, with all the resources and activities in the firm directed at generating customer satisfaction.

The adoption of the market concept by many firms in Western economies was precipitated by several factors.

- Intensity of competition increased both nationally and internationally, forcing organizations to place greater emphasis on consumer satisfaction.
- The level of consumer knowledge and sophistication has grown significantly. As consumers become increasingly aware of the various options available, only those products and services that are recognized as "need satisfying" will be purchased. Consumer awareness

has been aided by elaborate communication systems. The communication system has informed consumers of faulty products (such as General Motors recalling specific models of cars or trucks), price increases (such as U.S. Steel announcing a forthcoming price increase on rolled steel), and fraudulent advertising (such as the Federal Trade Commission investigating the claims of American Express). This increased awareness has enabled consumers to be much more discriminating in their purchase decisions.

• Production capabilities expanded in conjunction with the development of mass worldwide markets. Increased production capacity has led to economies in the scale in the production process. The added capacity can only be sold through successfully reaching mass markets by focusing on customer satisfaction.

• Finally, the need for innovative products for survival has forced firms to place their customers first. A key element to successful new product introductions–and between 80 to 90 percent fail–is knowing the needs and buying habits of the target group of customers.

RESEARCH METHODOLOGY

The research method consisted of personal interviews and observations in Hungary over six years since 1989 and supplemental contacts with representatives of the selected organizations in the United States as well as commercial counselors at Hungarian consulates. The interviews varied in length from fifteen-minute telephone conversations to half-day presentations by corporate officials. In addition, an extensive literature search was carried out covering electronic data bases in the United States and small circulation journals in Hungary. Each of the four firms was discussed with academic colleagues, industrial managers, and selected consultants with economic, financial, and market information obtained directly from the headquarters of each organization to the extent possible.

HUNGARY: A NATION OF CONTRASTS

In 1996, Hungary, a small Central European country of 10.5 million people, will celebrate its 1100th anniversary. For eleven centuries, this nation has barely survived at the crossroads of East and West, absorbing the culture, economics, and politics of one side, then the other. Years of Turkish, Russian, Austrian, and German subjugation did not obliterate the nation. Instead, Hungarians pride themselves as being distinctive citizens of Central Europe.

The major characteristic of Hungarians is the ability to survive, even to prosper, under adverse circumstances. Regimes come and go, but the culture remains. The traditions of Hungarian society put an emphasis on both common sense and intelligence. Education, which has become rather rigid, has a solid scientific and literary base.

From 1949 to 1989 Hungary experienced many periods of political repression and economic collectivization. But after 1968, the country embarked on what became known as "goulash communism"–an era of loosening the reins. Command and control slowly gave way to valuing managerial know-how. While the economy was certainly not market-driven or customer-oriented in the 1970s and 1980s, entrepreneurship still began to flourish. After 1989, major economic reforms began to take shape. From 1989 to 1991 the number of state-owned enterprises declined from 2,600 to 2,100 and their share of the value added in the economy declined from 51 to 35 percent. During the same period, the number of private enterprises quintupled to 36,600 and their share of the value added grew from 6 percent to 21 percent. The number of sole proprietorships almost doubled and their share of the value added grew from 6 percent to 10 percent (OECD, 1994). The economic transformation was certainly under way (Kornai, 1990).

But the road to a market economy is not easy; shifting from a socialist system is not completed overnight. The processes of liberalization, decentralization, and privatization are evolving; the pace is not fast and occasional setbacks occur (World Book, 1992). Yet the evidence is impressive and is further supported by the breadth and depth of foreign direct investments as well as the number of joint ventures and alliances between Hungarian and Western partners (Table 14.1).

Such ventures afford opportunities for reforming state enterprises, public agencies, and cooperatives. Tungsram and Videoton are two examples of privatizing, large investing, partnering, and contract manufacturing/ marketing.

HUNGARIAN ENTREPRENEURS

According to our own observation and reports of others, including those at the World Bank, the dynamics of entrepreneurship in Hungary is more complex and widespread than in most other former CMEA countries. Generally, Hungarian entrepreneurs in manufacturing resemble their counterparts in Poland, the Czech Republic, and Slovakia; they are fre-

TABLE 14.1. Major Foreign Direct Investments in Hungary

Domestic Company	Foreign Interest	Business	Investment ($ millions)
Tungsram	General Electric, USA	Lighting	350
GM Hungary	General Motors, USA	Engines, cars	250
Audi Engine	VW-Audi, Germany	Engines	200
Magyar Suzuki	Suzuki, Japan	Car assembly	180
Hungaria Insurance	Allianz, Austria	Insurance	124
Ford Hungaria	Ford, USA	Car components	123
Hunguard Glass	Guardian Glass, USA	Float glass	120
NMV Vegetable Oil	Ferruzzi, Italy	Oil, detergents	120
Hungarian Investments	Inst. Investments, UK	Investment fund	100
Compack Packing	Sara Lee, USA	Food packing	100
C/E International Bank	Intl. bank, various	Commercial banking	87
Dunapack	Prinzhorn, Austria	Paper	82
First Hungarian Invest.	Inst. Invest., USA	Investment fund	80
Malev	Alitalia, Italy	Airlines	77
Intercontinental Hotel	Mariott, USA	Hotel	77
Chinoin Pharmaceutical	Sanofi, France	Pharmaceuticals	75

Source: Adapted from *Invest in Hungary*, 1993, 4th quarter, Exhibit 4.

quently middle-aged men with a technical education and previous employment in a large, state-owned enterprise. Hungarian entrepreneurs also come from two other groups: quasiprivate enterprises or cooperatives, and new entrants with little or no experience in private business. One-third of Hungarian entrepreneurs owned another private business in the past; one-quarter owned more than one (Webster, 1993).

In examining the personality traits of the Hungarian entrepreneurs, clear differences emerge between them and their Polish, Czech, and Slovak counterparts. Compared to the others, Hungarians are more likely to describe themselves as high achievers, restless, and bored with routine; as eager to take risks; and as independents and loners (Table 14.2).

These Hungarian entrepreneurs also see themselves as less practical, less disciplined, and less concerned with control than their counterparts. They have a deep desire for information whether from domestic or foreign sources and are deeply passionate about their new ventures. Peko Steel

TABLE 14.2. Self-Described Qualities of Hungarian Manufacturing Entrepreneurs

Quality	No. of Responses	% of Responses
High achiever, easily bored with routine	52	19%
Risk-taker, willing to live with uncertainty	45	16%
Like to feel in control of what is going on	40	14%
A practical person with practical skills	36	13%
Highly disciplined, committed to hard work	33	12%
Independent, somewhat separate from others	32	11%
Self-confident, fairly sure of success	29	10%
Grew up in a difficult, troubled family	10	4%
Other	4	1%
TOTAL	**281**	**100%**

Note: Entrepreneurs were shown this list of personal qualities and were asked to choose the three that described them best. Sample consisted of 113 individuals, 94 men and 19 women.

Source: Webster (1993: 25).

and Graphisoft are our two examples of small Hungarian firms headed by the "new entrepreneur."

EAST-WEST COLLABORATION:
THE SEARCH FOR NEW MARKETS

The future of the Hungarian economy and its enterprises will depend much on the commitment of political leaders to reform measures. Another key factor is the extent to which East-West collaboration occurs; whether it is in the form of Western firms coming to Hungary or Hungarian enterprises seeking Western markets. For Hungary, foreign trade has been and will continue to be crucial. Traditionally, imports and exports combined to about 40 percent of GDP. Similarly, foreign investments and partnering now loom critical in rebuilding the economy and as a means to assimilate the knowledge and competencies required to compete in a free-market, competitive environment. The key is that the flow must be a two-way street, thereby overcoming the many impediments.

Hungary's attraction is its skilled labor force, its low wages, engineering know-how, and the pervasive entrepreneurial spirit. The country also offers a staging market for access to neighboring countries. Negative elements in the country include a 20 percent-plus inflation rate, an antiquated infrastructure, pollution, and bureaucratic rules (World Book, 1992). For Hungarian firms looking westward, the lure is the size of the export markets, domestic job creation, travel for managers, and infusion of technology and capital. Negative factors include Western resistance to "cheap imports" from the East, the cost of doing business, and the high probability of failure. Hungarian firms must learn about the complexities of distribution and promotion abroad in order to be successful.

These factors unfold in various ways in the four enterprises investigated. While each is examined in further detail below, there are some key facets.

• In the case of Tungsram, the absorption into the General Electric family assures its rejuvenation, particularly in terms of capital inflow and renovation, and becoming a major player in the global lighting markets. The price paid included a painful downsizing and the realization that wage increases would not be automatic, but rather tied to productivity improvements.

• For Videoton, the arrangement calls for an emphasis on contract manufacturing with well-known firms, such as IBM, Thompson, and Philips, assuring some job stability and access to markets.

• For the two small firms in the study, the key consideration was the promise of export markets. Peko Steel was optimistic that it could build on the remains of DAV, an old-fashioned steel mill, and believed that it could focus on selected steel users in neighboring countries. Capacity was not a problem, but antiquated technology, competitors, and difficulties in finding clients proved to be major obstacles. In the case of Graphisoft, its entry into Western markets, especially the United States, was eased due to low entry barriers and a partnership with Apple Computer. The timing was also right on its marketing of high-end architectural software.

EAST AND WEST:
IMPLEMENTING THE MARKET CONCEPT

While Peter Drucker once said that the purpose of a profit-seeking enterprise is to *create* customers, in today's competitive era, it is also essential to *retain* existing customers in a mutually beneficial, long-term relationship. In this context the market concept means delivering a product, or service, to a select group of clients, which meets or exceeds their expectations. In the past, enterprises in Eastern Europe seldom met this requirement or any other concerning timeliness of delivery, follow-up service, etc. It was a seller's market with buyers accepting what was delivered.

Following the radical transformation throughout the region in 1989 to 1990, enterprises found themselves in turmoil. Reliable sources of supply and the stable base of clients, often assured by the CMEA alliances, bilateral treaties, barter, and other long-term arrangements had suddenly disappeared. The progressive enterprises in the nations of Central and Eastern Europe now began to sense new opportunities. Even though the markets in the former USSR were no longer assured or had lost their buying power, the markets of the West and developing nations were open. Hungarian entrepreneurs began to evaluate these markets and implement the market concept in this new context.

While the market concept is being implemented in many Hungarian companies and especially in those whose outlook is favorable, there are situations in which such an effort has taken a different form. In several sectors of the Hungarian economy, especially in food, pharmaceuticals, tobacco, and retailing, Hungarian firms have been acquired by Western firms for their distribution channels, patent holdings, or contractual relationships. In some cases, the Hungarian firm was effectively shuttered after the acquisition and its product line replaced by higher-priced Western goods. The workforce was given a choice of early retirement, indefinite layoff, or termination. This procedure has not endeared such foreign firms to the Hungarian public.

What is common to the four enterprises reported in this study is their genuine dedication to becoming market-driven and customer-oriented. First, each firm recognized that it had to reassess its base of actual and potential clients in terms of customer expectations. Second, each realized that the external environment was not a forgiving one but rather was teeming with numerous competitors. Third, the delivery of the respective product or service had to carry not just the tangible item or verbal promise, but a high level of assured quality surrounded by presale and postsale service. These are the common market-oriented elements of Tungsram, Videoton, Peko Steel, and Graphisoft.

ENTERPRISE #1:
TUNGSRAM (GE LIGHTING SUBSIDIARY)

Tungsram is an old name in the history of Hungarian industry; it is a 100-year-old company with a proud tradition of making a wide variety of lamps and lighting systems. It has enjoyed good business relations with East and West; for example, it supplied headlights for many years to

Mercedes Benz. But during the 1949 to 1989 era, it operated in a controlled environment that enabled it to emphasize sheer volume, full employment, and personal passivity. Many factory lines were in dire need of renovation; marketing was hardly practiced. With the advent of privatization and the dissolution of its established trading patterns within the CMEA, Tungsram began seeking an alliance with a firm capable of improving both its marketing position and its marketing know-how.

General Electric is a large diversified U.S. firm with an avowed bent for market share, which was succinctly summarized by CEO Jack Welch in his famous statement about GE's far-flung collection of businesses: "Unless we are #1 or #2, we shall improve it, close it, or sell it" (Reich, 1992). GE was looking for acquisitions or joint venture opportunities in the new Eastern Europe. Tungsram's strength was in one of GE's original fields. GE has a solid record of making lamps and lighting equipment at Nela Park in Cleveland, Ohio as well as other locations around the world. Since GE's market share in Europe for this line of business in the 1980s was a very low 2 percent, investing in Tungsram would be a fine fit. GE brought to the table an emphasis on productivity, marketing know-how, cost containment, and product quality, elements that Tungsram was seeking from a prospective partner. Just as important, upon arrival, GE did not lay off many workers and installed an ex-Hungarian as chief executive. The original stake of 50 percent was purchased by GE from an Austrian bank for about $150 million (Bruner, 1992).

The honeymoon lasted about two to three years. GE became frustrated with continued losses and the slow pace of progress. By 1991 to 1992, GE decided to install a new leader, to lay off several thousand, and to increase its holding in Tungsram to 75 percent. It also allowed early retirement and trained some workers to become suppliers. Still, this was not enough and losses continued (Table 14.3).

According to *The New York Times*, "grand expectations collided with the grim realities of an embedded culture of waste . . . and indifference about customers and quality" (Perlez, 1994: C1. See also Legg, 1994; McClenahan, 1992; Schares, 1993). Hungarian workers were called lazy by U.S. managers who, in turn, were labeled pushy. The low productivity and lack of efficiency among Hungarian workers was also evident with Suzuki's entrance into the Hungarian market, leading to speculation that Hungarian production was below world standards (Okolicsani, 1992). The GE style of "action workouts" designed to get more productivity, coupled with wages falling behind inflation (wages were averaging $2/hr in mid-1994), fueled resentment on the part of workers, causing further motivational problems.

TABLE 14.3. Tungsram (GE): Selected Indicators

	1989	1990	1991	1992	1993	1994
Employees (thousands)	18.0	17.6	14.3	11.0	8.6	10.0
Ownership by GE	50%	56%	75%	75%	97%	99%
Investment by GE (mil US $)	150	90	90	280	280	280
Profit (Loss) (mil US $)	22(?)	loss	loss	(104)	even	prof.
GE's (Tungsram, Thorn) est. share of Eur. lamp market	3%	10%	17%	18%	18%	19%

Source: GE Lighting and author's estimate based on interviews.

Since the acquisition, productivity has improved manifold; some assembly line workers are being rehired; GE received another five-year tax holiday, and expects profits for 1994 and subsequent years. The dialogue between managers and workers continues, though the union is still upset. Building upon the 100-year-old Tungsram name, GE has seen its share rise to almost 20 percent of the European lighting market, and it is a solid #3 after Philips and Osram. The market is mature, so the key is aggressive selling to commercial, industrial, and residential end users, an already established customer base. While facing two solid, established competitors and the possibility of new competitors from developing nations, there is growing acceptance of GE-Tungsram's products among mass merchandisers in the U.S. market. The SWOT (Strengths, Weaknesses, Opportunities, Threats) analysis suggests that Tungsram can achieve its objectives and keep the parent company happy (Table 14.4).

As stated by John Betchkal, then Director of Corporate Communications for GE Lighting: "We came to Hungary for the long run and we expect that our investments will pay off by the end of the decade."

ENTERPRISE #2: VIDEOTON

Videoton was formed in 1938 and after 1945 became a dominant supplier of consumer and industrial electronics domestically and to neighboring nations, best known for its televisions and radios. The firm was assigned a key role in supplying military electronics to the USSR and other members of the CMEA, permitting it to expand into defense commu-

TABLE 14.4. SWOT Analysis for GE-Tungsram

Strengths
100-year tradition of brand, technology, product quality
Large financially strong parent
Global presence; combined with Thorn, 20% share in Europe
Downsizing, but retaining key talent as workers/suppliers
New management and merit system; upgraded/new facilities

Weaknesses
Major downsizing–morale and motivation problems
Attitudes and values hard to change; union objections
Bottlenecks and red tape with supplies and suppliers
Old-fashioned accounting/financial controls; change slow
Changes in top management; changes in training format

Opportunities
Competitors also have own problems, reorganizing
Market mature, but accepting new types of lamps and devices
Established client base: industrial/commercial/residential

Threats
Slow growth in the marketplace, especially Europe and USA
Two large competitors well established (Philips, Osram)
Developing nations' production facilities (India, Taiwan)
Complex distribution; shift of client base (DB, BMW to USA)

---

nications and security products. Typical of many state-owned companies in centrally planned economies, Videoton's structure was highly centralized and vertically integrated, controlling everything from means of production to distribution and sales channels. In addition, Videoton was also highly diversified, with its diversification decisions dictated by decrees of central planners rather than industry attractiveness (Kovacs, 1994).

In 1989, it was the industry leader, commanding 25 percent of Hungary's industrial electronics production. The collapse of the Soviet and COMECON markets, as well as the opening of formerly closed markets to foreign competition, had a devastating effect. With the exception of a small number of products that were sold in Western markets, all of Videoton's products were exported to the Soviet Union and other COMECON countries or sold to the Hungarian military. Reorganization proved to be painful and fruitless. From 1989 to 1991, revenues decreased from 21 bil

HUF to less than 6 bil HUF. By 1991, having lost more than 70 percent of its sales, the company was driven into bankruptcy. In early 1992, the company was privatized and purchased by a group of executives with entrepreneurial orientation; Euroinvest, a regional investment group; and the Hungarian Credit Bank, which took a controlling 60 percent share.

The newly privatized firm, still the largest Hungarian electronics enterprise, was given its marching orders by the new owners: Go and find Western partners and Western markets to utilize the excess production capacity. The former proved easier than the latter, but both goals are now being reached. The short-term strategy was survival; the long-run strategy growth. Western-style financial and accounting controls are being put in place. The organizational restructuring meant not only a slimmer workforce (about 5,300 in 1993) but the establishment of several independent profit centers. Unprofitable product lines are being terminated.

Videoton's immediate post-privatization marketing strategy can be described as ad hoc, opportunistic, and not tightly directed. The key concerns were: utilizing excess manufacturing capacity and space; retaining the skills of the existing labor force; avoiding further layoffs; generating cash flow; and stemming losses. In short, the early 1990s was truly an era of survival with reliance on orders from domestic firms and from small to medium size Austrian and German customers. While few sales provided high value-added activities, Videoton kept insisting on high product quality.

By 1993, Videoton's prospects were clearly improving; the firm had achieved a measure of financial stability (Table 14.5). Just as important, it signed up several Western partners for contract manufacturing. Repositioning the company as a subcontractor of electrical and mechanical com-

TABLE 14.5. Videoton: Selected Indicators

	1989	1990	1991	1992	1993	1994
Total Revenues (bil forints)	23.2	22.17	6.0	9.5	10.5	13.1
Operating Profit (Loss) (bil forints)	.5	(1.9)	(1.0)	(.3)	.1	.2
Revenue/Employee (forints)	1300	1400	550	1550	2200	2400

Note: Revenue by division in 1993 was as follows: contract manufacturing = 35%; consumer electronics = 16%; defense electronics = 9%; sales and service = 26%; all other = 14%.

ponents was paying off in several ways: jobs, capital, and technology infusion, and assured clientele. Philips of the Netherlands provided the early bulk of jobs and profits. At the end of 1994, IBM transferred its German magnetic head manufacturing to Videoton. A five-year cooperation agreement has been signed with IBM which promises both enhanced sales and further technology transfer. Videoton lined up other strategic partners: Akai, Alcoa, Fuba, Sony, and Mars Electronics. Since the corporate image and the brand names were still considered a solid asset in Central Europe and beyond, they are cultivated by Videoton which was eager to enhance its reputation further in Western markets. This reorientation emphasized its strengths and market opportunities, while minimizing weaknesses and threats (Table 14.6).

TABLE 14.6. SWOT Analysis for Videoton

Strengths
55-year tradition of quality manufacturing; brand name and corporate image
Experience/entrepreneurial managers; reorganized workforce
New partnerships/alliances; capital and technology infusion
Good location of plants; upgrading plant and equipment
Change focus from defense electronics; contract manufacturing

Weaknesses
Workforce cut back; wages higher than neighbor nations
R&D reduced significantly; little market research
Morale, motivation, training of workers; pension liability
Slow implementation of new accounting/financial controls
Contract manufacturing implies lack of control over destiny in 1990s

Opportunities
Diversified client base, receptive to old and new products
Large Western firms eager for low wage contract manufacturing
Capital infusion and technology, transfer likely to continue
Competitors also need to reorganize/redefine businesses

Threats
Expiring contracts will need to be replaced
Decline in defense electronics; saturating consumer goods
Sales and service from Hungary viewed with suspicion
Complex distribution and bureaucratic red tape abroad

ENTERPRISE #3: PEKO STEEL

During the past 15 years, global steel production capacity exceeded global steel demand by a wide margin. As a result, many old steel mills were closed in Western Europe, the United States, and elsewhere. After 1989, Polish, Hungarian, and other nations' old furnaces were shuttered, including Ozd Steel and Foundry. A year later, on the remains of this enterprise, Janos Petrenko established a small steel operation with 27 employees and called it Peko Steel Works (Brunner, 1994). The mill signed a leasing contract to operate certain facilities in the shut-down Ozd plant. The operation began with a credit line of 90 million HUF; by year end, Peko Steel had sales of 1,500 million HUF, 45 percent of it coming from abroad (Table 14.7).

Janos Petrenko is no ordinary businessman. Starting at the age of 15 in 1955 at the Ozd foundry, he moonlighted as a metallurgical technician. By 1978 he turned his second job into a full-time enterprise with a handful of workers. In the 1980s he won three grand prizes at the Budapest International Fair. While the initial year for Peko Steel was a success, the next year, 1991, proved to be painful, because the firm lost its cheap source of energy and the Hungarian government lifted tariffs on imported steel. Foreign markets proved tougher to enter than before. The workforce had to be slashed as sales and revenues decreased 50 percent. By finding some new customers in Hungary and abroad, sales rebounded in 1992, though not to the level of 1990.

During 1990 to 1993, Petrenko started other entrepreneurial ventures, such as servicing machinery, wholesaling, and commercial credit operations. His other personal commitments included intensive negotiations with energy firms and attending numerous trade shows. Petrenko also chose to establish branches or to hire agents in the West. Finally, he ran and was elected to Parliament. The far-flung operations of the company were carried out using family members and trusted colleagues. Despite some delegation, the various tasks were really undertaken or at least championed and/or supervised by the head of the enterprise, resulting in his near exhaustion. In early 1995, Petrenko decided to focus on his service and commercial ventures, and Peko Steel closed its doors. This was a painful but not surprising decision (Table 14.8).

While Petrenko undertook some limited market research and located a few clients for his steel output, he was fighting an uphill battle all the way–overcapacity in the industry, higher energy prices, foreign competition, and antiquated equipment. Petrenko could not emulate the lesson of the minimills in other countries which built their facilities anew, not on the skeletons of old mills. Beyond external factors, Petrenko overextended

TABLE 14.7. Peko Steel: Selected Indicators

	1990	1991	1992	1993
Turnover (Sales) (mil forints)	1500	800	1200	1500 (?)
Production Index (1990 = 100)	100	50	65	85 (?)
Employees (est.)	50	200	150	200
Export sales as % of total shipments	45%	35%	45%	50% (?)
No. of new non-steel ventures started by owner	–	2	6	14

Source: Peko Steel and author's estimate based on interviews.

TABLE 14.8. SWOT Analysis for Peko Steel

Strengths
Founder and family-run, entrepreneurship, loyal employees
Diversity of operations; branched into commercial services
Experience in steel industry; familiarity with technology
Private ownership; no overseeing by outsiders, board
Name recognition, political connections, trade show experience

Weaknesses
Limited funds, limited credit, antiquated accounting
Narrow marketing vision for extending steel sales
Managers with limited experience, low marketing skills
Other business operations demand more attention
Overextension, little market research, not known in West

Opportunities
Shutdown of state steel operations at home and abroad
Cost advantage over Western steelmaking companies
Physical distribution choices now broader in scope
End users ready to embrace small producer with drive

Threats
Global and local overcapacity in steelmaking and fabrication
Competition from other materials, foreign steel firms
Marketplace wants value-added products and expanded services
Experienced workers available but poor motivation and morale
No more protective tariffs or quotas from government

himself, a common occurrence among new entrepreneurs. The number of major new ventures proved to be too burdensome and in many ways too attractive when compared to the steel mill operations. The external environment and internal weaknesses overwhelmed Peko Steel.

ENTERPRISE #4: GRAPHISOFT

In 1980, a few enterprising mathematicians, fed up with bureaucratic state enterprises, established a computer software firm in Budapest. Two years later, the small operation, named Graphisoft, made a successful bid against larger competitors and obtained a contract to carry out computer modeling for a large Hungarian nuclear power plant. This provided a financial cushion and allowed the young entrepreneurs to design new programs for other industries and occupations. Displaying its three-dimensional modeling program for engineers at trade shows in West Germany in 1983 and 1984, Graphisoft was able to demonstrate its expertise and to obtain several hard-currency contracts.

Graphisoft then designed some key architectural software programs to run on Apple computers. While a few hundred users embraced the offering due to its low cost and appealing features, others balked because they were wedded to IBM compatible machines and Graphisoft's name was not well known. But by the late 1980s Apple's Macintosh line was upgraded to execute high performance engineering application. Graphisoft tied its fate to Apple and sold 1,000 ArchiCAD programs in 1988, 2,000 in 1989. It also developed yet another high-end design, TopCAD, and European users responded favorably.

By 1989, the company decided to take the risk and enter the largest, yet toughest markets of them all: the United States. Its two key executives, G. Bojar and G. Kafka personally conducted market research and to this day carry on both the financial calculations and the market assessment (Vecsenyi and Hisrich, 1994).

They found the U.S. marketplace different from the European. Competition was keener, promotion was more aggressive, and distribution channels were far-flung and complex. But a display of Graphisoft programs at an architect trade fair resulted in favorable reviews, word-of-mouth advertising, and eventually a user's club. Pricing of ArchiCAD and TopCAD was at the high end, but compared favorably with programs designed for mainframes and workstations. All these steps enhanced the corporate image and the brand names, and sales continued to climb in the 1990s. By the end of 1992, Graphisoft had established distribution in 45 countries, and had captured 30 percent of the global market for architectural programs operating with Macintosh computers, outselling Apple's own Claris software unit (Levine, 1993).

With a staff numbering about 60, mostly in Budapest, Graphisoft continues to improve its offerings, making them even more user-friendly. It also worked hard at competitive intelligence, benchmarking itself against rivals, especially Autodesk with its AutoCAD offering. Graphisoft must still improve its distribution channels in the United States. The dealer network is inadequate and follow-up service at client locations needs to be stronger. Graphisoft is now embarked on rectifying these matters and may add to its sales staff (Table 14.9). The company is hard at work in assessing trends in all regions, especially North America and Europe. Since there is clear indication of some saturation, Graphisoft is determined to

TABLE 14.9. SWOT Analysis for Graphisoft

Strengths
Early experience with small computers, software, and modeling
Easy to use products, constant upgrading, some services
Alliance with Apple Computer; cultivating relationship
Lower costs for programmers, designers; shoestring marketing
Penetrated European markets with skill; doing well in USA

Weaknesses
Narrow product line and end-use applications; must expand
While labor costs are lower, pays $30,000 per analyst in Hungary
Software program is compatible only with Apple, not IBM
Few strong ties with resellers, dealers, and distributors
Company is not as well-known as others; limited marketing

Opportunities
Current users are enamored with features offered; they like the programs
New end users are growing in number, even in Third World countries
Old buildings need restoration; constitute added market
Professionals want network capabilities; Graphisoft is moving there

Threats
Slow growth in number of architects and engineers in West
Schools of architecture have closed due to lack of demand
Saturation approaching in CAD products and services
Strong competitors in USA and Europe with money and reputation
Building relationships with dealers/users takes time and money

develop a new generation of architectural and engineering programs plus other offerings, including network applications (Table 14.10).

TABLE 14.10. Graphisoft: Selected Indicators

	1989	1990	1991	1992	1993
Turnover/Sales ($ thousands)	380	840	2400	4500	6000
Expenses ($ thousands)	880	1450	2560	3500	4500
Pretax Profit (Loss) ($ thousands)	(500)	(610)	(160)	1000	1500
Worldwide sales of MacCAD type programs (000 of units)	55.0	57.0	63.0	63.2	63.5
North American sales of high-end MacCAD programs (000 units)	15.4	16.2	18.2	19.4	20.0
Graphisoft sales of high-end MacCAD programs (thousands of units)	0	.1	.8	1.6	2.7

Source: Graphisoft and author's estimate based on interviews.

DISCUSSION

The unique aspects applicable to each organization are concerned with matching their strengths and weaknesses vis-á-vis opportunities and threats in the external environment.

The first level of assessment along these lines is the notion of a product-market matrix. While it is possible for any one organization to be in all four quadrants of such a matrix, even large enterprises see themselves as belonging to one quadrant at a given point in time. For GE-Tungsram, the combination of an established product in a mature market determines their location in the matrix, while Videoton is seeking to develop new products and adapt new technologies, thereby trying to re-create an established market. Graphisoft, while offering a new product is also creating a new market, as well as attempting to create further new markets through diversification. Peko Steel, although providing a traditional (old) product, attempted to develop new markets, albeit unsuccessfully (Table 14.11).

The second level of assessment addresses market focus, using another matrix to show country-market expansion. Graphisoft is demonstrating a narrow focus in both market and country, as opposed to GE-Tungsram, which is actively seeking diversification both in countries and markets

TABLE 14.11. Product-Market Matrix for Four Hungarian Enterprises

		MARKET	
		OLD	**NEW**
PRODUCT	**OLD**	Market Penetration GE-Tungsram	Market Development PEKO Steel
	NEW	Product Development Videoton	Diversification Graphisoft

served. Compromising between the two extremes of narrow focus and broad diversification, Peko Steel maintains geographic concentration while seeking market diversification. Videoton, on the other hand, is maintaining a market concentration, while seeking to expand its marketing outlets by diversifying into other countries (Table 14.12).

TABLE 14.12. Country-Market Expansion for Four Hungarian Enterprises

		MARKET	
		Concentration	**Diversification**
COUNTRY	**Concentration**	Narrow Product Focus Graphisoft	Country Focus PEKO Steel
	Diversification	Country Diversification Videoton	Global Conglomerate GE-Tungsram

GE-Tungsram needs to penetrate existing markets in all major regions around the globe with its quality lighting equipment and lamps. It must battle for market share against two key global competitors, Philips of the Netherlands and Osram, a subsidiary of Siemens (Germany). For Videoton, the emphasis is on rejuvenating the product line; it has to move away from defense electronics and old-line industrial systems into specific components manufactured on a contract basis, while at the same time improving their quality to permit their favorable competion in the international marketing arena. There is a need for entering new markets, a task in which its partners will assist. For Peko Steel, the key was on selling steel products to established as well as new customers in nearby countries. Finally, Graphisoft must penetrate the lucrative U.S. market with its newly designed architectural software, as well as with continued product innovations that can keep up with technologically improved computers.

CONCLUSION

This chapter has looked at marketing in a new context—how the marketing concept is evolving in Hungarian enterprises. Clearly, political and economic transformations have changed the landscape of Hungary. At the same time, many traditions, attitudes, and values have altered very little. The concepts of marketing orientation and entrepreneurship are alive and well among select Hungarians, especially those in small companies. In larger firms, it takes much longer to bring about the desired results.

By history and design, Hungary, a small nation, has long been reliant on foreign trade, investment, and business alliances. Involvement across national borders has grown by leaps and bounds after the tumultuous events of 1989. Western companies have entered Hungary in search of business and Hungarian firms have started penetrating Western markets. The early days of euphoria and hope for a "quick buck" have given way to cold reality, but even so, many opportunities remain.

What is most notable is that the reorientation toward the market concept, and specifically the focus on customer service, has not been accompanied by many formal market research activities. Much business intelligence is gathered on an ad hoc basis. Retaining old clients and finding new ones is still a matter of word-of-mouth, "old boy" networks and similar personal contacts, and in some cases political connections. Once survival is more assured and the environment less chaotic, it is likely that firms will implement more formal planning that will be preceded by more formal marketing intelligence activities.

Accomplishing the marketing task—delivering product or service that meets or exceeds expectations—will be no easy assignment, even in such large firms as Tungsram or Videoton. It is even more of a challenge for smaller enterprises. External and internal forces can combine to cause failure, as in the case of Peko Steel, or to cause success, as in the case of

Graphisoft. No firm can rest on its laurels; indeed, few firms continue to remain on top, year in, year out.

Achieving success requires commitment at the level of the individual, the group or division, the corporation, and ultimately the nation. It also means altering attitudes and social habits. While this can be done, it often takes years, as evidenced by the Tungsram workers. Companies may need to reorient themselves as shown in the example of Videoton's switch to contract manufacturing, and companies must establish distant markets as Graphisoft did. One key element that helps greatly is to have a well-to-do-parent, as GE is for Tungsram; strong partners infusing technology and capital, such as in Videoton; or a friendly ally, as Apple proved to be for Graphisoft. Going it alone is still very dangerous.

REFERENCES

Bruner, R. 1992. Tungsram's Leading Light. *International Management*, December: 42-45.

Bruner, R. 1994. The Wizard of Ozd (Peko Steel/J. Petrenko). *International Management*, November: 54-57.

Economist Intelligence Unit. 1994. *Hungary: A Survey*. London: EIU.

Fotex First American-Hungarian Annual Report, 1993.

Kornai, J. 1990. *The Road to a Free Economy.* New York: W.W. Norton.

Kovacs, P. 1994. Videoton Is Diversifying. *Hungarian Business Weekly*, November 9: 1-3.

Legg, G. 1994. No More Party Games: Electronics in Hungary. *EDN (Electronic Design News)*, August 20: 56-57.

Levine, J.B. 1993. Hungarian, High-Tech, and Programmed to Sell. *Business Week (Europe)*, March 15: 98.

McClenahan, J.S. 1992. Light in the East (GE Tungsram). *Industry Week*, March 2: 14-19.

OECD. 1994. Committee on Cooperation with Economies in Transition and Hungarian Central Statistical Office. *The National Accounts of Hungary*, Paris: OECD.

Okolicsanyi, Karoly. 1992. Hungary: A Car Industry is Born. *RFE/RL Research Report*, 1(19): 39-41.

Perlez, J. 1994. GE Finds Tough Going in Hungary. *The New York Times*, July 25: C-1, C-3.

Personal or phone interviews with selected officials at four organizations: Graphisoft, Peko Steel, Tungsram (GE), and Videoton.

Reich, L.S. 1992. Lighting the Path to Profit: GE's Control of the Electric Lamp Industry. *Business History Review*, Summer: 305-333.

Reynolds, P. and P. Young. 1992. *Eastern Promise: Privatization Strategy for Post-Communist Countries.* London: Adam Smith Institute.

Schares, G.E. 1993. GE Gropes for the On-Switch in Hungary. *Business Week (Europe)*, April 26: 102E-103E.

Vecsenyi, J. and R. Hisrich. 1994. Graphisoft: The Entry of a Hungarian Software Venture into the U.S. Market. In *Business Research and Management Challenges*, S. Peter, (Ed.). Budapest: International Management Center.

Webster, L.M. 1993. *The Emergence of Private Sector Manufacturing in Hungary: A Survey of Firms, Technical Paper No. 229*. Washington: World Bank.

World Bank. 1992. *Hungary: Reform and Decentralization of the Public Sector, Vols. I and II, Report No. 10061-HU*. Washington: World Bank.

Chapter 15

Patent Protection
for Central and Eastern Europe:
Lessons from the West

G. Scott Erickson

A recent focus by scholars on national innovation systems (NIS) has brought questions concerning technology-generation mechanisms squarely into the public policy debate. Where the issues were formerly highly theoretical and/or considered independently of unique national circumstances, scholars are beginning to consider the full scope of a country's environment for innovation from quite practical perspectives. This strain of the literature has raised interesting questions about the fit of concrete pieces of the NIS with a nation's peculiar strengths and weaknesses.

This discussion has generally been limited, however, to the major trading nations. Japan and the United States have received substantial attention, precisely because they are so different yet so successful in generating new technological products. The significant changes that the world economy has undergone in the past decade, however, beg the same question for countries outside the Global Triad (United States, Japan, European Union).

The issues are far different from those during the heyday of development studies considering the necessity of intellectual property protection in poorer nations. Given the rise of the Newly Industrialized Countries of Asia, the stabilization and growth of the economies in Central and South America, and the recent capitalistic intentions of Central and Eastern Europe, it is germane to consider the structure of national innovation systems in nations at unique stages of growth. Does one particular system

The author gratefully acknowledges the research assistance of Blake Jackson and the comments of two anonymous reviewers.

fit all? Should each incorporate U.S., European, or Japanese law as a whole, or should thought be given to the circumstances of individual regions or nations?

This chapter considers part of this question in relation to the countries of Central and Eastern Europe. A critical piece of any NIS is the patent system, designed to protect and disseminate technological information. By exploring the structure of the patent systems of the United States, Japan, and Germany, we can shed some light on the place patent law and practice have in generating technological output. The differences in the results of each system are enlightening and will allow room for recommendations on an optimal course for Central and Eastern Europe states seeking to modernize their economies.

BACKGROUND

National innovation system studies have grown out of a historical interest in considering which public policy spurs the greatest number of new technological products, an important potential source of national competitive advantage (Porter, 1990). Indeed, the concept that innovation drives capitalist economies dates to Schumpeter (1934), who also noted how the interactions between innovators and the political system could influence output. In recent years, the discussion has grown much more specific. Nelson (1982, 1984, 1990a, 1990b), for example, has done a substantial amount of work in this field, considering national differences in approaches to technology. These inquiries have focused on both national economic environments and specific governmental initiatives. Rosenberg's (1982) more micro-level analysis has also brought out some of these issues, and their joint work establishes the current state-of-the-art of NIS studies for individual countries (Nelson and Rosenberg, 1993).

Related work centers on these NIS's and measures impact by comparing relevant macroeconomic data. Patel and Pavitt (1987), Mowery (1992), and Mowery and Teece (1993) have considered Western Europe, the United States, and Japan, respectively, with an eye to the specific differences in the overall technology-generation environments and their visible impact on key indicators of innovation success.

The basic concept of a NIS is captured in Figure 15.1. Successful new product innovation efforts move from creative invention to commercial innovation. A great deal of attention in the earlier literature focused on firm-specific variables which influence this process. The impact of the size of the firm, its experience with the various stages of the process, the ability of firms to provide both freedom and structure, and other factors

FIGURE 15.1. The National Innovation System

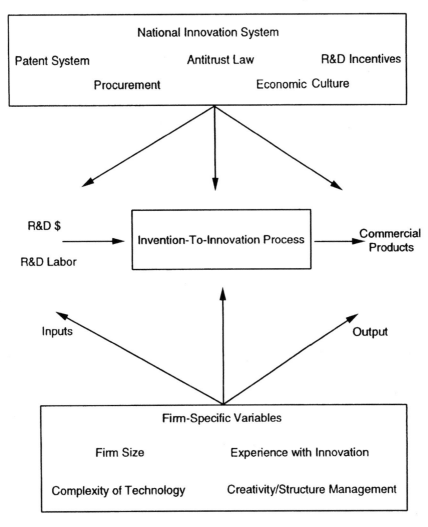

have been centerpieces of the literature on innovation management (Roberts, 1988, and Van de Ven, 1986 are excellent review articles of a substantial field).

The newer attention devoted to the environment within which innovation takes place has more to do with variables not controlled by the firm.

The national innovation system is essentially the total economic, political, cultural, and legal environment of technology-generation efforts. The pieces can obviously vary from nation to nation, but typical factors would include the patent system, government support of R&D, government procurement, and the overall economic culture (e.g., U.S. entrepreneurial vs. Japanese cooperative tendencies).

Past scholarship on specific parts of a NIS have suggested that changes in this environment can have an impact on firm behavior and, hence, on the overall generation of technology in a nation. The strengthening of judicial support of the U.S. patent system in the early 1980s, for example, seems to have resulted in significant changes in firm behavior (Kastriner, 1991; Shapiro, 1990). Nelson (1984) and Lichtenberg (1988) suggest that specific governmental activities can also have an impact. On the other hand, statutory change in the Japanese patent system has had very little effect on behavior because tradition-based administrative practice in the Japanese Patent Office did not change (Helfgott, 1990).

Discerning which initiatives or unintended changes in the environment will have impacts is the major question of NIS. At least part of the answer is found in the "fit" of technology-generation programs or systems with the economic culture of the country (Silverstein, 1991) and the impact of the full NIS, as a consistent package, producing innovations (Herbig and McCarty, 1993). The U.S. system, for example, seems to work precisely because it has evolved over time to suit the national character. Just about everything in patent law and elsewhere encourages the risk-taking, entrepreneurial behavior so celebrated in U.S. economic culture (Erickson, 1995). The full Japanese package has a similarly nice fit (Bowonder, Miyake, and Linstone, 1994a, 1994b) to a more cooperatively oriented nation dominated by innovative corporate giants. Generally, evolutionary changes in a NIS–changes that conditions reveal to be necessary–seem to work best. Sudden, discontinuous changes with no basis in other environmental needs have been less successful. Again, it is the ability of the NIS to work as a whole, with each piece supporting and reinforcing the others, that produces success.

This brings up the issue of sudden, discontinuous change in the economic system itself. NIS studies have tended to center only on the major trading nations, particularly the Global Triad. The newly capitalist nations of Central and Eastern Europe pose this issue outside of this traditional framework. On the one hand, there is no immediately obvious NIS in place as they seek to rapidly modernize, prepare themselves for entry in the EU, and join the international economy. On the other hand, the NIS of each country can essentially be designed from scratch to serve the particular needs of the region and the nations themselves.

Something of a past literature does exist, focusing on development economics and technology transfer. Usually this literature focused on full intellectual property protection or the total lack of it, however, with no middle ground. The issues still arise (Siebeck, 1990), but China's recent experience with the investment-killing impact of a lack of intellectual property protection should convince any remaining doubters of the need for protection if a nation seeks high-technology imports and investment. The debate needs to move beyond this choice to consider the type of intellectual property protection regime necessary to spur the behavior, both domestic and foreign, that a developing or newly capitalistic nation desires. Stamm (1991) has presented compelling evidence from Italy that, even among patent systems, the degree of strength has extremely important implications for investment flows.

To focus the discussion, then, this chapter will consider just one piece of the NIS: the patent system. The patent system is a good place to begin not only because the important issues of statute and behavior are both readily apparent, but also because the two most different patent systems among the countries belonging to the Organization for Cooperation and Development (OECD) have obvious and easily explained divergences which have received a great deal of attention in recent years. The United States quietly underwent an extended reexamination of its unique patent system in 1992 while Japan has had to defend its patent system against U.S. charges of discrimination as recently as 1988. Since these two nations represent the polar ends of a more-developed nation patent system continuum, we can use them to highlight the ways in which patent systems can differ in statute, practice, and impact. The German system, representative of the more middle-of-the-road European systems, can be easily compared once we establish these extremes.

PATENT SYSTEMS

The basic economic concept of patents is that potential innovators need some incentive to undertake inherently risky and expensive innovative activities. If competitors can simply copy an innovation once it appears on the market, and can do so without the tremendous sunk cost that successful innovative activities require, they will have a significant cost advantage. Since successful innovations must also generate enough profit to make up for unsuccessful attempts, the problem is magnified. Hence patents, a monopoly on rights to produce and sell the protected product, give innovators a stronger incentive to undertake such risky activities. Plant (1934) established this analytical basis for patents while Nordhaus (1969) provided an algebraic framework. In recent years, economic theory has focused more on game theory approaches to optimal patenting strategies (e.g., Dasgupta and Stiglitz, 1980) or theoretical workouts of optimal length and breadth of patent protection (Gilbert and Shapiro, 1990; Klemperer, 1990).

As noted earlier, however, the national innovation system approaches have more immediate applications to public policy debate. This type of analysis begins with a deeper understanding of the actual statutes and administrative practices in place and considers the data on output and the likely links between the two. As noted earlier, we are particularly fortunate to have detailed knowledge on the U.S. and Japanese patent systems because of recent policy debates over U.S. statutes (Advisory Commission 1992; *Hearings*, 1992; Wiggs, 1991), Japanese statutes and practice (*Hearing*, 1988), and scholarly examinations of the differences between these two systems (Helfgott, 1990; Kotabe, 1992; Ordover, 1991; Wineberg, 1988).

As a foundation for the discussion, consider Figure 15.2, a representation of the U.S. patent process. The United States is virtually the only nation left which employs a First-to-Invent (FTI) patent system. Under FTI, the true inventor is essentially guaranteed patent rights to the invention, regardless of who first files a patent application on the idea. As a result, "conception" is a critical date in patent law as it indicates when invention takes place; that is, the first time the idea occurred to the inventor.

Before a patent application can be filed, however, the invention must be Reduced-to-Practice (RTP) and proved to be workable. If the inventor then chooses to seek a patent, he or she files an application showing the invention to be useful, novel, and nonobvious. In short, there must be an "inventive leap" over previous technology. In the United States, this is a fairly stringent requirement, so slight variations in technology are not patentable. The application itself must reveal the "best mode" known to the inventor of practicing the invention, a declaration of all relevant prior art contained within the invention, a description of the invention, and the specific claims as to how the invention is different from known methods and hence worthy of patent protection.

The U.S. Patent and Trademark Office (USPTO) examines the application, granting the patent if it finds the invention meets the above-mentioned criteria. The grant itself gives monopoly protection over manufacture and use, but coincides with publication, disclosing the technology to public scrutiny. It is after the grant, generally, when any charges from third parties concerning oppositions to patent criteria or interference on true

FIGURE 15.2. U. S. Patent Process

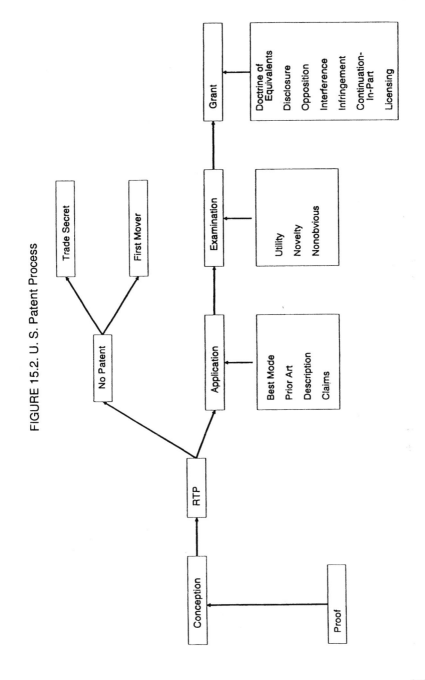

first invention arise. Similarly, opportunities for the inventor to deter third parties by charging infringement with the patented technology through unauthorized use, to file additional Continuation-in-Part applications extending the basic technology in new directions, or to pursue licensing agreements arise at this point.

This law and practice are unique to the United States among major trading nations. In the United States, patent protection essentially begins at conception, provided the inventor proceeds with some diligence in filing. As a result, a small entity need not worry about a larger entity with greater resources and more experience turning its conception into a commercial product and beating it to market. An inventor, large or small, can take the time to prove out the idea; design it for optimal manufacturing, marketing, and legal purposes; and then file a strong patent application. Once in place, the patents are interpreted very broadly, and any disagreements between applicant and the USPTO are subject to review by outside judicial authorities.

The effect of such a system is strikingly unique. The United States has a much better quality of innovation, i.e., a higher proportion of pioneering rather than incremental innovations (Erickson, 1994; Mowery and Teece, 1993), protected by much stronger and more far-reaching patents. This tendency to encourage risk-taking and going after the "big idea" is reflected in spending patterns as well, with R&D expenditures much more concentrated in the early phases of innovation (Mansfield, 1988a, 1988b; Rosenberg and Steinmueller, 1988). As a result, the innovation community in the United States is much more diverse, with a great deal more representation from small entity inventors, and with a much larger venture capital industry to support it (Mowery, 1992; Mowery and Teece, 1993). In short, the U.S. patent system supports the overall NIS tendency to encourage the "heroic entrepreneur" in addition to corporations (Erickson, 1995).

If the United States has the strongest patent protection and the greatest percentage of non-corporate inventors, Japan represents the opposite end of the continuum among major trading nations. Japan's innovation sector is dominated by large corporations, has relatively narrow and weak patents protecting mostly incremental innovations, promotes spending at the latter stages of innovation, and encourages not entrepreneurial risk-taking but cooperative cross-licensing.

In large part, the differences come from the overall economic culture of Japan, and the patent system incorporates most of these idiosyncrasies. Under Japanese patent law, no proof of conception is required because the nation operates under a First-to-File priority claim basis. The first party to file a patent application gains the patent. Since there is no need to reduce the idea to practice, proving workability, these patents are often quickly filed on very preliminary ideas. Further, since the Japanese Patent and Trademark Office (JPTO) has much looser utility, novelty, and nonobviousness requirements, these incremental technological advances do receive patents, but ones that tend to protect only very narrow slices of technology. The tendency is reinforced by the tradition of patents having only a single head claim. This requirement was discontinued over a decade ago, but examiners still tend to grant only very narrow patents based on few claims.

Once applications are received by the JPTO, procedures also differ markedly. Pre-grant oppositions are enthusiastically pursued, and once the application is granted, it is subject to a much more spirited post-grant opposition process as well as patent flooding—the practice of filing numerous nuisance patents on subjects bordering on the core technology of the key patent. The result is usually an inability to use the key patent in any substantive way unless opposers and rival patentees are cross-licensed. Any problems with the process are subject to review by the JPTO. Even if the courts do eventually get involved, they usually decide issues by referring back to the JPTO, so little independent review is available. As might be inferred, the JPTO is extremely busy, and the patent review process has become a bureaucratic nightmare, averaging five to seven years.

The key aspect is that success under the Japanese system requires quick movement from conception to filing, aggressive patent prosecutions, and an ability to differentiate high-technology products not on the basis of technological superiority and patent protection, but on the basis of manufacturing or marketing clout. All are weighted against small entities and geared to incremental innovations.

Western European patent systems tend to fall somewhere between these two extremes. The German system, for example, is very close to the Japanese system statutorily (the latter was modeled after it), but differs quite a bit in practice. Although post-grant oppositions are pursued with gusto, the resulting patents do tend to be broader than their Japanese counterparts. The Germans dropped pre-grant oppositions as part of their process just a few years ago, almost certainly because of the difficulties in competing with the Japanese in this part of the patent prosecution game.

The bottom line of patent systems in the major trading countries is that they are intended to generate ideas and their consequent development into commercial products. The better the protection offered to inventions and commercial innovations, the better will be the work behind the concepts. More risks will be taken. As a result, in considering the best patent system for a specific country, we want to look at its needs in terms of commercial product protection. The workability of the system within particular environments should also be an issue.

CENTRAL AND EASTERN EUROPE

The general picture of CEE is consistent with that of developing economies that would conceivably benefit from greater employment of technology. For decades, the Coordinating Committee on Export Controls (COCOM) system kept then-communist regimes from importing cutting-edge Western technologies with possible military applications. As a result, the region has some native innovation skills, particularly in military research areas, but is decidedly behind the curve in most technologies. There is a crying need for technology transfer as an aid to modernizing the various national economies (Govaere, 1991).

The current industrial structure is inherited from the centrally planned economies. It is characterized by monolithic firms that are being privatized at varying rates and in varying sizes, some whole, some not. A growing small-business sector is hatching within most of these countries, but with a few notable exceptions (Hungarian software, for example; see Smart and Miller, 1995), it is not at all clear that these new firms can be considered high-technology. Having learned their trade in a competitive vacuum, most managers at all levels are considered incompetent and most certainly not risk-takers (Staudt, 1994; Voss and Schepanski, 1994). The workers have skills but are nonetheless unproductive (Kraljic, 1990).

In terms of technological products, then, what are the most basic needs of these economies? Clearly technology transfer is an overriding immediate concern. Where a country like the United States may seek to "grow its own" innovations while also providing an attractive environment for importing technology, Central and Eastern European nations need to actively seek outside technologies. Not only do they need to catch up in terms of the current state of the art, but they do not seem to have the innovative, manufacturing, or marketing muscle necessary to create and produce new products. Cutting-edge infrastructure (power, communications, transportation) technologies are particularly important as these nations seek to modernize (Bock, 1994).

In line with this short-term need, the best of all possible worlds would include not only imported technology, but technology accompanied by capital (especially in the form of physical investments), production facilities providing skilled jobs, and the necessary training in the use of unfamiliar technologies. Therefore, rather than simply gaining innovative consumer products (for example, imported from production facilities elsewhere) the ideal plan for Central and Eastern European nations would include large-scale investment in high-technology production facilities employing domestic workers and providing both managerial skills training and an entrepreneurial attitude.

Since industrial and consumer markets are still in early development stages, what factors would encourage this sort of overseas investment in the area? A number of compelling features suggest that the right sort of protection environment might prove attractive to outsiders. Initially, Central and Eastern Europe provides opportunities to essentially build from scratch and hence move more quickly along new technological trajectories. Innovations are often grouped into categories according to whether they are incremental, following closely on what came before, or pioneering, establishing new paradigms within which future incremental innovations will follow. Often, because of an installed base utilizing a previous technology, a new trajectory will take some time before it is generally accepted, simply because of the cost of reworking the old base (David, 1985). In the Central and Eastern European countries, since the old base is so poor, opportunities exist to more rapidly incorporate new ideas.

This pattern is already being seen in certain areas. The example receiving the most attention concerns communication. This region has a limited established copper-wire grid. As a result, replacing the old technology with improved fiber optics connections is less of a problem since the new technology can be plugged into more of a vacuum. Indeed, a number of businesses are simply jumping the step of establishing physical links in the first place by passing directly to cellular phone technologies (Levine, 1993). The willingness to employ unfamiliar technologies and the ease of establishing the new base make this area particularly attractive to outside firms seeking to sell their most up-to-date wares.

A second major opportunity that should encourage outside technology transfer through investment is found in the skilled, low-cost labor force. In general, low-cost labor is, by definition, unskilled. Consequently, an area whose labor is capable of high productivity but has been mismanaged because of a poor economic incentive structure and incompetent supervisors, should be extremely attractive to outside firms seeking to produce and market high-technology goods.

This idea feeds directly into a third major incentive to incorporate the Central and Eastern European countries into high-tech investment patterns. Long-range plans include incorporation into the EU, so a strong manufacturing and marketing base in the relatively low-cost Central and Eastern European countries will well serve Western Hemisphere and Asian nations intending to target the EU. As the countries modernize and are folded into the general European community, the labor cost advantages will decrease, but the short-term advantages of low-cost skilled labor will be replaced by this direct access to the EU from a modern, established base.

So the Central and Eastern European countries have strong incentives to encourage outside investment in high-technology goods and production. Just as important, they have certain characteristics that would seem to make them particularly attractive target nations for such technology transfer. Given these circumstances, what type of intellectual property system would seem to be most appropriate? Consider first some evidence on how the various Western systems perform in encouraging outside technologies to enter their markets while investing in local R&D and training.

Table 15.1 presents several pieces of data concerning these factors for a number of OECD countries. The countries are subjectively divided into technology-generating (producing substantial domestic innovation relative to world levels) and nontechnology-generating (satisfied to import most technologies). This distinction is necessary because some of the figures for the technology-generating countries are subject to bias in one direction since their domestic innovation sectors are so large, and in the opposite direction because their markets for innovative products are often large and attractive to outside firms. The United States, for example, remains the largest single market in the world for goods, hence virtually all new technologies will come to the U.S. market but still have to compete with the large number of domestic innovations. On the other hand, we know the most about the intellectual property protection systems in these countries, and can thus talk more intelligently about them than we can the perhaps more germane nontechnology-generating nations. As a result, both groups are included in the table and the following analysis.

It should also be noted that using macro-level evidence in this manner is fraught with peril because of all the different variables entering into technology generation in a given nation. Consequently, drawing conclusions based on differences in any single indicator becomes problematic. What we are doing here is considering a number of indicators, with the idea that the preponderance of the evidence may point to conclusions that can be reached with a greater degree of comfort. Large differences in the indicators also help to remove some of the fear that country-specific bias may influence them more than actual technology-generation variations.

Dependency ratio refers to the percentage of patent applications received from nonresident or foreign sources. Countries with a relatively high dependency ratio are dependent on the importation of outside technology. This number is highly affected by the intentions of the nation to produce its own technology, of course, as well as the size and attractive-

TABLE 15.1. Technology Indicators

	Dependency Ratio (1991)	Inventiveness Coefficient (1991)	Technology Balance of Payments (U.S. $m) (1991 Purchasing Power Parity)	Foreign R&D Percentage (1991)	U.S. R&D Expenditures (per capita) (U.S. $m) (1991)	U.S. R&D Employment (per capita) (1991)
U.S.	1.00	3.5	+13,815	11.0%	--	--
Japan	0.13	27.1	− 6,179	0.1%	1.16	15,887
Germany	1.89	4.1	− 1,652	3.1%	31.36	3,354
France	4.96	2.2	− 614	11.4%	15.27	8,150
U.K.	3.53	3.4	− 634	16.0%	27.96	2,854
Italy	--	--	--	8.6%	32.68	13,132
Belgium	56.80	0.7	− 379	0.5%	5.66	9,092
Canada	16.08	0.8	+ 35	18.1%	14.19	2,596
Denmark	32.01	2.1	− 110	4.4%	--	--
Netherlands	26.36	1.1	− 666	2.4%	31.65	4,306
Portugal	33.85	0.1	--	--	--	--
Spain	19.87	0.6	− 1,538	10.0%	--	--

ness of the domestic market. As a result, small differences in the numbers do not amount to much. However, the status of the Japanese ratio as a stark outlier reflects the dominance of Japanese technology in Japan and suggests that this system is not predisposed to importing technology for practice by foreign companies.

A similar story is told by the *inventiveness coefficient*. This number reflects the rate of resident patent applications per 10,000 population. Again, small differences can be explained by a number of factors, but the dramatic difference in the Japanese number again suggests that the innovation climate is highly geared to domestic innovation and resident patents. Does this mean that the Japanese have a higher level of technological output, a factor the patent system may influence and will be highly desirable for countries in Central and Eastern Europe in the long run? Studies suggest not (Mowery and Teece, 1993; Erickson, 1994). The Japanese generate many patents, but they tend not to encompass the same amount of technology as U.S. or European patents. Predictably, the underlying inventions tend to be more incremental and dependent on imported pioneering technologies. While the Japanese patent system does not, in and of itself, "cause" these results, it certainly plays a part in an overall innovation environment that does.

Moreover, as noted earlier, the top priority of Central and Eastern European countries would seem to be attracting investment, not promoting their own innovations. In this respect the Japanese system offers a number of contradictory facts. In terms of *technology balance of payments* (licensing royalties flowing into the country compared to those flowing out), Japan runs a net deficit of dramatic proportions. For a nation importing technology, this is not surprising, but given the above figures about Japan's reliance on own-country patents, it is curious. The only other major trading nation running similar numbers is South Korea (from a separate source with differently calculated numbers, National Science Board, 1993). South Korea is notorious for its run-ins with the United States over weak intellectual property rights. Net royalty deficits of this size suggest a nation in which outside high-technology companies are hesitant to invest, preferring to license domestic firms and let them handle production, marketing, and patent prosecution. This is not the ideal picture for CEE nations whose needs go beyond licensing rights.

A similar story is told by the figures concerning the percentage of R&D done by foreign firms *(Foreign R&D percentage), U.S. R&D expenditures* in other nations, and *U.S. R&D employment* in other nations. A nation receiving not only technology, but capital expenditures and employment as well should rate highly on the first two scales. The last category is calculated as domestic population corresponding to each foreign-generated R&D job. Hence, a large number here indicates a relatively low level of foreign R&D employment in the targeted country. The Japanese system, the weakest patent regime among major trading nations, rates markedly lower on all measures. A low need by foreign firms to adapt to the environment may explain some of the lower ratings in nontechnology-generating countries since little local R&D needs to be done; but this does not explain the Japanese numbers. The tendency of Italy, also fairly notorious for weaker intellectual property protection, to be the nation closest to Japan in the latter two ratings also lends some credence to the argument that a weaker patent system causes some fear in potential investors.

The overall conclusion of these numbers is that a weak intellectual property protection system is not likely to generate the type of technology transfer, investment, and employment patterns that the countries in Central and Eastern Europe should be seeking. Some minimum level of coverage, beyond that of Japan, seems necessary. Does that mean that these nations should aim for maximum protection, such as that promised by the United States? Short-term, the choice would seem to make little difference. The major advantage of the United States system is its seeming ability to encourage entrepreneurial innovation from smaller entities. Central and Eastern European nations have small business, but not capable high-tech entrepreneurial firms.

In the long run, however, they may seek this path. One major issue in Central and Eastern European nations is establishing the capitalist motivation/reward system (Kraljic, 1990; Staudt, 1994; Voss and Schepanski, 1994), and the example of a Polish or Czech Bill Gates would go a long way to planting this seed in the minds of coming generations. Furthermore, one goal of importing technology and facilities surely is to train domestic labor, and one long-term outcome of such training should again be a capability to generate unique at-home innovations. As the foreign employers are successful, so should they be able to spin off domestic entrepreneurs creating their own high-tech market niches. The wild capitalism seen in this area since liberalization suggests that the people respond well to market signals (*The Economist*, 1993), and if market rewards are provided for innovation, they may very well respond. So why not structure the system to enable small entities to compete? Theoretically, strong patent statutes seem to be appropriate.

The logistics of the United States, Japanese, or other systems are another issue. Once again, the Japanese system does not appear to be a good fit in terms of the resources and needs of these nations. Japanese patent prosecutions require large staffs of patent attorneys and engineers learned in the key technologies of their companies and their competitors. Since so much of the game concerns pursuing and answering pre-grant and post-grant oppositions, as well as flooding activities, any firm intending to compete seriously in Japan's intellectual property game must resign itself to a certain critical mass in its patenting operations. This tendency does not seem to lend itself well to a newly capitalistic economy. German and other EU systems have less of an emphasis on sizable patent departments, but they are also larger and busier than those found in most of their U.S. counterparts.

The U.S. system is not a panacea either, however. The discovery process necessary to uncover the true inventor in interference proceedings is costly and lengthy. Moreover, it does not allow foreign evidence of conception. This part of U.S. law is blatantly discriminatory and is obviously not appropriate for any country likely to import most of its technology in the near future. First-to-Invent includes positive factors, but ease of determining the true first inventor is not one of them.

One thing that can be done in a customized patent system, however, is to solidify the rules of proof in such procedures. As just noted, U.S. interference proceedings can be extraordinarily lengthy and expensive. The reason is the difficulty involved in identifying the moment of conception in inventors' bound laboratory notebooks. A system requiring a different, more positive sort of proof could eliminate many such problems without denying the strengths of a FTI system. Such proofs could be anything from preliminary filings to establish conception dates, fleshed out later when more information is available, to the simple procedure of requiring inventors to notarize important laboratory findings. The latter, of course, would be much easier to administer and extend to foreign proofs of invention without any hints of discrimination. Moreover, any opportunity to limit the already bulging governmental bureaucracies of these nations (Kraljic, 1990) should not be ignored.

The overall recommendation for Central and Eastern European nations, as shown in Table 15.2, is a strong system of intellectual property protection. The U.S. side of the patent system continuum is not a bad place to start for nations seeking to import technology, investment, and employment in the short term, and which may have the potential for entrepreneurial innovation in the long-run. U.S. FTI law can be substantially simplified, made more workable, and made less discriminatory, factors that may add even more attractiveness to new patent systems. It is a structure on which to construct customized systems that can appeal to the needs, and take advantage of the strengths, of each individual country.

TABLE 15.2. An "Ideal" Central and Eastern European Patent System

OBJECTIVES	FEATURES
Protection:	
Short-term Technology Transfer (Foreign technology imports & investment)	Strong Patent Protection
Long-term Entrepreneurial Opportunity (Home-grown, small entity technological development)	Strong Patent Protection
Administration:	
Priority Claim Mitigate advantages of scale and experience	First-to-Invent
Prosecution Limit opportunities for legal maneuvers and "gamesmanship"	First-to-Invent; structure oppositions so as to minimize purely legalistic use
Proofs of Invention Easy to determine and nondiscriminatory	Official documentation of conception, acceptance of appropriate foreign documentation

CONCLUSIONS

In order to attain their long-term economic objectives, the countries of Central and Eastern Europe must accomplish a number of short-term tasks. They need to encourage an inflow of investment capital. The best form for these investment funds would be job-creating infrastructure and manufacturing projects based on cutting-edge technologies. In creating an environment to appeal to investors seeking homes for such projects, however, Central and Eastern European nations should avoid the bureaucratic and legalistic swamps that swallow up scarce professional resources. Hence, the optimal environment would protect new technologies and encourage investment while providing easily understood and administered regulations.

Consequently, the optimal design for a national innovation system is not one currently found anywhere in the world. As with most matters in the newly capitalistic economies, the unique situation in which they find themselves requires tailored, and perhaps previously unseen, solutions. As discussed in this chapter, the patent system is an illuminating example. The patent system is, of course, only one piece of a national innovation system and does not in and of itself generate particular technological results. It is necessary, however, to have the goals and practices of the patent system fit with other pieces of the NIS, so that all parts work together toward the desired result.

The patent system recommended in this chapter is a hybrid First-to-Invent system, providing strong protection for foreign patentees in the short term and for would-be entrepreneurs in the long. This level of protection, the data suggest, will better ensure positive flows of both new technologies and physical investment. Moreover, because so many other political uncertainties exist in these countries, the more intellectual property protection concerns can be alleviated through strong patents, the better for the peace of mind of foreign investors. And, in the long run, this system would provide the best prospects for a homegrown entrepreneurial sector.

Logistically, the system also has advantages. More narrowly protected systems tend to require large patent department staffs to engineer around competing products and practice administrative gamesmanship. By improving on the basic FTI system, this proposal would remove many of these requirements while simplifying the process of discovering the true first inventor. The system would be bureaucratically manageable, simpler for individuals and companies to administer, and less open to abuse. All are important considerations for countries with limited professional resources and oversized governmental agencies.

This proposal is only a rough sketch, of course, and the devil is always in the details. But it seems a good point from which to begin discussion on the particular needs of individual countries, and how each can structure pieces of a national innovation system to best take advantage of national prospects. The countries in Central and Eastern Europe are a phenomenon we have never seen before, and they offer tremendous opportunities to observe how the free market and regulation interact within an economy. Regardless of decisions made on patent law, we need to track the results and learn from the experience.

REFERENCES

The Advisory Commission on Patent Law Reform. 1992. *A report to the secretary of commerce*, (August).

Bock, J. 1994. Innovation as creative destruction: The role of small businesses in the commonwealth of independent states (CIS). *International Journal of Technology Management*, 9(8): 856-863.

Bowonder, B., Miyake, T., and Linstone, H.A. 1994a. The Japanese institutional mechanisms for industrial growth: A systems perspective-part I. *Technological Forecasting and Social Change*, 47: 229-254.

Bowonder, B., Miyake, T., and Linstone, H.A. 1994b. The Japanese institutional mechanisms for industrial growth: A systems perspective-part II. *Technological Forecasting and Social Change*, 47: 309-344.

Dasgupta, P. and Stiglitz, J. 1980. Industrial structure and the nature of innovative activity. *The Economic Journal*, 90 (June): 266-93.

David, P.A. 1985. Clio and the economics of QWERTY. *American Economics Association: Papers & Proceedings*, 75:2 (May): 332-337.

The Economist. 1993. Rejoined, a survey of eastern Europe. (March 13): 1-22.

Erickson, G.S. 1994. International indicators of the quality of technological output. In H. Kahalas, Y.R. Puri, and K. Suchow (Eds.), *Global Competitiveness*, proceedings of the 1994 ASC U.S. Competitiveness in the Global Marketplace Conference: 425-436.

Erickson, G.S. 1995. Generating national technological output: The influence of a national patent system. *Advances in Competitiveness Research*, 3(1): 86-109.

Gilbert, R. and Shapiro, C. 1990. Optimal patent length and breadth. *RAND Journal of Economics*, 21(1): 106-112.

Govaere, I. 1991. The impact of intellectual property protection on technology transfer between the EC and the central and eastern European countries. *Journal of World Trade*, 25(5): 57-76.

Hearing before the subcommittee on foreign commerce and tourism of the committee on commerce, science, and transportation, Senate. 1988. Effect of the Japanese patent system on American business. Washington, DC: U.S. Government Printing Office.

Hearings before the Senate subcommittee of patents, copyrights, and trademarks and the House subcommittee of intellectual property and judicial administration of the Senate and House committees on the judiciary on the patent system harmonization act of 1992 (S.2605 and H.R.4978). 1992. Transcript, (April 30).

Helfgott, S. 1990. Cultural differences between the U.S. and Japanese patent systems. *Journal of the Patent and Trademark Office Society*, (March): 231-238.

Herbig, P.A. and McCarty, C. 1993. National management of innovation: Interactions of culture and structure. *Multinational Business Review*, (Spring): 19-26.

Kastriner, L.G. 1991. The revival of confidence in the patent system. *Journal of the Patent and Trademark Office Society*, (January): 5-23.

Klemperer, P. 1990. How broad should the scope of patent rights be? *The RAND Journal of Economics*, 21(1): 113-130.

Kotabe, M. 1992. A comparative study of U.S. and Japanese patent systems. *Journal of International Business Studies*, 21(1): 113-130.

Kraljic, P. 1990. The economic gap separating east and west. *Columbia Journal of World Business*, (Winter): 14-19.

Levine, J. 1993. For emerging countries, cellular is no luxury. *Business Week*, (April 5): 60.

Lichtenberg, F.R. 1988. The private R&D investment response to federal design and technical competitions. *The American Economic Review*, 78(3): 550-559.

Mansfield, E. 1988a. Industrial R&D in Japan and the United States: A comparative study. *American Economics Association: Papers and Proceedings*, 78(2): 1157-1168.

Mansfield, E. 1988b. The speed and cost of industrial innovation in Japan and the United States: External vs. internal technology. *Management Science*, 34(10): 223-228.

Mowery, D.C. 1992. The U.S. national innovation system: Origins and prospects for change. *Research Policy*, 21: 125-143.

Mowery, D.C. and Teece, D.J. 1993. Japan's growing capabilities in industrial technology: Implications for U.S. managers and policymakers. *California Management Review*, 35(2): 9-34.

National Science Board. 1993. *Science & engineering indicators–1993*. Washington, DC: U.S. Government Printing Office.

Nelson, R.R. (Ed.) 1982. *Government and technical progress: A cross-industry analysis*. New York: Pergamon Press.

Nelson, R.R. 1984. *High technology policies: A five-nation comparison*. Washington, DC: American Enterprise Institute for Public Policy Research.

Nelson, R.R. 1990a. Capitalism as an engine of social progress. *Research Policy*, 19: 193-214.

Nelson, R.R. 1990b. U.S. technological leadership: Where did it come from and where did it go? *Research Policy*, 19: 117-132.

Nelson, R.R. and Rosenberg, N. 1993. *National innovation systems: A comparative analysis*. New York: Oxford University Press.

Nordhaus, W.D. 1969. *Innovation, growth and welfare: A theoretical treatment of technological change*. Cambridge, MA: The MIT Press.

Ordover, J. 1991. A patent system for both diffusion and exclusion. *Journal of Economic Perspectives*, 5(1): 43-60.

Organization for Economic Cooperation and Development. 1994. *Main science and technology indicators*. Paris: OECD Publications (2).

Patel, P. and Pavitt, K. 1987. Is western Europe losing the technological race? *Research Policy*, 16: 59-85.

Plant, A. 1934. The economic theory concerning patents for inventions. *Economica*, (February): 30-51.

Porter, M.E. 1990. *The competitive advantage of nations*. New York: The Free Press.

Roberts, E.B. 1988. Managing invention and innovation. *Research-Technology Management*, (January/February): 11-29.

Rosenberg, N. 1982. *Inside the black box: Technology and economics*. Cambridge: Cambridge University Press.

Rosenberg, N. and Steinmueller, W.E. 1988. Why are Americans such poor imitators? *American Economics Association: Papers and Proceedings*, 78(2): 229-234.

Schumpeter, J.A. 1934. *The theory of economic development*. Cambridge, MA: Harvard University Press.

Shapiro, A. 1990. Responding to the changing patent system. *Research-Technology Management*, (September/October): 38-43.

Siebeck, W.E. (Ed.) with Evenson, R.E., Lesser, W., and Primo Brago, C.A. 1990. *Strengthening protection of intellectual property in developing countries: A survey of the literature*. Washington DC: The World Bank.

Silverstein, D. 1991. Patents, science and innovation: Historical linkages and implications for global technological competitiveness. *Rutgers Computer & Technology Law Review*, 17: 261-319.

Smart, T.R. and Miller, K.R. 1995. Putting Hungarian high tech on the map. *Business Week*, (September 4): 107.

Stamm, O.A. 1991. GATT negotiations for the protection of new technologies. *Journal of the Patent and Trademark Office Society*, (September): 680-699.

Staudt, E. 1994. Innovation barriers on the way from the planned to the market economy: The management of non-routine processes. *International Journal of Technology Management*, 9(8): 799-817.

Van de Ven, A.H. 1986. Central problems in the management of innovation. *Management Science*, 12(5): 590-607.

Voss, P. and Schepanski, N. 1994. Rising from the ruins: Innovation in the five new German länder. *International Journal of Technology Management*, 9(8): 822-832.

Wiggs, B.R. 1991. Canada's first-to-file experience–Should the U.S. make the move? *Journal of the Patent and Trademark Office Society*, (July): 493-513.

Wineberg, A. 1988. The Japanese patent system: A non-tariff barrier to foreign businesses? *Journal of World Trade*, (February): 11-22.

Chapter 16

Reactions to Organizational Structure: A Comparison of Employees in the United States and Bulgaria

Lynn E. Miller
Richard M.Weiss

The challenge of identifying fundamental structural contingencies–relationships of contextual factors (such as size and technology) to dimensions of organizational structure (such as formalization and hierarchy)–would be substantially complicated by the observation of cross-national variations in context-structure relationships. In their seminal work on the "culture free" thesis, Hickson, McMillan, Azumi, and Horvath (1979) described the prospect of establishing separate social sciences for different countries or cultures as "terrifying" (p. 29) and a "nightmare" (p. 26).

Fortunately, although some national variations have been noted, substantial research has supported the existence of organizational contingencies that hold true across national and cultural boundaries (see Zeffane, 1989, for a review of this research). Nevertheless, contextual factors account for only some of the variation in organizational structures. The particular forms of organizations may be influenced, as least in part, by historically and culturally determined preferences and expectations. As examples, Lincoln, Hanada, and Olson (1981) found that employees of Japanese ancestry were more likely to value vertical and horizontal complexity than were Caucasian employees in the same companies. Japanese employees also expressed greater preference for paternalistic company practices (see also Kelly and Reeser, 1973). Agarwal (1993) found that U.S. employees reacted more negatively to formalization than did those in India.

In recent years, management scholars have begun to direct substantial attention to the rapid changes being faced by managers in the formerly socialist countries of Central and Eastern Europe (Luthans, Welsh, and Rosenkrantz, 1993; Pearce, 1991). Many writers have expressed concern that the historical and cultural characteristics of that region may limit the successfulness of interventions based on theory and research from the United States and western Europe (McNulty, 1992; Perlaki, 1994; Welsh, Luthans, and Sommer, 1993).

In this study, we attempted to learn how employees from the United States and Bulgaria differ in their reactions to dimensions of organizational structure. Although we begin with an historical overview of management practices in Bulgaria, our assumption is that simply knowing what cross-national structural differences *exist* is not as important as knowing how employees *react* to those structural dimensions. For example, Kakar (1971) noted that although Indians expect parental authority relations, they prefer supervisors with low levels of assertiveness. Particularly in countries where the status quo is being challenged, knowledge of past practices alone may be of limited utility when proposing organizational interventions or new ventures.

SOCIALIST STRUCTURES AND REFORMS

During its communist period from 1944 to 1989, Bulgaria was considered the Soviet Union's most trusted ally, sometimes being referred to as the USSR's "Sixteenth Republic" (Kiezun, 1991; Zonis and Semler, 1992). The obsequious Todor Zhivkov, the head of the Bulgarian Communist Party from 1954 until the 1989 coup staged by Gorbachev-style reformers, nurtured his own and Bulgaria's standing with the Soviets through many changes in Soviet leadership. As a result, Bulgaria enjoyed substantial Soviet subsidies.

Bulgaria's economic structures and mechanisms were largely an importation of the Soviet system (Kiezun 1991; Petkov and Thirkell, 1991). Thus, the Soviet principles of "one man management" and "democratic centralism" became the basis for industrial administration in Bulgaria. Combined, these principles imply that although the head of each enterprise has authority and responsibility for decision making, these decisions are to be informed by the collective views of subordinates (Vlachoutsicos and Lawrence, 1990; Petkov and Thirkell, 1991). In practice, there is reason to believe that the actual participation by workers often was low, with much of it taking place indirectly via party or union representatives, or with workers attending meetings but not joining in discussions of substantive issues.

Work was organized largely according to Taylor's principles of scientific management, with efficient production being the primary goal. High levels of centralization, formalization of production procedures, and division of labor were the hallmarks of this approach, and little emphasis was placed on creativity and innovation (Perlaki, 1994; Yanowitch, 1985). Kiezun described Bulgaria's "style of working" as "characterized by tight bureaucratization and rigidity in carrying out instructions to the letter" (1991: 26). Yet, the dynamics of a centrally planned economy resulted in full employment and labor shortages, which strengthened the position of labor and weakened management control (Lane, 1987). In Bulgaria, as in the Soviet Union, the levels of turnover, absenteeism, alcoholism, and "loafing" were extremely high (Petkov and Thirkell, 1991; Leites, 1985; Shlapentokh, 1989). Systems of promotion, pay rates, bonuses, overtime, and awards were often based on social loyalties, rather than on performance, thereby further undermining worker motivation (Petkov and Thirkell, 1991; Yanowitch, 1985).

In the early 1980s, "progressive" workplace reforms were introduced in both the Soviet Union and Bulgaria (Petkov and Thirkell, 1991; Yanowitch, 1985). By decree, the use of work teams—brigades—as the fundamental basis for the organization of enterprises became widely implemented. The concepts of humanization through job rotation, work group self-management, and enlarging/consolidating fragmented jobs had long been consistent with socialist ideology, but previously had been subordinated to faith in mechanization and automation as humanizing (Yanowitch, 1985). In the 1970s, however, participation and autonomy emerged as dominant themes in the Soviet management literature, partly in response to the results of Western reforms, such as Swedish experiments in job redesign. To a great extent, brigade-based structures were justified as potential production tools that would enhance coordination and cooperation and, by tying compensation to group performance, would result in the exertion of normative pressures on "loafers, drunkards, and shirkers" (Yanowitch, 1985).

Yanowitch (1985) noted that Soviet workplace humanization efforts also included the formalization of policies regarding promotion and occupational advancement as a response to the many complaints regarding the arbitrary nature of such policies. Whether brigade structures were implemented as true reforms is unclear. Administrators and conservative scholars expressed concerns that granting brigades substantial autonomy and decision-making responsibility could result in collective resistance to management's goals (Yanowitch, 1985). For example, concern was expressed that the brigade's normative influence could be directed at "rate busters" as well as "loafers." There is evidence that many brigades were "on paper" only, and that managers often resisted the delegation of significant managerial authority. An eight-plant study in the USSR (Klivets, 1983, cited by Yanowitch, 1985) indicated that the majority of managers believed that foremen and "administration," rather than brigades, were the appropriate sources of authority for decisions regarding functions such as planning and distributing work assignments, norm-setting, and introducing new technology. Although the 1986 Labor Code required the election of brigade leaders in Bulgaria, 87 percent of the candidates were nominated by management or the party or trade union, while only 13 percent were nominated by the collective (brigade) (Petkov and Thirkell, 1991). Yanowitch (1985) cited a number of Soviet writers who noted that the mandate for self-managing work brigades was received with skepticism by workers who viewed it as simply another management "campaign" designed to heighten work intensity.

CULTURAL VALUES OF AMERICANS AND BULGARIANS

Perlaki (1994) applied Hofstede's (1980, 1991) well-known framework of cultural values to describe the values held by citizens of the various formerly socialist countries of Central and Eastern Europe. Perlaki suggested that Americans and Bulgarians are likely to differ on three major value dimensions. First, he argued that Americans are likely to have more of an *individualistic* orientation than Bulgarians, i.e., Americans are more likely to accept and value self-interested and autonomous behavior, whereas Bulgarians are more likely to value behavior directed toward the collective interests of the larger group. Second, the two countries are likely to differ in *power distance*, with Bulgarians being more likely to accept social inequalities, such as the inequality between superiors and subordinates, as legitimate and justified. Third, the cultures are likely to differ in *uncertainty avoidance*, with Bulgarians being more likely than Americans to prefer structured to ambiguous situations.

Agarwal (1993) argued that differences in cultural values can predict how members of a given culture will tend to react to different organizational structures. In the United States and other cultures that value individualism, low power distance, and ambiguity, we would expect to find resistance to organizational structures that limit individual autonomy and, instead, a preference for structures that allow greater subordinate participation in decision making. In Bulgaria and other countries with a tradition of socialism and centralized control, collectivist ideologies have long justified the subordination of individual interests for the good of society. We would expect to find a greater willingness in such societies to accept centralized and formalized control. Given the history of Bulgarian job design reforms, we may even find that lower level employees eye participative structures with cynicism. Welsh, Luthans, and Sommers (1993), for example, speculated that the failure of their participative intervention in a Russian textile factory may have been attributable to the facade of participation that workers had often experienced in the past.

PREDICTED REACTIONS
TO ORGANIZATIONAL STRUCTURE

In examining employee reactions to organizational structure, it is important to identify the ways in which such controls are implemented. For example, Organ and Greene (1981) found that a sample of scientists and engineers in the United States had positive reactions to formalization *that clarified job expectations*. Agarwal (1993), however, found that *monitoring conducted to ensure compliance with formalized rules and procedures* led to negative reactions among American (although not among Indian) salespersons.

Similarly, centralization that requires employees to check with superiors when making decisions pertinent to their own task performance should restrict autonomy and result in greater dissatisfaction than centralization that merely precludes involvement in decisions with an indirect impact on one's task performance.

The present study used a variety of measures of centralization and formalization to determine their impact on employee satisfaction. We used an "objective" (or "institutional") measure of formalization (based on Pugh, Hickson, Hinings, and Turner, 1968) that asked about the existence of documentation such as written job descriptions, manuals of rules, etc. We also used two "perceptual" measures developed by Aiken and Hage (1966, 1968) and modified by Miller and Weiss (1991). One of these perceptual measures, the job specificity scale, asks respondents to indicate the extent to which job procedures are spelled out (e.g., "Whatever situation arises we have procedures to follow in dealing with it."). Hypothesis One was based on the expectation that Bulgaria's mechanistic production system had cultivated a reliance on formalized procedures for job performance, although we were curious to see whether a distaste for previous structures had emerged since the fall of communism.

> *Hypothesis One:* An "objective" formalization measure and job specificity will have stronger positive relationships with job satisfaction for the Bulgarian sample than for the U.S. sample.

The second perceptual measure of formalization, the rule observation scale, asks about the extent to which employees are monitored for rule violations. Hypothesis Two was based on the expectation that Americans would view such surveillance as being a patronizing and intrusive restriction of their autonomy, but that Bulgarians would accept it as a necessary form of control in a collectivist system, and might even embrace it as necessary for ensuring an equitable distribution of rewards:

> *Hypothesis Two:* Rule observation will have a stronger inverse relationship with job satisfaction for the U.S. sample than for the Bulgarian sample.

We used two measures of centralization: participation in decision making and hierarchy of authority (Aiken and Hage, 1966, as modified by Miller and Weiss, 1991). The first measure indexed the degree to which decision making had been decentralized by asking about employee involvement in various decisions, such as the adoption of new policies or the hiring of new staff. We expected that the U.S. sample would respond more positively to involvement in decision making because participation is consistent with low power distance values, and because we assumed that the Bulgarians were more likely to have had experience with participation being used as a manipulative facade:

> *Hypothesis Three:* Participation in decision making will have a stronger positive relationship with job satisfaction for the United States than for the Bulgarian sample.

The hierarchy of authority measure asks respondents about the extent to which employees must obtain approval from superiors before taking action. Hypothesis Four was based on the assumption that employees in the United States would react negatively to constraints on autonomy that increase the sense of inequality between superior and subordinate:

> *Hypothesis Four:* Hierarchy of authority will have a stronger inverse relationship with job satisfaction for the United States than for the Bulgarian sample.

In studying the reactions of United States and Indian salespeople to characteristics of organizational structure, Agarwal (1993) argued that salespeople want and expect substantial autonomy, and therefore should react particularly negatively when autonomy is constrained. Because non-sales employees with high levels of autonomy are often individuals who have sought out higher level positions that offer such freedom, we thought that high-autonomy employees in general might react negatively to structural constraints. On the other hand, the literatures concerning substitutes for leadership and employee reactions to task-oriented leadership (Kerr and Jermier, 1978; Yukl, 1981) suggest that individuals with high autonomy might be more receptive to structural constraints than individuals with low autonomy, whose performance is already likely to be circumscribed by sequential interdependence, low job scope, and close supervision. To explore these issues we decided to split our United States and Bulgarian samples into subsamples with low and high autonomy. We did not make any a priori hypotheses regarding differences that might exist between the low- and high-autonomy subsamples.

DATA COLLECTION

In the United States, we surveyed 246 full- and part-time employees from a wide variety of organizations. Questionnaires were completed by respondents at two universities who attended undergraduate (n = 118) or graduate (n = 128) business classes. Some of the respondents were employed part time, but the majority held full-time employment and attended class at night.

In Bulgaria, questionnaires were completed by 109 respondents, about two-thirds of whom were students attending graduate business classes conducted by professors from the United States and sponsored by the U.S. Agency for International Development. The remaining responses were from co-workers of these students. A wide variety of organizations were represented; as examples, respondents worked in the transportation, production, government, banking, research, and telecommunications industries. Many of the respondents were highly educated, with advanced degrees in technical fields. Although precise figures are not available, the vast majority held full-time employment.

As described more fully above, three measures of formalization were included in the questionnaire: "objective" formalization (four items), job specificity (four items), and rule observation (two items). They also completed two measures of centralization: participation in decision making (a four-item measure of decentralization) and hierarchy of authority (five items).

Autonomy was assessed with Miller and Weiss' (1991) five-item modification of Aiken and Hage's (1966) job codification scale. Although this scale originally was developed by Aiken and Hage to measure the extent to which job descriptions are formalized in writing, there is clear agreement that the items on this scale (e.g., "How things are done here is left up to persons doing the work") are better conceptualized as providing a perceptual measure of job autonomy (Dewar, Whetten, and Boje, 1980; Miller and Weiss, 1991; Pierce and Dunham, 1978). The U.S. and Bulgarian samples had the same median scores on this scale, and a median split was used to divide each country sample into low- and high-autonomy groups. In each country, a substantial number of respondents scored at the median, and these respondents were arbitrarily placed in the "high-autonomy" groups.

A measure of technology, Hage and Aiken's (1969) four-item task routineness scale, was used as a control variable in regression analyses. Because task routineness is commonly known to be a determinant of both structure and job satisfaction, we decided to control for its effects in our analyses. We intended to control for organizational size as well, but this measure was unusable due to a translation problem: Some of the respondents in the Bulgarian sample understood our size measure to refer to the size of their work brigade rather than the size of the entire enterprise. Although size is known to correlate with some dimensions of organizational structure, it appears to be related to job satisfaction only indirectly via structural measures, if at all (Berger and Cummings, 1979). Analyses with data from our U.S. sample indicated that organizational size (the log of the number of employees) was not a significant predictor of job satisfaction either before or after controlling for structure and task routineness ($r = .06$, $p = .32$; beta $= .06$, $p = .52$).

Job satisfaction was assessed with a two-item global satisfaction measure from the Michigan Organizational Assessment Questionnaire (Seashore, Lawler, Mirvis, and Cammann, 1982): "All in all, I am satisfied with my job" and "In general, I like working here."

AMERICAN AND BULGARIAN REACTIONS TO ORGANIZATIONAL STRUCTURE

Table 16.1 shows the results of t-tests of the differences between the two country samples in job satisfaction, organizational structure, autonomy, and task routineness. The reader should be cautious not to overinter-

TABLE 16.1. Differences in Job Satisfaction, Structure, Autonomy, and Routineness Scores

VARIABLE	BULGARIAN MEAN	U.S. MEAN	P-VALUE
Job Satisfaction	10.31	9.98	n.s.
"Objective" Formalization	6.76	6.34	p<.003
Job Specificity	10.19	11.43	p<.001
Rule Observation	5.30	3.86	p<.001
Participation in Decision Making	8.80	9.30	n.s.
Hierarchy of Authority	13.90	10.45	p<.001
Autonomy	11.45	11.34	n.s.
Task Routineness	10.32	9.98	n.s.

Note: N's range from 102 to 106 for the Bulgarian sample, and from 238 to 245 for the U.S. sample due to missing data for some variables.

pret the mean differences between the two countries, because no attempt was made to match the industries, organizations, or respondents represented in the two samples. For example, although the Bulgarians described their enterprises as more "mechanistic" (that is, as being more hierarchical, more likely to have formalized documentation, and more likely to monitor for rule violations), that difference could be attributable either to true cultural differences or merely to our Bulgarian respondents' organizations being larger or more likely to be mass production facilities. On the other hand, the nonsignificant mean differences between the two samples in terms of job satisfaction, autonomy, and task routineness are reassuring. Previous research has indicated that levels of job satisfaction reported by employees in Central and Eastern European countries are comparable to levels elsewhere (Yanowitch, 1985); a significant American-Bulgarian difference in job satisfaction could signify that our samples were unusual in some way. Also, the observed similarity in autonomy and task routineness for our two samples suggests that the nature of the work being performed did not differ dramatically between the two countries.

Table 16.2 provides the results of regression analyses using the structure and routineness variables to predict job satisfaction for the American and Bulgarian subsamples with low and high levels of autonomy. The

TABLE 16.2. Standardized Coefficients from Regressions Predicting Job Satisfaction for High- and Low-Autonomy Subsamples of U.S. and Bulgarian Respondents

| | LOW AUTONOMY | | HIGH AUTONOMY | |
INDEPENDENT VARIABLE	AMERICAN	BULGARIAN	AMERICAN	BULGARIAN
"Objective" formalization	−.10	.06	.09	−.18
Job Specificity	.24*	.39*	.10	.46**
Rule Observation	.08	−.04	−.24**	−.04
Participation in Decision Making	.24**	−.16	−.01	.35*
Hierarchy of Authority	−.31**	−.42*	−.24**	−.18
Task Routineness	−.32**	−.29*	−.20**	−.23*
Adjusted R-Squared	.37	.26	.24	.22
Sample Size	91	32	143	59

*p < .05.
**p < .01.

control variable, task routineness, was negatively related to job satisfaction in all analyses. For both American and Bulgarian respondents with *low levels of autonomy*, hierarchy of authority was a significant inverse predictor of job satisfaction, while job specificity was a significant positive predictor. The only difference between the two subsamples was that U.S. respondents with low autonomy reported greater job satisfaction when they participated more in decision making. For Bulgarians with low autonomy, participation had an inverse, although nonsignificant, relationship with job satisfaction. Thus, for the low-autonomy subsamples, only Hypothesis Three, which predicted that Americans would react more positively to participation than the Bulgarians would, was supported.

For respondents with *high levels of autonomy*, the results in Table 16.2 provide partial support for Hypothesis One, which predicted that Bulgarians would react more positively to "objective" formalization and job specificity than would Americans. Specifically, we found that the high-autonomy Bulgarians did have a significant job specificity-satisfaction relationship, whereas the Americans did not. Hypotheses Two and Four, which predicted stronger inverse relationships of rule observation and hierarchy for the U.S. sample than for the Bulgarian sample, were both supported.

However, unlike the results for the low-autonomy groups, participation was associated with significantly higher levels of job satisfaction for the high-autonomy Bulgarians, but not the Americans. This result thus contradicted Hypothesis Three.

DISCUSSION OF FINDINGS

The results of the present study suggest that the autonomy level of the employee may be an important determinant of how employees react to various dimensions of structure. The American and Bulgarian employees with *low levels of autonomy* had similar reactions to organizational structure. Low-autonomy employees from both countries reacted negatively to having to obtain approval for actions through a hierarchy of authority, and reacted positively to formalization in which jobs and procedures were specified. Unexpectedly, neither group had an adverse reaction to monitoring to ensure compliance with the rules. The only difference we observed between the two low-autonomy subsamples was that employees from the United States reacted more positively to participation in decision making than did employees from Bulgaria. In general, these results suggest that employees are willing to accept the formal controls that may accompany work that is performed nonautonomously. The need to obtain approval for one's actions in an already constrained job apparently is not welcome, however; perhaps it is perceived as excessive control.

American and Bulgarian employees with *high levels of autonomy* did react differently from each other to the structural characteristics of their organizations. As we had expected, Americans reacted more negatively to constraints on their autonomy. They were more dissatisfied to the extent that they had to go through the organizational hierarchy to obtain approval for their actions and to the extent that they were observed for rule infractions. While the Bulgarians reacted positively to the formal specification of jobs and procedures, high-autonomy employees from the United States did not. On the other hand, Americans with high levels of autonomy did not react positively to participation in decision making, whereas the Bulgarians did.

The literature on participative leadership suggests some reasons for why participative decentralization was more strongly related to satisfaction for the Bulgarian respondents with high autonomy and for the American respondents with low autonomy than for the other groups. Path-goal theorists have argued that participation may influence satisfaction via two different mechanisms (House and Mitchell, 1974; Yukl, 1981). First, participation can increase role clarity on an unstructured task for individuals with low tolerance for ambiguity. Consistent with this proposition, Schuler

(1976) found that individuals with high authoritarianism considered participation to be satisfying, but only on unstructured tasks. Individuals from Bulgaria and other cultures that value both power distance and uncertainty avoidance may welcome participation as a mechanism for clarifying expectations, but only when they perform autonomous or otherwise unstructured work.

The second way in which participation may influence satisfaction is by making work more intrinsically rewarding for individuals who have high needs for autonomy. For Americans and individuals from other cultures that value individualism and low power distance, participation may be an important method for providing intrinsic rewards, particularly when the job offers little autonomy.

IMPLICATIONS

In an earlier study, Agarwal (1993) predicted that salespeople in the United States, who are members of a low power distance/high individualism culture, would react negatively to organizational constraints on their otherwise high levels of autonomy. He expected that salespeople in India, who are more likely to accept high power distance and low individualism, would not react as negatively to structural constraints. Using formalization measures to operationalize structure, Agarwal supported his hypotheses and found evidence that—much like the Bulgarians with high autonomy in our study—Indian salespeople reacted *positively* to some types of formalization. Agarwal recommended that subsequent cross-national studies of the impact of organizational structure include task factors, such as autonomy and routineness, as well as additional structural factors, such as participation in decision making. Thus, the present study can be seen as both confirming and extending Agarwal's work.

Taken together, these two studies suggest that Hofstede's cultural values taxonomy may prove to be very useful for identifying cultures in which organizational structures are likely to have differing effects. Rather than having to examine employee reactions to organizational structures in every country that might be of interest, it may be possible to use Hofstede's framework to accurately predict how much formalization and centralization will be acceptable to people in different cultures. This information could be very useful for organizations expanding to other regions or consultants involved in organizational development in various countries. Although drawing generalizations about the values of entire nations is dangerous in that it ignores the vast individual differences that exist within a culture, it appears that the various historical, political, cultural, and other forces that influence a nation's peoples may create some meaningful and identifiable patterns of values and related behaviors (Clark, 1990).

Even more dangerous than overgeneralizing about the value systems of entire nations is assuming that management approaches can be exported to other regions without regard for cultural differences. Since the fall of communism, scholars and practitioners have been eager to offer their expertise to countries struggling to change their administrative and economic systems. Yet very little research has been conducted to determine how practices and structures in the formerly socialist countries differ from those of the West (Luthans, Welsh, and Rosenkrantz, 1993; Pearce, 1991; Perlaki, 1994). The present results suggest that some of our structures and approaches may not be eagerly embraced by people with very different traditions.

REFERENCES

Agarwal, S. 1993. Influence of formalization on role stress, organizational commitment, and work alienation of salespersons: A cross-national comparative study. *Journal of International Business Studies*, 24: 714-739.

Aiken, M., and Hage, J. 1966. Organizational alienation: A comparative analysis. *American Sociological Review*, 31: 497-509.

Aiken, M., and Hage, J. 1968. Organizational interdependence and intra-organization structure. *American Sociological Review*, 33: 912-930.

Berger, C.J., and Cummings, L.L. 1979. Organizational structure, attitudes, and behaviors. In B.M. Staw (Ed.), *Research in Organizational Behavior*, Vol. 1: 169-208. Greenwich, CT: JAI Press.

Clark, T. 1990. International marketing and national character: A review and proposal for an integrative theory. *Journal of Marketing*, 54: 66-77.

Dewar, R.D., Whetten, D.A., and Boje, D. 1980. An examination of the reliability and validity of the Aiken and Hage scales of centralization, formalization, and task routineness. *Administrative Science Quarterly*, 25: 120-126.

Hage, J., and Aiken, M. 1969. Routine technology, social structure, and organizational goals. *Administrative Science Quarterly*, 14: 366-376.

Hickson, D.J., McMillan, C.J., Azumi, K., and Horvath, D. 1979. Grounds for comparative organization theory: Quicksand or hard core? In C.J. Lammers and D.J. Hickson (Eds.), *Organizations alike and unalike*: 25-41. London: Routledge & Kegan Paul.

Hofstede, G. 1980. *Culture's consequences*. Beverly Hills, CA: Sage.

Hofstede, G. 1991. *Cultures and organizations: Software of the mind*. London: McGraw-Hill.

House, R.J., and Mitchell, T.R. 1974. Path-goal theory of leadership. *Contemporary Business*, 3: 81-98.

Kakar, S. 1971. Authority patterns and subordinate behavior in Indian organizations. *Administrative Science Quarterly*, 16: 298-307.

Kelly, L., and Reeser, C. 1973. The persistence of culture as a determinant of differentiated attitudes on the part of American managers of Japanese ancestry. *Academy of Management Journal*, 16: 67-76.

Kerr, S., and Jermier, J. 1978. Substitutes for leadership: Their meaning and measurement. *Organizational Behavior and Human Performance*, 22: 375-403.

Kiezun, W. 1991. *Management in socialist countries*. New York: Walter de Gruyter.

Lane, D. 1987. *Soviet labour and the ethics of communism, full employment and the labour process in the USSR*. Brighton: Sussex, UK. Wheatsheaf Books.

Leites, A. 1985. *Soviet style in management*. New York: Crane, Russak & Co.

Lincoln, J.R., Hanada, M., and Olson, J. 1981. Cultural orientations and individual reactions to organizations: A study of employees of Japanese-owned firms. *Administrative Science Quarterly*, 26: 93-115.

Luthans, F., Welsh, D.H.B., and Rosenkrantz, S.A. 1993. What do Russian managers really do? An observational study with comparison to U.S. managers. *Journal of International Business Studies*, 24: 741-761.

McNulty, N.G. 1992. Management education in Eastern Europe: 'Fore and after. *Academy of Management Executive*, 64: 78-87.

Miller, L. E., and Weiss, R.M. 1991. Factor analytic study of the Aiken and Hage measures of perceived organizational structure and technology. *Psychological Reports*, 68: 1379-1386.

Organ, D.W., and Greene, C.N. 1981. The effects of formalization on professional involvement: A compensatory process approach. *Administrative Science Quarterly*, 26: 237-252.

Pearce, J.L. 1991. From socialism to capitalism: The effects of Hungarian human resources practices. *Academy of Management Executive*, 5(4): 75-88.

Perlaki, I. 1994. Organizational development in Eastern Europe: Learning to build culture-specific OD theories. *Journal of Applied Behavioral Science*, 30: 297-312.

Petkov, K., and Thirkell, J.E.M. 1991. *Labour relations in Eastern Europe*. New York: London.

Pierce, J.L., and Dunham, R.B. 1978. An empirical demonstration of the convergence of common macro- and micro-organization measures. *Academy of Management Journal*, 21: 410-418.

Pugh, D.S., Hickson, D.J., Hinings, C.R., and Turner, C. 1968. Dimensions of organization structure. *Administrative Science Quarterly*, 13: 65-105.

Seashore, S.E., Lawler, E.E., Mirvis, P., and Cammann, C. (Eds.). 1982. *Observing and measuring change: A guide to field practice*. New York: Wiley.

Schuler, R.S. 1976. Participation with supervisor and subordinate authoritarianism: A path-goal reconciliation. *Administrative Science Quarterly*, 21: 320-325.

Shlapentokh, M. 1989. *Public and private life of the Soviet people*. New York: Oxford University Press.

Vlachoutsicos, C., and Lawrence, P. 1990. What we don't know about Soviet management. *Harvard Business Review*, Nov.-Dec.: 50-63.

Welsh, D.H.B., Luthans, F., and Sommer, S.M. 1993. Managing Russian factory workers: The impact of U.S.-based behavioral and participative techniques. *Academy of Management Journal*, 36: 58-79.

Yanowitch, M. 1985. *Work in the Soviet Union: Attitudes and issues.* Armonk, NY: Sharpe.

Yukl, G.A. 1981. *Leadership in organizations.* Englewood Cliffs, NJ: Prentice-Hall, 1981.

Zeffane, R.M. 1989. Organization structures and contingencies in different nations: Algeria, Britain, and France. *Social Science Research,* 18: 331-369.

Zonis, M., and Semler, D. 1992. *The east European opportunity.* New York: Wiley.

Chapter 17

Dual Restructuring: Survival of Newly Privatized Companies in Eastern Europe

Fritz Kröger

After a nearly 40 years of centrally planned regimes, Eastern European companies are facing a difficult challenge. Given the depressed economic situation domestically, they strive to gain access to Western markets quickly, but are not yet capable of meeting these markets' requirements. Their situation corresponds roughly to the situation in Germany after the Second World War. The rapid development of industry, later referred to as the "Wirtschaftswunder" (economic miracle), could only be accomplished with the assistance of foreign governments and the influx of primarily American companies. Today, similar efforts are under way by Western governments, and companies based in Western Europe, America and Asia are establishing themselves in Central and Eastern Europe and forming linkages with local firms.

In Western Europe, especially in Germany, expansion into Central and Eastern Europe is pursued for a variety of reasons: The competitive position of many German companies and of other West European competitors is weakening. Entire sectors of industry are faced with economic decline. Traditional markets have almost reached saturation. Competition from both Japan and the Asian "tigers," and the United States together with Mexico, is steadily increasing in Germany's traditional domestic markets. German companies, which pay very high taxes and are burdened with the highest labor costs in the world, are pressured to enhance their productivity and to search for new markets.

Traditional management approaches and management concepts such as downsizing and reengineering will help to some extent to compensate for the high cost. However, established ways of thinking have to be abandoned, because it is not enough to marginally improve one's competitive position: completely new strategic alternatives are needed to achieve the necessary breakthroughs.

The logical approach in this situation is to combine the strengths of German firms (or other Western firms) with those of their counterparts further east. While suffering from high cost, Western firms possess technological know-how, financial power, and marketing expertise. However, often these advantages are insufficient to achieve sustainable advantage given the high cost of doing business. In contrast, the newly privatized Eastern European competitors are in a complementary situation whereby as formerly state-owned entities they also suffer from inadequate competitive ability, albeit for different reasons. Rather than high costs, their main problems are an unfavorable situation on the domestic market, weak distribution channels, a lack of marketing know-how, and insufficient customer orientation.

Thus, by combining their value-added chains, Western and Eastern companies can create a decisive competitive advantages for both sides (Bronder, 1993; Porter, 1980; Porter, 1990):

- The German company relocates value-adding activities to East European neighbors who are close, both geographically and culturally. For the German company this relocation provides a partial solution to its labor cost problem and also creates improved access to the developing Eastern European markets.
- At the same time, the Eastern European companies are given improved employment opportunities and access to Western markets. In addition, they benefit from the continuous transfer of know-how, especially in the marketing and sales areas. Thus, they can develop faster and more successfully than comparable privatized companies without Western partners.

These competitive advantages, however, are only realized when both sides–East and West–closely integrate their value-adding processes and actively exploit the potential for synergy (Zentes, 1992). This interdependence requires major changes in the companies involved: "Dual Restructuring." The completely redefined value-added chain will dramatically change the overall structure of company performance. Thus, it is not only necessary to radically restructure the "underdeveloped" Eastern company, but also the Western European organization which is relocating some of its activities (Yip, 1992).

- The Western company first reduces its vertical integration by relocating manufacturing steps that are cost-drivers and involve noncore competencies (Harrigan, 1983). It can thus focus on marketing and sales. Only after the partnership has consolidated, will more sensitive activities such as R&D activities be relocated.

- Eastern companies optimize their manufacturing process in order to develop into a quality supplier over the long term rather than remaining a low-tech supplier. With selective transfer of know-how by the Western partner or owner, the Eastern company will provide impetus for economic growth in Eastern Europe in the medium term.

INCREASING COMPETITIVE PRESSURE
IN THE WEST

German companies operate in an environment characterized by constantly increasing competitive pressure. Success is possible only if company performance is optimal as to the success factors, time, quality, and cost; if the market is supplied accordingly; and if new lucrative markets can be identified and developed. A simple competitive strategy based on only one of these three factors can no longer ensure survival. Successful companies increase their flexibility in a way that they can grow in at least one dimension, without neglecting the other two to such an extent that competitors perceive an opportunity to position themselves more favorably.

- *Cost:* Compared worldwide, German companies employ the most qualified workforce with a high educational level and high productivity. However, the average cost of labor in Germany is the highest in the world. In comparison, labor costs in Hungary are far below the labor costs of Portugal or South Korea, which themselves are only a fraction of those in Germany. Labor costs in Russia, Bulgaria, or Romania are even lower.

  In order to achieve acceptable unit costs, even a quality leader must produce as cost-effectively as possible. A competitor who offers nearly comparable quality at lower prices generally can catch up quite quickly with one that has a head start based only on quality.

- *Time:* The rapid development in key technologies—e.g., microelectronics, new materials, or biotechnology—shows that only companies which utilize the key technologies in a timely and consistent manner will achieve competitive advantage. As product life cycles accelerate, the time span during which a technology offers its developer a competitive advantage continues to decrease. For example, the advantage achieved with the development of a high performance chip remains only until a competitor has closed the performance gap or introduced a chip which is twice as advanced—which is often within a matter of months. Technological innovation, therefore, only grants a temporary advantage following Schumpeter's dictum of "creative destruction." As a consequence, innovators need to employ a strategy that renders their own innovation obsolete—a strategy used by Intel.

While the need to achieve flexibility has been increasing, German companies have become complacent and bureaucratic due to their growth in recent decades. Changing toward leaner structures is a long-term process and often results in frictional loss due to ownership rights being at risk. Medium-size companies may be more flexible, but they may have difficulties in covering the costs of high flexibility and permanent innovativeness.

Besides being able to meet customers' desires, a quick response to market changes is necessary. The dominant market position achieved by the competitor who first enters a new market leads to a competitive advantage that is difficult for followers to recover. This can best be seen by the market positions taken by the "pioneers" of the consumer goods industry in Eastern Europe. Philip Morris, Coca-Cola, or Nestle will benefit for a number of years from their willingness to assume risks when they established themselves in these emerging markets. (For several case studies see Zentes, 1991, Part 3.)

- *Quality:* For a long time, "Made in Germany" was synonymous with high quality and engineering and withstood any comparison to the competition. Today, however, German automotive manufacturers, for example, spend more time than their Japanese rivals eliminating manufacturing mistakes than producing a car that, from an engineering perspective, is almost at par (Womack, Jones, and Roos, 1990). The much vaunted concept of quality is not doing very well in Germany. Proven quality concepts, which interestingly enough did not originate in Germany, such as Total Quality Management, are prophylactic and thus oriented toward cost reduction by preventing mistakes instead of eliminating them. Many German companies are engaged in trying to catch up with the competition from overseas.

  In addition, many German products exceed customer requirements, thus becoming too complex. Overcomplexity no longer constitutes a promising driving factor for differentiation, if it ever did. Increasingly, quality is becoming service-related rather than product-related. Technically brilliant products with impressive, but unwanted, superfluous features are often no longer required and thus not purchased. Compared to other leading industrialized nations, German manufacturers pay too little attention to "the voice of the customer." Thus far, "deproliferation"–the reduction of complexity–has been realized by only a few companies.

In sum, for German companies traditional solutions are not enough in this grave situation. Solutions are required not only to result in marginal cost reductions but also to dramatically redefine the company's cost position, enabling "quantum leap improvements." Customer-oriented business processes have to be defined and reorganized, and the existing reengineering potential must be realized. The reduction of vertical integration that is sometimes a by-product of reengineering projects has resulted in lower labor cost, in that low-value-adding activities have been shifted to low-wage countries. An example of this is the textile industry. However, over time the great physical and also cultural distances from such sites can create new problems.

The opening of the East provides huge potential nearby with very attractive cost structures and resources. German companies are linked to this region both traditionally and for reasons of geographical proximity. They need to take advantage of the existing potential in order to provide new opportunities for both themselves and the economies of the East (Koch, 1991).

NEEDS OF EAST EUROPEAN COMPANIES

The fall of the "Iron Curtain" was the most radical and far-reaching historical event since the Second World War. Market-oriented Western companies suddenly gained access to a region with almost 427 million inhabitants (Central Europe with the Czech Republic, Hungary, Poland, Slovenia, and Slovakia; the Baltic states of Lithuania, Estonia, and Latvia; the former Soviet Union and the Balkans with Albania, Romania, Bulgaria, Macedonia, and former Yugoslavia). In spite of significant political, legal, and economical problems, the potential of this region should not go to waste. Economic growth is an important prerequisite for political stability, and this is also in Western Europe's interest.

The East and Central European countries provide not only a rich store of natural resources such as natural gas, oil, and coal, as well as agricultural products, but also an enormous potential workforce. More than 50 percent of the population of the former Soviet Union–approximately 200 million people–are in the workforce, and many of them are highly qualified, as evidenced by Soviet Union's leading position in the aircraft, military, and aerospace industries. Valuable R&D resources in the areas of metallurgy, physics, chemicals, and electronics are available at 80 percent less than comparable resources would cost in Western countries. The difference in labor costs per hour is even more dramatic, amounting to less than 5 percent of a work hour in the West.

Central and Eastern Europe and the former Soviet Union constitute one of the world's largest markets to be developed. There is great accumulated demand for both consumer and capital goods. The long-term development of a sound market is one of the challenges for ensuring the survival of both Western and Eastern companies. Companies can reduce their dependence on saturated Western markets. Even if buying power on the local level for products and services produced in the West is inadequate, barter transactions could be made between East and West.

Besides the immediate benefit for the investor, the Eastern partner country will also benefit from the influx of foreign firms via cooperation and acquisitions due to increasing income and growing know-how.

DUAL RESTRUCTURING

Dual restructuring divides the value-added chain of a product between Western and Eastern companies in such a way that significant improvements in competitive advantage can be achieved for both.

The result is a division of labor with which both the Eastern and Western companies can be shaped to meet the future. Dual restructuring provides optimal structuring of two complementary companies. In the most extreme case, this sometimes results in a "green field" solution for Western investors. All advantages the Western company achieves propels economic recovery in the East and drives market development.

Detailed analyses are required to answer the questions about which activities should be relocated to the East, how to find the appropriate partner, how to propel the engagement forward, and how to control the restructuring and market-entry processes. Only with a clear picture of the situation for both sides and of the requirements of the current and future markets can measures be developed.

From the Western investor's standpoint, dual restructuring follows a five-step approach:

1. *Analysis of the relocation potential of value-added activities.*
   All value-added activities of the Western company have to be assessed as to their suitability for relocation, based on net benefits and strategic significance.

2. *Identifying the Eastern European location.*
Decisions on appropriate countries and industries have to be made before the search for an Eastern European country or plant is initiated. A wide range of factors has to be considered when selecting a target company; for instance, the possible contribution to the desired competitive advantage, and the compatibility of cultures and manufacturing structures. (For country-specific considerations see Zentes, 1991, Part 2.)

3. *Competitive analysis.*
Besides analyzing existing markets, the chances of market entry by rivals must be analyzed (Porter, 1990). A thorough product/market/ competitor analysis is needed, and the result has a significant effect on selecting country, partner, and site.

4. *Form of engagement.*
Once the activities to be relocated have been identified, the form of the entrepreneurial engagement in the East has to be defined. Actions range from long-term delivery agreements with Eastern companies to acquisitions. The decisive factor is the engagement's objective. Is it the realization of short-term cost targets, or the long-term penetration of a new market, or both?

5. *Implementation of dual restructuring.*
Redistributing activities automatically means that the value-added chain must be oriented toward both sides in order to realize potential benefits. The activities in the West and in the East have to be coordinated and harmonized with reference to the common objective, requiring not only new structures but also new control processes. If the levels of quality and reliability are acceptable, a simple supplier relationship is sufficient. The greater the need for restructuring the Eastern company and the more important the components, products, and activities to be relocated are for the Western company, the more necessary it is to forge, a close legal link (Steinberg, 1991).

Dual restructuring is an attractive option for German industry, particularly for mature industries such as steel manufacturing and mechanical engineering. Other candidates are industries that are under considerable pressure due to saturated markets, such as the automotive industry. In fact many companies in these industries were among the first to take advantage of the opening in the East.

New complementary value-added chains need to be developed partnerships between Eastern and Western companies. At first, the East will supply low-tech products, components, and raw materials to assume its place in a worldwide value-added alliance, while the Western partners concentrate their efforts on high-tech products, design, engineering, and related services. In the medium term, this will lead to a partial shift of high-tech product manufacture to locations in the East which will receive an increased share of value added and the related transfer of know-how.

These tasks require visionary new structures, supported by detailed knowledge on restructuring, extensive insight into local conditions, and the ability to implement the restructuring processes as quickly as possible. Thus, an experienced consultant can provide valuable assistance, by, for instance, significantly reducing the time required.

ILLUSTRATIVE CASE:
JAGENBERG MASCHINENBAU GmbH

The experience of Jagenberg Maschinenbau GmbH & Co. KG shows how a company from the highly competitive machine manufacturing industry can improve its competitiveness by taking advantage of an East European location and thereby turning losing operations into profit generators. In addition to machine manufacturing, Jagenberg was also active in the paper industry, foil technology, and packaging; its 1993 sales were DM 777 million.

Problem: High Cost

One of Jagenberg's main concerns was its cost disadvantage in the area of conventional small parts production. Small German manufacturers could produce the parts as subcontractors at hourly rates between DM 45 and 60, whereas Jagenberg's hourly costs exceeded DM 100. It was expected that through staff reductions and renegotiated employment agreements cost could be reduced. However, the savings were insufficient to regain cost competitiveness in small-parts production.

Options

When management, under the leadership of CEO, Dr. Wolf-Peter Müller, met to decide on the fate of small part manufacturing, the alternatives became clear:

- The first option was to close down conventional parts production at Jagenberg and outsource to small independent suppliers. Jagenberg units, primarily paper production, would be permitted to purchase directly from the suppliers and thereby avoid the high overhead that

Jagenberg would have to charge its units. The disadvantage, of course, was a reduction in sales for the company as a whole.

- The second option meant to try to lower costs even further, beyond what was possible under Option #1. It was this idea that led to the expansion to Eastern Europe. At the current location, no further savings were possible beyond what had already been examined, and attractive locations could not be found in lower cost West European countries such as Great Britain, Italy, or Portugal. Thus, in early 1993 management decided to find a suitable location somewhere in Central or Eastern Europe. Later, Dr. Müller explained: "One precondition for me as the CEO was to develop the East European location on the basis of reconfiguring the mechanical engineering business in order to regain profitability."

Dual Restructuring: Developing the Concept

On April 1, 1993, machine manufacturing was split from the paper division and established as a legally independent subsidiary of the Jagenberg concern. In the shortened fiscal year 1993, it produced losses in the tens of millions. Eighty percent of the new company's business originated in the production of parts and components for Jagenberg's paper production business, 5 percent for the other divisions, and 15 percent for outside customers. The cost reduction measures discussed earlier were quickly implemented: By the end of 1994 the workforce had been cut by 20 percent to 426 employees and total sales were DM 74 million.

Immediately after the decision to relocate, the search began for a suitable site in Eastern Europe for Jagenberg's parts manufacturing and assembly operations. The logical place to start was in the Czech Republic since already in 1989, Jagenberg had subcontracted the maintenance of their packaging machinery to affiliates of the Czech Milcom corporation. Thus, some kind of cooperation and basic mutual understanding were already in place. Jagenberg's managers were reasonably confident that Milcom's strong track record in machine manufacturing and the geographical proximity to Jagenberg's location in Germany would yield the envisioned cost reductions and not be compensated by excessive quality, handling, and transportation costs. Dual restructuring thus became a top priority: In May 1993 senior executives of Jagenberg visited the Czech Republic and Slovakia to examine potential candidates for a joint venture.

At the same time, Jagenberg also identified the functions to be relocated. These were found among steps in the production process that could be handled with relatively easy-to-operate, conventional machinery that had high-cost labor requirements and where price competition was intense.

The criteria for determining the optimal partner were defined in detail. The ideal partner had to be prepared to reconfigure its workforce into a newly established joint-venture company. (See also Fröhlich, 1991, for various aspects of East-West joint ventures.) The ideal partner had to have a track record in small lot size production of machine parts, given Jagenberg's reputation as a producer of special machinery. Also, Jagenberg wanted to contribute its own machinery from sites in Western Europe as a fixed asset investment to the joint venture. Its machine tool capacity was vastly under-utilized, partly due to other, unrelated relocations within the Jagenberg group. Therefore, the Eastern partner needed to have sufficient factory space available in order to accommodate the machinery. Furthermore, the partner needed to be located in an area that provided a sufficiently larger pool of workers for subsequent expansion. A final concern was labor productivity. At all sites, Jagenberg engineers carefully scrutinized working speed, reliability, and quality.

Dual Restructuring: Implementation

After four companies had been visited—two in the Czech Republic and two in Slovakia—Jagenberg selected Vuma in Novè Mesto, Slovakia. Vuma was an expert manufacturer of prototypes and small lot sizes. Also, some of the turnaround measures needed after the privatization had already been implemented. Vuma's workforce in 1993 stood at 700 compared to 2,000 originally, and was expected to be reduced further to 500 by year-end 1994.

The geographical distance between Novè Mesto and Neuss, Jagenberg's location in Germany, was 1,400 km with good roads ending within 15 km of Vuma's company gates. This turned out to be an important factor, since the closest candidate visited by Jagenberg was located in the Tatra mountains where access was difficult, especially during the winter months. One final favorable aspect of the Vuma site was that a nearby machine tool factory was scheduled to close which ensured Jagenberg of a large pool of skilled workers.

In June 1993, Jagenberg's Board of Directors approved the joint venture. At the time, Slovakian law prohibited establishing a foreign-owned company without local participation. It was therefore decided that Jagenberg's initial share in the joint venture called Vuma Jagenberg would be 20 percent and Vuma would hold 80 percent of the shares. The agreement further stipulated that Jagenberg would acquire 51 percent as soon as relative productivity, which then stood at 1 to 4, reached a ratio of 1 to 2 compared to the west German plant. Jagenberg's cautious approach manifested itself in other ways as well: For example, until Jagenberg acquired a majority ownership, its machinery would be leased by the joint venture.

Soon after the agreement was signed and the machinery transferred, Vuma Jagenberg received its first test orders. It quickly became clear that the cost savings were dramatic: Vuma Jagenberg's transfer price was DM 23 per production hour plus a DM 2 transportation charge, compared to DM 60 for a small west German supplier.

Twenty-five Vuma employees were brought to Jagenberg's plant in Neuss. Among them was the head of production of Vuma Jagenberg, who was responsible for selecting the most qualified for the training period in western Germany. This proved to be successful because it enhanced the understanding among the parties. In mid-1994 Vuma Jagenberg employed 73 workers; an expansion to 120 was planned for the near future.

Restructuring has been executed quickly and efficiently. A west German expert was assigned to the joint venture for six months in order to supervise the installation of equipment, to instruct employees, to organize production, and to acquaint the employees with Jagenberg's policies. Jagenberg's accounting system was replicated in the joint venture and a premium-based wage system was introduced in order to improve motivation and productivity.

A simple, efficient management information system was installed and plans called for a major system enhancement once Jagenberg obtained a majority position. Vuma Jagenberg was linked to the German data processing system for order management.

Materials management was the only major problem. The Slovakians encountered difficulties in obtaining the necessary input; thus Jagenberg had to organize weekly truck transports of finished parts from Vuma to Neuss. On the return trip, the truck was used to distribute semi-finished parts.

The faster-than-expected increase in employment was due to two reasons: First, a large volume of finished parts for paper technology could be produced at Vuma Jagenberg; and second Vuma Jagenberg became a primary location for the components assembly for the packaging business.

Dual Restructuring: Lessons

Jagenberg Maschinenbau exemplifies successful cost-induced dual restructuring. Market considerations were of minor significance in the relocation decision, even if in the future the market should improve appreciably. However, once the venture is in place, it appears that Vuma Jagenberg might profitably be used as a staging site for additional relocations in Central/Eastern Europe. In 1995, test production of major parts in the East suggests a 60 percent cost reduction compared to Western Europe.

Learning from Jagenberg Maschinenbau the key success factors of the dual restructuring project were:

- Initially relocate only uncritical, labor-intensive steps of the operation and only after previously testing for quality.
- Include local employees in on-site decision making and utilize their contacts to the maximum extent.
- Split off from the parent company only those areas that are necessary. This way the parent company can concentrate on its core competencies.

By the end of 1994, less than two years after the initial decision, Jagenberg was in the enviable position of being able to offer its customers finished parts and components with a competitive blending of Western and Eastern cost positions. Compared to 1993, losses had been reduced by 50 percent and a balanced result for 1995 was considered a demanding yet realistic objective. This was not only exceptional for Jagenberg but also for the German machine industry at large which had experienced losses in recent years. While it was painful to reduce personnel in order to bring costs under control, the parent company considered the cuts necessary. Even labor representatives were convinced that a smaller but competitive workforce was better than continued losses and eventual bankruptcy. It turned out that this careful approach positioned Jagenberg for future adaptation and growth.

When asked what he should have done differently, Dr. Wolf-Peter Müller replied: "Perhaps our approach was too cautious and we should have tried to acquire a majority right from the beginning. As to the floor space, we've already reached the capacity limit. A larger building would have been better. But otherwise, we would use the same approach."

REFERENCES

Bronder, C. 1993. *Kooperationsmanagement: Unternehmensdynamik durch strategische Allianzen.* Frankfurt/New York: Campus Publishing.

Fröhlich, A. 1991. *Ost-West Joint Ventures.* Baden-Baden: Nomos Verlag.

Harrigan, K.R. 1983. *Strategies for vertical integration.* Lexington, MA: Lexington Books.

Koch, H. 1991. Rein oder raus. *Manager Magazin,* No. 8: 118-124.

Porter, M.E. 1980. *Competitive strategy.* New York: The Free Press

Porter, M.E. 1990. *The Competitive advantage of nations.* New York: The Free Press

Yip, G.S. 1992. *Total global strategy. Managing for worldwide competitive advantage.* Englewood Cliffs, NJ: Prentice-Hall.

Womack, J.P., Jones, D.T., and Roos, D. 1990. *The machine that changed the world.* New York: Rawson Associates.

Zentes, J. 1992. (Ed.) *Ost-West Joint Ventures.* Stuttgart: Schäffer-Poeschel Verlag.

PART V:
EMPLOYEES AND CONSUMERS
IN A NEW CONTEXT

Chapter 18

Labor Relations and Policies in Hungary and Poland: Implications for Western Human Resource Managers

Jacob M. Chacko
Piotr Chelminski

With a population of 38 million people, Poland is one of the largest and most populated countries of the former COMECON (Council for Economic Cooperation and Development) nations. Hungary, sometimes referred to as the "jewel of the Eastern European Crown," has a population of 10.5 million people (Dent, 1992). Hungary and Poland possess a well-educated and inexpensive labor force when compared to the Western European countries. The free-market policies implemented by the Hungarian and the Polish governments have had a significant impact on the labor market in the two countries. The transition toward an economic system governed by free-market principles has resulted in intense competition in the labor market. To understand the current labor issues it is imperative to review the historical developments in labor relations in the two countries.

Between the late 1940s and early 1990s three distinct periods in labor movement can be identified in both countries, which, in spite of the Soviet influence on labor policies, differ significantly (Table 18.1).

EMERGING LABOR ISSUES IN POLAND AND HUNGARY

Employment

After World War II, Central and Eastern European nations experienced rapid industrialization under communism. In spite of high demand for

293

TABLE 18.1. Labor Policies in Hungary and Poland During the 1940s to 1990s

Poland	Hungary[a]
Soviet Model (late 1940s-1980) • communist regime determined all aspects of labor relations • assumed homogeneity of interests between the labor and management • labor unions were established and controlled by the state • labor laws were devised and enforced to punish rather than protect workers • collective disputes treated as subversive activity • full employment policy mandated by the constitution • sporadic labor strikes (1956, 1970, 1976) • privately owned farms were not affected by labor policies	*Soviet Model (1950-1968)* • communist regime determined all aspects of labor relations • assumed homogeneity of interests between the labor and management • labor unions were established and controlled by the state • collective disputes treated as subversive activity • labor laws were devised and enforced to punish rather than protect workers • social upheaval in 1956 • full employment policy mandated by the constitution
Solidarity Model (1980-1989) • workers established the first independent labor union–"Solidarity" (resembling labor unions of Western nations) • Solidarity's demands pertained to the society as a whole, and were economic, political, and social in nature • full employment policy still mandated by the constitution • in 1981 the union was delegalized and later reinstated • Solidarity evolved into a political power with majority representation in senate by 1989	*Liberalized Soviet Model (1968-1988)* • recognized labor-management conflicts • though not adequate, increased importance given to workers' rights • labor unions continued to be controlled by the government • legitimized labor disputes • full employment policy still mandated by the constitution
Transition Model (1989-Present) • drastic changes in labor market due to implementation of free-market principles • workers face unemployment for the first time in 40 years (unemployment rate of 16.9 percent)[b] • reduced government intervention in labor policies • declining role played by labor unions	*Transition Model (1989-Present)* • drastic changes in labor market due to implementation of free-market principles • workers face unemployment for the first time in 40 years (unemployement rate of 11 percent)[b] • reduced government intervention in labor policies • restructured labor unions • declining role played by labor unions

Sources: (a) Hethy (1992), (b) Graczyk (1995).

labor due to the rapid industrial growth, the cost of labor remained low due to government wage controls. To create higher output the production system relied on increased inputs rather than on improving productivity. The low productivity, combined with inappropriate wage differentials, poor training, high labor turnover, and hoarding of labor aided the communist regimes in achieving the constitutionally mandated full employment. Together, these factors resulted in a wasteful usage of the workforce. In early 1995, six years since the decision to embrace the market system, the situation was not very much different in most state-owned enterprises. Wages were still low and local workers' councils resisted any proposed layoffs. However, in the private sector labor practices were moving toward Western labor management practices which reduced the inefficiencies of the old system.

To deal with the high rate of unemployment accompanying the transition, governments in both countries established a safety net for displaced workers. In 1989, the Polish government introduced the *Employment Act*, initially amended in 1990 and again in 1992. It recognized the unemployed as a legitimate employment category for the first time in over 50 years and stipulated benefits for the unemployed. Under the 1992 version, the monthly unemployment benefits were set at 36 percent of the average national monthly salary instead of being linked to the salary previously received by the displaced worker. The duration of benefits was reduced to one year. This amendment resulted in a 27 percent reduction in the number of registered unemployed eligible for benefits (Brown, 1992).

A similar legislation, also known as the *Employment Act*, was enacted by the Hungarian government (Hars, Kovari, and Nagy, 1991). In reality, the unemployment compensation in Poland and Hungary is grossly inadequate for subsistence which is all the more significant since, in 1995, unemployment in Poland was close to 17 percent and in Hungary about 11 percent. Due to the high level of unemployment, the responsibilities of the governmental labor offices were expanded to include such activities as arranging for retraining and organizing public works programs, in addition to assisting the unemployed in finding suitable jobs.

The communist full employment policy provided the labor force with little or no experience in job search. Unlike their Western counterparts, to this day workers in Poland and Hungary take a passive stance when it comes to exploring job opportunities. Several additional factors aggravate the situation. Severe housing shortages make it expensive and difficult for people to relocate. Also, people are less accustomed to leaving behind their families and communities (Etzioni, 1991). To alleviate the geographic imbalance in unemployment, the Polish government offers tax breaks to companies investing in high unemployment regions.

Since unemployment is a new phenomenon in the two nations, it has had a major psychological impact on individuals who lost their jobs as well as on their families. The right to work and job security, both guaranteed under the communist system, are believed to be birthrights. Thus, even the economically justified layoffs cause more severe feelings of rejection among Central and Eastern European workers than in the West (Bednarzik, 1990). This makes provision of a safety net particularly important, as the unbalanced labor market, coupled with a deteriorating standard of living could result in social unrest that could undermine the nations' political and economic system which is still in its infancy.

Wage Policies

In the socialist command economy, the government was responsible for regulating each enterprise's wage fund and for fixing wage scales for workers in different job classifications. Even though the implementation of free-market principles calls for demand and supply to set wage rates, some level of governmental intervention over wages beyond what is customary in developed market economies seems necessary during the transition process to manage inflationary pressures.

In Poland's state-owned enterprises, wages are not yet established by the market; rather, they are controlled through the *Indexation Law.* This law stipulates that wage increases should not exceed the rate of inflation and mandates a progressive 100 to 500 percent penalty tax on state employers who increase their total payrolls above the government set limit (Ash, 1992; Chelminski, Manakkalathil, and Tangsrud, 1994). Hungary has minimum wage regulations in place and the government has been adjusting the minimum wages to help those with subsistence-level incomes. In early 1991, the minimum monthly compensation was set at HUF 7,800, which translated into slightly above U.S. $100.00 at the 1991 exchange rate (Cukor and Kovari, 1991). Also, to combat the relatively high inflation, it was suggested that the government, along with the trade unions and other interested parties, implement a temporary system of collective bargaining that would limit excessive nominal wage increases for certain managerial positions in some industries (Cukor and Kovari, 1991). In this way, the governments attempted to maintain a tight relationship between wage increases and the rate of inflation. The deflationary policies have been critical in deterring hyperinflation, but they also have contributed to a sharp decline in real wages. The decline in purchasing power is exacerbated by the cutbacks in nonwage subsidies enjoyed by labor under the previous system.

In early 1995, the average monthly salary in Poland was approximately ZI 650.00 (U.S. $270). Employers must pay a 45 percent social security tax and a 2 percent unemployment tax on the total wage sum (Price Waterhouse, 1992). In Hungary, the employers contribute 44 percent of the gross wages toward the national social insurance system (Gray and Karp, 1995). In spite of the high taxes on wages levied on employers, the cost of Polish and Hungarian labor is still lower than in most of the so-called low-wage nations. For instance, in 1991, the average hourly cost of labor including taxes in these two nations was about U.S. $1.45-2.20, while the hourly wages including benefits were U.S. $2.17 in Mexico, U.S. $3.58 in Hong Kong, U.S. $4.32 in South Korea, U.S. $4.38 in Singapore, and U.S. $4.42 in Taiwan (Baker, Smith, and Weiner, 1993). In addition, in Poland and Hungary, the health care system is fully financed by the government. The wages in both Poland and Hungary should remain below the Western European standards for many years to come. A study by the Central European Economic Review shows the estimated number of years that it will most likely take to achieve about 75 percent of the average level of income in the European Union (Table 18.2).

Worker Training

The literacy rate of 98 percent among Poles and Hungarians (*The World Almanac*, 1994), along with the fact that a majority of individuals have received vocational training, points to the effectiveness of the educational system in these countries. Eight years of elementary education is compulsory; after that students have the option of vocational training or secondary education, which prepares candidates for college level education. Another inherent strength of the educational systems in the two nations, unlike that of most developing countries, is that it ensures equal access to

TABLE 18.2. Estimated Number of Years to Achieve 75 Percent of the Average European Union Income Based on GDP Growth in Poland and Hungary

Annual GDP Growth	Hungary	Poland
3 percent	35 years	44 years
4 percent	26 years	33 years
6 percent	18 years	22 years

Source: Graczyk, 1995: 50.

education for both men and women. Women in the workplace were granted equal opportunity under communism. However, with regard to managerial positions, the *glass ceiling* is as prevalent in Poland and Hungary as in the West.

Labor Unions

During the communist era, virtually all workers in Poland and Hungary were members of the government-sponsored union. The trade unions were bureaucratic government agencies that did not represent workers, but rather served the state in the process of imposition of new production plans and task formulation. Labor disputes and collective bargaining between employers and employees were practically nonexistent. The reforms initiated in 1968 in Hungary, and in 1980 in Poland changed the organization and functions somewhat. However, the transformations in 1989 have had an even greater impact on the role and structure of labor unions (see Table 18.1).

Current goals of Polish and Hungarian labor unions are quite similar to those of Western labor unions. In Poland, the role of the Solidarity Union as an instrument of positive social, political, and economic change has given way to one of being a conventional worker-oriented organization which may cause some concern among Western investors, especially from North America (Dowling and Schuler, 1990; Freeman and Medoff, 1987).

In 1992, 83 percent of the Polish labor force was unionized mainly in three large organizations, down from virtually 100 percent membership earlier. This decline is due to a general disillusionment among workers with the bureaucracy of the communist unions, and later, with the Solidarity's having become a political party and the ruling elite.

In Hungary, labor unions have also experienced tremendous change. The National Council of Trade Unions declared representation of workers as its exclusive function and proclaimed its independence from any political party. In 1990, the council was reorganized into a National Confederation of Hungarian Trade Unions. The bureaucratic structure of the old union was dismantled and the organization was put under close control of the member unions. In spite of these changes, union membership has dropped from 98 to 75 percent of the workforce (Dent, 1992). Several professional groups have left the national union and formed alternative smaller organizations and workers' councils (Mako and Simonyi, 1992).

Sociocultural Aspects of Labor

The lack of incentives to foster initiative and hard work under the communist system has left the labor force and the management ill-prepared to perform effectively and efficiently in a free-market economy. Guaranteed full employment and the inefficient utilization of labor in industry have raised a labor force used to working slowly, not taking initiative, not accepting job responsibilities, and often missing work.

Central and Eastern European workers tended to entertain less formal relationships with management which led to greater levels of social interaction outside of the workplace than in the case of Western companies. The informal nature of work relationships resulted in less formal enforcement of organizational hierarchy (Riff, 1994). This also makes it difficult to implement labor reduction policies, as managers are reluctant to layoff subordinates who often are their close friends.

In general, Poles and Hungarians are eager to work for Western corporations as these companies often offer better career advancement opportunities and higher remuneration than local firms. However, a part of the labor force in the two nations is somewhat hostile toward Western investment for a number of reasons:

- Some workers are reluctant to work for foreigners, just as some Americans are reluctant to work for Japanese in America (Galbraith, 1992).
- Although they renounce socialism, Central and East European workers also dislike the capitalist class structure (Tayeb, 1992). This attitude may be due to communist propaganda which emphasized the ideological equality of the communist society, while exaggerating the economic and social differences between the classes in capitalist nations.
- Workers fear continued layoffs as new management looks for greater production efficiencies (Chelminski, Manakkalathil, and Tangsrud, 1994).
- Workers feel that the state enterprises, which theoretically belong to them, are being sold to foreigners at bargain prices.
- Many workers are uncomfortable with the Western style of management, a reflection of the work habits acquired during the Communist era (Chelminski, Manakkalathil, and Tangsrud, 1994).

IMPLICATIONS AND RECOMMENDATIONS FOR WESTERN INVESTORS

Poland and Hungary are often portrayed in business press as having a relatively inexpensive labor force which is true even when payroll taxes are included. The government-imposed cap on wages for state-owned enterprises in Poland, and collective bargaining aimed at keeping wages low in Hungary, when coupled with the prevailing rate of unemployment, should keep wages low in the foreseeable future. As a result, these nations constitute a favorable environment for companies with labor intensive operations.

The advantage of low-cost labor is to some extent diminished by the relatively low productivity of the Polish and the Hungarian workers. Inadequate emphasis on quality of goods and services is another trait that was inherited from the communist system. The workers and managers still lack an understanding of the importance of product quality in the market place. The modification of personality traits and work habits of post-communist societies could take a considerable amount of time. However, higher monetary benefits, combined with restructuring inefficient operations, have proven to be an effective means of change in the short run (Chelminski, Manakkalathil, and Tangrud, 1994).

Implications for Western Investors

To increase productivity, it is imperative for Western employers to develop effective incentive programs that will improve motivation, encourage initiative, and reduce moonlighting. It is obvious that paying higher wages than state-owned companies is one way of achieving these objectives. However, higher wages will not necessarily eliminate the need to provide other benefits to which workers have become accustomed under the previous system such as housing, day care facilities, education, in-house medical care, transportation, subsidized vacation plans, etc.

Another problem inherited from the Communist era is the lifelong job security enjoyed by workers which has reduced the incentive to perform at their highest potential. A solution to this predicament would be the formulation of an effective performance evaluation and termination policy based on a cost-benefit analysis of low versus high labor turnover.

The relative immobility of the labor force should be of concern to potential investors. Companies have to seek out the optimal balance between the availability of a higher quality but more expensive labor force, and the potential tax breaks sometimes offered by the government to encourage investment in regions of high unemployment. However, the mobility constraints will make it difficult to attract qualified managers and high quality workers if a plant were to be located in a rural area. In such instance investors might want to consider developing community housing.

It is important to understand the existing level of technological development in these nations to ensure adequate training and time for adjustment in trying to introduce more advanced production methods. Companies need to consider various options ranging from on-site training to sending workers to company training centers abroad. Training needs to emphasize the importance of customer service, a concept foreign to workers in a seller's market. The high rate of literacy of the labor force should simplify and expedite their training. However, the language barrier could be a constraint as very few blue collar workers in Poland or Hungary speak a Western language.

The full employment policy of previous governments provided workers with a high degree of job security, thus, most lack job-seeking skills. When hiring blue-collar workers, employers need to be creative and develop appropriate methods of recruitment, since traditional Western recruiting processes may prove ineffective in these countries. To acquire high-quality workers, employers must follow a proactive recruiting strategy. Rather than relying on local labor offices which are inefficient and crowded with low-quality workers, employers should advertise in local and national newspapers and magazines.

As in any international venture, cross-cultural sensitivity training is imperative for both expatriate managers and local workers. In managing the labor force in Hungary and Poland, Westerners must realize that they are dealing with a labor force that is more educated and sophisticated than they might have expected. It is also important to be aware of the less formal hierarchical relationships that prevail on factory floors. Cultural understanding and closer social interaction will not only aid in effective management, but also diminish the anti-Western sentiments among the workers.

A crucial difference between the Polish and Hungarian labor is in the propensity to protest and strike. Poland has one of the most active labor forces in the world. As exemplified by the Solidarity movement, Polish labor has had a history of strikes and uprisings against authority. While instrumental in bringing about the downfall of the old communist system, labor's propensity to protest and strike could prove to be disadvantageous to attracting Western investors. Hungarians, on the other hand, do not have a tradition of strikes. Although workers have the right to strike, they do not seem to exercise it to the extent of their Polish counterparts.

The haste with which legislation has been passed during the transitional period gives rise to the concern that laws are neither comprehensive nor in their final form. Thus, investors should anticipate changes in labor laws and clarify doubts with appropriate governmental agencies.

In sum, the central location of Poland and Hungary, combined with favorable labor force characteristics, makes them attractive sites in Eastern

Europe. These countries can be considered as gateways due not only to their relatively inexpensive and well-educated labor force, but also to their geographical and cultural proximity to the main markets in the West and further East. The domestic market potential of Poland and Hungary is another lure to investors.

Many labor-related problems that are of concern to Western managers still exist in the two nations. Ultimately, with the full adoption of a market economy, the labor environment will become more similar to that of the West, though it remains to be seen how long this change will take. It is important for both present and prospective investors to realize that Poland and Hungary are strategic markets of the future. Therefore, companies should plan to invest in these countries on a long-term basis, avoiding a short-term strategy that hinges solely upon capitalizing on low wages. With proper planning and realistic anticipation of potential problems, Western investors should be able to capitalize on the opportunities with which they are presented.

REFERENCES

Ash, N. 1992. Poland: Model in a muddle. *Euromoney Supplement*, April: 58.

Baker, S., G. Smith, and E. Weiner. 1993. The Mexican worker. *Business Week*, April 19: 84.

Bednarzik, R. 1990. Helping Poland cope with unemployment. *Monthly Labor Review*, December: 27.

Brown, B. 1992. Transforming postcommunist labor markets: The Polish case. *RFE/RL Research Report*, August: 50-56.

Chelminski, P., J. Manakkalathil, and R. Tangsrud. 1994. The Polish work force: Implication to western investors. *Business & the Contemporary World*, 1: 102-111.

Cukor, E. and G. Kovari. 1991. Wage trends in Hungary. *International Labour Review*, 2: 177-189.

Dent, B. 1992. Rendszervaltas is only a word. *New Statesman & Society*, April 3: 30-31.

Dowling, P. and R. Schuler. 1990. *International Dimensions of Human Resource Management*. Boston, MA: PWS-Kent Publishing Company.

Etzioni, A. 1991. Eastern Europe: The wealth of lessons. *Challenge*, July/August: 8.

Freeman, R. and J. Medoff. 1987. What do unions do? In L. Simeon and B. Nissen (Eds.), *Theories of the Labor Movement*. Detroit, MI: Wayne State University Press: 300-320.

Galbraith, J. 1992. The rush to capitalism. In D. Kennett and M. Lieberman (Eds.), *The Road to Capitalism: Economic Transformation in Eastern Europe and the Former Soviet Union*. Orlando, FL: The Dryden Press: 92-96.

Graczyk, M. 1995. Awangarda fortuny. *Wprost*, March 5: 51-55.

Gray, K. and R. Karp. 1995. Economic reforms in Eastern Europe: Privatization in Hungary. *Proceedings of Academy of International Business Southwest Regional Meeting*, March: 167-175.

Hars, A., G. Kovari, and G. Nagy. 1991. Hungary faces unemployment. *International Labour Review*, 2: 165-175.

Héthy, L. 1992. Hungary's changing labour relations system. In Széll, G. (Ed.), *Labour relations in trandition in Eastern Europe*: 175-182. Berlin, New York: Walter de Gruyter.

Mako, C. and A. Simonyi. 1990. Social spaces and acting society. In Széll, G. (Ed.), *Labour relations in transition in Eastern Europe*: 29-84. Berlin, New York: Walter de Gruyter.

Price Waterhouse. 1992. *Doing Business in Poland: Information Guide*. Warsaw: Price Waterhouse.

Riff, M. 1994. How to combat anti-western attitudes. *Journal of European Business*, January/February: 12-14.

Tayeb, M. 1992. Capitalism, socialism, and business organizations. In G. Szell, (Ed.), *Labor Relations in Transition in Eastern Europe*. Berlin: Walter de Gruyter, Inc.

The World Almanac. 1994. Nations of the World. Mahwah, NJ: Funk & Wagnalls Corporation.

Chapter 19

Russian Pay Practices, Preferences, and Distributive Justice Judgments: Implications for Joint Ventures

Jane K. Giacobbe-Miller
Daniel J. Miller
Vladimir I. Victorov

As Central and Eastern European countries strive to transform their command economies to market-driven economies there has been a call for assistance from the West. An abundance of programs have sprung up throughout Central and Eastern Europe for the purpose of providing training and consultation in the development of managerial skills in marketing, finance, accounting, and administration. At the same time, joint venture activity has increased dramatically as Western companies seek to expand their product markets overseas.

Joint ventures in Central and Eastern European countries have encountered numerous challenges, some related to the bureaucracies in the various countries while others seemingly relate to cultural differences between these and Western countries. Many joint ventures appear to be "feeling their way through" the adaptation of managerial systems from the West and their experiences can be helpful in determining which (if any) systems can be fully transferred.

However, in the quest to bring about rapid, systematic change in a politically volatile environment there has been little effort to explore the basic values and beliefs of the citizenries of Central and Eastern Europe. These underlying values have important implications for the appropriate design of managerial systems. Of particular interest to many joint ventures, as well as economists from both the East and West is the design of compensation systems that will both stimulate productivity and enhance worker perceptions of fairness. The appropriate design of compensation systems is dependent on a variety of factors, including the historical development of pay systems in Central and Eastern Europe and prevailing practices since attempts to transform these economies has begun. Basic values of the citizenry are also important, as most current workers have spent a lifetime working under socialist systems and principles. To further complicate the situation, all of the Central and Eastern European countries currently have parallel systems, with significant numbers of state-owned organizations still operating in their economies. Yet, joint ventures, cooperatives, and privately owned enterprises are rapidly growing in number. Therefore, workers in joint ventures have not only their historical employment in state-owned enterprises as a point of comparison, but also the continued existence of state-owned enterprises which probably employ some of their friends and family.

This article focuses on Russia, one of the primary Central and Eastern European countries undergoing transformation to a market economy. The purpose of this chapter is twofold: first, we will explore historical and current pay practices in state-owned and joint-venture enterprises in Russia. Second, we report our findings from three studies of Russian perceptions of pay fairness relating to different bases for allocating pay. From our analysis of pay practices and our study results we draw tentative conclusions about compensation systems design for joint ventures in Russia. We begin with an examination of historical pay practices based on our belief that the past informs the present.

RUSSIAN PAY PRACTICES (1917-1992)

In theory, compensation systems should be designed to reflect the culture of the workers who will be subject to them. The culture of Russia has been described as "collectivist." In this context, collectivism refers to a system in which the members of the collective are expected to take care of each other and where group goals are dominant over individual goals (Triandis et. al., 1992). Collectivist cultures are often associated with pay systems that are based on group performance, although some collectivist cultures base payment on the personal needs of employees (Gomez-Mejia and Welbourne, 1994). In addition to a longstanding tradition of collectivism that dates back to the medieval Russian peasant commune, pay practices from the time of the Russian Revolution are rooted in the works of Marx and Engels (Flakierski, 1992).

A primary theme throughout this period was the need for communist countries to strive for equality. One of the prominent philosophies espoused by Marx was: "From each according to his ability; to each according to his need" (Marx, 1942: 566). However, Marx recognized that not all workers contribute equally or even in accordance with their abilities. He therefore maintained that each worker should receive a wage that is in proportion to the work performed (Marx and Engels, 1974). The "work performed," however, was differentiated only by the duration or intensity of labor (Marx and Engels, 1974); supporting the notion that there should be little differentiation in wages, Engels maintained that even differences in worker skill or education should not be recognized for pay purposes (Engels, 1954).

The period immediately following the Revolution was characterized by a fascination with equality. Primarily, moral incentives appealing to the workers' sense of obligation to the collective good were used to stimulate worker productivity. Lenin, however, the architect of the revolution and the new socialist state, soon realized that moral incentives were inadequate to motivate the Russian workers. Contemporaneous with Lenin's efforts to run the new command economy was the advent of Scientific Management (Taylorism) in the West. While Lenin viewed much of Taylor's work as the epitome of exploitative capitalism, he did see merit in the idea of linking pay to productivity through a piece-rate system. Thus, piece-rates and bonuses became a part of the communist pay system, a pattern that has continued to the present (Kiezen, 1991).

Despite persistent efforts to link pay to productivity there are a number of features of the historical pay system and economy in Russia that have undermined these efforts. These features reflect, in part, the ongoing tension between the need for efficiency and the desire for egalitarianism that has plagued socialist countries from their inception (Flakierski, 1992). These include the overarching low-wage/high nonwage policies that persist to this day in state-owned enterprises; the notorious "wage leveling" policies that resulted in part from egalitarian values and in part from labor shortages; the pattern of pay differentials; and Russian managerial practices. These features have effectively severed any connection between pay and productivity. Each of these will be discussed, along with their implications for contemporary pay systems in joint ventures.

A Low-Wage/High Nonwage Policy

For the last several decades the Soviet Union has pursued a low-wage policy while social consumption funds provided for workers' basic needs. This was wholly consistent with Marx's basic premise that monetary wages would disappear in a Communist society as each worker contributed according to his or her ability for the betterment of the collective. Social consumption funds, which emulate a combination of government and private employer benefits in the United States, were allocated by the central government for education, health, pension, benefits, and subsidies for most basic needs–especially housing and food. Consistent with Communist doctrine, wages were kept purposefully low through state-determined pay scales, a practice made possible by monopolizing the means of production (Shcherbakov, 1991).

The problem with the low-wage/high nonwage approach to compensation is threefold. First, it is difficult to create clear linkages between nonwage incentives and productivity, particularly since a cash-equivalent value of some benefits is not readily apparent. Further, some workers will value particular benefits more highly than other workers (Standing, 1991). Thus some benefits may not have an incentive or reward value for some workers. Finally, when wages are extremely low relative to nonwages, the incentive value of modest cash bonuses is inconsequential.

Further complications arise with the lack of a hard currency in Russia. Heretofore basic needs have been provided and controlled by the state (as employer), thus wages were not particularly effective in enhancing a worker's standard of living in such areas as housing, education, and health care. Wages could provide luxuries; however, the price of quality consumer goods is very high which requires extraordinary bonuses to be paid. Finally, savings have not been an attractive option with the current runaway inflation in Russia.

Western management practices assume that money is a motivator. However, it is difficult to determine from past experience whether this is true in Russia as well. Research conducted in Russia in the 1970s and 1980s indicates that differences in salary were not important to Russian workers in choosing jobs. Rather, workers were more likely to focus on housing accommodations and working conditions as a reason for leaving a job, as well as opportunities to enhance their skills. One explanation for these results is that wages have been kept so low that it is really the nonwage benefits that have differentiated jobs from the worker's perspective (Standing, 1991). Accordingly, it is unknown whether pay would be an effective motivator in the Russian culture if wages were more important in determining a worker's standard of living.

Wage-Leveling Policies

The works of Marx and Engels made clear that an important distinction between socialism and capitalism was the stress on egalitarianism (Flakierski, 1992). However, it was recognized that initially some degree of differential payment was necessary as the system evolved into communism. In the 1920s the Soviet government centralized wage scales for manual and nonmanual workers (Shcherbakov, 1991). Soviet theory for differentiating occupational pay was based on differences in skill, working conditions, the importance of the industry to the national economy, the regional location, and the type of enterprise. In practice, however, the philosophy of egalitarianism influenced the pay structure, and chronic labor shortages resulted in relatively low pay differentiation. Over time, the earnings of highly educated technical workers have approximated those of manual workers.

The Pattern of Pay Differentials

It has been suggested that the problem with productivity in the former Soviet Union can be attributed more to the pattern of pay differentials than to wage leveling. Two aspects of pay differentiation are particularly noteworthy. First, wages in general have favored manufacturing–a pattern that was defensible during the industrial revolution but is inappropriate in a service or information economy. The emphasis on manufacturing has been attributed to the Soviet belief that material production was more important in creating wealth for the citizenry (Flakierski, 1992). Second, occupational wage differentials declined drastically during the 1970s and 1980s, from a 200 percent differential in 1970 to a 10 percent differential in 1986 (Flakierski, 1992). This has given rise to a situation where wages in some occupations requiring low levels of education exceed those of jobs requiring high levels. The latter situation has been attributed in part to the socialist concept of "socially useful work" differentiating between "productive and unproductive" labor (Standing, 1991). This situation has created considerable concern in that there are structural disincentives for acquiring the education and skills that are necessary for economic growth and development (Shcherbakov, 1991).

Managerial Practices

As noted previously, pay systems in Russia have often been comprised of low wages supplemented by piece-rates and bonuses. Piece-rate payments were quite modest, resulting in little or no incentive for productivity improvements. Bonuses were often awarded when productivity targets were met or exceeded. However, bonuses were usually distributed equally among the workers regardless of their individual contributions (Kirsch, 1972). Taken together, wages, piece-rates, and bonuses still resulted in low overall wage payments relative to high nonwage payments from social consumption funds (Vodopivec, 1991).

In addition, performance evaluation systems that would theoretically support a linkage between productivity and pay were (and are) virtually nonexistent in Russia. Based on a recent experience of one joint venture in

Russia the concept of providing performance feedback was completely unfamiliar to the Russian employees (Puffer, 1992).

Finally, it should be noted that worker participation in firm decision making is a fundamental feature of socialist systems. In its most basic form workers meet to discuss and decide on basic business strategies. In addition, workers are routinely involved in a Russian version of continuous improvement efforts (Kiezen, 1991).

RUSSIAN PAY PRACTICES (1992-PRESENT)

Wage/Nonwage Trends

Even as recently as 1987, governmental tax practices exacerbated the trend toward higher social consumption wages and lower cash wages. The 1987 State Enterprise Act imposed a 75 percent tax on wages beyond specified minimum levels. This induced enterprises to provide additional goods and services as bonuses and incentives in lieu of direct cash payments. These goods and services have been as basic as direct distribution of food to employees and their families which allowed them to avoid the long queues of Russians waiting for food (Standing, 1991).

The low wage/high nonwage policies of the former Soviet state are changing in state-owned enterprises. Many nonwage benefits are being abolished by the Russian government. For example, housing subsidies in some areas are being phased out over the next five years. At the end of this five-year period, rents for housing will no longer be controlled. Similarly, the controls on food prices have already been eliminated. For workers of state-owned enterprises whose pay is significantly less than those of joint ventures, there is a noticeable erosion of their standard of living through inflation and reduced subsidies for the basic needs such as food and housing.

In contrast, joint ventures are free to establish wages as they deem appropriate, without the shackles of past enterprise practices. Initially, joint ventures discovered that pay has to be significantly higher than that of state-owned enterprises in order to compensate workers for the loss of job security and some social consumption benefits—although many joint ventures still offer significant nonwage benefits. Also, as an initial step during the years of consumer shortages, joint ventures discovered the importance of bartering arrangements that allow for goods and services as substitutes for wage incentives. In what is perhaps a conscious attempt to more directly link wages to productivity, one joint venture rewarded workers by giving them artificial "cash currency" that could be used to purchase Western consumer products from a catalogue (Puffer, 1992).

The situation in Russia is rapidly changing, however, and will undoubtedly have undergone more change since this chapter was written. Consumer goods shortages have all but disappeared in some areas. Also, foreign currency exchange offices are now plentiful in some areas. As a result, using goods and services as a substitute for wage incentives may no longer make sense.

Wage Leveling and Pay Differentiation

In 1986, Gorbachev sought to reform the pay structure by differentiating wages on the basis of education, quality of work, and skill. However, the reform was too expensive given the prevailing economic conditions. Also, despite conscious efforts to reform, the trend toward increased wage leveling continued throughout the 1980s. Labor shortages for unpleasant jobs generally associated with low skill, created pressures against increased wage differentiation (Flakierski, 1992). While the effects of past practices continue to affect current pay structures, the present state of compensation in Russia is one of tremendous diversity across organizations. Minimum wages are still established by the state, but beyond this, organizations may pay what is deemed appropriate although wages above a certain threshold are subject to high taxes. Most noteworthy, there is a large and growing disparity between payment by state-owned organizations and privately owned or joint-venture firms.

Implications for Joint Ventures

Low Wage/High Nonwage Practices

Contrary to the most recent past, joint ventures in Russia are best advised to use direct wage incentives which can now be used by the workers to purchase whatever they desire. Also, workers can now convert rubles to hard currency for savings, and as a hedge against the rapid inflation of the Russian ruble.

Further, it is imperative for managers of joint ventures in Russia to now recognize the ineffectiveness of small direct cash incentives, as has been past Russian practice. Consumer goods that are now available are primarily imported and priced comparably with markets around the world. On average Russian workers cannot afford these goods and small cash incentives will not improve their ability to do so. Thus, joint ventures are best advised to offer cash incentives that approximate those of workers in Western market economies.

Wage Leveling and the Pattern of Pay Differentials
for Joint Ventures

Wage leveling is considered a primary source of low labor productivity in Russia–largely the result of no incentive for education and skill development. This has led to a devaluation of skills critical to science and technology (Shcherbakov, 1991) which could severely hamper Russia's ability to function in the information-based economy. Further, it is believed that the lack of a relationship between wages and quality/quantity of work has caused a loss of motivation. Joint ventures in Russia have the opportunity to reverse this trend by recognizing education and skill as primary factors for pay differentiation.

There are two pay systems that would facilitate this objective. One is the "point plan" system of job evaluation that is the predominant system for establishing wage structures in the United States. This system involves the ranking of jobs based on "compensational factors" such as education or skill required for the job. Pay is determined according to the overall ranking of the job in the organizational hierarchy. A second approach might be a "pay for knowledge" or "pay for skills" system that is used in some team-based organizations. This system pays workers based on what they know or the skills they possess, rather than the job itself. Either of these systems would create linkages between pay and skill or education acquisition. There is some concern, however, that even these systems will not be sufficient to stimulate productivity. Rather, the effectiveness of pay systems might be further enhanced by directly linking pay to productivity, perhaps through a profit-sharing approach (Vodopivec, 1991).

However, managers in joint ventures must realize that they, too, may have difficulties attracting labor to unpleasant jobs, particularly when employment in a joint venture is associated with a loss of job security and social consumption fund benefits. Therefore, pay for unskilled workers in joint ventures may have to exceed that of state-owned enterprises and differentiation based on skill or education must occur beyond that point. Pay systems in joint ventures may have to be more compressed than those in the United States. This is not to suggest that the degree of wage differentiation in the United States is optimal. In fact, pay disparities in the United States exceed those of other Western free-market economies and have been the subject of considerable criticism (Helms and Crowder, 1995).

Managerial Practices for Joint Ventures

As joint ventures seek to staff their enterprises with Russian workers, they need to be aware of the historical experience of workers under socialism. The absence of performance feedback systems and the equal distribution of bonuses undermined efforts to stimulate worker productivity. While it has been deemed "imperative" that worker productivity be stimulated, all of the necessary systems to establish such linkages represent a dramatic change to the previous experience of Russian workers. Accordingly, joint ventures in Russia would be best advised to ease into practices that will create strong linkages between worker productivity and pay as well as practices that create huge disparities in workers' incomes. While dramatic and abrupt change may seem the most effective way to stimulate productivity, one must be continuously aware of the fragile nature of the political transformation. Firms that create great disparities in pay among workers could well be viewed as "heartless" and symbolic of the exploitative systems the Russian workers once found despicable. During the period of transition, where Russians have experienced primarily the pain of economic transformation and few, if any, benefits from a market economy, the image of ruthless capitalism could well undermine the very purposes of Western involvement.

In addition, joint ventures should recognize and embrace the long history of worker participation in Russia. While worker participation has historically been an important part of the managerial practices of Western Europe, its popularity has spread to the remainder of the Western economies, including the United States. It would be entirely appropriate to continue worker participation in joint ventures in Russia, particularly in the design of systems that represent dramatic changes. For example, one firm reports success in involving employees in the design of a new pay system that is based on individual employee performance (Puffer, 1992). Likewise, worker participation would be appropriate for the design of performance appraisal, discipline, and discharge systems. (See also Chapter 17 in this volume.)

RESEARCH ON RUSSIAN PAY PREFERENCES

Our review of the literature regarding Russian pay practices found conflicting views about what would likely be the preferences of Russians for various types of pay systems. On the one hand, Russians have a long history of egalitarianism, both in practice and in principle. This would suggest a preference for equalized pay regardless of productivity. However, soon after the Russian Revolution, Lenin realized that equalized payment and moral incentives were insufficient for the motivation of workers. As a result, Lenin instituted a system of individual piece-rates and bonuses that were tied to group productivity. If motivation and perceptions of fairness are linked among Russian workers–considerable research in the United States supports this linkage among U.S. workers–Russian workers have seemingly rejected equalized payment as exemplified by their reduced productivity.

With awareness of the importance of designing compensation systems that fit with the culture of the workforce, we have developed a stream of research that explores Russian pay preferences, perceptions of pay fairness, and worker productivity under various forms of pay allocation. At the time of this writing, our research is still in progress. The following reports what we have learned.

Study One

Our first study was very basic and exploratory. We were interested in the general rules of pay distribution that would be selected by Russian managers. Our sample was comprised of 21 Russian managers who were enrolled in a training program at a university in the northeastern United States. The managers were given a simple scenario in which they were asked to imagine that they had a bonus of 100,000 rubles–at the time of the experiment a considerable sum–to divide among employees as a reward for their hard work. They were then asked whether they would divide the rubles equally, according to need, according to individual productivity, or based on some other criterion. Of the 21 managers, 20 indicated that payment should be according to individual productivity. However, the majority of these focused on effort rather than results as the measure of productivity.[1] The remaining manager indicated that he would divide the bonus according to individual need. These results should be interpreted in light of the fact that these managers had self-selected into a program that teaches Western management practices; many had relocated to the United States for a period of one to two years. It is therefore reasonable to assume that they had seemingly accepted Western management practices and perhaps had considerable knowledge about them.

Study Two

Our second study was more elaborate, and included 125 Russian students who were enrolled in a technical university in St. Petersburg, Russia

---

1. The distinction between effort and results is important in the literature. In fact, the definition of productivity as effort rather than results has been a persistent feature of Soviet pay systems since the Revolution. This feature has been identified as a major inhibitor of worker productivity–used in the Western sense of results (Shcherbakov, 1991).

and 88 U.S. students who were enrolled in business courses in two universities in the northeastern United States. Participants were asked to first complete a questionnaire and scenario role-play and then to participate in an experiment involving various forms of pay allocation.

Similar to our first study, participants were asked to assume the role of a manager responsible for allocating a bonus to a work unit that assembles computer keyboards. However, in this study a description of each employee was provided. The descriptions gave information about the employee's marital status, number of children, household income, and productivity. Based on this information the participants distributed the bonus and subsequently were asked to report their basis for the allocation decisions. The results produced striking contrasts between U.S. and Russian subjects. A clear majority (59 percent) of the U.S. subjects distributed the bonuses on the basis of individual productivity, although a significant number (27 percent) also distributed the bonus equally. The criterion of need was clearly rejected by the U.S. subjects as only 9 percent indicated need as their basis for allocation. In contrast, 55 percent of the Russian subjects distributed the bonuses on the basis of individual need as determined by the marital status, children, and household incomes of the hypothetical employees. Individual productivity was a strong, but secondary factor for pay distribution (36 percent). Russians clearly avoided use of the equality rule for distribution (8 percent).

The second part of the study involved an experiment in which subjects were asked to perform a task of sorting index cards. Productivity was measured as the number of correctly alphabetized cards that a subject could sort in a ten-minute interval. Subjects were assigned to one of three experimental groups. The first group was told that payment would be made according to their individual productivity. The second group was told that payment would be made according to the group's productivity and that each group member would be paid the same. The third group was given a choice as to whether they chose to be paid equally or on the basis of their individual productivity. After the task was completed, subjects were asked to report their perceived fairness of the pay allocation. We also collected productivity information across the three experimental conditions.

The results of our study indicated that:

1. When given a choice, both Russian and U.S. subjects chose to be paid based on their individual productivity.
2. When assigned to a payment condition, both Russian and U.S. subjects reported the greatest perceived fairness when payment was based on individual productivity.

3. Productivity was the highest for U.S. subjects when they were performing under conditions where pay was based on individual productivity.
4. Productivity did not vary for the Russian subjects under any of the experimental conditions.
5. For both Russian and U.S. subjects, the opportunity to choose the terms of payment produced a heightened sense of satisfaction with pay, over and above the satisfaction experienced when working under the preferred allocation rule.

Study Three

We have just completed data collection for a third study. The sample for this study is comprised of 100 Russian managers who are currently employed by state-owned or joint ventures in Russia. This study is also a scenario role-play. Its primary distinguishing factor from the second study is the inclusion of an additional variable, co-worker relations, which is thought to be important in collectivist cultures. While the results are preliminary, it appears that this group of Russian managers:

1. Prefer payment based primarily on individual productivity.
2. Give significant, but secondary weight to co-worker relations as a basis for pay.
3. Recognize the importance of workers' need in making pay allocations.
4. Reject equal distributions regardless of individual productivity.

Results

Across the three studies, one result is consistent. Both the Russian and U.S. subjects prefer to allocate bonuses based on individual productivity. Neither group prefers equal distributions. Need appears to be a more important criterion for awarding pay for the Russian subjects, although the students (as future workers) appeared to be influenced more by need than were the managers. In contrast, need is explicitly rejected by the U.S. subjects.

Implications of These Studies for Joint Ventures

The results of our studies thus far seem to indicate that there may be some degree of transferability of U.S. pay systems to the Russian culture, particularly if the pay system is based on individual productivity. Despite the Russian collectivist culture, it appears that the Russians in our studies prefer payments based on individualized productivity. However, unlike our U.S. subjects, Russians appear to be sensitive to the needs of individual workers. Taken together, these results suggest that in order for pay systems to be perceived as fair and acceptable to Russian workers they should seek to blend these two principles for pay distribution.

What we would suggest is not that pay should be allocated according to individual need (as some collectivist cultures do) but rather that individual need should be somewhat equalized through benefits that emulate those of large corporations in Western Europe and the United States. These might include typical benefits such as employer-paid medical insurance, pensions, and subsidized cafeterias, day care, and tuition. Benefits packages could also include subsidized transportation services as are often provided in France or, as in the Philippines, direct distribution of food (Dowling, Schuler, and Welch, 1994). Mortgage assistance would also be appropriate as Russia makes opportunities available for ownership of private property. Currently, home ownership is well beyond the reach of the average Russian citizen. While these kinds of benefits are not the same as employer-provided housing, health care, education, day care, summer camps, and food, they would at least provide a safety net for employees and assistance with skill development and acquisition of additional education. We are cognizant of the fact that a heavy emphasis on employer-provided benefits is contrary to trends in the United States, where employers are seeking to transfer the costs of benefits to employees. However, the "middle ground" of generous benefits as opposed to direct provision of basic needs would be an appropriate step during the transformation to a market economy.

It is noteworthy that our Russian subjects indicate a strong aversion to the equal distribution of pay. Our Russian participants believe that this is a conscious backlash to the failed socialist practices of the past. Similar results have been observed in recent studies conducted in China (Chen, 1995). This result suggests that, contrary to what we might have expected in a collectivist culture, some of the pay practices in the United States that accompany team-based management, such as gain-sharing and profit-sharing, may be inappropriate in Russia at this time.

In addition, it is clear that participation in decision making–exemplified by the presence of a "choice" in the basis for pay allocation in our experiments–has a positive effect on Russians' perceptions of fairness. Similar results have been observed in the United States which have led to the widespread use of participatory management practices. This suggests that where possible, joint ventures in Russia should involve employees in the development of compensation systems and supporting practices (e.g., performance appraisal systems). Employee involvement will not only likely improve perceptions of fairness but will also lead to the development of systems that more appropriately fit the Russian culture.

CONCLUSIONS

We feel that there is much to be learned about the Russian culture that has important implications for effective management practices. More than providing answers, our research raises many questions:

1. What is the optimal mix of wages and benefits for Russian workers during the transition to a market economy?

While many have clearly indicated the need to dramatically change the current wage/nonwage ratio, our second study suggests that future workers (i.e., current students) still believe that employers should provide for the basic needs of their employees. Our third study, with managers, indicates that need is an important criterion as well, although not as important as productivity. How might employers meet the needs of the economy and the workers simultaneously?

2. How might the current pay structures be changed to create incentives for skills and education acquisition?

There is considerable concern that the current wage system creates disincentives for the acquisition of education and skills that are crucial to the Russian economy in the information economy. However, the low wage/high nonwage system has made differentials for education and skills negligible. A job evaluation system such as a point plan might be useful, but could prove to be quite expensive if unskilled workers need to be paid comparably to the state-owned employee market in order to attract and retain them. Highly educated and skilled workers would then have to be paid much higher than their counterparts in state-owned enterprises.

3. What kinds of incentives are appropriate in an economy where consumer products are extremely expensive and small additional cash payments will not necessarily improve an employee's standard of living?

Current joint ventures in Russia have experimented with awarding goods and services for good performance. This can be problematic, however, if workers do not uniformly value the goods and services awarded by the employer. With consumer goods more widely available in Russia today, cash incentives seem most useful now. However, they must be significant enough to be noticeable. How much is enough? Continued experimentation by joint ventures may offer the answer to this question.

4. How might pay be better linked to productivity?

This, of course, is a question that is also relevant for Western managerial systems. However, most Western companies at least have a system of performance evaluation, with established performance standards. The question then becomes what kind of performance standards would be deemed as fair and acceptable to Russian workers. The piece-rate system utilized in our experiments is familiar to Russian workers and was deemed acceptable. However, piece-rate systems are not generally appropriate for white-collar jobs. Performance standards in the United States have evolved over many decades and have been continuously adapted to reflect current managerial values and job contents. We should be extremely cautious in assuming that similar performance standards would be acceptable and fair to Russian workers. Again, worker participation in the development of performance standards and appraisal systems would be appropriate.

In conclusion, our strongest recommendation to organizations seeking to establish joint ventures in Russia is to thoroughly research the past managerial practices of firms in their industry and to familiarize themselves with the culture of their employees. *It should not be assumed that what is effective in the United States or other Western cultures will be effective in Russia.* Perhaps the best approach would be to involve Russian workers and managers in the design of pay and other managerial systems. This would likely maximize the chances that these systems will be acceptable to Russian workers, and effective and efficient for the organization.

REFERENCES

Chen, C.C. 1995. New trends in rewards allocation preferences: A Sino-U.S. comparison. *Academy of Management Journal*, 38: 408-428.

Dowling, P.J., Schuler, R.S., and Welch, D.E. 1994. *International Dimensions of Human Resource Management*. Belmont, CA: Wadsworth Publishing Co.

Engels, F. 1954. *Anti-Duhring*. Moscow: Progress Publishers.

Flakierski, H. 1992. Income inequalities in the former Soviet Union and its republics. *International Journal of Sociology*, 22(3): 1-86.

Gomez-Mejia, L.R. and Welbourne, T. 1994. Compensation strategies in a global context. In R.A. Noe, J.R. Hollenbeck, B. Gerhart and P.M. Wright (Eds.), *Readings in Human Resource Management*. Homewood, IL: Irwin Publishing Co: 561-562.

Helms, M. and Crowder, M. 1995. International Executive Compensation. In Mendenhall, M. and Oddou, G. (Eds.), *Readings and Cases in International Human Resource Management*. Cincinnati, OH: Southwestern Publishing Co: 394-404.

Kiezen, W. 1991. *Management in Socialist Countries: USSR and Central Europe*. New York: de Gruyter.

Kirsch, J.L. 1972. *Soviet Wages: Changes in Structure and Administration from 1956*. Cambridge, MA: The MIT Press.

Marx, K. 1942. Critique of the Gotha Programme. In Marx, K. *Selected Works*, Vol. 2. New York: International Publishers, pp. 550-601.

Marx, K. and Engels, F. 1974. *Werke*. Vol. 23. Berlin: Dietz Verlag.

Puffer, S.M. 1992. *The Russian Management Revolution*. Armonk, NY: M.E. Sharpe.

Shcherbakov, V.I. 1991. Remuneration of labor in the USSR: Problems and prospects. *International Labor Review*, 130(2): 227-236.

Standing, G. 1991. Wages and work motivation in the Soviet labor market. *International Labor Review*, 130(2): 237-253.

Triandis, H.C., Bontempo, R., Villareal, M.J., Asai, M., and Lucca, N. 1992. Individualism and collectivism: Cross-cultural perspectives on self-in-group relationships. *Journal of Personality and Social Psychology*, 54(2): 323-338.

Vodopivec, M. 1991. The labor market and the transition of socialist economies. *Comparative Economic Studies*, 23(2): 123-158.

Chapter 20

Life and Consumption Styles in the New Bundeslanders Five Years After the Collapse of the Berlin Wall

Christoph B. Melchers

Since the opening of the East German market, following the collapse of the Berlin Wall in November 1989, retailers, advertising agencies, and market researchers have found themselves time and again confronted with unexpected problems. Shortly after reunification the prevailing opinion was that East Germany would, within a few years, proceed on the same trajectory that West Germany had traveled over a period of 40 years. However, only a few months into the transition, marketers noticed confusing consumer behavior patterns in stark contrast with this perspective. Many German and foreign firms were disappointed by the results of their marketing efforts which were supposed to be tailored to the specific needs of the East Germans. The purpose of the research reported here is to shed light on these confusing experiences and gain insight into the East Germans' buying behavior and underlying motivations.

A first clue in deciphering this confusing mix of attitudes and behaviors is the realization that present attitudes and behaviors continue to be influenced by those acquired during the socialist era. The more insecure individuals feel in the new environment and with the vast consumption opportunities, the more likely they will seek safety in previously acquired, familiar behaviors. To understand and correctly forecast East German

---

Translated by Arieh Ullmann.

consumer behavior, it is necessary to trace the development of lifestyles and conditions under the old regime through the turbulent transition to the present "Unified Germany in Year Five."

METHODOLOGICAL FOUNDATIONS

This research is based on in-depth interviews conducted with 120 men and women in 27 locations in former East Germany (for an extensive report see Melchers and Relin, 1993) based on a morphological approach. This method uses unstructured interviews and thus prevents the problems associated with standardized questionnaires where individuals' replies frequently are conditioned by their perceptions of what is expected. The selection of the interviewees was carefully structured to ensure a representative distribution in terms of age and employment categories.

Morphological market psychology derives from morphological psychology which seeks to systematically represent fundamental human needs (for an overview see Salber 1968; 1969; 1983; 1986; 1988; regarding its applications in marketing see Melchers 1991a; 1991b; 1993a; 1993b; 1994; 1995). It emphasizes three relationships, each of which contain a static and dynamic extreme. Similar to magnetism, the tensions between the polar needs complement each other and thereby form a hexagonal system that we call "Tension of Needs" (ToN) (Figure 20.1).

- The need for individual safety is placed opposite the need to abandon safety, to experience dynamics and change. The desire for change without safety is as intolerable as its opposite.
- The need to be socially adapted—which provides safety—is juxtaposed by the desire to fulfill individual intentions and preferences and to secure individual freedom—which implies accepting risk and the consequences of one's decisions.
- Individual skills provide a sense of stability while they also provoke a desire to go beyond and to attain new levels and accomplishments.

According to morphological theory, normally these tension-filled relationships oscillate. For example, in a market economy individuals abandon secure situations time and again in favor of change which leads to new and different, yet stable situations. Usually, society grants individuals sufficient freedom to lead a life between social adaptation and individuality. People are permitted to pursue objectives that may transcend their current capabilities but that may someday become part of their skills repertory.

FIGURE 20.1. Basic Tension of Needs Hexagon

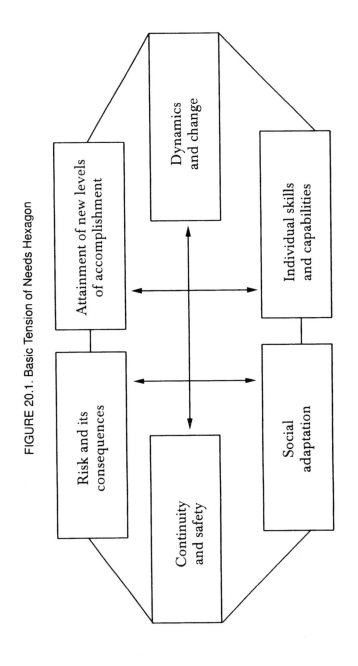

Consumption plays an important part in regulating these tensions: Acquiring certain products can provide security; other products offer a chance to change one's life. Products enable individuals to set themselves apart from the rest of society on the one hand, and to adapt to society on the other hand. Consumption is a way to pursue certain goals in life which currently may not be attainable but which some day may be reached via personal effort.

LOCKED-OUT DYNAMICS: LIFE IN THE GDR

Life Conditions in the GDR: Interruption of ToN

Examining the conditions in the former GDR in the context of ToN, it is evident that individual freedom was constrained which prevented the back and forth movement between the poles of the basic needs. Individual dynamics was taboo; it was nearly impossible to escape the state-imposed existential safety. Life was completely secure and, overall, rather boring. Individual engagement had to comply with the state's objectives; adaptation was in demand. It made little sense to perfect one's skills, because there were few chances to embark for "higher," more ambitious goals. Life in the GDR had been reduced to the static poles of ToN: security, adaptation, and status quo in terms of individual skills (Figure 20.2).

The state replaced consumption as the mediator between various needs with an anticonsumption ideology. The socialist vision of society was supposed to provide the all-encompassing medium to resolve any existential tensions. Consumption was reduced to the role of replenishing consumed energy.

However, this state-imposed construct was unable to provide for the psychological needs of its citizens—the psychological and political laws did not mesh. The socialist system was deficient in that it was unable to accommodate individual needs for dynamics and individuation. When dealing with matters of the psyche, nothing can simply disappear; it reemerges, oftentimes in strange forms. In East Germany, a way to deal with the desire for risk was to shift it to the private sphere, for example by seeking a divorce—the result was a record high divorce rate in the GDR.

Thus, people in the GDR were compelled to find substitutes for the locked-out dynamics. One of the most important substitutes was consumption. Disposed of its role as a mediator of ToN consumption manifested itself in the socialist form of "hunting and gathering." Interpreting hunting and gathering in the GDR within the context of the ToN hexagon, its substitute function for the individual living in the GDR becomes clear.

FIGURE 20.2. Truncated Tension of Needs Hexagon

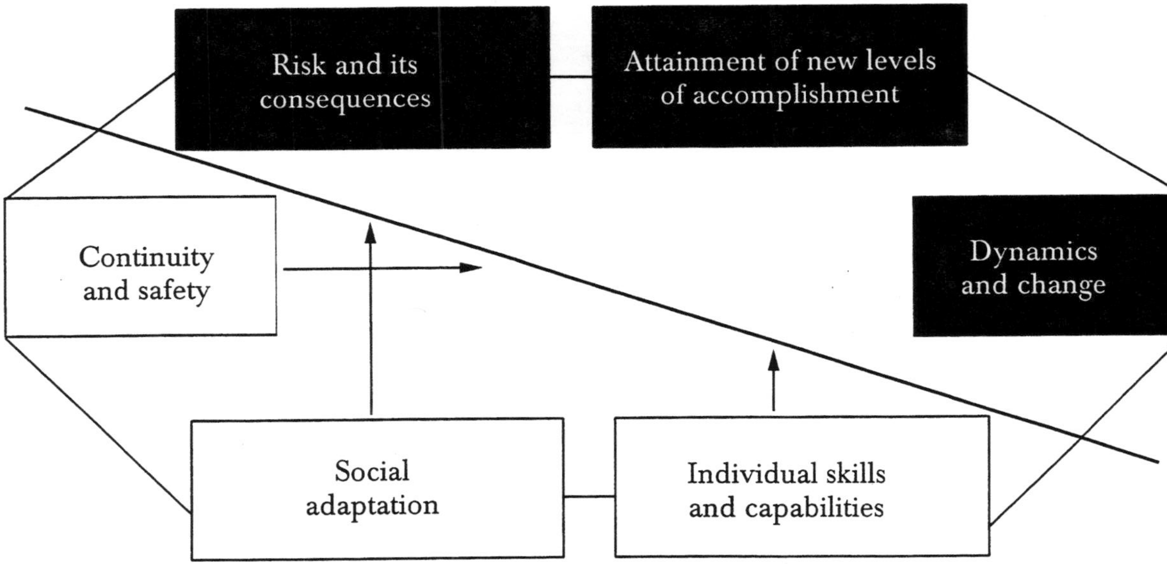
Risk and its consequences
Attainment of new levels of accomplishment
Continuity and safety
Dynamics and change
Social adaptation
Individual skills and capabilities

Consumption Styles in the GDR

Varieties of Hunting and Gathering as a Substitute for Dynamics

The difficult supply conditions prevailing under socialism transformed consumption into an ideal substitute for the truncated opportunities for psychological development. For the GDR citizenry, hunting and gathering scarce consumption goods became a universal surrogate for dynamics. One could never be sure whether a certain product was available or not. The everyday version of this uniform style of consumption consisted in patiently dealing with the meager supply available in "regular" stores: waiting in line; continuously inquiring for goods that one expected to need at some point in the future; and hoarding products one expected to have a need for some day. The moments when these items were finally discovered were relished with a feeling of joy; they were symbols of a small victory over paralyzing everyday life.

To escape the prevailing paralysis and to experience something exciting was the goal of every GDR citizen for which a broad range of opportunities existed: purchasing goods in the hyper-expensive Delikat or Exquisit chain stores; legally permitted travel to Eastern Europe; or acquiring goods from the West. People mobilized their capabilities and skills in a growing barter-based shadow economy where, with a little bit of luck and ingenuity, almost everything was to be found.

Escape from Uniformity: Consumption as a Substitute for Dynamics and Excitement

Apartment, dacha[1], and car served as pillars for the escape from the unattractive, uniform public sphere. Here it was possible to express individuality and to develop one's abilities. And the unavoidable hunting and gathering to purchase spare parts, building materials, furniture, and kitchen gadgets turned into a time- and energy-consuming experience.

Escape from Adaptation: Consumption as a Means for Individuation and Differentiation

Consumption replaced experiencing true risks. By displaying conspicuous consumption it was possible to differentiate oneself from the uniform masses and to provoke questions. Especially useful for this purpose were

---

1. Russian for cottage, i.e., a small house out of town near a lake, etc.

goods from the West which thereby acquired fetishist characteristics. During certain periods it was politically quite risky to own products from the West. For example, if during the 1960s a student managed to acquire a pair of blue jeans from the West and decided to wear them, this not only attracted the attention and envy of classmates but also brought an admonition by the principal.

Hunting and Gathering as Proof of One's Abilities: Consumption as a Substitute for Individual Development

Due to extensive controls, most GDR citizens were unable to deploy their abilities and skills in the pursuit of their personal goals or for the sake of their own development. Instead of following the socialist ideology and offering their skills for the development of socialism within the parameters set by the state, citizens invested their talents in outfitting their private lives. However lethargic on their jobs, in their private sphere GDR citizens displayed all sorts of ingenuity and skills. Trading services for money or goods, do-it-yourself work in their apartments, houses, or dachas, or work on their cars improved their standard of living and at the same time provided a sense of having tricked the state.

The result was a widespread shadow economy, the socialist equivalent of the Western market system: Indeed, those who were adept in moving within the "socialist mini-capitalism" experienced fewer problems in adapting to the market economy after reunification.

Lifestyles in the GDR

Based on the manifold behaviors of the GDR citizenry, eight typical lifestyles can be distinguished that form the foundation of today's lifestyles and consumption patterns in the New Bundeslanders.

"Loyalists" included the convinced socialists who felt that in East Germany their participation in the development of socialism was of global historical importance. They were satisfied with the state and explained its deficiencies as temporary phenomena characteristic of a transitory stage on the path to socialism. Loyalists were present in all sectors of GDR's society: in the state bureaucracy, schools, factories. Of course, the prevailing economy of scarcity was painful for them, too. However, their ideology demanded they consider consumption to be of minor importance for life. Many could even resist the tempting opportunities of obtaining Western products.

The "Disillusioned" originally displayed a positive attitude toward socialism. However, confrontations with state organizations regarding their political views, experiences of being spied upon and of outright oppression, as well as disappointed hopes for a career, or the omnipresent economic scarcities in daily life caused by widespread inefficiency, made many of these former loyalists realize that their state had abandoned the right path. Only reluctantly did the Disillusioned participate in public life. In spite of their cynicism and sarcasm they tried to secure private gain. Oftentimes, consuming Western products was one way to express their criticism of the socialist system.

The "Saturated on a Small Scale" encompassed many GDR citizens of middle and old age. By patiently cultivating "relationships" over many years, they had managed to gain access to the products they desired. After waiting for many years they had finally obtained for themselves a good apartment or a house; after persisting for ten or fifteen years they had been permitted to buy a Trabant, the East German standard car; and they had discovered sources for Western goods and scarce products from the East. Retirees were permitted to visit relatives in West Germany and thus had fewer difficulties in obtaining Western goods. Their standard of life was entirely owed to the state which, however, did not convince them of its proclamations. After reunification the egos of the Saturated on a Small Scale were badly shaken because all those products which they had acquired with a great deal of patience and persistence meant little by Western standards.

"Escapists" had perfected their flight into their private sphere. The had reduced their participation in public life and on the job to the unavoidable minimum, while their leisure time activities became the true center of their lives. They focused all their disposable energies on their hobbies: gardening, do-it-yourself, building a dacha, family life, and children. Escapists were active in procuring the necessary materials for their hobbies; as often as possible they tried to obtain Western products. Their orientation toward their private life continued after reunification albeit for different reasons.

In their innermost thoughts, "Secret Capitalists" had always been supporters of the despised capitalist economic system. They focused their energies on activities related to the shadow economy to such an extent that this turned into a second job for many. Frequently, Secret Capitalists achieved an unusually high standard of living. Emotionally, they seesawed between pride of having achieved so much by tricking the state against all odds, and depression when they realized from watching West German television that, no matter what their standard was, compared to the West they would remain second class forever.

Those that the state could not do without were the "Indispensables." Because of this, the state granted them privileges that the rest of the people were not permitted to have, without demanding superficial loyalties in exchange. The Indispensables–top athletes, the elite in the arts, technology, and the sciences–provided hard currency and international recognition. In exchange, they were given a passport and the permission to own large amounts of Western currency. Indispensables had always lived with one leg in the West; all they had to do after reunification was to pull over the other as well.

"Socialist Managers" comprised the top echelons of the Nomenklatura–less due to their capabilities than based on their immaculate personnel files which enabled them to pursue careers in the political and economic systems. Socialist Managers could be found in export-oriented industrial kombinates[2] and export-import enterprises that brought in hard currency which was urgently needed. Also part of this group were a few high level party functionaries and journalists. Due to their continued contacts with the West, Socialist Managers always had one leg "over there," although they loudly proclaimed to be in the service of Socialism. It was no surprise that after the turning point they found themselves quickly at the top.

The "Oppositionists" expressed their criticism of the prevailing regime by emphasizing the deficient realization of the socialist ideals. They were convinced a third path existed between socialism and capitalism, and they maintained intensive communication with like-minded individuals in the West. Many of them were victims of prolonged spying of which they were not always aware. They were less interested in the pursuit of material things because the conflict with the prevailing system assured them of an adequate level of dynamism in their lives.

THE TRANSITION
FROM SOCIALISM TO CAPITALISM

Little changed immediately after and because of the transition, since the state, which shielded the individual from most risks and changes, did not change within a few days or months. By the same token, human beings living in such a state could not take advantage of the suddenly expanded options available to them overnight. Rather, their consumptive behavior continued to be shaped by the circumstances in the defunct GDR.

The Wall Opens: Hunting and Gathering
in Neighboring Territory

Whoever happened to be in West Berlin a few days after the Wall crumbled could observe how people who are hunters and gatherers react to

---

2. Large, highly diversified and vertically integrated industrial complexes.

the neighbor's plentiful hunting grounds known only from TV. As always, they hoarded when an opportunity for consumption had presented itself–with the added pleasure of doing it in the territory of the much-envied West Germans. With the familiar and anxious question utmost in their minds–"Who knows when this will be possible again?"–combined with the habit of building inventories, the GDR citizens attacked the well-stocked shelves. The buying frenzy of the "Ossis"[3] can in no way be explained by a need "to catch up." Rather, their compulsive behavior was rooted in their old GDR habits. Their hoarding activities enabled them to continue their habit of hunting and gathering.

After Reunification: Rediscovered Dynamism

After reunification the former GDR citizens experienced a totally alien system: The traditional separation of the fundamental needs vanished and with it the limitation on individual options characteristic of the socialist system. New opportunities arose, and new risks, too. The sudden freedom demanded new behaviors that the East Germans never had the opportunity to practice. Just as their counterparts in Socialism, decision makers in the West never considered the psychological realities of the former GDR inhabitants in designing the transition to a market economy. For most of the East Germans, the sudden change from one system to the other was simply too much. Pressured to take advantage of the new opportunities and to present themselves as the new citizens of this system, most of them were totally helpless.

By contrast, the "West" invaded East Germany with caravans of automobiles, and armies of commercial agents and sales reps. New shops quickly established themselves, stocked with West German products and accompanied by noisy advertising. With much ado the dilapidated road system and the partly desolate cities were being renovated. At work a new wind made itself noticed: the old jog-trot was no longer permitted. The GDR economy collapsed and tens of thousands became unemployed. Given these circumstances, the East Germans were eanthing but happy. For them, the newfound dynamism was too vehement. The familiar feeling of security was lost. No wonder then that the first booming product in the East was the insurance policy. Instead of gaining access to the new opportunities available in a market economy, the East Germans sought security by falling back on habitual behaviors commensurate with their

---

3. West German nickname for East Germans.

own state of development. So as not to get lost in the midst of these oscillating ToN, the people sought to avoid the dynamic poles.

CITIZENS OF THE NEW BUNDESLANDERS: THE UNKNOWN CONSUMER

Several typical styles of consumption can be distinguished among the former GDR inhabitants and traced back to previous lifestyles under socialism. In the following we briefly discuss these lifestyles, their origins, and the related consumption styles.

The Silenced Lifestyle: Movement on Enemy Territory

In the GDR, the Silenced were part of the "system implementers": They were teachers, public servants, low-level functionaries, and workers, and "Socialism was their life." After reunification they were quasi "kidnapped" by capitalism. They do not agree with the new situation, and consider themselves disadvantaged. For them, the calamity forecasted by socialism before the transition has happened to the fullest extent. The "class enemy" has won and now holds an overwhelming position: Thus it is best to keep quiet. Apparently the Silenced are resigned to accept the new conditions; however, deep in their hearts they believe that some day their hour will come. When striking up a conversation with them, they point to unemployment, plant closings, and rent increases to prove that socialism is the better system after all–and confide that they hope the GDR system will return.

Typical Consumption Styles: Value Fetishism, Bargain Hunting

Following their persistent belief in socialist values the Silenced continue to reject consumption and adopt a frugal lifestyle (Table 20.1). They buy the necessary minimum without enthusiasm and focus on the practical usefulness of products. They have no understanding whatsoever for the value of brand names. By restraining themselves they also try to withstand the undeniable temptations of the West.

The Plaintiff Lifestyle: Set Out in the Desert

In the GDR, today's Plaintiffs belonged partially to those followers who had arranged themselves inconspicuously with the system. Without values

TABLE 20.1. Consumption Styles in the New Bundeslanders

Value Fetishism
A product's usefulness is deemed the sole legitimate criterion. Price/value ratios of products are scrutinized. Advertisements based on emotions are rejected as a defensive mechanism against the influx of a Western lifestyle. "Value" is sometimes used as a pretense for hiding a desire for prestige when purchasing a product.

Budgeted Outfitting of Personal Sphere
Emphasis on outfitting one's personal sphere and on products used at home, thereby avoiding the suspicion of consuming for prestige purposes and complying with the prevailing socialist ethos. Extremely stingy and emphasize practical usefulness of products (see Value Fetishism).

Bargain Hunting
Focus on special promotions and sales of everyday products and more expensive items enables continuation of hunting-and-gathering style of consumption. Such sales share many features with GDR shopping, e.g., limited time offers, or waiting in line. Bargain hunters also like to shop in poorly stocked shops or on Monday mornings before the shelves are restocked from the weekend. Quote: "It's good to hear a salesperson say: We don't have it in stock!"

Dry Runs
Practicing shopping (window shopping, catalog viewing) without actual purchase. Allows practicing one's taste; getting acquainted with product offerings; dealing with aggressive sales pitch unknown in the GDR where salespeople were mere distribution clerks. Dry runs are occasionally legitimized due to lack of funds (which often is not true).

Cultivating Hobbies
Besides products for daily consumption, frequent purchases for hobbies (e.g., motor bikes, photography, wines) with emphasis on quality and price/value. Level of ownership frequently par with Western counterparts.

Buying Westernization
Frequent purchase of predominantly Western products in order to better understand the essence of the West and to assimilate to Western lifestyle. Minimize differences from West Germans.

Selective Shopping Euphoria
Effort to extend post-transition shopping euphoria. Due to financial limitations, shifted to low cost items. Frequently extensive purchases of specific products (e.g., CDs, pocket books, candy, lipsticks).

Demonstrating Saturation
Restraint in purchasing Western products (the only ones bought). Need for Western products satisfied before or immediately after transition thanks to contacts with the West, and/or high income.

and interests of their own, they appreciated the system's security and at the same time vied for the promising West. The nucleus among the Plaintiffs, however, is comprised of the Saturated on a Small Scale who, after the transition, experienced a loss in value of their former significant assets. Based on their experiences during the first years, the Plaintiffs feel overwhelmed by the market economy, if not disappointed and cheated. Without the security of socialism, they are confused by their failed experiments to adjust themselves to the new opportunities. Having succumbed to the manifold temptations of a consumer society, many are in financial distress and eager to "take revenge" against the capitalists. Their frustration expresses itself in continued complaints and in their feelings of victimization. A position of internal opposition is widespread among the older generation, the unemployed, and retired. Plaintiffs develop a tendency to glorify the situation in the GDR; however, they have no desire to see it return.

Typical Consumption Style: Budgeted Outfitting of Personal Sphere, Bargain Hunting

Distrustful of the temptations of the market economy, the Plaintiffs have turned the precise calculation of the price/value ratio of all products into a cherished hobby. They take advantage of all available consulting services for consumers, carefully study consumer reports, and react vehemently against all advertising that uses emotional appeals instead of objective data. Plaintiffs are also suspicious of brand names–after all, it is the inherent value of a product that they are interested in, not its brand recognition.

The Help-Seeker Lifestyle: Self-Pity as a Motto for Life

In the GDR the Help Seekers were part of the Intimidated. Just as in the past, today they tend to view themselves as threatened and overwhelmed by "the situation." Their extreme need for security leads them to feel threatened by even small changes in their lives and compels them to seek help and advice from all sorts of organizations. Everything is "too much" and unknown: "What will the state pay in case of illness?" "What papers do I need to travel abroad?" "How do I complete a tax form?" "Which is the best VCR among the many brands and models?" All these questions make the Help Seekers feel neglected. They seek refuge in their private sphere but do not really enjoy it; all opportunities for enjoyment are spoiled by fear and self-pity.

*Typical Consumption Styles: Dry Runs, Value Fetishism, Budgeted
Outfitting of Personal Sphere, Bargain Hunting*

Help Seekers' incapability for enjoyment is reflected in their consumption styles: Occasionally, they may dream of extravagant luxuries; however, they would never dare to carry out their dreams. Correspondingly, Help Seekers study catalogs with great interest; here they can live their wishes without facing the consequences. Often these consumers emphasize that they would not buy even if they had the necessary financial resources—which, in fact, turns out to be a pretense because frequently Help Seekers do own sufficient funds for safety reasons.

The Hermit Lifestyle: Escape from the New Dynamism

Even more so after the transition than before, the apartment is the Hermit's bastion. Just as before, Hermits have problems adapting to society. They try to succeed "out there" in professional life. However, whenever and as often as possible they seek refuge in their private sphere where their true life takes place. In the GDR Hermits had to take part in collectivist public life; now the security of the private home is used to compensate for the hectic everyday life.

*Typical Consumption Styles: Budgeted Outfitting of Personal Sphere,
Value Fetishism, Bargain Hunting, Cultivating Hobbies*

Hermits use the increased supply of goods first and foremost to equip their private oasis by purchasing products that enhance their life at home. Especially important are electronic products: Hermits love to withdraw behind their computers and VCRs.

The Tolerater Lifestyle: Careful Adjustment

Patience was the Toleraters' virtue during the GDR era. As Escapists they tended to reject socialism. They did not resist participating in the compulsory activities yet conserved their energies for their private lives. Now they follow a new slogan: "Keep going; some day things will get better." For Toleraters the new conditions provide an opportunity to carefully heal the schism in their way of life. They aim to establish a balance between professional and personal life. They actively deal with the new situation but remain inconspicuous–unlike the Bossis[4] or Plaintiffs. Instead, they try to get used to the new way of life and to find harmony between their new and old ways.

Typical Consumption Styles: Budgeted Outfitting of Private Sphere, Cultivating Hobbies

The previously prevailing discrepancy of their lifestyle, and the Toleraters' carefulness is clearly visible in their style of consumption. On the one hand they are part of the group of "reasonable" consumers who live frugally and take advantage of sales and discounts. On the other hand, for their homes and hobbies, they occasionally splurge and succumb to one or more extravagancies.

The Bossis Lifestyle: Attack is the Best Defense

During the times of the GDR, Bossis[4] tried hard to implement their ideas of consumption; as Secret Capitalists their lifestyle was active and materialistic. Now they seek to escape the sentiment of being constrained and second class, from which they suffered before. Bossis usually are young; life as capitalists is more of an opportunity than a stress for them. Accordingly, they view the new freedom in positive terms. Bossis are hard workers and take advantage of the opportunities that present themselves in a market economy; frequently they become entrepreneurs. Thanks to their capitalist activities in the GDR, Bossis are prepared to deal with the related challenges. Changes in behavior only take place if Bossis consider the old habits as no longer up to date. In order to establish harmony between work and lifestyle Bossis orient themselves by the examples set by the West and like to experiment when buying.

Typical Consumption Styles: Buying Westernization, Cultivating Hobbies, Selective Shopping Euphoria

Since they try to be as indistinguishable as possible from the West Germans, Bossis purchase only goods from the West–even if those produced in the former GDR are par with Western standards. Instead, Bossis pursue Western status symbols and frequently are excessive consumers.

---

4. A playful combination of "Ossi" for East Germans and the English "boss" which is also used in colloquial German. Thus, Bossis are East Germans in leading positions or who aspire to such positions.

Oftentimes, they expand hobbies and preferences already cultivated in the GDR, made possible thanks to the more abundant opportunities available to them now.

The Wossis Lifestyle: Over-Identification with Everything New

Whereas Bossis displayed activism and self-confidence in GDR times, Wossis[5] belong to the group of Secret Capitalists who in the GDR managed to climb the career ladder via adaptation and integration. Wossis try hard to abandon their pasts—and thereby employ the kind of behavior that characterized their past: adaptation. Their biggest concern is not being able to adapt to the prevailing order. Thus Wossis stumble over their own perception of a Western lifestyle and through overidentification frequently convey the image of an East German caricature of a Westerner.

Typical Consumption Styles: Buying Westernization, Selective Shopping Euphoria

The Omniscient Lifestyle: New Game, New Happiness

The consumer types discussed so far experienced a change in their situation which they also perceived as such. This does not pertain to the Omniscients: They maintain a lifestyle that dates back to the pretransition era. As former indespensibles or Socialist Managers, they have good reasons for emphasizing that they are used to the conditions prevailing in a market economy. However, sometimes they, too, fail to understand the new situation. Frequently they mention that their experience of conducting business under socialism and capitalism puts them in a better position than their Western counterparts aspiring to leading positions. However, behind their effort to have an answer for everything, they are hiding their anxiety about the risks inherent in their new dynamic lifestyle.

Typical Consumption Styles: Demonstrate Saturation, Selective Shopping Euphoria

Omniscients not only know everything, they also own everything there is. They seek to set themselves apart from the rest by demonstrating

---

5. Also a play with words, this time a combination of "Ossi" and the East Germans' corresponding nickname for West Germans "Wessi." (Many East Germans prefer the nickname "Westler" to avoid the West German habit of using diminutives as abbreviations.) Thus, a "Wessi" is an East German who very much would like to be like a West German.

through their buying behavior that whatever may be novel for the rest has long been familiar to them. Accordingly, Omniscients entertain their guests with exotic delicacies while at the same time displaying a critical attitude and restraint when shopping.

The Idealist Lifestyle: Emphasize Theory

Idealists include social activists, intellectuals, artists, and individuals from the theater scene. During the GDR era they often criticized the system, and as the Oppositionists they depended on the support of their Western colleagues. After the transition they adopted a style of consumption that is dominated by ideas and principles. They do not disapprove of the opportunities offered, including consumption, per se; however, they use them selectively, corresponding with their critical posture.

Typical Consumption Styles: Cultivating Hobbies, Buying Westernization

Idealists remain oriented toward the West as they did in the GDR. In the West, as before in the East, Idealists are concerned with social issues. Enjoyment and individuality are acceptable, yet their buying decisions are all too often determined by social involvement. For example, an Idealist may purchase a bed frame made of iron instead of mahogany to save tropical forests, or he may abstain from buying French wines in response to the French government's decision to resume nuclear tests. In this way Idealists discover ways to express individualistic preferences.

East Germany in Year Five

As shown in the preceding sections, the lifestyles in the New Bundeslanders have developed from those existing in the GDR. The people in the GDR experienced the sudden transition from socialism to capitalism and the related acceleration of everyday life as a threat, and thus sought to deal with the challenges by relying on old behavioral patterns. On the one hand, East Germans are maintaining their habitual attitudes toward consumption while on the other hand they are recognizing that they have to reorient themselves given the changed conditions. However, this reorientation will not happen overnight. For a large number of East Germans hunting and gathering continues, albeit in new forms. Consequently, these consumers require a supply that can balance the dual tendencies for status quo and reorientation.

SAMPLE PRODUCT CATEGORIES

Given the typical characteristics of East Germans' consumption style it is evident that only a few of them indicate a Western orientation. How the aforementioned consumption styles manifest themselves concretely can be made clear by looking at a few products categories. The meanings of and values associated with certain product specify consumption as a general category.

Travel

Since traveling to the West was forbidden for most of the people in the GDR, it was assumed that after the borders opened, travel activity to the West would be high. However, actual levels lag far behind expectations. Investigations indicate that being allowed to travel is different from being able to do so. Obstacles such as insufficient language skills, lack of knowledge about how do deal with hotels, and more traffic in the streets made East German travelers feel awkward and lost. East German citizens were accustomed to spending their vacations in state-owned vacation homes. There they would meet friends and old acquaintances; also, they were catered to around the clock from food to medical treatment. For this reason, group travels are the most attractive because they provide a feeling of security. Often, former GDR inhabitants travel in self-organized groups with friends, family, and colleagues from work. In terms of destinations, West Germany and Austria are preferred because of the cultural similarities. Only a few dare to travel to other countries, and if they do, it is mainly in organized groups accompanied by professional guides.

Beverages, Cigarettes

In contrast to other products, alcoholic beverages and cigarettes were readily available in the GDR in many variants. Consumption of alcohol and cigarettes were part of the comforts of personal life beyond the civic duties. Thus many types of alcoholic beverages were available, which corresponded well to existing preferences and were consumed in large quantities even though consumers criticized the poor quality. In contrast, East Germans were very satisfied with the supply of cigarettes and believed that their brands were of equal quality to those available in the West. Coffee was available in the GDR; its quality, however, was poor. It was typically available in Intershop stores[6] and frequently given as presents whereby certain Western brands stood for top quality and were known throughout the GDR.

Current consumer behavior indicates how much East Germans like their traditional after-work escapism and would like to continue with this habit: On the one hand they adhere to their ingrained consumption while on the other hand reunification allows them to expand their consumption of these types of products. Especially the Plaintiffs, Hermits, Help Seekers, and Toleraters take advantage of the expanded supply to improve their domestic oasis for enjoyment. More frequently than others they continue to buy Eastern brands. Concerning Western brands, they prefer to stay on secure territory in that they purchase those they were already familiar with during GDR times via presents sent from the West. However, these groups feel very insecure regarding top quality brands. They are under the impression that "only the brand name counts" which does not sit well with their Value Fetishism. Therefore, it is primarily the Bossis, Wossis, and Omniscients who consume these brands. This is especially true for alcoholic beverages in that these groups have completely switched to Western brands and also adapted their preferences correspondingly: dry instead of sweet wine, less hard liquor, and more wines and champagne. Omniscients like to demonstrate their sophistication by relying on exotic brands.

Prepared and Frozen Food

Prepared and frozen foods were scarce in the GDR. At best, frozen food departments in grocery stores carried mixed vegetables and poultry. Fish sticks were in high demand but were rarely available. As watchers of West German TV, East Germans envied Western consumers for the readily available prepared food.

In terms of eating habits the transition has not created havoc for the East Germans: They appreciate the much larger selection and are satisfied with the prevailing price/value ratio. They often purchase poultry, fish sticks, fish, prepared food in cans, and soups in bags. Heavy, filling products are popular, which correspond to traditional preferences. Items labeled "light" are primarily desired by Western-oriented consumer types.

Basically, modern foods are appreciated by all GDR consumers. They fulfill the desire for an easier everyday life and do not remind people of the dark sides of capitalism. Those who orient themselves primarily by value principles occasionally fear that frozen foods diminish the value of preparing food at home; nevertheless the convenience of frozen foods

---

6. Hard currency stores selling Western goods.

carries the day. Consumers displaying Budgeted Outfitting of Personal Sphere wholeheartedly appreciate the time-saving aspects of prepared foods. Bargain Hunters vie for discount offers in frozen and prepared foods; Bossis, Wossis, and Omniscients favor low calorie and low cholesterol products.

Cosmetics

Cosmetics were difficult to obtain in the GDR and the quality was poor. According to socialist doctrine the "socialist woman" had to take care of herself and be beautiful, but should avoid a lack of solidarity by trying to outdo other women or by being conspicuous in her appearance. The continued popularity of cosmetics, which started right after reunification, is therefore quite surprising.

Our research indicates that cosmetics are good "transition products" that assist buyers in finding their way into a Western lifestyle. For instance, women can sample cosmetics and perfumes at home and learn from relatives living in the West and in this way take a tentative step toward a Western identity. However, if women do not feel comfortable with their new look and if their friends and colleagues react unfavorably, cosmetics and perfume can be easily washed off and new types tried in the hope of better results. Cosmetics thus are more flexible and cheaper than clothes as a way to explore "temporary metamorphoses."

Printed Media

During GDR times, West German magazines and newspapers were very popular and frequently were smuggled into the country. They provided different information and viewpoints than the tightly controlled state media. After reunification, unexpected problems arose with the then readily available printed media.

East Germans were disturbed by the fact that different opinions could be found in the same magazine and that editorials did not provide instructions on how a report or event had to be interpreted. East Germans disliked the ideological uniformity of the press of previous times; however, they were overwhelmed and irritated by the plurality of opinions. In addition, the printed media demanded a different way of reading compared to the habit of working through articles in the GDR press as though reading chapters in a textbook—which was necessary in order to be able to correctly represent the Party's position. Instead of articles and speeches covering several pages, Western magazines offer short and easily digestible pieces written for fast consumption–which many new citizens find terribly "superficial."

Thus, especially those journals and magazines that tried to reflect the diversity of life in the Federal Republic had a hard time in the new Bundeslanders where citizens were looking for orientation in a turbulent environment. In contrast, daily newspapers offering concrete suggestions for everyday life in the new situation sold well.

FUTURE OF CONSUMPTION IN THE NEW BUNDESLANDERS

No Uniform Consumers

The uniform Eastern consumer does not exist; it is a fiction of Western managers which originated in the image of a "consumption gap" widely held immediately after reunification. If we want to help the East German citizens reorient themselves and lead them toward more frequent purchases of Western products, it is essential that incorrect models be discarded. For example, one popular hypothesis claims "The people in the East want to Westernize as quickly as possible!" Marketing strategies that were developed based on this premise ignored important differences between East and West. Another theory claimed: "People in the East want to become Westernized, but they need more time!" The corresponding marketing strategy emphasized: "Back to the Sixties!"

Research suggests that the situation is not that simple. In order to use the results of this investigation for marketing strategies, two conclusions need to be considered:

- The "people in the East" do not exist. Instead, there are new types of lifestyles and consumer groups.
- Target marketing is critical, with product groups and consumer groups as the main parameters.

Future Consumption Patterns: A Matter of Generations

- Factor lifestyle. Only those individuals who displayed an active and individualistic lifestyle and had a good grasp of the subtler forms of hunting and gathering will Westernize quickly. Westernization for the others will take years and they may never become truly westernized.
- Factor Product Group. For each lifestyle there are specific supporting product groups with high purchase affinity.

- Factor Age. Those who have internalized the role of private consumption in the GDR over decades–typically individuals aged 30 and older at the time of transition–will not be able to switch entirely to a Western style of consumption. Instead, they will continue their habitual yet slightly adapted forms of hunting and gathering.
- Factor Socioeconomic Development. As long as the economy in the new Bundeslanders lags behind the West and self-confidence of the East Germans remains weak, the development of Western life and consumption styles will be inhibited–both for young and old. If Western conditions are perceived as unfriendly and overwhelming, East Germans are likely to fall back on habits practiced in the GDR–as often has been often the case in recent years. However, if the new conditions are considered open and accessible, East Germans will be more willing to adapt. Overall, it will take the inhabitants of the former GDR a generation to fully blend into a Western lifestyle.

REFERENCES

Melchers, Christoph B. 1991a. Typen von Verbraucherverhalten jenseits des Verbrauchers. In: G. Breuning (Ed.), *Bericht über den 26. Kongress der Deutschen Marktforschung*: 55-73. Würzburg: BVM Series, Volume 20.

_____ 1991b. Kreativitätsunterstützende morphologische Motivforschung–Die Bild-Regie in der Haarpflege. *Zwischenschritte*, 10(2): 5-25.

_____ 1993a. Morphologische Marktpsychologie. In: H. Fitzek and A. Schulte (Eds.), *Bericht über den Kongress Wirklichkeit als Ereignis*: 28-58. Cologne: Bouvier Publ.

_____ 1993b. Das Image qualitativer Methoden. *planung & analyse*, (3): 46-51.

_____ 1994. Gruppendiskussionen in der Marktforschung. Part I. *planung & analyse*, (2): 5-9; Part II. *planung & analyse*, (3): 32-36.

_____ 1995. Werbe-Zielgruppen. Ein Beitrag zur qualitativen Präzisierung der Mediaplanung. *planung & analyse*, (3): 48-56.

_____ and Relin, M. 1993. *Der unbekannte Konsument–Konsumstile in den neuen Bundesländern*. Hamburg: Stern Bibliothek.

Salber, W. 1968. *The Psychische Gegenstand*. Bonn: H. Bouvier u. Co. Publ.

_____ 1969. *Wirkungseinheiten*. Wuppertal: A. Henn Publ.

_____ 1983. *Psychologie in Bildern*. Bonn: Bouvier Publ. Herbert Grundmann.

_____ 1986. *Morphologie des seelischen Geschehens*. Cologne: Tavros Edition. Moll & Eckhardt oHG Arbeitskreis Morphologische Psychologie e.V.

_____ 1988. *Kleine Werbung für das Paradox*. Cologne: Tavros Edition, Moll & Eckhardt oHG Arbeitskreis Morphologische Psychologie e.V.

Chapter 21

Epilogue:
The Managerial Challenge
in Transition Economies

Arieh A. Ullmann

If there is one single area of agreement regarding the transformation in Central and Eastern Europe, it is that the size and complexity of the task and the time needed for positioning these nations on a path to prosperity and political stability have been vastly underestimated by everyone: by the politicians on both sides of the vanished Iron Curtain, by the experts of national and international assistance agencies, the scores of consultants, business executives and scholars in the West, and, last but not least, the people of Central and Eastern Europe themselves. Some accomplishments can be recorded, though, for example: the formation of more or less democratic regimes and a decentralization of power in practically all countries of the region; the success of Poland's reforms (Johnson and Loveman, 1995; Perlez, 1996); the emergence of financial markets and private ownership; Opel's world class assembly operations in Eisenach as the successor to the East German Wartburg plant (Haasen, 1996). But there are other, less promising signs, too. First, the political backlash threatening to return communists to power is no longer mere speculation. Even in Berlin, surely the single best location for creating mutual understanding between East and West, the October 1995 state elections yielded an ominous result: With 36 percent of the vote in the eastern part of the city, the successors to the East German SED (Socialist Unity Party) may have established themselves as a force to be reckoned with at least at the local level (*Neue Zürcher Zeitung,* 1995). Second, many of the CMEA (Council for Mutual Economic Assistance) countries continue to suffer from high inflation, and large sections of society remain impoverished.

343

Only Poland and Slovenia are close to reaching the pretransition level of output of their economies (*Transition*, 1996b: 27). Third, hundreds of enterprises that are still owned by the state or have been converted to a *de jure* privatized status are waiting to be turned around or dismantled. And fourth, confusion and cynicism abound in vast segments of the populace concerning the blessings of the market economy. I remember the elderly woman carrying a live chicken on her way home from the market in Radauţi in northern Romania in May 1993 telling me: "Under Ceausescu, at least we had enough food and it was cheap!"

The purpose of this final chapter is to tie together some of what has been learned about managing in transforming economies into a comprehensive theory-based context. This should provide a better understanding of the nature of the challenges that managers and entrepreneurs have to contend with in the future. This concluding section will suggest that the notion of a convergent development of the region toward a Western-style structure in terms of the economies and governments is perhaps simplistic and that observed conduct seemingly in conflict with the expectations of Western experts may, in fact, reflect a combination of traditions and the prevailing environment.

REVOLUTIONARY TRANSFORMATION OF SOCIETY: THEORETICAL UNDERPINNINGS

For a theoretical starting point, I will rely on an expanded version of the punctuated equilibrium theory which has served as the theoretical reference point for several contributions in this volume (Gersick, 1991; Romanelli and Tushman, 1994; Tushman and Romanelli, 1985; for applications in this volume see Newman and Nollen, Chapter 8; and Savitt, Chapter 9). To serve the purpose of understanding the transformation in Central and Eastern Europe, the theory needs to be expanded in important ways. First, so far it has been applied primarily to a variety of systems in their interactions with a dynamic environment (see the examples in Gersick, 1991). The impetus for revolutionary change, which implies a change in a system's "deep structure" (Gersick, 1991: 13), is localized outside the system itself in its environment, even though internal causes are not *a priori* excluded (Gersick, 1991). However, in their empirical study of microcomputer producers Romanelli and Tushman found no confirmation for internal performance crises leading to revolutionary transformations (Romanelli and Tushman, 1994). In contrast, as Frohlich and Oppenheimer in Chapter 1 point out, it was not so much an identifiable discontinuity in the environment which led to the collapse of communism–even though U.S. President Reagan's arms race may have contributed to its demise–than the conditions within the system itself.[1] Second, punctuated equilibrium theory does not explicitly concern itself with differences in the impact of revolutionary change on the internal structure of complex, differentiated systems. In order to apply punctuated equilibrium theory fruitfully in the context of the transformation in Central and Eastern Europe, it needs to be situated in a multi-level context.

To achieve this expansion of punctuated equilibrium theory I will rely on a neo-Marxist model developed by the German political scientist Claus Offe which he uses to discuss problems of late capitalism (Offe, 1973). In contrast to punctuated equilibrium theory, neo-Marxist theory concerns itself with internally caused crises that are the result of the interplay between contradictory forces in society. To rely on such a model in this context seems appropriate given the long tradition of Marxist theory to analyze and understand the occurrence of crises and revolutionary changes, even though it may appear somewhat ironic to apply it for investigating issues related to the collapse of communism.[2] Relying on a combination of Marxist theory and systems theory, Offe conceptualizes society as being comprised of three subsystems: the political-administrative subsystem, the economic-technical subsystem,[3] and the sociocultural subsystem. These three subsystems interact with the environment (other societies, physical environment) as well as with each other, each of them providing essential inputs to the other two. Through its policies, the political-administrative subsystem compensates for and ameliorates the deficiencies caused by the economic-technical subsystem's pursuit of profit and provides a social safety net and other essential public goods to the sociocultural subsystem. In return, the political-administrative subsystem relies on taxes generated by the economic-technical subsystem and on legitimacy conferred to by the sociocultural subsystem. The

---

1. I am not suggesting that the environment needs to be held constant. It is more a matter of relative change. For example, in case of an illness, the change in the organism's performance (internal change) is far greater than the changes occurring in the environment.

2. It is surprising that none of the proponents of punctuated equilibrium theory has noted the connection to the extensive body of literature relying on Marx's theory, e.g., Crosser (1960), Mandel (1978), Shonfield (1965). For a different approach to predict the breakup of the Soviet Union, see Collins (1995).

3. The inclusion of the technological system as part of the economic subsystem is my extension of Offe's model. Given that the creation and application of new technology is closely intertwined with economic considerations and, to a large extent, occurs in enterprises, this seems to be a justifiable modification. See also Habermas' use of Offe's model (Habermas, 1973: 37) and Erickson (Chapter 15).

economic-technical subsystem supplies goods to the sociocultural subsystem and receives work in exchange. According to Jürgen Habermas different forms of society are characterized by varying degrees of differentiation and coupling among the three subsystems and by different dominant organizational principles. Consequently, each form of society is prone to be victim of a distinctive type of crisis (Habermas, 1973). In the language of systems theory crises arise, if the structure of a system allows for fewer problem solutions than are needed to ensure the system's continued existence (Habermas, 1973: 11). For a fundamental change of a system to be experienced as a discontinuity or revolution, a second, subjectivist, definition is required: Society loses its identity if, over the course of time, generations no longer recognize themselves and thus perceive a discontinuity in traditions (Habermas, 1973: 13). In other words, society is defined simultaneously as a system and as a symbolically structured environment. Viewed from this perspective, punctuated equilibrium theories as they have been used heretofore are lower-level theories which deal with a system's reaction to environmental change, whereas the neo-Marxist model addresses internally caused revolutionary change at a higher level. A third element of an expanded punctuated equilibrium theory is the concept of system-specific time. Time has two dimensions. First, there is the objective dimension which is measured in hours and fractions or multiples thereof as units related to the rotation of the earth around the sun and of the moon around the earth. Second, there is the subjective dimension which is specific to a given system, for example, biological and geological time. I argue that social systems, too, have their specific time even though the latter is more flexible than biological time as history has shown. In the economic-technical subsystem, for instance, specific time varies greatly from industry to industry, a generation in the electric utility industry is far longer than in computer chips. Industry specific time also varies across objective time, which is evident, for example, when comparing the rate of innovation in a historical context. There is ample evidence that the system-specific time of the sociocultural subsystem is to be much longer measured in objective time units than that of the political-administrative or the economic-technical subsystem. Douglass North remarked that "although formal rules may change overnight as the result of political and judicial decisions, informal constraints embodied in customs, traditions, and codes of conduct are much more impervious to deliberate policies" (1990: 6). Thus, the key elements of the sociocultural subsystem that shape individual and collective behavior tend to persist while the political-administrative and economic-technical subsystems undergo revolutionary change. Witness, for example, the ethnic wars in former Yugoslavia and the Soviet Union, the Germans' "need for superiority" which Norbert Elias identified in the German Federal Republic in the 1970s but which was already noted by Friedrich Naumann during World War I (Autenrieth, 1993).

Habermas demonstrates how different kinds of societal systems in human history are characterized by different organizational principles[4] (e.g., familial relationships in tribal societies, classes in feudal Europe), display varying degrees of subsystem differentiation and, correspondingly, experience different types of crises. In late capitalism where, compared to laissez-faire capitalism, the political-administrative subsystem intervenes in the economic-technical subsystem to a much higher degree than by merely ensuring the framework for market-based exchanges, economic crises tend to be perceived as crises of the political-administrative subsystem.[5] This applies to a much higher degree for the system labeled "real socialism." Based on Marxist-Leninist theory, the Party, as the sole and true representative of the interests of all workers, through the government, dominated all aspects of life and directly regulated and controlled all three societal subsystems. Thus, the system-specific crisis in socialist system is a political crisis, since the other two subsystems are tightly coupled to the governing political-administrative subsystem. Both punctuated equilibrium and Marxist theory share a perspective of long equilibrium periods where in the language of punctuated equilibrium theory incremental change and adaptation regimes prevail to be followed by short bursts of revolutionary change and organizational re-creation, or, in the language of Marxism, the contradictions in society

---

4. Organizational principles are defined as "highly abstract rules which arise out of rare evolutionary thrusts, and as emergent features characterize a new level of development" (Habermas, 1973: 18). They are thus akin to deep structures defined as "the set of fundamental 'choices' a system has made of (1) the basic parts into which its units will be organized and (2) the basic activity pattern that will maintain its existence." (Gersick, 1991: 14)

5. In the view of its proponents, late capitalism *qua* capitalism continues to be plagued by the fundamental contradictions already determined by Marx. However, it has undergone changes in important ways to reflect developments that have occurred since Marx's time: technological development, globalization, expansion of the service sector, and more sophisticated public policies to regulate the economy. "Late capitalism is the epoch in history of the development of the capitalist mode of production in which the contradiction between the growth of the forces of production and the survival of the capitalist relations of production assumes an explosive form." (Mandel, 1978: 563)

accumulate and finally erupt in revolutions that change the fundamental organizing principles of society.

CRISIS OF COMMUNISM

In the 1980s, most motivational capital for achieving the noble goals of socialism had long been consumed. Few, if any, still believed that the East's "real socialism" would ever overtake the West in terms of standard of living as the Soviet Premier Nikita Khrushchev had claimed when, in 1961, he banged his shoe on the podium in the United Nations. What had remained was the hope for a life, albeit dull, in a comfortable and dense social cocoon spun by the omnipotent state. Instead, the failure of socialism in terms of national output, productivity growth, changes in real per capita income and consumption became increasingly clear: The East had lost ground and continued to fall further and further behind. What changed in the 1980s was that the poor state of the economy was being discussed quite openly by the communist leadership (Berliner, 1987; Hewett, 1988). Given the politicized nature of the economy, the deterioration of the economic-technical subsystem was seen as a crisis of the political-administrative system. "The intense desire [of Central and Eastern Europe, A.A.U.] to rejoin the economies of Western Europe reflects both an attraction to the obvious achievements of Western Europe and a revulsion against the failures under communism. The low per capita incomes in Eastern Europe do not fully explain the pervasive sense of frustration in the region. It is one thing to be poor, but it is quite another to have become impoverished needlessly as a result of the failure of the communist system. It is the sense of unnecessary decay, as much as the deprivation itself, that motivates the impulse of change" (Lipton and Sachs, 1990: 76). While some argue that the communist leaders could have prevailed and weathered the crisis (Lavigne, 1995), they tried reforms instead, encouraged an open discussion of the reasons for the dismal economic performance (Glasnost), and opened the door to private economic activities. The "socialist mixed economy" (Szelényi and Kostello, 1996: 1089) replaced pure central planning. Once the threat of open repression by the state was shaky, the political-administrative subsystem suddenly needed a much larger supply of legitimacy from the sociocultural subsystem to continue its existence. Instead, the opposite occurred, the population made it clear that there was no longer a legitimate basis for the political-administrative system in its current form. The monopoly of the Party was swept away and the crisis culminated in the fall of the Berlin Wall on November 9, 1989.

The transformation which followed and which, in many ways, is still ongoing, entails indeed a change of "deep structures" or "organizational principles" of systems at many levels. So far, most of the changes have taken place only in two of the three subsystems: Wholesale replacement of the institutions, legal framework, and raison dêtre of the political-administrative subsystem; in the economic-technical subsystem development of property rights, of the institutional and legal framework needed for a market economy, restructuring of an excessively concentrated industry and outmoded capital stock and of a new banking system; and creation of a private sector (Ernst, Alexeev, and Marer, 1996). At the sociocultural level, orientations, values, and attitudes need to be changed to conform to the changes in the other two subsystems (Peng and Heath, 1996). But little seems to have happened in this regard; values reinforced by decades of socialism such as the dominance of distributive justice over commutative justice persist and hinder the transition process (Pavett and Whitney, 1995). Several studies indicate that disillusionment with Soviet-style socialism is far from implying approval of Western-style capitalism (Nelson, 1995).

TRANSFORMATION
OF THE STATE-OWNED FIRM

The gradual erosion of the central planning system in the 1980s which, in 1989 and 1990, culminated in a collapse has not been accompanied, *pari passu*, with the development of a market system. As a consequence, firms are operating in an institutional vacuum under extreme uncertainty. Old frameworks have ceased to exist, yet linger on in the behaviors of economic actors, and new arrangements are not yet fully developed, or if they are, often only on paper and not in the acts of decision makers and bureaucrats. The situation is exacerbated by the uncertainty at the political level which has greatly hampered the road from plan to market in many nations in the region. All too often, the formation of the new market-based economic-technical subsystem is mired in a confusing mix of nationalism, ideological and ethnic conflicts, and distributive games. Following North (1990) who pointed out that economic activity is shaped by the institutional framework which provides the rules of the game, we should expect distinctive differences in behavior at the firm level compared to that in established market economies.

For a start let us illustrate the implication for a state-owned firm[6] arising from the revolutionary change at the societal level using microeconomic theory. In socialism, firms were tied into the Council for Mutual Economic Assistance network which included the state-owned enterprises in all member countries and established a strict division of labor in terms of industries and products. Frequently, there was only one producer for a given product; intermediary and end products had to be shipped for further processing and distribution from country to country. Procurement of a firm's inputs as well as distribution of its outputs were handled not by the firm itself, but by state agencies. (For an extensive treatment of the case of the German Democratic Republic see Albach, 1994; in this volume see Newman and Nollen, Chapter 8). Likewise, specialized state agencies were responsible for imports and exports; market entry by new firms was not permitted.

When the Iron Curtain disappeared, this rigid system of monopolists and monopsonists fell apart. On the demand side, the heretofore price-inelastic demand curve became elastic and shifted to the left as the state-owned monopolist suddenly encountered competitors from the West. Although Western products tended to be more expensive, they quickly gained market share. For example, in Romania in the early 1990s domestic toothpaste and cigarettes were rapidly replaced with pricey imported brands. In the state-owned socialist firm marginal costs remained high, the contraction in demand resulted in severe losses. On the supply side, the socialist firm produced well beyond the market-based efficiency frontier. It wasted capital by hoarding supplies to prepare itself for unexpected shortages, and it wasted labor because maintaining full employment corresponded to socialist ideology. Also, as a socialist entity it managed a wide array of services for its employees and their families (see Newman and Nollen, Chapter 8). In terms of relative factor prices, labor was relatively less expensive which, while conflicting with the prevailing ideology according to which capital was supposed to be interest free, is evident from the much older capital structure of the East. With the emergence of competing products, the efficiency frontier moved to the left implying a more efficient process requiring less labor and less, albeit

---

6. We are less concerned here with the legal process of privatization of a firm; from a managerial viewpoint this is not the main issue. The more critical question is whether the firm has already begun the transformation to an entity that can sustain competition in the emergent new environment. Thus, the term "state-owned" or "socialist" firm used here is to be understood as synonymous to a pre-transformation firm irrespective of its legal status.

more modern, capital per unit of output. Hence, in order to become competitive a firm operating at the socialist efficiency frontier faced the formidable task of (1) downsizing its labor force, (2) moving to a different production function which (3) required considerable investments in new production technology from the West, (4) training its workers on the new machinery, and (5) shedding the ancillary service functions. Due to the demise of the state agencies in charge of procurement and distribution, the transforming firm also had to (6) search for suppliers and (7) find new markets. The latter task was complicated by the fact that the established markets in the CMEA countries virtually disappeared overnight due to the contraction of the economies, the influx of Western goods, and the requirement for hard-currency payments.

Using a "generic" SWOT (Strengths, Weaknesses, Opportunities, Threats) chart, the challenge to management of a transforming state-owned firm in the early days of the transition to a market economy presented itself as follows (see Danis et al., Chapter 14).

TABLE 21.1. Generic SWOT Chart of a State-Owned Socialist Firm

Strengths
- unclear since change so fundamental

Weaknesses
- obsolete products
- poor product quality
- obsolete production technology
- no distribution system
- little firsthand market knowledge
- traditional supply lines interrupted
- inadequately trained labor force
- management inexperienced in market economy
- high debt owed to state and other firms
- no financial reserves
- inadequate control and information systems
- distrust in the new system

Opportunities
- subcontractor to Western efficiency seeking firm
- joint venture with Western firm
- total/partial buyout by Western firm
- find new products in demand

Threats
- political instability
- inflation
- rudimentary economic infrastructure
- changing industry structure:
  − entry of strong competitors
  − traditional markets disappearing
  − suppliers disappearing
- shifting consumer preferences

In terms of punctuated equilibrium theory the changing environment demanded nothing less than organizational re-creation or transformation: changes in strategy (product, market, technology, competitive timing); a shift in power from the state to management and the new owners; changes in structure (less vertical integration, creating of a marketing function, spinoff of social services), and controls (bureaucratic to market-oriented), as well as a change in organizational core values (Tushman and Romanelli, 1985: 179). The firm described in Table 21.1 represents an extreme yet not unlikely case as evidenced by the furniture manufacturer reported by Lutz and Davis in Chapter 7. Differences existed between the various countries in Central and Eastern Europe given their history and previous reform experiments that offered openings to the West to a varying extent with Hungary and Poland on one side of the spectrum and Albania, Romania, and Russia at the opposite end (see Savitt's and Hefner and Woodward's studies in Chapters 9 and 10, respectively, and Ernst, Alexeev, and Marer [1996]). Company-specific differences also existed in that some firms, especially those which as exporters, brought in hard currency, were in a better position at the onset of the transformation (see the case of Královopolská described in Chapter 8) However, even under the best circumstances the difficulties of transforming these enterprises into competitive entities were and are staggering, given the fact that the task of improving the performance of state-owned companies even in a more benign environment is fraught with difficulties (World Bank, 1995).

Punctuated equilibrium theory suggests that a sense of urgency and optimism, outside assistance and leadership are vital ingredients for successfully accomplishing revolutionary change in organizations (Gersick, 1991; Kotter, 1995; Tushman and Romanelli, 1985). Indeed, some of the studies reported in this volume corroborate this finding: the successful transformation of Královopolská relied on superb leadership (Chapter 8) and the failure of Skala (Chapter 9) was caused by its absence; the turnaround of Tungsram and of Poland's sugar refiners is owed to foreign direct investment by a Western firm which injected much-needed skills (Chapters 14 and 10, respectively); Videoton's success rested on a combination of leadership and Western partners (Chapter 14); and First Rate Furniture Firm, even though it had received new equipment and was inundated with inquiries that provided potentially valuable information about market opportunities and internal strengths, was caught in a downward spin lacking critical resources (Chapter 7).

It is reasonable to assume that the share of state-owned firms which have access to these resources represents a minority. Managers are poorly prepared for the new demands (Chapter 5; Csath, 1989, Penrice, 1995), and the reservoir of skilled executives that could succeed those in power steeped in the old ways is minuscule, albeit growing. The amount of foreign direct investment in Central and Eastern Europe of $14 billion in 1995 (*Transition*, 1996b: 25) is far below what would be needed to create sizeable foreign presence in a significant share of state-owned enterprises. Correspondingly, several studies report that firms' conduct reflected more of a reorientation than a re-creation especially among the larger ones. Ernst, Alexeev, and Marer (1996) mention that the predominant change in state-owned firms was to shift emphasis from procurement to marketing and finance, as well as to prune the product mix and focus only on those products in demand. Other changes such as the introduction of new technology, the creation of new products and structural alignments occurred less frequently. A 1994 survey of 231 managers from the region indicates that only 29 percent of the changes introduced since the onset of the transition were strategic (Penrice, 1995).

How, then, can these firms, which represent the overwhelming majority in terms of value of assets and share of employment, continue to exist? Following North's argument that a society's institutional framework constrains and regulates economic activity (North, 1990: 3), the "correct" strategy needs to be tailored to transition economies where dual regimes coexist. Traditional microeconomic theory and punctuated equilibrium theory assume functioning markets as the relevant environment. However, even in developed market economies such as the United States, aspects other than market efficiency can play a critical role as the Chrysler bailout demonstrates. As has been mentioned in the introduction there is plenty of evidence that in Central and Eastern Europe privatization or corporatization in many instances has only occurred on paper. (See, e.g., Filatotchev et al., 1996.) Often, the state continues to control the companies through the privatization agency holding the shares (Mujzel, 1994), albeit to a lesser extent given the weakened position of the government in most nations in the region. Insider control is likely to prevail in may instances via a coalition of management and workers with a vested interest in the status quo as seems to be the case in Russia (McFaul and Perlmutter, 1995). By astute use of the politically sensitive threat of massive unemployment and widespread bankruptcies, these entities can continue their existence with minimal adjustments in their strategic orientations assured that the government will continue to bail them out— what Kornai labeled "the soft budget constraint" (Kornai, 1980). The critical resource for this strategy to work is the network of informal relationships established by all state-owned enterprises long before the onset of the transition as a means to procure resources and to negotiate with the state bureaucracies. Whereas the formal CMEA network collapsed in 1990, the informal endured and is being redeployed in an innovative fashion to deal with the extreme level of uncertainty. David Stark (1996) has shown how in Hungary the largest 200 corporations and top 25 banks together with the state agency in charge of privatization and institutions of local government have created a new form of *keiretsu* or *chaebol* of intertwined cross-ownerships combining a vast number of formally independent state enterprises, "privatized" shareholding companies, and "newly created" limited liability companies, the latter being frequently spin-offs of the other two. He views this as an organizational hedging strategy to deal with extreme levels of uncertainty:

> Under conditions not simply of market uncertainty but of organizational uncertainty, there can be multiple (and intertwined) strategies for survival–based in some cases on *profitability* but in others on *eligibility*. Where your success is judged, and the resources placed at your disposal determined, sometimes by your market share and sometimes by the number of workers you employ in a region; sometimes by your price-earnings ratio and sometimes by your "strategic importance"; and, when even the absolute size of your losses can be transformed into an asset yielding an income stream, you might be wise to diversify your portfolio, to be able to shift your accounts, to be equally skilled in applying for loans as in applying for job creation subsidies, to have a multilingual command of the grammar of credit worthiness and the syntax of debt forgiveness." (1996: 1014-1025, emphasis in the original)

Thus, according to Stark, a new form of property is being created which he calls "recombinant property"[7] that blurs the public and private domain, enterprise boundaries, and the boundedness of justificatory principles. Similar combinations of privatized firms with extensive cross-holdings and bank and state participation can also be observed in Russia's financial-industrial groups (Gornov, 1996). Evidently, old-line managers are well prepared for this particular kind of portfolio management deployed as a hedge against the unique uncertainty prevailing in transition economies, far better than they would be for the rules of a pure market-based game. Recombinant property also takes into consideration the absence of institutional trust in post-communist societies. As Pearce, Branyiczki, and Bakacsi (1994) show, under communism there was wide-

---

7. Thus, the creative use of informal networks currently is more a strategy for survival than for growth as Peng and Heath (1996) propose.

spread use of person-based reward systems reflecting pervasive distrust in organizations. There is good reason to assume that this is also true in interorganizational dealings—a fact that is discussed by Michael Mauws and Nelson Phillips in Chapter 3. Institutional trust, i.e., assurance that transactions are conducted with full respect of sanctioned principles, is essential for a functioning market economy, but it takes time to develop (Creed and Miles, 1996). In a market economy actors expect that their counterparts will adhere to the law and fulfill their part of a contract as negotiated. For example, they expect a handshake between strangers representing contracting parties to be upheld, and bidding processes to adhere to announced principles and to be free of favoritism. This is not true for socialist societies where managers were engaged in never ending political games with internal and external stakeholders aimed at maximizing power (for a vivid description see Kostera, Proppé, and Szatkowski, 1995). Their research indicates that much of the pretransition role of the manager continues to prevail in the ongoing transition period (Kostera, Proppé, and Szatkowski, 1995: 643). Managers' hesitance to play by the market rules only is supported by the unions which want to secure jobs, and by politicians who are reluctant to be held responsible for even higher rates of unemployment. At the same time, politicians are eager to show Western donors that they are proceeding withprivatization to attract further financial support. Is it therefore surprising that state-owned enterprises are reluctant to abandon "irrational behavior" (Mujzel, 1994: 137) by limiting themselves to improving efficiency, failing to search for new markets, insisting on further government support, etc. (Starodubrovskaya, 1995)? The finding that companies have embarked on reorientations and not re-creations as suggested by the punctuated equilibrium paradigm may reflect a measuring error in that the research design fails to include the institutional level, the network, and only focuses on the individual firm. Recombinant property allows managers to effectively utilize old, familiar strategies in postsocialist metamorphosis. These strategies buy time to acquire the new skills and train the employees in the new ways of thinking that are so difficult to learn, or, in the eyes of these managers, replace the need for re-creation altogether (Penrice, 1995). These strategies open an alley to rely on a wide network to secure the missing resources and to meet on a familiar territory of informal networking to counteract and circumvent the harsher aspects of a market economy.

NEWLY FORMED FIRMS

Prima facie the statistics on new firm creation in Central and Eastern Europe indicate a dramatic change in the makeup of these economies. In

Poland the number of private domestic corporations increased from 53,500 in 1990 to 110,200 as of September 30, 1994; the number of individually owned firms rose from 813,000 in 1989 to 1,784,000 by the end of 1993. The number of state-owned firms declined from its peak in 1990 of 8,400 firms to 5,100 by September 30, 1994 (Ernst, Alexeev, and Marer, 1996: 88). In Hungary, between December 1988 and May 1994 the number of shareholding companies rose from 116 to 2,679, limited liability companies from 450 to 79,395, whereas the number of state enterprises declined from 2,378 to 892 (Stark, 1996: 1000). The previous section suggested, however, that a fair number of these privatized companies and entrepreneurial ventures are, in fact, captives of large entities of the recombinant property sector. In addition, a significant number of the very small ventures are one-person operations owned by individuals who have other jobs and may have been created primarily for tax evasion purposes. In this section, I want to focus on those entrepreneurs who are "true" entrepreneurs in the Western understanding who have created viable enterprises outside of the recombinant property sector and not as fly-by-night operations. (For a profile of a generation of early entrepreneurs see Abell and Köllermeier, 1993.)

Entrepreneurs have already existed under communism where as reformers and inventors they worked within the system and, at the same time, as independent minded rule-breakers strove to change it (Kiser, 1989). What changed in the aftermath of the collapse was that the activity of the entrepreneur became legal, although its social acceptance is still questionable. Anybody who traveled in Central and Eastern Europe shortly after the collapse of the old system can attest to the fact that the entrepreneurial spirit is alive and well. As one successful Romanian entrepreneur in the metal fabricating industry and former member of the *nomenklatura* whose firm provided work for close to 100 employees explained to me in May 1993: "You know, this is the Wild West of the 1990s." Initially, the entrepreneurial zest manifested itself primarily in taking advantage of the opportunities created by the prevailing shortages: the cigarette vendor at the street corner; the Poles with the huge shopping bags in Berlin who bought everything from bananas to toilet paperand carried them back in their Ladas; the two young Romanians I met on an overcrowded Russian bus on their way from northern Romania across the Ukraine to Poland where they would purchase a few tires and bring them back the same way to their home town to be sold at a profit. As the supply situation changed these vendors were compelled either to find new niches, to expand operations or to exit the market altogether.

Entrepreneurs face an even tougher environment than the decision makers in state-owned companies. They do not have access to state support and face a population which is suspicious of individuals who display ambition, creativity, and are constantly looking for unmet needs in the market and who, if successful, very quickly can afford luxury items the simple state employee can only dream of. They have to negotiate with banks which are unaccustomed to dealing with entrepreneurs and reluctant to lend money. The high tax burden on profits combined with the value-added tax is a serious impediment. The lack of reliable market information, the lack of managerial and accounting skills as well as the threat of foreign competition provide additional obstacles and are likely to result in a higher mortality rate of startups than in the West. Also, entrepreneurs do not have an informal network of contacts that can be tapped for help, and the creation of networks akin to those in the West has been difficult. External initiatives to set up such business roundtables akin to those in the West to compensate for their lack in these economies have been difficult. My own experience in Bucharest, Romania, suggests that entrepreneurs are distrustful of anyone reflecting a characteristic of all post-communist societies. They are reluctant to share information with fellow entrepreneurs and still have to learn that informal trading of information can create mutual gains. Also, similar to what John Kmetz in Chapter 4 reports, entrepreneurs are recruited from different strata of society, and individuals who under socialism were ostracized by the ruling elite are reluctant to mingle with former *nomenklatura* members. Obviously, no one can expect these rifts to disappear overnight. However, entrepreneurs have one big advantage compared to executives in state-owned firms–their personalities. Unlike their counterparts, they are willing to take risks and try to play the new game of the market. They do not shy away from making decisions and working hard to make their dreams come true (for example see Abell and Köllermeier, 1993; Milbank, 1995; and Miller, Comes, and Simpson, 1995). The case studies indicate that outside assistance in a variety of forms is frequently a critical ingredient as is the entrepreneurs' ability to create a strong organizational culture. Marx's account of the two print shops in Romania in Chapter 12 offers a prime example: Not so much by virtue of their expertise but more through their example did the Americans provide critical skills. The concrete day-to-day practice of Christian principles offered a foundation on which the founders were able to build a strong organizational culture that permitted the members of the organization to rise above the prevailing attitudes. However, in terms of employment and GDP contribution the entrepreneurial sector is still small. In this regard it is interesting to note, for example, how often the same entrepreneurs are featured in articles in the business press.

RESOLVING THE LEGITIMACY PROBLEM

As initially pointed out, "real socialism" was unable to deal with the legitimacy crisis that developed by the end of the 1980s. However, the transition to Western-style capitalism with a large private sector is equally risky in that it may cost the political-administrative subsystem the needed support by a populace that is not ideologically predisposed toward Western capitalism. On the one hand, the window of opportunity for a "big-bang," fast-reform approach as in Poland has closed in the meantime. To many countries in the region it never may have been open, because it requires a strong government. On the other hand, a gradualist approach more or less emulating the Chinese model is inflicting extensive pain on the populace and thus is also risking to consume the legitimacy capital created in the early days of the transition. Thus, the political- administrative system is caught in a dilemma which will become more pressing the longer the unsatisfactory status of the economy continues.

The creation of a "post-socialist mixed" economy provides a way out of the quandary in that it affords the political-administrative system the same multilingual capability as it does to the managers. The truly private sector with a significant foreign presence as a discernible entity within the economic-technical subsystem and the rising class of entrepreneurs can be made responsible for arising failures and thereby a looming crisis deflected, all the more so in that this tactic allows to kindle latent xenophobic sentiments. At the same time, the existence of a recombinant property sector as part of the economic-technical subsystem provides an opportunity to claim any gains in the standard of living.

At the time of writing it is too early to speculate about the durability of the emerging structure of the economy that is made up, we claim, part of recombinant capital, part of a market sectorcomprised of foreign-owned or influenced firms and, finally, the entrepreneurial private sector. However, as Mauws and Phillips in Chapter 3 point out, it seems just as bold to expect a resurrection of a neoconvergence theory and to assume that these economies, ignoring their past, will within a generation convert to a carbon copy of the Western form of a market economy. Much will depend on the overall success of the economic-technical subsystem—which to a large part is in the hands of the political-administrative system. Studies show that democratic freedom is having a positive influence on the economy (de Melo, Denizer, and Gelb, 1995; Kaminski, Wang, and Winters, 1995) which implies that in open societies managers have a better chance of operating businesses successfully. A possibly unique form of a mixed market system will have to earn its legitimacy in Central and Eastern Europe by raising the standard of living not of a few, but of the population at large–just as was the case in West Germany after World War II. Thus, the successes and failures of the enterprises and their managers including those described in the preceding chapters have a far bigger significance in Central and Eastern Europe than in the West.

TRANSFORMATION, ENTREPRENEURSHIP, AND THE FUTURE OF DEMOCRACY

At the eve of the first free presidential elections in Russia, much ink is flowing speculating about the future course of Russia and its economy should Gennady Zyuganov, the Communist party candidate, win. In the eyes of the West, a victory of Boris Yeltsin is seen as a vote for a continued opening of the Russian Federation toward political freedom and a decentralized, market-based economy. This view ignores the fact that Russia has always been governed by autocratic rule and that the Russians' first encounter with capitalism has been a far cry from the pious, thrifty, and industrious individuals described by Max Weber. "[But] the advance guard of capitalism that arrived in Moscow was armies of speculators, barons of the black market, gangs of drug dealers, armed, aggressive racketeers, brutal, ruthless, powerful mafias" (Kapuscinski, 1996: 69). This traumatic experience coincided with another, equally difficult psychological shock–the breakup of the Soviet Union. Little wonder then that Russians long for order and for social security as indicated by a survey conducted by the University of Strathclyde (Kramer, 1996). Even when ignoring criminality there is increasing empirical evidence that "former cadres are the main winners of market transition" (Szelényi and Kostello, 1996: 1085). In Russia, 75 percent of the new political elite and 61 percent of the new business elite are said to come from the old Soviet nomenklatura (*Transition,* 1996a). This is not all that surprising given the fact that the role of a manager in state-owned firms was a station on a political career (Kostera, Proppé, and Szatkowski, 1995) and that these individuals enjoy a significant information advantage under a recombinant property regime but also as entrepreneurs. Given the strong showing of the communists and the nationalists, the weakened status of the central government and the poor showing of the democrats, all of this would suggest that Boris Yeltsin will have to find a way to simultaneously reestablish a sense of order and safety, to satisfy the widespread longing for the Russians' self-image as a grand nation, and to continue invigorating the economy in a way that will also address the demands of the old-new business elite. By the same token, Gennady Zyuganov, too, will have to take into consideration that Russia today is a far more pluralist society and that powerful groups have emerged that will resist relinquishing their recent gains. Furthermore, Russia today is much poorer than ten years ago and will have to rely on continued support from the West, such as the $10.2 billion three-year financial stabilization loan granted by the International Monetary Fund. Zyuganov seems to be aware of the irreversibility of recent changes. His vague program, while heavily criticized, promises a slowdown of the transformation process, more state intervention in the economy and restrictions on foreign investments coupled with increased payments to those who have lost out during the transition (Thornhill, 1996). Thus, since either president will have to take the desires of the population and the prevailing realities into account, it may very well be that in the short run the differences between the two candidates' future course will not be as large as often depicted—unless a coup d'état is instigated. Most likely, no matter who will win, the emerging form of government will be a far cry from a Western-style democracy. Within this overall context, the "free-market" sector will have a role to play as will foreign companies, although there will be many restrictions imposed on them. Yet, as the examples of other countries have shown, totalitarian rule is not completely at odds with a market- driven economic-technical subsystem or sector within the latter until a relatively high level of economic development is reached.

REFERENCES

Abell, D. F., and Köllermeier, T. (Eds.) 1993. *Dynamic entrepreneurship in Central and Eastern Europe.* The Hague: DELWEL Publishers.

Albach, H. (1994). The transformation of firms and markets: A network approach to economic transformation processes in East Germany. *Acta Universitatis Upsaliensis: Studia oeconomicae negotiorum;* Vol. 34. Uppsala: Uppsala University.

Autenrieth, C. 1993. Impact of system culture on West and East German managers: A new topic of intercultural management research. *The International Executive,* 35(1): 73-88.

Berliner, J. 1987. Organizational restructuring of the Soviet economy. In U.S. Congress, Joint Economic Committee (Ed.) *Gorbachev's Economic Plans,* Vol. 1. Washington, DC: U.S. Government Printing Office.

Collins, R. 1995. Prediction in macrosociology: The case of the Soviet collapse. *American Journal of Sociology,* 100(6): 1552-1593.

Creed, W.E.D., and Miles, R.E. 1996. Trust in organizations. A conceptual framework linking organizational forms, managerial philosophies, and the opportunity costs of controls. In Kramer R.M. and Tyler, T.R. (Eds.) *Trust in organizations. Frontiers of theory and research.* Thousand Oaks, CA: Sage: 16-38.

Crosser, P. K. 1960. *State capitalism in the economy of the U.S.* New York: Bookman Associates.

Csath, M. 1989. Management education for developing entrepreneurship in Hungary. In J. Davies, M. Easterby-Smith, S. Mann and M. Tanton (Eds.) *The challenge to Western management development.* London/New York: Routledge: 137-151.

de Melo, M., Denizer, C., and Gelb, A. 1995. From plan to market: Patterns of transition. *Transition,* 6(11-12): 4-6.

Ernst, M., Alexeev, M., and Marer, P. 1996. *Transforming the core. Restructuring industrial enterprises in Russia and Central Europe.* Boulder, CO: Westview Press.

Filatotchev, I., Hoskisson, R.E., Buck, T., and Wright, M. 1996. Corporate restructuring in Russian privatizations: Implications for U.S. investors. *California Management Review* 38(2): 87-105.

Gersick, C.J.G. 1991. Revolutionary change theories: A multilevel exploitation of the punctuated equilibrium paradigm. *Academy of Management Review,* 16(1): 10-36.

Gornov, S. 1996. Funding the FIGS. *Business in Russia.* 65: 40-41.

Haasen, A. 1996. Opel Eisenach GmbH–creating a high-productivity workplace. *Organizational Dynamics,* (Spring): 80-85.

Habermas, J. 1973. *Legitimationsprobleme im Spätkapitalismus.* Frankfurt am Main: Suhrkamp Publ. (engl. *Legitimation crisis,* Boston: Beacon Press, 1975).

Hewett, E. 1988. *Reforming the Soviet economy: Equality versus efficiency.* Washington, DC: Brookings Institute.

Johnson, S. and Loveman, G. 1995. Starting over: Poland after communism. *Harvard Business Review,* (March-April): 44-56.

Kaminski, B., Wang, Z.K., and Winters, L.A. 1995. Trade performance depends on bold reform. *Transition,* 6(9-10): 17-19.

Kapuscinski, R. 1996. A normal life. *Time* (May 27): 68-72.

Kiser III, J.W. 1989. *Communist entrepreneurs. Unknown innovators in the global economy.* New York: Franklin Watts.

Kornai, J. 1980. *Economics of shortage.* Amsterdam: North-Holland.

Kostera, M., Proppé, M., and Szatkowski, M. 1995. Staging the new romantic hero in the old cynical theatre: On managers, roles and change in Poland. *Journal of Organizational Behavior,* 16: 631-646.

Kotter, J. P. 1995. Leading change: Why transformation efforts fail. *Harvard Business Review* (March-April): 59-67.

Kramer, M. 1996. Russia '96. *Time* (May 27): 46-57.

Lavigne, M. 1995. *The economics of transition: From socialist economy to market economy.* New York: St. Martin's Press.

Lipton, D., and Sachs, J. 1990. Privatization in Eastern Europe: The case of Poland. *Brookings Papers on Economic Activity,* 2: 293-333.

Mandel, E. 1978. *Late capitalism.* London: Verso.

McFaul, M., and Perlmutter, T. (Eds.) 1995. *Privatization, conversion, and enterprise reform in Russia.* Boulder, CO: Westview Press.

Milbank, D. 1995. Polish entrepreneurs revitalize economy but battle huge odds. *The Wall Street Journal,* No. 62 (March 30):A1, A6.

Miller, K.L., Comes, F.J., and Simpson, P. 1995. Poland: Rising star of Europe. *Business Week,* (December 4): 64-70.

Mujzel, J. 1994. State-owned enterprises in transition: Prospects amidst crisis. In M. Jackson and V. Bilsen (Eds.) *Company management and capital market in the transition.* Aldershot: Avebury: 117-144.

Nelson, D. N. 1995. Syndromes of public withdrawal in postcommunism. *Transition,* 6(1-2): 13- 15.

Neue Zürcher Zeitung. 1995. Bonner Wundlecken nach der Berliner Wahl. No. 247 (October 24): 3.

North, D. C. 1990. *Institutions, institutional change, and economic performance.* Cambridge MA: Harvard University Press.

Offe, C. 1973. Krisen des Krisenmanagements. In Jänicke, M. (Ed.) *Herrschaft und Krise.* Opladen: Westdeutscher Verlag: 197-223.

Pavett, C.M., and Whitney, G. 1995. Privatization, human resource practices, and affect: Comparative case analysis in a transforming economy. *Journal of International Management,* 1(4): 343-372.

Pearce, J.L., Branyiczki, I., and Bakacsi, G. 1994. Person-based reward systems: A theory of organizational reward practices in reform-communist organizations. *Journal of Organizational Behavior,* 15: 261-282.

Peng, M. W., and Heath, P. S. 1996. The growth of the firm in planned economies in transition: Institutions, organizations, and strategic choice. *Academy of Management Review,* 21(2): 492-528.

Penrice, D. 1995. The post-communist world. The obstacles to change. *Harvard Business Review* (January-February): 14.

Perlez, J. 1996. A bourgeoisie blooms and goes shopping. Poland's market reforms take hold. *The New York Times,* May 14: D1, D6.

Romanelli, E., and Tushman, M. L. 1994. Organizational Transformation as punctuated equilibrium: An empirical test. *Academy of Management Journal,* 37(4): 1141-1166.

Shonfield, A. 1965. *Modern Capitalism.* London: Oxford University Press

Stark, D. 1996. Recombinant property in East European capitalism. *American Journal of Sociology,* 101(4): 993-1027.

Starodubrovskaya, I. 1995. Attitudes of enterprise managers toward market transition. In M. McFaul and T. Perlmutter (Eds.) *Privatization, conversion, and enterprise reform in Russia.* Boulder, CO: Westview: 57-68.

Szelényi, I., and Kostello, E. 1996. The market transition debate: Toward a synthesis? *American Journal of Sociology,* 101(4): 1082-1096.

Thornhill, J. (1996) Zyuganov leaves voters guessing over true instincts. *Financial Times,* June 10, p. 2.

Transition, 1996a. Milestones of Transition. 7(1): 16-20.

Transition, 1996b. Milestones of Transition. 7(3-4): 25-27.

Tushman, M. L. and Romanelli E. 1985. Organizational evolution: A metamorphosis model of convergence and reorientation. In L. L. Cummings and B. M. Staw (Eds.) *Research in Organization Behavior*, 7: 171-122. Greenwich, CT: JAI Press.

World Bank 1995. *Bureaucrats in business. The economics and politics of government ownership.* Oxford: Oxford University Press.

Index

Page numbers followed by the letter "t" indicate tables; "i" indicate illustrations/figures; "n" indicate notes.